Orthodox Christianity and Nationalism in Nineteenth-Century Southeastern Europe

ORTHODOX CHRISTIANITY AND CONTEMPORARY THOUGHT

SERIES EDITORS
George E. Demacopoulos and Aristotle Papanikolaou

This series consists of books that seek to bring Orthodox Christianity into an engagement with contemporary forms of thought. Its goal is to promote (1) historical studies in Orthodox Christianity that are interdisciplinary, employ a variety of methods, and speak to contemporary issues; and (2) constructive theological arguments in conversation with patristic sources and that focus on contemporary questions ranging from the traditional theological and philosophical themes of God and human identity to cultural, political, economic, and ethical concerns. The books in the series explore both the relevancy of Orthodox Christianity to contemporary challenges and the impact of contemporary modes of thought on Orthodox self-understandings.

Orthodox Christianity and Nationalism in Nineteenth-Century Southeastern Europe

EDITED BY
LUCIAN N. LEUSTEAN

FORDHAM UNIVERSITY PRESS
New York • 2014

Frontispiece: Southeastern Europe in the nineteenth century
(*Source:* Mina Moshkeri Upton, LSE Design Unit)

Copyright © 2014 Fordham University Press

All rights reserved. No part of this publication may be reproduced, stored in a retrieval system, or transmitted in any form or by any means—electronic, mechanical, photocopy, recording, or any other—except for brief quotations in printed reviews, without the prior permission of the publisher.

Fordham University Press has no responsibility for the persistence or accuracy of URLs for external or third-party Internet websites referred to in this publication and does not guarantee that any content on such websites is, or will remain, accurate or appropriate.

Fordham University Press also publishes its books in a variety of electronic formats. Some content that appears in print may not be available in electronic books.

Library of Congress Cataloging-in-Publication Data

Orthodox Christianity and nationalism in nineteenth-century southeastern Europe / edited by Lucian N. Leustean.
      pages cm. — (Orthodox Christianity and contemporary thought)
   Includes bibliographical references and index.
   ISBN 978-0-8232-5606-8 (cloth : alk. paper)
   1. Orthodox Eastern Church—Balkan Peninsula. 2. Nationalism—Religious aspects. 3. Nationalism—Balkan Peninsula. I. Leustean, Lucian, editor of compilation.
   BX750.B3O774 2014
   281.9'496—dc23

2013047225

Printed in the United States of America

16 15 14   5 4 3 2 1

First edition

Contents

Acknowledgments		ix
1	Orthodox Christianity and Nationalism: An Introduction *Lucian N. Leustean*	1
2	The Ecumenical Patriarchate *Paschalis M. Kitromilides*	14
3	The Orthodox Church of Greece *Dimitris Stamatopoulos*	34
4	The Serbian Orthodox Church *Bojan Aleksov*	65
5	The Romanian Orthodox Church *Lucian N. Leustean*	101
6	The Bulgarian Orthodox Church *Daniela Kalkandjieva*	164
	Postscript *Lucian N. Leustean*	203
Notes		207
List of Contributors		263
Index		267

Acknowledgments

The idea for this volume has been with me since my doctoral studies in the Department of Government at the London School of Economics and Political Science (LSE). As an executive member of the Association for the Study of Ethnicity and Nationalism (ASEN) at the LSE, and writing a thesis on Romanian Orthodoxy, I benefited enormously from attending the weekly doctoral workshops on "Nationalism and Ethnicity" that were run in the first year by Professor Emeritus Anthony Smith and, upon his retirement, by Professor John Breuilly. Debates between the former's ethno-symbolist view and the latter's modernist approach to nationalism have informed this volume and put into perspective the issues it addresses. I am grateful to Dr. John Hutchinson, John Madeley, and colleagues in ASEN for the discussions we had on the interplay between religion and nationalism.

Despite the relatively large number of books on Southeastern Europe, there remains little investigation into the ways in which, in the nineteenth century, the predominantly Orthodox churches faced the growing nationalist ideology and the concept of the nation. By bringing together experts from Southeastern European countries, this volume sheds light on the relationship between Eastern Orthodox churches, nationalism, and the nation-building process. I am grateful to the contributors to this volume for conducting archival research and presenting material based on primary sources. Their expertise has been extremely valuable in taking into account both vernacular publications and in offering detailed data on the period.

I am also grateful to Professor Aristotle Papanikolaou and Dr. George Demacopoulos for welcoming this volume into their book series Orthodox Christianity and Contemporary Thought; Fredric W. Nachbaur, director, and William C. Cerbone at Fordham University Press for their constant support and encouragement while I was working on this project; the Press's three anonymous reviewers who provided useful comments; and for the kind and generous support of the team at the Press.

This volume has benefited from discussion on religion and nationalism with a large number of scholars. In particular, I am grateful to Professor Daniel Chirot for his comments on the history of Romania; Professor Simon Dixon for his comments on the Russian Orthodox Church in the nineteenth century; Professor Dominic Lieven for confirming, against the general misconception, that, on his return from Russia, Napoleon Bonaparte did not travel through the principalities of Moldavia and Wallachia; Dr. Alex Drace-Francis for providing a number of sources on Western travelers in Wallachia and Moldavia; Professor Paschalis Kitromilides, who, in addition to writing the chapter on the Ecumenical Patriarchate, has provided useful feedback on the chapters on Greece and Bulgaria; and Dr. Dimitris Stamatopoulos who, in addition to writing the chapter on the Church of Greece, identified many lay names of nineteenth-century Ecumenical Patriarchs. I would also like to acknowledge the pioneering works of Professor Emeritus Keith Hitchins and Professor Emeritus Mircea Păcurariu on Romanian Orthodoxy in the nineteenth century, which were influential in my writing of the Romanian chapter. Some findings of this volume were presented at the conference on Eastern Christianity in Post-Imperial Societies at the Central European University, Budapest; the Consultation on Orthodox Ecclesiology at St. George's House, Windsor Castle; the Conference on Orthodox Ecclesiology and Modernity at the Centre for Russian, Soviet, Central and Eastern European Studies of the University of St. Andrews; and the Conference on Ecclesiology and Nationalism in a Postmodern Era at the Volos Academy for Theological Studies. My thanks go to the organizers of these events and the constructive comments of their participants.

Last, but not least, I am grateful to Deborah, Clara, and Maia for sharing with me this journey into the nineteenth century. I would like to dedicate this volume to my wife, Deborah, for always accompanying me on my intellectual journeys and for making this one of the most exciting.

CHAPTER

1

ORTHODOX CHRISTIANITY AND NATIONALISM: AN INTRODUCTION

Lucian N. Leustean

On the morning of January 5, 1859, at the end of the liturgy in the Orthodox cathedral in Iași, the capital of the principality of Moldavia, Father Neofit Scriban addressed the congregation. He had given many sermons in the cathedral; however, on this particular date Father Neofit faced an unusual audience. Among the faithful who regularly worshipped at the relics of Saint Parascheva, the protector of Moldavia, were the members of the assembly who would decide the future of the principality. They had a specific mission: to elect a new prince, a key figure in their plan to unite Moldavia with the neighboring principality of Wallachia. Father Neofit, a supporter of the unionist cause and fully aware of the significance of the moment, stated:

> Brethren, Jesus Christ has said that "For where two or three have gathered together in My name, I am there in their midst." You, Brethren, are not two, or three, but a real gathering in the name of God. God is in your midst. You are here in the name of the Romanian nation [and] the Romanian nation is in your midst. On the flag under which you have assembled, the flag of the Romanian nation, great events, the Romanian faith, unity, are written in large letters. The church, which is founded on faith, blesses the flag of this faith. . . . You, Brethren, through the faith of the Romanian nation, by remaining faithful to this flag, will find the same strength as the church [finds] in its own saints. The faith of the Romanian nation

was not, is not, and will not be anything else, but the unity of all Romanians in a single state, the only anchor of salvation, the only port in which the national boat could be saved from surrounding waves.

You, Brethren, have gathered here in the church of Stephen the Great; looking at the altar that he raised to the God of your parents, I think that, through this [altar], you will be able to enter into the wishes of this hero of our nation. You, [remember that] by leaving this place, you are leaving [in order to fulfill] a great gesture that for many centuries has been lost for us; you are about to elect a successor to this great hero; therefore, as his true sons, you could not be anything other than the true expression of his wishes.

Myself, [as] last year, from this altar, I said and I will continue to say that this great hero has told us that "the God of our parents will send us a Redeemer who will heal our wounds and accomplish our wishes." May your chosen leader today be the redeemer expected by the Romanian nation. May he heal its wounds and achieve its wishes. Therefore, Brethren, may your election today be that of a real Messiah of Romania. God and the world are looking at you, the church is blessing you and the whole Romanian nation is waiting for you![1]

A few hours after Father Neofit's sermon, the assembly elected Alexandru Ioan Cuza to be the prince of the principality of Moldavia; a few days later, on January 24, 1859, the assembly of the neighboring principality of Wallachia decided that Cuza should also be their prince, thus confirming the unification of the two states. A new country was inscribed on the map of Southeastern Europe, titled "The United Principalities of Wallachia and Moldavia," also known as "The United Romanian Principalities."

Orthodox Christianity in Nineteenth-Century Southeastern Europe

The intrinsic link between Orthodox Christianity and the idea of the nation, as presented in Father Neofit's sermon was one of the most significant concepts that ran through Southeastern Europe during the nineteenth century. Close relations between the religious and political elites, as in Moldavia, were paralleled throughout the region. Orthodox churches, from hierarchs to ordinary clergy and the faithful, engaged in the spread of the nationalist ideology and, in most cases, worked together with political elites in supporting the emergence of national states. Political state independence was followed by churches claiming their own victories against the centralized religious authority of Constantinople to the extent that, by the end of the nineteenth century, independent (autocephalous) churches were internationally recognized as national seats of religious power.

The establishment of independent Orthodox churches was a gradual process. After the French Revolution, the spread of modern nationalism throughout Europe raised significant challenges for the Orthodox commonwealth. The Greeks, Serbs, and Romanians began revolutionary campaigns asserting independence from the Ottoman Porte, with political revolutions followed closely by religious actions. Within the Ottoman Empire and its *Rum Millet* system, the Ecumenical Patriarch represented the "ethnarch," holding both religious and political office to represent the Orthodox faithful in its relation with the Sublime Porte.

Conflict between the Porte and the Ecumenical Patriarchate reached a dramatic level in 1821 when Greece declared its independence. Accused of treason and of supporting the insurgents, Ecumenical Patriarch Gregory V (1797–99; 1806–8; 1818–21) was hanged outside the central gates of the patriarchal palace on Easter Sunday, April 10, 1821, the most important religious festival of the church. The execution of the patriarch had a direct impact on Orthodox mobilization. The faithful perceived the patriarch as a martyr and a model for their nation-states. From mere priests to top clergy, the authority of the Ecumenical Patriarchate was considered to have been marred by Ottoman rule and only the building of national churches was regarded as the means to achieve statehood.

The first Orthodox church in Southeastern Europe to challenge the religious authority of the Ecumenical Patriarchate was that of Greece. In 1833, Greek hierarchs declared autocephaly, a position that was recognized by Constantinople only in 1850. Seeking the political support of other European powers, Greece instituted the monarchy. The new head of state, King Othon (1833–62), was a Roman Catholic whose wife was German Evangelical. He was not forced to convert to Orthodoxy but the 1843 constitution stated that his successors should be brought up in the Orthodox faith. The monarchy left its legacy on church-state relations by transforming the church into a state institution.[2] Politically, Greece promoted the "Great Idea" (*Megali Idea*), which advocated the expansion of frontiers and the incorporation of Greek-inhabited territories that were under Ottoman rule. This policy began in 1864 when Greece included the Ionian islands and continued in 1881 with the expansion to Thessaly and parts of Epirus, in 1912 to Macedonia and Crete and in 1945 to the Dodecanese. Greece's political ambitions led to military conflict with Turkey and the 1923 Treaty of Lausanne stipulated massive population exchanges between the two countries. Belonging to and practicing the Orthodox faith was associated with being part of the Greek nation and was the condition of deportation from Asia Minor to Greece.

In Serbia, diplomatic discussions after Karađorđe's First Uprising (1804–13) and Miloš Obrenović's Second Uprising (1815) resulted in 1830 in the proclamation of Serbian autonomy under Ottoman rule. Church developments paralleled those in the political sphere and in 1831, the church was granted autonomy from the Ecumenical Patriarchate, while in the 1838 and 1869 constitutions, Orthodoxy was declared as the state religion. In 1878 Serbia was recognized by the Congress of Berlin as an independent kingdom and in 1879 King Milan Obrenović (prince 1868–82; king 1882–89) and Metropolitan Mihailo Jovanović of Belgrade (1859–81; 1889–98) obtained autocephaly from Constantinople.[3] The establishment of the Kingdom of Serbs, Croats, and Slovenes after the First World War led to a new status for the Serbian Orthodox Church. In 1919 the church was raised to the rank of patriarchate and Metropolitan Dimitrije Pavlović (1920–30) became its first patriarch. The patriarch occupied a position in the Royal Council and members of the Orthodox clergy held seats in the National Assembly. The political unification of the South Slavs was perceived by the church hierarchy as the religious unification of the Serbian Orthodox Church; consequently, the church extended its influence to political affairs.

In Romania, the 1859 union between the principalities of Wallachia and Moldavia under the rule of Prince Alexandru Ioan Cuza (1859–66) was closely connected to the rise of the Romanian Orthodox Church outside the jurisdictional authority of the Ecumenical Patriarch. Imposing his control of the church, Cuza introduced the secularization of monastery estates, declared Romanian as the only language spoken in religious rituals, and established a synod that followed his rule. Comparable to Greece's political trajectory, Romanian political leaders sought support from European powers and elected the Roman Catholic Prince Carol I from the Hohenzollern-Sigmaringen family (prince 1866–81; king 1881–1914) as head of state. In 1865 the Romanian Orthodox Church declared autocephaly, which in 1885 was recognized by Constantinople. The proclamation of the Romanian independent kingdom in 1881 was accompanied by increasing state control of the church, which led to ecclesiastical instability. The establishment of Greater Romania in 1918 with the incorporation of the territories of Transylvania, Banat, Bukovina, and Bessarabia was followed by the reorganization of the church. In 1925, the parliament raised the church to the rank of patriarchate and Metropolitan Miron Cristea was elected its first patriarch (1925–39).[4]

The case of Bulgaria offered a unique example of church-state relations in Southeastern Europe, as the struggle for ecclesiastical independence from the Ecumenical Patriarchate took place before the emergence of the Bulgarian state.[5] The first claims of autonomy came after the Crimean War (1854–56) and resulted in 1870 in the establishment of a Bulgarian Exarchate. The exarchate was set up by the Ottoman government and comprised thirteen dioceses under Constantinople's jurisdiction. Bulgarian hierarchs demanded a national church; however, in 1872 a synod under the leadership of the Ecumenical Patriarch Anthimos VI (1845–48; 1853–55; 1871–73) rejected their request, condemning the doctrine of *ethno-phyletism* that asserted the emergence of ecclesiastical organization on ethnic lines. The synod refused to recognize the Bulgarian Exarchate, declaring it a schismatic church. This position continued after Bulgaria became an autonomous principality in 1878 and an independent kingdom in 1908. Bulgaria's first constitution of 1879 stated that the church remained united with the Ecumenical Patriarchate.

Orthodox Christianity and the Idea of the Nation

This volume focuses on the relationship between Orthodox churches, nationalism, and the nation-state-building process in Southeastern Europe in the nineteenth century. By providing a historical approach to church-state relations in the predominantly Orthodox states of this region—namely, Greece, Serbia, Romania, and Bulgaria, it offers an insight into the ways in which Orthodox churches engaged with the nationalist ideology. In addition to an analysis of these churches, the volume includes a chapter on the Ecumenical Patriarchate's position toward the spread of nationalism, highlighting the challenges posed by the declarations of autocephaly in the region.

Despite nationalism being the prime ideological motor of the nineteenth century, in most cases Orthodox churches achieved their national fulfillment only after the First World War. As a general rule, the volume follows a steady chronological analysis from the first to the last decades of the nineteenth century and, where significant, also predates this period (in the case of the Bulgarian church) or follows on from it (in the case of the Greek, Serbian, and Romanian churches). For example, the memories of the Bulgarian medieval state and its relation with Byzantium remained potent for the political imaginary of the church and the ways in which hierarchs engaged with Constantinople. The issue of *ethno-phyletism* that claimed a connection between ethnicity and the church had its roots not only in the establishment of the Bulgarian Exarchate but also in the medieval position of the church in Bulgaria.

Although the title of each chapter uses the contemporary name of each church, the reader is urged to take into account their ethnic diversity during this period. From this perspective, the volume investigates "national" historiographies and the ways in which Orthodox churches perceived the concept of the nation by addressing the following questions: To what extent did Orthodox churches support the nation-building processes in Southeastern Europe? The emergence of new nation-states was a complex phenomenon and some church factions remained loyal to the Ottoman Porte, claiming indissoluble ties with the Ecumenical Patriarchate. What role did the religious and political leadership in Southeastern Europe have in the establishment of national Orthodox churches? In Greece and Romania hierarchs were appointed by the regime and religious leaders were actively engaged in political issues. Did nationalism in Southeastern Europe take a religious form during the nineteenth century? Orthodox churches in Bessarabia under Russian rule and in the Austro-Hungarian territories of Transylvania and Bukovina retained not only contact with Romanians in Wallachia and Moldavia but also were prime actors in promoting the national identity of their faithful.

Despite a significant volume of literature on nation-state building in Southeastern Europe, there remains little analysis on the ways in which churches participated in this process. Orthodox churches retained not only transnational ties throughout the region but were also significant social, economic, and political actors capable of mobilizing the masses in support of the national ideology. This study demonstrates how, from a theoretical perspective, the actions of Orthodox churches in the nineteenth century oscillated between the four main paradigms of nationalism—namely, modernism, ethno-symbolism, perennialism, and primordialism.

Modernism, the predominant theoretical paradigm in the literature, argues that nationalism was both a novel phenomenon with a clearly identifiable historical origin—that is, the time of the French Revolution—and a process of "invention."[6] This view has been supported by Elie Kedourie in a rather bold statement that started the very first chapter of his influential book *Nationalism*, in which he pointed out that "Nationalism is a doctrine invented in Europe at the beginning of the nineteenth century."[7] The nationalist ideology had not only a political dimension but also a strong religious influence. It affected all social and political strata by transforming, in Émile Durkheim's words, "things purely secular . . . into sacred things: these were the Fatherland, Liberty, Reason. A religion tended to become established which had its dogmas, altars and feasts."[8]

The concepts of "Fatherland," "Liberty," and "Reason" were in contradiction with the jurisdictional nature of Orthodox Christianity. For the Orthodox commonwealth of Southeastern Europe, the Ecumenical Patriarchate in Constantinople held both spiritual and political office, in a tradition that went back to the Byzantine Empire. In Orthodoxy the relationship between church and state has been characterized by the concept of *symphonia* (συμφωνία) or the "system of coreciprocity" (Σύστημα συναλληλίας; Latin: *consonantia*) in which religious and political rulers worked together toward "achieving a sublime destiny" of the faithful.[9] After the fall of Constantinople in 1453, the *Rum Millet* system preserved the religious authority of the Ecumenical Patriarchate over the ethnic communities of the Ottoman Empire.[10]

In the nineteenth century, the legacy of *symphonia* was evident in the work of religious and political leaders in their joint struggle to obtain national independence, identifying their common enemy not only in the political structure of the Ottoman Empire but also in the religious authority of the Ecumenical Patriarchate. Close relations between the religious and political spheres were evident across the region, with political elites playing the prime role in acquiring national independence while ensuring that churches supported the processes of achieving statehood. In both Greece and Romania, political leaders were influential in organizing church synods that fostered nationalist views and ultimately led to national autocephaly.

It is without doubt that the nation-states that appeared on the map of Southeastern Europe were the product of "political movements seeking or exercising state power," as claimed in John Breuilly's modernist interpretation of nationalism.[11] However, political movements had also to take into account the predominant religious confession of the region. Nationalism resonated among the people of Southeastern Europe not only due to political aspirations but also due to mobilization of Orthodox churches in this process. As Paschalis Kitromilides has pointed out, "Nationalism became a real, as opposed to a theoretical problem for Orthodoxy, once the peoples of the Balkans rose up in arms against Ottoman rule in the early nineteenth century."[12] Orthodox churches were capable of developing both national and transnational ties that benefited the former at the expense of the decreasing influence of Ottoman rule and of the Ecumenical Patriarchate.

Orthodox churches adapted to the modern character of nationalism through innovatory changes, the most significant of which was education, a prime factor in fostering national cohesion. The establishment of primary schools, seminaries, and faculties of theology in the region ensured both the training of the clergy and provided a unified view of the nation. From this perspective, education within the church milieu promoted both the processes of "invention" and "imagination" of the nation.[13] Father Neofit's sermon at the start of this chapter is an example of "inventing" the Romanian nation in the principalities of Wallachia and Moldavia. On the other hand, Romanians living in the adjoining territories of Transylvania, Bukovina, and Bessarabia found in the education promoted by their own Orthodox communities the most important valuable means of "imagining" the unified nation, a reality that would take place only in 1918 in Greater Romania.

Education was paralleled by support for the nationalist ideology from a wide range of social strata throughout the region. In Bulgaria, most hierarchs were appointed by Constantinople; many of them did not know the native language, and national mobilization was pioneered by craftsmen and tradesmen rather than the church. The establishment of local councils throughout Bulgaria proved to be the motors of national awakening and ultimately led to demands for a national church. The councils refused to pay financial support to the Ecumenical Patriarchate and forced the Greek hierarchs and clergy to leave their parishes, which were then occupied by native clergy. Furthermore, the councils instructed the local church hierarchy to omit the name of the Patriarch of Constantinople during the liturgy. These actions came from politically constituted bodies rather than from the local Orthodox church, demonstrating a modernist view of nationalism.

In contrast to the Bulgarian case, other countries in the region showed the active support of the church for nation-state building. During the Greek War of Independence, hierarchs worked closely with their secular counterparts, while the active involvement of the church was clearly evident in the 1859 unification of Wallachia and Moldavia, which would probably not have been possible if the church had not opposed the 1857 fraudulent election for Moldavian ad-hoc Divan Assembly by mobilizing large section of the population against the political authorities.

Although the nationalist ideology was a modern phenomenon, Orthodox churches influenced the nation-building process through reviving the Byzantine dream of a Christian state.[14] Anthony D. Smith's ethno-symbolic view of nationalism argues that "nationalism is much more than a political ideology; it is also a form of culture and 'religion'."[15] As such, religious and political leaders incorporated myths and symbols in order to give coherence to their nationalist programs. Orthodox mythologization was strongly encouraged by the political leadership and found support in the masses. From this perspective, church hierarchs became "moral innovators" of the nation,[16] reminding the faithful of the Byzantine model of *symphonia* and support for both a national church and a unified nation-state.

In Greece, the process of mythologization led both the church and state to support the "Great Idea," of which the long-term aim was the reestablishment of the Byzantine Empire. In Serbia, the nineteenth century saw the rise of the cult of Prince Rastko Nemanjić who became known as Saint Sava, the founder of the Serbian autocephalous church in the thirteenth century, a cult that would gradually acquire a predominantly mythical role in the national consciousness. In Wallachia and Moldavia, religious and political leaders looked back to the Middle Ages, promoting to the rank of "national" figures previous rulers of the principalities such as Stephen the Great and Michael the Brave. These figures became not only models to follow but also protectors of the Romanian nation. In Bulgaria, although the church hierarchy retained a marginal political role and was not involved in the election of Prince Ferdinand of Coburg-Gotha, the state endorsed the process of mythologization. The prince declared himself to be a "tsar," thereby recalling the glorious past of the Bulgarian Empire, and claimed to be a descendent of the Byzantine emperors. In the Balkan Wars (1912–13) he even supported the idea that if his side won he should be crowned in the Church of Saint Sophia in Constantinople.[17]

The third theoretical paradigm of nationalism, perennialism, which claims that nations could be traced to immemorial times, was also present in the thinking of Orthodox churches. Greece looked back to ancient times, promoting the idea that modern Greece was the direct product of the Hellenic classical age. In particular, the writings of Adamantios Korais (1748–1833), which deplored the religious and political decadence of the Ottoman Empire, resonated among the Greek intellectual elite. Korais's influence would be visible in Konstantinos Paparrigopoulos's five-volume *History of the Great Nation*, published between 1860 and 1877, which connected ancient Greece, the Byzantine Empire, and the modern state.[18] In Bulgaria, the *Istoriya Slavyano-Bolgarskaya* (Slavonic-Bulgarian History) written in 1762 by Father Paisii of Hiledar was one of the most influential publications before the 1878 liberation of the country. Paisii was extremely critical of Ottoman rule and the Ecumenical Patriarchate, claiming that only a return to the glories of the past could unite the Bulgarian nation. Romania witnessed a similar process with both religious and political leaders referencing the Roman times and claiming the unity of the nation throughout centuries on the basis of their common Latin-derived language in a territory surrounded by Slavic-speaking neighbors.

For Bulgaria and Serbia, the perennialist concept conflicted with competing religious jurisdictions and geographical boundaries of their nations. The Bulgarian Church claimed to be a direct descendent of the Bulgarian Patriarchate (927–1018), which initially had its first headquarters in Preslav, and was located in Ohrid during the First Bulgarian State (1018) and as part of the Patriarchate of Tûrnovo (1235–1393), while the Serbian Church saw its territory fragmented between the Patriarchate of Peć (1346–1463 in medieval Serbia and 1557–1766 in the Ottoman Empire), the Karlovci Metropolitanate (1691–1920 in the Habsburg Empire), and Orthodox churches in Dalmatia, Bosnia-Herzegovina, and Montenegro.

Although the involvement of Orthodox churches with the nationalist ideology can be identified within all three previous paradigms of nationalism, it is perhaps the fourth type, primordialism, which came closest to Orthodox theological thinking. Primordialism, in the words of Anthony D. Smith, claims that "nations . . . share with God the attributes of existing before all things and of originating everything."[19] By referring to God and the origins of "all things," primordialism promoted a theological understanding of the nation.

The concept of a nation could be found in the earliest writings of the Christian church. Throughout centuries the concept of *ethnos* stated in the New Testament, "go and make disciples of all the nations [*ethnos*]" (Matt. 28: 19; Mark 16: 15–16), has been at the core of the Orthodox Church's engagement with the secular world. The New Testament's *ethnos* took a jurisdictional approach by being reproduced in Apostolic Canon 34, which clearly delineated relations between the clergy.[20] However, the *ethnos* of both the New Testament and Apostolic Canon 34 are in contradiction with the modern concept of the nation. As Lucian Turcescu points out, the former relates to "Christians of non-Jewish descent living together regardless of their ethnic origins" while the later has been the result of the spread of modern nationalism after the French Revolution.[21] Finding a commonly agreed view of the meaning of the nation was a thorny issue throughout the nineteenth century; furthermore, this issue remains contested today. While many church hierarchs have welcomed the emergence of their nation-states and autocephalous churches, claiming that they were instituted by God, there have also been voices stating that Orthodox churches should reject the concept of the nation. According to the latter view, the church, as the body of all faithful, is above the construction of the nation and only the *eschaton*, the second return of Christ, will enable nations to achieve their national potential as the will of God.

The eschatological and primordialist interpretations of nationalism produced one of the most debatable decisions taken within Orthodox commonwealth during the nineteenth century—namely, the 1872 Ecumenical Patriarchate's condemnation of *ethno-phyletism*, which affected the recognition of the Bulgarian Exarchate as the church of the Bulgarian nation. The refusal to recognize an ethnic Bulgarian Church until 1945, with the church having its headquarters in Constantinople rather than in Sofia, had a long-term societal effect, with Bulgarians being the least religious in Southeastern Europe. By contrast, in those cases where Orthodox churches acquired autocephaly and were an integral part of the nation-building process, levels of religiosity were high.

Primordialism was present not only in the 1872 condemnation of the Ecumenical Patriarchate but also among local Orthodox churches. After the 1861 Karlovci Congress that decided upon the reorganization of Orthodox churches in the Habsburg Empire, the religious leaders in Bukovina refused to unite their church with their Romanian fellows in Transylvania.

Bishop Eugenie Hacman claimed that due to the multiethnic character of the Bukovinian diocese, which also comprised Ruthenians, his church had its own distinct identity in the Habsburg Empire. He criticized the involvement of laymen in church structures in Transylvania and suggested that the Orthodox Church should follow the religious organization of the first centuries in which only the clergy were in charge of the church. Hacman's refusal to unite with Transylvania resulted in the rather unusual Metropolitanate of Bukovina and Dalmatia, which brought together Romanian, Ruthenian, and Serbian faithful, with their bishops meeting annually in Vienna. The establishment of this metropolitanate showed the difficulty of finding a commonly agreed concept of the nation that looked back to the first Christian centuries rather than welcome a modern interpretation of nationalism.

Throughout the nineteenth century, Orthodox churches remained at the core of nation-building processes by supporting both the elite and the faithful in the construction of the nation. Through religious ceremonies and jurisdictional organizations, the churches reminded the faithful of the Byzantine model of church and state. Myths, religious symbols, and liturgical ceremonials continued to bring the Orthodox people together, even if they were subjects of different political authorities. Questions of identity brought them together (they were all Orthodox) while the growth and institutionalization of nationalism created borders that challenged religious identity. Thus, for example, was an Orthodox believer in Bucharest an Orthodox Romanian or a Romanian Orthodox? Religious and national identities both overlapped and raised conflicts.

Although Orthodox churches had not faced the challenges of nationalism before the nineteenth century, they had engaged with concepts of ethnicity and identity throughout their existence. From this perspective, the words of Gennadius Scholarius, the first Ecumenical Patriarch after the 1453 fall of Constantinople, are a reminder of the search for personal and collective identity within the Orthodox commonwealth: "Though I am a Hellene by birth, yet I would never say that I was a Hellene. For I do not believe as the Hellenes believed. I should like to take my name from my faith and, if anyone asked me what I am, to reply 'a Christian.' Though my father dwelt in Thessaly . . . I do not call myself a Thessalian, but a Byzantine. For I am of Byzantium."[22]

For Gennadius Scholarius, the Byzantine Empire as a Christian structure took precedence over territorial identity. Identification with contrasting concepts such as that of being "a Christian," "a Thessalian," "of Byzantium," or belonging to a specific territory, would continue to preoccupy the Orthodox faithful. The dialogue between the church and the nation lies at the heart of this volume.

Note on Transliteration

National changes on the map of Southeastern Europe have perhaps most clearly been reflected in cities being known under different names, according to either their ethnic composition or political status—for example, Cernăuți in Romanian (as part of Greater Romania), Chernivtsi in Ukrainian (as it is known today), Czerniowce in Polish (as part of Galicia), and Czernowitz in German (as part of the Austro-Hungarian Empire). This volume uses Greek, Serbian, Romanian, and Bulgarian spelling of the names of people, cities, and regions—for example, Karlovci, Tûrnovo, Cernăuți, and Chișinău—except in cases where the English terms are well-known, such as Belgrade, Bucharest, Wallachia, Bukovina, and Bessarabia. The proper names of hierarchs are those that were used by their churches (for example, Prokopije Ivačković in Serbian and Procopie Ivașcovici in Romanian).

CHAPTER

2

THE ECUMENICAL PATRIARCHATE

Paschalis M. Kitromilides

The impact of the major force shaping European modernity in the nineteenth century, nationalism, upon the foremost institution around which Orthodox society traditionally cohered in Southeastern Europe, the Patriarchate of Constantinople, forms a complex story that can be seen to unfold on many levels. The response of the patriarchate to the secular challenge of nationalism was equally complicated and could be traced in many contexts. To avoid confusion, anachronism, and unfairness in attempting to recover, at least partly, this story, one precondition must emphatically be borne in mind: an understanding of the encounter of the patriarchate with nationalism should not be reduced to a power struggle over simply the control and direction of the Orthodox community, but it should be seen and interpreted as the response of a religious institution to the challenge posed to its core values and self-definition derived from a centuries-old tradition by a secular threat to this heritage—a threat from which the church saw as its nonnegotiable duty to safeguard the Orthodox community. This is the core of the historic encounter to be sketched in outline in what follows. Losing sight of the deeper spiritual and ideological incompatibilities of the two world-views locked up in the encounter would reduce the story to a confusing record of personal conflicts, antagonisms over power, and violent disagreements concerning the prospects of the Christian community in the Ottoman Empire. The approach to be followed here will involve an attempt to gauge and appraise the response of the Ecumenical Patriarchate as the foremost repository and self-conscious guardian of the Orthodox religious tradition to nationalism.

The initial encounter of the Orthodox Church and its institutional exponent, the Patriarchate of Constantinople, with the challenges of modern secular thought had, of course, taken place before the age of nationalism. The earliest such encounters had been well under way in the eighteenth century in the interplay of the Orthodox tradition with the Enlightenment. As I have attempted to suggest on a number of previous occasions, that earlier encounter too was more complex and nuanced than it has often been assumed by conventional historiographical approaches. As a rule, the Orthodox Church, especially before the period of the French Revolution, manifested a noteworthy openness to the exponents of modern secular learning and, as long as questions of doctrine remained untouched, it proved quite prepared to enlist them in its projects for the education of the faithful.[1]

Even after 1789, and despite the intensification of ideological confrontations between proponents and opponents of modern ideas in the Orthodox community both within and without the Ottoman Empire, the church's openness to the Enlightenment made possible the emergence of a remarkable phenomenon that could be described as "ecclesiastical Enlightenment." This was represented by a number of senior prelates who occupied leading positions in the hierarchy during the first two decades of the nineteenth century and in their pastoral work that appeared sincerely devoted to the modernization and improvement of education, attracting the admiration and approval of important and outspoken leaders of secular thought such as Adamantios Korais.[2]

One particular manifestation of the impact of the Enlightenment and its expectations of cultural refinement upon the inner life of the church was registered in the style and diction of the official documents issued by the secretariat of the patriarchate or by the Holy Synod. A conscious turn to a more learned style, reflecting a deeper command of ancient Greek is noticeable already in the mid-seventeenth century and it became a generalized tendency from the mid-eighteenth century onwards. The new style is obvious in the dating of patriarchal documents where the ancient Greek names of months are preferred to those of the Roman calendar; it is also reflected in the tendency to hellenize episcopal titles by making place names conform to Greek grammar and "by hunting names with an air of Hellenism."[3] The most eloquent and literal record of the "prevalence of

Hellenic spirit" in the praxis of the church was the special concern for the use of language. The chronographer of the Ecumenical Patriarchate, Manuel Gedeon, makes a quite strong point of this: "The most splendid and powerful means of strengthening and preserving Hellenism inviolate in its integrity, was for the Patriarchate of Constantinople and the other patriarchates the pure Greek language, free from the cacophony of foreign accretions and this was the language in official patriarchal documents drafted by the chief secretaries, who as a rule were also the head teachers of the patriarchal academy."[4]

Such had been the intellectual substratum of the work of the church. In the period of the Enlightenment, concern for the proper use of language became a distinctive feature of patriarchal practice in Constantinople, and, according to Gedeon, it set a precedent and a standard for the nineteenth century. I have dwelled on this aspect of ecclesiastical practice not only on account of the intrinsic interest of the subject but also in order to illustrate a broader interpretative problem. The concern for language and the special care for the proper usage of Greek could be easily interpreted as an intellectual expression of the spirit of nationalism, thus confirming a conventional historiographical view of long standing that saw the Orthodox Church as a primary agent of Greek nationalism. The cultural initiatives connected with the proper use of language could thus be seen as a precocious manifestation of such a secular spirit in the bosom of the church.

In fact, such a reading of the evidence, plausible as it appears at first sight, would only betray the characteristic inability to grasp the historicity of pertinent phenomena, and a total misunderstanding of the character of ecclesiastical practice. Concern for the proper use of Greek did not possess for the church ethnic significance, let alone nationalist meaning. It rather confirmed its status within the cultural tradition of Orthodoxy that went back to the Greek fathers of the fourth century. It should thus be seen as a reclaiming and an affirmation of an ancient religious identity with a distinctly ecumenical content, rather than as a sign of a form of ethnic awareness.

The question of language, and the easy ways in which it can be misunderstood and misinterpreted, illustrates the broader cognitive and methodological problems facing any attempt to understand and interpret, or even simply to narrate, the story of the attitude of the church toward modern secular systems of values and, most particularly, toward the complexities and conflicts involved in the advent of nationalism within the ethnic communities over whose spiritual life the Orthodox Church had presided for millennia. In the particular case of the Ecumenical Patriarchate, the question of nationalism could be seen to present serious challenges to the church on many levels: spiritual, pastoral, political, and administrative.

Nationalism was a force of change transforming European societies in the direction of modernity. Ipso facto, therefore, the nexus of modernity and nationalism involved a confrontation with the church. In a context of ethnic heterogeneity and national pluralism such as that of Orthodox Christianity in the age of nationalism, the confrontation between the Ecumenical Patriarchate and national modernity could be traced—primarily for reasons of analytical efficacy—on three levels: firstly, on the level of relations with the new national states of the Balkans, which, as an integral part of their nation-building projects, claimed the independence of their local churches from Constantinople; secondly, on the level of governance of the Orthodox community within the Ottoman Empire, a community that since the Fall of 1453 had been defined in terms of religion and had been placed under the jurisdiction of its ecclesiastical leadership; and, thirdly, on the level of relations with the Ottoman state, once the empire itself was set, rather belatedly, into the orbit of nationalist transformation.

The Orthodox Church and the Advent of National States in the Balkans

On the level of the relations of the Ecumenical Patriarchate with the new Orthodox national states of the Balkans, one can discern quite clearly the inner logic of ecclesiastical attitudes toward the array of secular changes represented by nationalism. Between the 1830s and the 1880s, a process of drastic changes transformed the political map of Southeastern Europe as, one after another, the Orthodox nationalities of the region acceded to independent statehood: Greece, Serbia, and Romania became sovereign kingdoms, Greece in 1830 after a ten year war of independence, Serbia in 1878 after a protracted period of autonomy under Ottoman suzerainty since 1831, and Romania in 1881 after the union of the principalities of Wallachia and Moldavia in 1859 and the election of a European prince as head of the new autonomous state in 1865.

The new nation-states demonstrated a particular sense of urgency to integrate the Orthodox Church in their nation-building projects by detaching its local branches within their new state borders from Constantinople and proclaiming them autocephalous.[5] Inevitably, this created problems with Constantinople. The Ecumenical Patriarchate did not, in principle, object to autocephaly. There were serious precedents to the recognition of autocephaly in medieval Orthodoxy, as in the cases of the medieval patriarchates of the Bulgarian and Serbian empires that had remained in complete canonical communion with Constantinople until their abolition by the Ottomans following the disappearance of the states to which they had been attached. Furthermore, Constantinople had proceeded at the close of the sixteenth century with the granting of autocephaly and patriarchal status to the Orthodox Church within the Russian Empire, thus creating a fifth Orthodox patriarchate in 1589.[6]

The objections Constantinople voiced to the new autocephalies of the age of nationalism were directed primarily at the unilateralism whereby the new secular states attempted to impose their will on the church. This can explain the different forms the question of autocephaly took in the Serbian case, on the one hand, and in the Greek and Romanian cases on the other. Serbian political and ecclesiastical authorities in the autonomous principality of Serbia in 1831 and the sovereign kingdom of Serbia in 1879 took the formal steps required by canon law by applying to the Synod of Constantinople for ecclesiastical autonomy first and autocephaly subsequently, receiving both smoothly with the blessing of the Ecumenical Patriarchate. By contrast, Greece and Romania proclaimed unilaterally their churches independent of Constantinople, putting the claims of nationalist sensibility before the formalities of canon law. This secular modus operandi created serious problems in the Orthodox communion. Constantinople totally rejected the unilateral actions creating Greek autocephaly with the consequence of a schism between the autocephalous Church of Greece and the Orthodox communion lasting from 1833 to 1852. Another schism appeared in the making on account of Romanian state policies in the ecclesiastical domain without prior consultation with Constantinople in the 1860s, the 1870s and the 1880s. In both the Greek and Romanian cases, the conflicts were healed and full communion restored once the formalities required by canon law were finally followed, the national governments and their local churches applying for autocephaly on the grounds of their accession to political independence and receiving their new status by means of an official document, *Patriarchal Tomos*, issued by the Synod of the Ecumenical Patriarchate.[7]

The way Constantinople, under a number of different patriarchs and at points in time at some distance from each other,[8] handled the question of the autocephaly of national churches illustrates, characteristically, the fundamentally different logic of Orthodox ecclesiology from the secular values of nationalism.[9] This became even more obvious in the protracted and sad story of the Bulgarian ecclesiastical question. In the case of the Bulgarian Orthodox community, the aspiration to ecclesiastical emancipation preceded the claim of independent statehood as a preparatory stage of national assertion, paving the way to state sovereignty. The Bulgarians were latecomers to nationalism, in comparison to the other Balkan Orthodox communities, but once they did, their commitment and enthusiasm were second to none. They expressed their aspirations by clamoring for an independent Bulgarian Church, as a herald, obviously, of an independent Bulgarian state. It would be reasonable to suppose, in view of the extreme intermixture of nationalities and ethnic communities in the region, that the aspiration to set up an independent Bulgarian ecclesiastical entity was also a means to attempt an initial delineation of the territorial basis of a future Bulgarian state.

The first Bulgarian claims to ecclesiastical autonomy were voiced after the Crimean War (1854–56). In order to accommodate the demands of their Bulgarian flock, two Ecumenical Patriarchs, Joachim II in 1861 and Gregory VI in 1867, proposed arrangements for ecclesiastical autonomy in predominantly ethnic Bulgarian areas under the spiritual jurisdiction of Constantinople. Since there was no Bulgarian state, the Ecumenical Patriarchate judged that there was no canonical basis for anything else. This proved unsatisfactory to the Bulgarians who were actively encouraged in their aspirations by Russian foreign policy and by the broader Panslavist movement. In 1870, with the support of the Russian ambassador in Istanbul, Count Ignatiev, the Bulgarians managed to obtain an edict from the Sublime Porte setting up an autonomous Bulgarian Exarchate in thirteen dioceses that belonged to the jurisdiction of the Ecumenical Patriarchate.

The synod of the patriarchate rejected this proposed arrangement as uncanonical and proceeded to the convocation of a major synod of the Orthodox patriarchates to consider the issue. Russia abstained, but the other Orthodox patriarchates and the autocephalous Church of Cyprus agreed to take part. The synod met in Istanbul in late August 1872, and, by September 17, it concluded that the Bulgarian claims were uncanonical and the demand for a separate church along ethnic lines represented the heresy of *ethno-phyletism*. The exarchate was proclaimed schismatic, condemned, and its ecclesiastical leaders were defrocked and excommunicated. The Bulgarian schism introduced intense conflicts into the Orthodox community and caused tremendous suffering to large numbers of people in Macedonia, Thrace, and Eastern Rumelia, who paid the heavy costs for the secular values that had crept into the church and brought about this confrontation over essentially secular issues of power and politics. The Patriarchate of Constantinople, nevertheless, was consistent in its attitude in facing up to this challenge of secular nationalism: the absence of an independent state in the Bulgarian case could not warrant the canonical steps that had led to autocephaly in the cases of Greece, Serbia, and Romania. The schism lingered on until 1945 when it was settled in less than a month once certain formalities were transacted by the Bulgarian Church under Exarch Stephen.[10]

The Ecumenical Patriarchate and the Governance of the Orthodox Community in the Ottoman Empire

The Bulgarian Orthodox was not the only group that questioned the authority of the Ecumenical Patriarchate after the Crimean War. The broader changes that marked the government of the Ottoman Empire during the age of reforms, ushered in by the *Hatt-i Humayun* of 1856, raised the expectations of the Greek Orthodox flock of the Ecumenical Patriarchate as well as for a different, more active role in the administration of the church and in the management of the affairs of their own community. Up until then, the church and the affairs of the community were managed through an oligarchic system of power-sharing between the incumbent patriarch and a group of about eight senior metropolitans who occupied the thrones of sees in the vicinity of Constantinople.

This was the system of *gerontismos*, government by the elders, instituted around the middle of the eighteenth century as a way of breaking the patriarch's monopoly of power.[11] Lay influence was extensively exercised to be sure, especially by Orthodox officials and dignitaries of the Porte like the grand dragomans and the princes of Wallachia and Moldavia, as rule members of the Phanariot families. Increasingly, as the nineteenth century progressed, lay influence in the affairs of the church was wielded by persons of great wealth who had risen to prominence through success in commerce and banking and had amassed enormous fortunes. All these forms of influence, however, remained informal and noninstitutionalized and very often involved unwarranted intervention of laymen in purely ecclesiastical issues beyond their competence, which, inevitably, bred corruption.

The new claims voiced after 1856, precisely involved a demand for formal institutionalized representation of the lay element in the administration of the church, and this could be only connected with the rise of secularization marking the age, of which nationalism was a particular expression in the Christian communities of the Ottoman Empire. The picture, of course, was neither uniform nor predictable as to who stood where or as to the consistency of the positions adopted. All this was determined by circumstances, short-term alliances, and calculations of interests. As a result of the movement of lay assertion in the affairs of the church, nevertheless, major institutional changes came into place whereby the old oligarchic system of government by the elder metropolitans was abolished and was replaced by a new system by which the governance of the church was entrusted to a Holy Synod of twelve prelates, drawn from the entire body of the hierarchy, renewable every two years[12] while affairs of the Orthodox community were managed by a "permanent mixed council," composed by eight elected lay members and four metropolitans. Both bodies were presided over by the patriarch, and the two together formed an electoral college, broadened with the addition of lay dignitaries and other representatives from the parishes of Constantinople and the provinces, which elected the patriarch.[13]

These institutional changes were provided for by the "General Regulations," enacted officially on January 27, 1862 as part of the broader structure of Ottoman reforms that sought to modernize and make government more accountable in the empire. The "General Regulations" were the product of protracted negotiations in the Orthodox community that took years to transact, following the initial edict of the Sublime Porte concerning the introduction of reforms. An initial "national assembly," composed of representatives and dignitaries of the Orthodox community, was convoked between 1858 and 1860 with the charge to draft the regulations that would implement the reforms among the Orthodox. The assembly produced the draft that eventually, after further revisions, was enacted as the General Regulations in 1862. The text and its various specific provisions, however, remained an object of contention and it was repeatedly subjected to revisions by other assemblies in 1870 and 1872 and by successive appeals of the two bodies to the Porte.[14]

The institutionalized presence of the lay element provided outlets for the introduction of nationalist sensibilities and conflicts into the affairs of the church, and it also fostered the emergence of many-sided conflicts between the lay element and the leadership of the church, which attempted in most instances to maintain a nonnational approach to ecclesiastical and community affairs on the basis of the traditions of Christian ecumenicity, as noted above, for instance, in the attempts to accommodate Bulgarian claims before the schism.

The wider story of the politics of the Orthodox community in the Ottoman Empire in the age of reforms is certainly beyond the scope of the present essay, which attempts to bring some order to the consideration of the equally complex question of the encounter of the Ecumenical Patriarchate with the protean challenge of secular nationalism. On this level of analysis, the relevance of the story of the new institutional arrangements brought about by the application of the Ottoman reforms in the system of governance of the Orthodox community consists in the recognition of the outlets it provided whereby nationalism and national passions influenced the policy options and decisions of the church. The formal presence of the laity, with its own divisions, factions, conflicting views and interests in the process of ecclesiastical governance, and especially direct lay participation in patriarchal elections, influenced in significant ways, through various forms of dependence and patronage, the policies of the patriarchate.[15]

On the evidence of the historical record, it was largely the pressure, coming from lay elements in the Orthodox community, who had been converted to the values of Greek nationalism, that, in the 1860s and 1870s, led to the escalation of the conflict with the Bulgarian Orthodox that culminated in the schism. It was such elements, influenced largely by the nationalist politics of Epaminondas Deligiorgis, prime minister of Greece in the mid-1860s and in the early 1870s, that, against the more moderate counsel of senior leaders of the Orthodox community in Constantinople, pushed for a sharp showdown with the Bulgarians, motivated to a considerable degree by anti-Russian attitudes. It was characteristic of the climate of the time that at the Synod of 1872, the Patriarch Cyril of Jerusalem, who wished for moderation toward Bulgarian aspirations, was subjected to threats and forced to remain away.[16]

The Bulgarian question remained the crucible of the church's encounter with nationalism. As Bulgarian activities on behalf of the exarchate escalated in Macedonia and Thrace, and the Greek state became more actively involved to protect Greek interests in the regions, the panorthodox policies preferred by Patriarchs Joachim II and Joachim III went unheeded by a younger generation of prelates, who had to face the consequences of the schism on the ground. Thus these younger prelates were forced, very often by pastoral necessity, to align themselves with Greek nationalism and to espouse its values. This group of senior clergymen included some of the most dynamic and gifted bishops of the Ecumenical Patriarchate, charismatic men like Chrysostom of Drama and then of Smyrna and Germanos of Kastoria and then of Amasya. Their conversion to nationalism through their involvement in irredentist politics in Macedonia signaled, in a way, what the wave of the future would bring in the relationship of the Ecumenical Patriarchate to nationalism.[17]

Concurrently, in another domain of the church's traditional concerns, that of education and cultural life, the wave of ethnonationalism was also actively transforming the mentality and values of the younger generations of its flock through the active promotion of Greek cultural policies in the Orthodox communities of the Ottoman Empire, both in the Balkans and Asia Minor. These cultural policies, through the foundation of schools and nurseries, the training of teachers, and the active encouragement of the foundation of local cultural associations, aimed at, and to a considerable extent, did achieve the cultivation of Greek national consciousness among the Orthodox populations of the empire, even in distant and isolated regions in the far interior of Asia Minor.[18] The church, which in fulfilling its pastoral duties had been traditionally the leading agent in the education of the faithful, could not, of course, oppose educational initiatives that did not threaten Orthodox doctrine (as similar initiatives of Western missionary groups did), and, therefore, the process of the nationalization of its flock through the expansion of the network of Greek schools proceeded apace in the new environment of freedom, toleration, and equality made possible by the institutional context of Ottoman reforms.

The process of the internal and initially inadvertent nationalization of the Orthodox Church in the course of the nineteenth century could be more clearly illustrated if we turned our attention for a moment to the insular microcosm of the Orthodox Church of Cyprus. Although Cyprus is an autocephalous church and does not belong to the jurisdiction of Constantinople, under Ottoman rule the two churches became closely identified and ties in the nineteenth century were particularly close to the point that developments in the ecclesiastical life of Cyprus followed closely the broader patterns unfolding on a much larger scale in the extensive territorial jurisdiction of the Patriarchate of Constantinople in Asia Minor and the Balkans.

Cyprus had gained ecclesiastical autocephaly at the Third Ecumenical Council at Ephesus in 431. It thus ranked sixth after Rome and the four Eastern patriarchates in ecclesiastical seniority. Under the medieval Frankish kingdom and the subsequent period of Venetian rule, the autocephaly of the Church of Cyprus was suppressed by Rome (1260–1571), but it was restored by a synod of Orthodox patriarchs held in Constantinople in 1572, following the Ottoman conquest of the island the previous year.

Under archbishops Chrysanthos (1767–1810) and Kyprianos (1810–21), the Church of Cyprus went through a period of revival and reconstruction, taking many initiatives in the cultural domain. Archbishop Kyprianos was a genuine representative of the ecclesiastical Enlightenment noted above and took important measures in the field of education,[19] establishing a higher "Hellenic school" in Nicosia in 1812 and supporting, in 1819, the initiation of a "Philological Gymnasium" in Limassol, modeled after the Philological Gymnasium of Smyrna, one of the foremost hearths of the culture of the Enlightenment in the Greek world. All this creative energy shown by the Cypriot exponent of the ecclesiastical Enlightenment came to a tragic end in 1821, when the archbishop, the three metropolitans, Chrysanthos of Paphos, Meletios of Kition, Lavrentios of Kyrenia, and hundreds of other senior ecclesiastical dignitaries and lay notables fell victims to the savagery and rapacity of a local Ottoman governor, who staged a major massacre on July 9, 1821, and in subsequent weeks.

Thus the Church of Cyprus shared in the martyrdom brought upon the Orthodox hierarchy throughout the Ottoman Empire in reprisal for the Greek revolution in 1821. Later on, this legacy of martyrdom supplied a powerful symbolic impetus to the growth of Greek nationalism in Cyprus, endowing it with its "ethnomartyr" founding fathers.

The history of the Church of Cyprus for the remainder of Ottoman rule down to the British occupation of 1878, was, in fact, a protracted endeavor to recover from the heavy blow dealt to it by the tragedy of 1821. The 1820s was a decade of instability in the church with three prelates alternating on the archiepiscopal throne, but during the relatively longer reign of archbishop Panaretos (1827–40), a systematic effort at reconstruction was undertaken with the convocation of two assemblies of senior clergy and lay notables in 1830 and 1839, which provided especially for the organization of the island's Orthodox community and the establishment of schools. An important initiative took place in 1828, shortly after Panaretos's accession, whereby the archbishop, the bishops, and lay notables of Cyprus signed an appeal to the first head of state of liberated Greece, Governor Ioannis Capodistrias, to take measures for the inclusion of Cyprus within the borders of the fledging new state. This appeal set a pattern that was going to be repeated on many occasions for the rest of the nineteenth and during the twentieth century, with the Church of Cyprus leading the movement for the incorporation of the island in the Kingdom of Greece.

Although Archbishop Panaretos was expelled from his throne with an imperial command in 1840, in the age of reforms that marked the last phase of Ottoman rule in Cyprus, the Orthodox Church on the island enjoyed relative tranquility and respect. Three archbishops at the close of the Ottoman period received high Ottoman decorations, marking the new age in the relations of the Orthodox Church with the Ottoman state. The new climate allowed the church to concentrate on its internal reconstruction and the promotion of Greek education. In her educational projects, the Church of Cyprus was repeatedly assisted by Constantinople, especially by the *Syllogos*, the Greek Literary Association of Constantinople. Ties with the Ecumenical Patriarchate remained close throughout this period and Constantinople was constantly the main point of reference for the Church of Cyprus. Clergy from the island began being trained at the new Theological School established by Constantinople in 1844 on the island of Halki in the Sea of Marmara. These cultural initiatives and expanding ties with the new Greek state and major centers of Greek diaspora and ecclesiastical life around the Eastern Mediterranean, especially with Alexandria and Jerusalem, contributed decisively to strengthening the sense of Greek identity in Cyprus and laid the foundations for the future growth of a dynamic nationalist movement in the island.

Meanwhile at the center of the empire and the Orthodox Church, the return of Patriarch Joachim III to the throne in 1901, with the support of the neo-Phanariot group in the lay leadership of the Orthodox community, who saw in the preservation of the Ottoman Empire the safest guarantee for the survival and prosperity of the church and its flock, acted as a brake that slowed the wholesale conversion of the Ecumenical Patriarchate toward nationalism. Amid all other Orthodox churches that had been transformed into national churches and, led by the Church of Russia, were pursuing active nationalist strategies, the Ecumenical Patriarchate under Patriarch Joachim still held out, professing the values of Christian universalism and ecumenicity.[20] The patriarch passed away on November 13, 1912, literally on the morrow of the outbreak of the first Balkan War. The Greek army had just taken Thessaloniki on October 26, the day of the city's patron saint, St. Dimitrios. In the age of Balkan Wars and of the Great War that followed, the resistance of the Ecumenical Patriarchate to nationalism finally withered away. Ten years later, in the wake of Greece's Asia Minor disaster, the patriarchate paid the heaviest of costs for this transient flirtation with nationalism, with the martyrdom and eventual expulsion of its flock from its historic hearths in the land of the seven Churches of the Apocalypse.[21]

The Church and the Ottoman State

Since its reestablishment by Mehmet the Conqueror in 1454, the Patriarchate of Constantinople had functioned as an institution of the Ottoman imperial order. Upon their accession, the patriarchs, in their personal capacity as leaders of their religious community, were issued imperial edicts (*berats*) recognizing their status and detailing their duties, especially their foremost obligation to secure the loyalty and submission of their Christian flock to their Ottoman master.[22] Despite the official recognition of their status as religious leaders of a significant part of the population of the empire, the patriarchs, as a rule, suffered the consequences of the arbitrariness of despotic power. This is reflected in the frequency of changes on the patriarchal throne, some patriarchs serving only a few months or even weeks, many of them returning to the throne for second, third, or even further terms and several falling victims to martyrdom, including some of the most prominent ones such as Cyril I, Gregory V, and Cyril VI.

Of the many cases of patriarchal martyrdom under Ottoman rule, the story of Patriarch Gregory V is particularly revealing in connection with the multiple facets of the church's relation to secular thought, in general, and to nationalism, in particular. Gregory came to the ecumenical throne in 1798 from the Metropolis of Smyrna. His background linked him with the movements of revival of Orthodox spirituality emanating from Mount Athos earlier in the eighteenth century. When he ascended the throne of Constantinople in 1798, the Ottoman Empire was in dire straits, besieged by the pressures of the age of revolution on all sides: French revolutionary troops had just occupied the Ionian islands on the empire's Western front, Napoleon had landed in Egypt, putting the empire's territorial integrity in serious jeopardy, separatist movements by local toparchs were threatening the empire from within, and revolutionary initiatives inspired by Jacobinism like the one led by Rhigas Velestinlis were rising among the Christian subjects of the empire. The Sublime Porte, in a state of alarm, obviously pressed the patriarch to do something to keep his flock in line and to secure its loyalty to the empire. The patriarch did not need to be convinced. Deeply committed to Christian culture and to the cultivation of the faith of his flock through the improvement of education and intent on fulfilling his pastoral responsibilities by establishing, on safe foundations, the canonical order in the church, the patriarch did not think that any form of disloyalty to the Ottoman state could be conducive to anything edifying for the Orthodox community. For him, as for most of his predecessors, the legitimacy of the Ottoman state was a fundamental premise of the condition of the earthly existence and conduct of the church. Hence the patriarch's active campaign against the revolutionary ideas of liberty and equality that were infiltrating the conscience of a segment of his flock came as a natural consequence. This campaign was particularly notable in 1798—the critical year of Napoleon's landing in Egypt—and included the patriarch's famous encyclical to the inhabitants of the Ionian islands, warning about the pernicious spiritual consequences of French revolutionary principles, the condemnation of the revolutionary initiative of Rhigas Velestinlis, and the publication of the track *Paternal instruction*, which attempted to systematically reinterpret the terms liberty and equality to make them conform to the idea of submission to the Ottoman state.[23]

All these expressions of official ecclesiastical policy reflected the distance the Orthodox Church wished to maintain from modern secular ideas in order to keep the faithful within its fold and expressed with sincerity an ancient tradition of which the Patriarchate of Constantinople felt itself to be the guardian. The patriarch's attitude remained consistent in his following two patriarchates (1806–8 and 1819–21). His third patriarchate coincided with the escalation of the ideological preparation of the Greek struggle for freedom and the outbreak of the war of independence. The patriarch remained consistently opposed to all these movements, fearing—rightly as it turned out—that they would lead to violent reprisals by the Ottomans that might put the very physical survival of the Christian people in jeopardy. Gregory's last patriarchate turned into an active campaign to contain the radical effects of secular ideas among his flock and to strengthen the bases of traditional Orthodox culture. Among other initiatives, the patriarch set up a patriarchal press, appointed a patriarchal censor and invited Orthodox scholars to submit their works for publication. Counter-Enlightenment initiatives among the learned laity, both within the Ottoman Empire and in the diaspora, were encouraged, including the publication in Vienna of the journal *Kalliope* in 1819, as a forum of conservative opinion against the liberal *Ermis o Logios,* also published in Vienna, and the radical journal *Melissa*, published in Paris. The most important initiative of the period was the attempt to bring Greek education in line by affirming the control of the church over the main high schools of the Greek world and closing down, through the initiative of local metropolitans, the major institutions following a predominantly secular curriculum like the Philological Gymnasium in Smyrna and the High School of Chios. Just as the Greek war of independence was breaking out in March 1821, the patriarch convoked a synod in Constantinople that issued a condemnation of "philosophical lessons," meaning exactly the curricula of the Enlightenment introduced into Greek high schools.[24] The best-known measure of ideological control came at the very end of Gregory's third patriarchate and involved the encyclicals disowning the revolt against Ottoman rule led by Alexander Ypsilantis in Moldavia. The month of March 1821 was marked by many parallel initiatives, including an encyclical of March 11, 1821, confirming that the condemnation of the outbreak of the revolt "had been signed amid a torrent of tears on the holy altar."[25]

All this, however, "an authentic expression of ecclesiastical politics under Ottoman rule" as it has been rightly characterized by Gregory's most objective modern biographer,[26] did not assuage the Ottomans' panic at the revolutionary outbreak, neither did it convince them of the loyalty of the Orthodox Church. On April 10, 1821, Easter Sunday, the Patriarch Gregory V and four senior prelates resident in Istanbul, Dionysios of Ephesus, Athanasios of Nicomedia, Gregory of Derkoi, and Evgenios of Anchialos, were executed for high treason. The patriarch, who had celebrated Easter liturgy at midnight, was hung from the central gate of the patriarchate at Phanar in Istanbul; his body was given over to a mob and eventually thrown into the Bosporus. The gate of the patriarchate where the patriarch had been hung has remained closed ever since.

The patriarch's martyrdom at the outbreak of the Greek revolution despite his active opposition to secular values and to any form of liberation initiatives throughout his tenure of the patriarchal throne, transformed him immediately into an icon of Greek nationalism. Throughout the period of the liberation struggle in the 1820s, his name became a slogan for the fighters of Greek freedom and later, in the independent Greek state, he was ceremoniously incorporated among the protagonists of the liberation of Greece. Somewhat ironically, in the 1870s, his statue was erected outside the University of Athens next to that of Rhigas Velestinlis, whose political ideas he had condemned as "full of rottenness."

On the centennial of his martyrdom in 1921, Patriarch Gregory V was canonized by the synod of the autocephalous Church of Greece, an initiative faced with skepticism by Constantinople at the time[27] although subsequently the patriarch as an "hieromartyr" was included in the patriarchate's calendar of saints. It is interesting to note that whereas for the Church of Greece Gregory V is an "ethnomartyr," the Church of Constantinople prefers to refer to him as an "hieromartyr," recalling and connecting him to the tradition of the early church and associating him with such great and popular early saintly bishops like Charalambos and Eleftherios martyred by the Romans.

The story of Patriarch Gregory V is extremely important, as it reveals the whole nexus between Orthodoxy and nationalism. As it should be clear from the brief survey of the patriarch's pastoral activity and ecclesiastical policies above, he remained, throughout, with impressive consistency, dedicated to the spiritual, canonical, and pastoral traditions of Orthodoxy that ipso facto turned him into an opponent of the multiple expressions of secularism, including its foremost political manifestation, nationalism. This, in fact, was an authentic expression of the Orthodox position, which Gregory incarnated with a deep sense of responsibility with his life and death. His martyrdom, nevertheless, delivered him to the ideology of Greek nationalism and to the historiography that embodied this ideology, for which Gregory's antinationalist policies and his skepticism about plans for the liberation of Greece remained a source of profound embarrassment. Throughout the nineteenth and repeatedly during the twentieth century, there have been historiographical attempts to "exonerate" the patriarch from the charge of "collaborationism" with the "foreign and infidel tyrants" of the Greek nation leveled against him by equally ideologically motivated arguments of historians and other commentators with a leftist or "progressive" orientation. Of course, both positions are simply symptomatic of anachronistic thinking, ideological prejudice, and an inability to recover and judge on its own terms, taking into account its religious premises, the ways the Orthodox Church, with the Ecumenical Patriarchate at its head, strove against enormous odds to discharge its pastoral duties and to preserve the Orthodox faith within the institutional framework set by the Ottoman state.

It was precisely this institutional framework that seemed to be changing in the age of reforms. For about a quarter of a century, from the 1850s to the 1870s, the official Ottoman recognition of the equality of all subjects of the empire and the project of a common Ottoman identity regardless of religion or ethnic origin involved ipso facto a new attitude toward Orthodoxy and the Ecumenical Patriarchate. The frequent changes of the holders of the patriarchal office continued throughout the nineteenth century, but the incumbent patriarchs were treated with respect and accorded state honors and top decorations that symbolized the new status of equality and toleration to which the empire aspired.

A small, little known social event late in 1851 reflected the new climate and the hopes it nurtured. On December 15 of that year, the reigning Sultan Abdul Mecid I (1839–61) in a gesture suggesting great favor and good will, graced with his presence the wedding of the daughter of one of the most prominent Orthodox dignitaries at the time, Stefanos Vogoridis, who had served the Porte in various capacities, including that of Prince of Samos. According to a detailed eyewitness account, the sultan arrived at the church where the wedding was blessed and remained standing with his hands crossed throughout the ceremony, saying that he had taken an oath never to sit down on occasions at which the name of the Lord was mentioned.[28]

The *Hatt-i Humayun* of February 18, 1856, provided the formal context for the new condition of the church in the Ottoman Empire by affirming the rights and privileges that would secure its free and unfettered functioning: it recognized the spiritual privileges and exemptions of Christian communities, secured the complete religious freedom of all religious confessions, granted permission to build and repair places of worship, schools, and philanthropic establishments, forbade forced religious conversions, proclaimed the complete equality of all subjects of the empire, forbade discrimination in favor of any religious community, granted to all the right to assume and exercise public offices, dignities, and visit state schools, it ordered the establishment of mixed courts, gave the option of buying exemption from military service, granted the right of property ownership to foreign subjects, and guaranteed complete religious toleration.[29]

The new position of the church in the Ottoman Empire was best reflected in ecclesiastical architecture. Whereas for centuries Orthodox churches were built behind high walls and under tiled roofs, which made them as inconspicuous as possible, as can still be seen today in the old walled city of Istanbul, in the second half of the nineteenth century, during the age of reforms and subsequently, new imposing church buildings were erected with impressive domes and belfries. Some of the best known examples of this new ecclesiastical architecture include the Holy Trinity Church in Pera, which still dominates Taxim square in Istanbul, Holy Trinity in Kadiköy, St. Kyriaki, and Panagia Elpida in Kumkapi in Istanbul. Most of all, the best sign of the self-confidence and optimism that the Orthodox community in the Ottoman Empire enjoyed in this period is provided by the domed building of the Patriarchal Great School, built in 1882, which still dominates with its red-brick structure the northern shore of the Golden Horn.

The official Ottoman attitudes, which made possible the public affirmation of Orthodox religious identity in the Ottoman Empire in the age of reforms and its aftermath, were not to last for very long. New needs and priorities in the government of the Ottoman Empire under Sultan Abludhamid II (1876–1909) changed the climate of recognition and acceptance of the pluralism of Ottoman society that had given prominence to the Orthodox Church. The rise of nationalism among the Christian communities of the empire eventually forced upon the Sublime Porte the recognition of the necessity of a new form of legitimization of state power and a new source of loyalty to imperial authority. This new source of legitimacy and loyalty was provided by nationalism. Sultan Abludhamid, as caliph of Islam, turned first to Islamic nationalism, but this became increasingly Turkified in order to attract the loyalty of the main population group in the empire.[30] In this context, the old struggle between Christianity and Islam was revived and recast in modern: that is, nationalist terms. It was a kind of ideological "Cold War," as it has been aptly suggested,[31] in which the survival of the one meant the destruction of the other. The ideological militancy that replaced the spirit of toleration of the age of reform destroyed the social theory of Young Ottomanism, which had sustained the introduction of the first Ottoman constitution in 1876 and had visualized a basically multicultural transformation of the empire.[32] With the reversal of the prospects of pluralism in the Ottoman Empire, the differentiated official attitude toward Orthodoxy also disappeared. The Hamidian government attempted to break the power and freedom of action of the church by curtailing its traditional privileges that had been confirmed and strengthened by the *Hatt-i Humayun*. The first attempt was made in 1883 through an attempt to reformulate the text of the *berats* issued for two newly elected metropolitans. This provoked serious protests on the part of the church, leading eventually to the resignation of Patriarch Joachim III in 1884.[33] All this led to a protracted conflict between the Ecumenical Patriarchate and the Sublime Porte over the so called "privileges" of the church. The confrontation lasted for decades and was never resolved, but it did provoke an extensive literature on the traditional privileges of the Orthodox community.

After the turn of the century and the advent of the Young Turk movement, the Orthodox Church and the Ecumenical Patriarchate would experience the suspicion, exclusiveness, and hostility of Turkish nationalism, which would seal its history in the twentieth century.

List of Ecumenical Patriarchs

Neophytos VII, 1798–1801
Gregory V (Georgios Aggelopoulos), 1797–1798, 1806–1808, 1818–1821
Kallinikos V, 1801–1806, 1808–1809
Jeremiah IV, 1809–1813
Cyril VI (Konstantinos Serpentzoglou), 1813–1818

Evgenios II, 1821–1822
Anthimos III (Anthimos Horianopoulos), 1822–1824
Chrysanthos (Chrysanthos Manoleas), 1824–1826
Agathangelos, 1826–1830
Constantios I (Sinaitis), 1830–1834
Constantios II 1834–1835
Gregory VI (Georgios Fourtouniadis), 1835–1840, 1867–1871
Anthimos IV (Anthimos Vamvakis), 1840–1841
Anthimos V, 1841–1842
Germanos IV, 1842–1845, 1852–1853
Meletios III (Meletios Pagkalos), 1845
Anthimos VI (Anthimos Ioannidis), 1845–1848, 1853–1855, 1871–1873
Cyril VII (Konstantinos), 1855–1860
Joachim II (Ioannis Kokkodis), 1860–1863, 1873–1878
Sophronios III (Stavros Meydantzoglou), 1863–1866
Joachim III (Ioannis Devetzis or Dimitriadis), 1878–1884, 1901–1912
Joachim IV (Nikolaos Krousouloudis), 1884–1887
Dionysios V (Dionysios Charitonidis), 1887–1891
Neophytos VIII (Joachim Papakonstantinou), 1891–1894
Anthimos VII (Aggelos Tsatsos), 1895–1897
Constantinos V (Konstantinos Valiadis), 1897–1901

CHAPTER 3

THE ORTHODOX CHURCH OF GREECE

Dimitris Stamatopoulos

The founding of the Greek autocephalous church marked a significant stage in the creation of nationalized churches in the Balkans, which had formerly been under the control of the Ecumenical Patriarchate of Constantinople.[1] The establishment of the church in 1833 and its recognition by the patriarchate in 1850 formed the prelude to the progressive dissolution of the Orthodox flock in the Ottoman Balkans.[2] However, the prototype for this situation (the creation of a nation-state in Southeastern Europe) did not necessarily entail some sort of originality in the organization of the new institution. As was the case in the adoption of other state, judicial, and educational institutions, the models for imitation were corresponding institutions, mainly those of Western states, but also of Russia. The "imitation" or "transfusion" of Western institutions was of course not a straight path; rather, the transference of Western or imperial models comprised a complex and often contradictory process.

Consequently, although the establishment of the Greek autocephalous church was the result of political pressure exercised by the English and French embassies on the newly formed Greek state, with the goal of weakening Russian influence,[3] its founding seemed to replicate core elements of the Russian ecclesiastical model.[4] At the same time, the creation of the first nationalized church in the Balkans evinced the contradictory historical conditions of the period: internal political antagonism among supporters of the English, French, and Russian parties concerning the general orientation of the new state, ideological opposition between the epigones of the modern Greek Enlightenment and their adversaries, and theoretical conflict between supporters of a civil state model of church-state relations and those who insisted on the ideals of Orthodox ecumenism as represented by the Ecumenical Patriarchate.

Since the modern Greek state formed a battlefield for rival foreign policies, and above all rival ideological orientations, its founding and development should be considered in relation to the influence of European imperial nationalism on its institutions.[5] Modern historiography has become accustomed to dealing with the nation-state as being naturally and deliberately opposed to the existence of imperial states; however, doing so neglects to take into account the hybrid character of the nineteenth century. At the same time that nation-states were seeking to simulate empires, empires—particularly those of Eastern and Southeastern Europe—were attempting to nationalize their populations on the basis of the dominant identity of the ruling dynasty. Just when those traditional continental empires of Eastern and Southeastern Europe were setting in motion the processes for modernizing their state structures, they were under pressure from the economic and military superiority of the Western colonial empires. The influences of both the Eastern and Western type of imperial discourses can be traced in the founding and evolution of the nationalized church, even though its functionality concerned the classic operations of homogenization and the formation of a new national identity.

For this reason, the proclamation of the Greek autocephalous church was characterized by some interesting paradoxes: an autocephalous Orthodox Church had as its head a Catholic monarch, Othon (Otto Friedrich Ludwig von Wittelsbach, son of the king of Bavaria, Ludwig I), while the ideological prime movers of this endeavor were individuals such as the (Lutheran) regent Georg Ludwig von Maurer and his (Greek Orthodox) counselor Theoklitos Farmakidis, who, although they were supported by the British and French embassies, imposed a model for ecclesiastical governance inspired by that of the Russian Standing Holy Synod as imposed by Peter the Great in the early eighteenth century.

Thus the new church needed to respond simultaneously to two different problems: first, that of the dependence of the Greek Church on the patriarchate, and second, that of the subjugation of the church to the state. Both problems had made their appearance, together with a pressing need for their resolution, even before the arrival of the young king Othon and his councilor-regents.[6] The establishment of the Bulgarian Exarchate (1870),[7] as well as the recognition of the Serbian Church (1879) and Romanian Church (1885) that followed, ignited ethnic conflicts in the geographic region of Macedonia.[8]

The Prelude to the Founding of the Autocephalous Church

After six years of war with the Ottomans (the revolution had broken out in February 1821 in Moldavia and Wallachia, and in March had spread to the Peloponnese, Aegean islands, and Central Greece), at the Fourth National Assembly in Troizen (April 1827), the Greeks took the decision to call Ioannis Capodistrias back from abroad to serve as the first governor of the newly created Greek state. Capodistrias, a former deputy minister of foreign affairs for Russia, had been largely responsible for the recognition of the revolutionaries by the European diplomatic community (against the wishes of Klemens von Metternich, chancellor of the Habsburg monarchy and the adviser of the Holy Alliance) and would govern Greece until his assassination in 1831. Capodistrias's arrival in 1828 marked a suspension of the democratic institutions enacted up to that point by the revolutionary national assemblies. Although his centralized, authoritarian government set in motion the process for the establishment of an autocephalous church, and generally, for the founding of new state institutions, at the same time it marked the defeat and gradual marginalization of the liberal ideas of the Enlightenment tradition as represented primarily by the students and supporters of Adamantios Korais. Paradoxically, it severed liberal reform from its ideological presuppositions.[9]

The ecclesiastical metropolises of the Peloponnese, which was the central region of revolutionary activity, had become subject to the jurisdiction of the Ecumenical Patriarchate upon its final conquest by the Ottomans in 1718. Central Greece and the Aegean islands, which with the Peloponnese comprised the core of the first Greek state, had been subject to the Ottomans and consequently to the Ecumenical Patriarchate since the fifteen century.[10]

As early as Ioannis Capodistrias's return to Greece, the question of dependence on the patriarchate had been posed in political terms, since the Ecumenical Patriarch Agathangelos (who was probably of Bulgarian origin) had, at the demand of the Sublime Porte, sent a letter to the revolutionary Greeks, proposing a compromise with the Ottoman Empire in exchange for a general truce. Capodistrias rejected the patriarch's proposal, and, although he acknowledged him as the "head of the Holy Church," it was clear that the patriarchate could only function as a mechanism of Ottoman authority. It was Capodistrias who first established (on September 12, 1829) a Ministry "of Ecclesiastical [Affairs] and Public Education." Its new minister, Nikolaos Chrysogelos, in instructions sent to the metropolitans "concerning the performance of their duties"—while considering that the application of the holy regulations in cases involving family law was the inalienable work of the bishops—forbade the ordainment of new priests or the promotion of already-ordained prelates in new bishoprics until the state's final settlement of this issue through "general provisions."

As Gerasimos Konidaris has correctly pointed out, through his actions Capodistrias demonstrated that, as a defender of the civil-state model, he too would prefer the subjugation of church to state.[11] However, it remains an open question whether he chose this path in concert with the patriarchate, as Chrysostomos Papadopoulos has maintained. Konidaris attempted to refute this view by developing an argument concerning the governor's "civil state" beliefs. In fact, Capodistrias's correspondence with Patriarch Agathangelos's successor Constantios I showed that both sides appeared to have had common ground for discussion of the resolution of individual subjects; however, the question of ending the patriarchate's control, and above all that of the governance of the ecclesiastical provinces of Greece, was never posed.[12]

The Establishment of the Greek Autocephalous Church

Capodistrias's assassination in front of the door of Saint Spyridon in Nafplion in 1831 as a result of the Peloponnesian notables' reaction to his policy of centralization certainly upset the political stage, at the expense of Russian foreign policy in Greece. On December 5, 1831, at the Fifth National Assembly convened in Argos two months after the assassination, a higher ecclesiastical authority deemed the Ecclesiastical Council was formed; its provisions contained a reference to a particular "Greek" church, as the new minister "for Ecclesiastical Affairs," Iakovos Rizos Neroulos, also referred to it. The first person to explicitly support the founding of the Greek autocephalous was Adamantios Korais, who in 1833 expressed the opinion that "the clergy are not compelled to acknowledge the Patriarch of Constantinople as their leader, as long as Constantinople remains tainted as the capital of a lawless tyrant. On the contrary, they should be ruled by a synod of prelates who will be freely chosen by priests and laity, as the ancient church did, and as the church of fellow-believing Russians continues to do today."[13]

Korais, the most important intellectual of the modern Greek Enlightenment, had been living on a permanent basis in Paris since the French Revolution. Despite the fact that he himself never visited liberated Greece, he emerged as the most important opponent of conservative clerical circles, and provided the ideological inspiration for ecclesiastical reform.[14]

Korais's proposal enraged the world of the patriarchate, and there were many who proposed excommunication, which Patriarch Constantios I rejected. What is interesting, however, is that the solution Korais proposed was not based (ostensibly) on a Western, but on a Russian model. Such an argument significantly weakened the position of Russophiles in the newly formed state. The essence of the problem was not just the impending reforms, but also whether their approval would be a matter solely for the state or whether it would need to be given by the patriarchate.

In the end, Adamantios Korais's line of argument was followed by the cleric Theoklitos Farmakidis, who, as one of the most prominent supporters of the pro-English party and an opponent of Capodistrias, undertook to finalize the plan that had been hammered out by Maurer.[15] For Farmakidis, "political autonomy without ecclesiastical autonomy is utterly unreasonable."[16] What a position like this entailed was a refusal by the Greek state to accept that the founding of the Greek Church was an act that required the approval of the patriarchate.[17] This stance was accepted by Maurer, who naturally wished to ensure the long-term absolutist authority of the new monarch. Moreover, if the example of the Russian Church was that on which Farmakidis relied, the model of the Bavarian Consistorium was that which Maurer imposed as the basic solution to the problem of the new church's formation. In reality, the Church of Greece emerged as a hybrid of these two sources of influence.

With a royal decree of March 15, 1833, a lay-clerical commission was created (with Farmakidis as a member, and the competent minister, Spyridon Trikoupis, as chair). This commission undertook to formulate a plan for the organization of the Greek Church, and on July 23, 1833, the Organic Law on the Autocephalous Church of Greece was published.

According to this law, the spiritual head of the church was Jesus Christ. However, with regard to its governance, it now had the king as head. A five-member Holy Synod of the King of Greece was stipulated as the highest ecclesiastical authority of governance, with its members appointed by the king, and a royal councilor present at its meetings (along the model of the Russian Holy Synod). In addition to higher clergy, priests and monks also had the right to participate in the Holy Synod. The king would have the right to convene the body, but not to intervene at the doctrinal level. To a large extent, the articles of the Organic Law were those published in 1818 on the basis of which the Bavarian Consistorium had been organized.[18] Maurer insisted on the originality of the Greek case, claiming that the Holy Synod of the Church of Greece was much freer and more independent than the corresponding Russian one.[19] Farmakidis was appointed the Holy Synod's first secretary, a key position for its governance, since the secretary was permitted to take part in discussions although he did not have the right to vote.

Although the source of inspiration for the establishment of a standing Holy Synod was the Russian model, the act of founding the Church of Greece met with a negative response from Russia. Russia maintained a strong foothold in the newly established state, since the Russo-Turkish war of 1828–29 and the Treaty of Adrianople were the main reasons that led Great Britain to recognize the Greek state in the London Protocol (February 1830). It was logical that the new state should become a field of competition between the Great Powers. Its basic political structure relied on the operation of three "parties" (in reality, loosely organized client networks) that reflected their strong influence: the "English," the "French," and the "Russian."[20] The "Russian party," led by Ioannis Capodistrias's brother Augustinos and the family of Theodoros Kolokotronis, who had played a leading role in the 1821 Revolution, had definitely been weakened after the governor's assassination. The issue of the reconstruction of the party's power was directly connected with the issue of whether or not an independent church would be founded by the patriarchate. Since one of the most powerful arguments of the Russian party was the common religious bond uniting the two peoples, Greek and Russian, it was logical that it would endeavor to prevent the founding of an independent Orthodox Church by the patriarchate. By contrast, the representatives of the French and English parties realized that their main opponent could be weakened by the proclamation of an autocephalous church.

As expected, the consul of Russia publicly opposed the proclamation ceremony and his successor demanded that Othon abandon his Roman Catholic faith and convert to Orthodoxy, precipitating a rupture between Russia and the new king. However, Russia's stance should not be solely interpreted as the result of domestic tensions within the Greek kingdom. Naturally, Russia viewed with concern the ever-increasing influence of the British and French consulates/embassies at Othon's court, while at the same time it was gaining a powerful foothold within the Ottoman Empire (following the signature of the Treaty of Hünkâr İskelesi in July of 1833, which provided for mutual assistance between Russia and the Ottoman Empire in case of attack by a foreign power).[21] Russia appears to have worried that independence from the patriarchate meant not only the weakening of Ottoman, but also of Russian influence in the Greek kingdom. The Russian factor was often decisive in the elevation of patriarchs in Constantinople, as had recently been confirmed in 1835 with the election of the pro-Russian Patriarch Gregory VI.[22] Thus, this was the real goal of ecclesiastical reform—namely, the weakening of the bases of support of Russian policy in the newly formed state, for which the patriarchate could, under some conditions, be a capable intermediary. Russia knew that its influence would be stronger if the "Orthodox link" was mediated by the Patriarchate of Constantinople; not all the patriarchs were pro-Russian, but in the independent autocephalous church of a state dependent on the English, pro-Russian archbishops would be unlikely to emerge.

Surrounding this central political conflict was a second ongoing conflict, one involving the degree of secularization of the Greek Church and the role of its higher clergy. It was no accident that one of the first conflicts between the Greek government and the higher clergy was caused by the fact that the Organic Law allowed participation on an equal basis in the Holy Synod of priests and monks (Farmakidis, for example, was a priest). According to the higher prelates, such a reform "contravened Apostolic and Synodic Laws";[23] in response, the competent minister gave the example of the Russian Holy Synod, in which priests were permitted to participate. This negative confrontation of the authority of the higher clergy with the regent reached its climax with the appointment of bishops in the newly formed state. On November 20, 1833, ten permanent and thirty temporary bishoprics of the Church of Greece were designated by royal decree. The temporary bishoprics were designated following pressure by the Holy Synod for those metropolitans and bishops who had taken part in the revolution and been expelled from provinces in the Ottoman Empire to assume hieratic offices. The establishment of bishoprics actually led to a complete equivalency of prelates, since the hierarchy among metropolitans, archbishops, and bishops ended. The metropolitans would be mere bishops, preserving their title only in honorary form.[24] Egalitarianism among the bishops made it easier for the state to intervene in the internal workings of the church (as in the Russian example), even if this did not necessarily imply a "popularization" or secularization of the institution of the church.

A source of tension was created concerning the handling of marriage and divorce cases when Maurer issued an order on the basis of which divorces would be subject to the competency of civil courts. On May 15, 1835, the Holy Synod notified the higher clergy through an encyclical that "since marriage [is] seen as a civil contract, and will henceforth be tried by the civil courts, we are released from this duty, and limited only to marriage, and to the issuing of a divorce for a case that has already been tried by the civil courts, when you are asked to do so by the latter."[25] With its encyclical of March 31, 1834, the church had already stipulated that the bishop's permission was required for a marriage to be performed. The loss of control over the issuance of divorces was very important with regard to the clergy's sovereign role in Greek society.

Apart from cases of divorce, which had always been the monopoly of the Orthodox clergy in the management of family-law cases in the Ottoman Empire, the regency also raised doubts about another field where the clergy had confirmed its social hegemony: the holy canons concerning impediments to marriage. Thus, for example, marriages of the fifth degree (by marriage) and sixth degree (by blood) were permitted, when at the same time they were forbidden by the patriarchate for the Orthodox flock of the Ottoman Empire.[26]

In addition to church matters, the regency also interfered in the affairs of monasteries, which were differentiated into stavropegial (i.e., those directly subject to the Patriarchate of Constantinople), parish-provincial (i.e., those subject to the jurisdiction of a local bishop), and founders (also subject to the patriarchate, but governed by the founder or his descendents). In Greece in 1833, there were around 563 monasteries and *metochia* (dependencies of monasteries): 545 for men and 18 for women. The number of monks was about 3,000. Of them, 277 lived alone, while the yearly income of the monasteries was calculated at 600,000 drachmas.[27] Maurer, probably exaggerating, increased the number of monks to 8,000, and their income to 2,149,980 drachmas, and considered that the monasteries possessed around a quarter of the land of the Greek kingdom. Certainly ecclesiastical wealth had grown during the period of Ottoman rule, which had resulted in the deterioration of the situation of landless farmers and those with small plots. On December 19, 1833, the new minister for ecclesiastical affairs, Konstantinos Schinas, sent a text with guidelines (instructions) to the Holy Synod, on the basis of which monasteries with fewer than six monks were dissolved, and their monks would have to move to larger monasteries. Those with a larger number of monks had to pay a double tax (i.e., twice the usual one-tenth), with the goal of improving ecclesiastical affairs and education. The lands from the dissolved monasteries were auctioned off, although the monks who had abandoned them had priority in the auction, should they choose to remain as renters. However, since many abbots believed that the inventory of the monasteries was for purposes of taxation, they declared small numbers of monks, which resulted in a very large number of monasteries being dissolved, especially in 1834.[28] These provisions mainly concerned the stavropegial and parish monasteries, but spread to the founders' monasteries as well, since many founders or their descendents only rarely held the title to ownership, resulting in their property being expropriated as well. In the end, 412 out of 563 monasteries were dissolved.

The question of the expropriation of monastic property had been connected with that of the founding of the Central Ecclesiastical Fund, from which the salaries of the clergy would be paid. The fund was in fact established in December 1834, but its revenues (from the sale of objects belonging to portable monastery property, the yearly rental of monastery real estate, and the "double tenth" paid by the remaining monasteries) were never sufficient to fund clerical salaries, since they also provided for the financial needs of ecclesiastical schools and archaeological excavations. The fund was dissolved in the following years and not reestablished until 1909; payment of the clergy would be effected only in the 1930s.

The Problem of Recognition: The Ecumenical Patriarchate and the Greek Autocephalous Church

On July 21, 1834, Maurer was removed from the position of regent and left Greece. However, the question of the recognition of the Church of

Greece by the Ecumenical Patriarchate remained. In October, Konstantinos Oikonomos, a former professor in the Philological Gymnasium of Smyrna and an intellectual with close ties to the patriarchate and Russia, arrived in Greece. During the years that followed, Oikonomos would emerge as Farmakidis's most significant ideological opponent, exerting pressure on the patriarchate for recognition of the Greek autocephalous church. A number of groups of intellectuals formed around these two personalities, trading accusations for about seventeen years.

Although the Holy Synod of the Church of Greece was entirely based on the theoretical legitimation of the denunciation of Pietism (*Theosophism*) by Theofilos Kaïris[29]—which the Ecumenical Patriarchate had expressed during the reign of Gregory VI—the patriarch who followed him, Anthimos IV, refused to accept the relevant encyclical, declaring that he "had no knowledge of the existence of such a voluntarily formed Holy Synod in the Greek state, and that the provinces of this state were under the spiritual jurisdiction of the Ecumenical Patriarchate."[30] This stance increased pressure not only on the Holy Synod, but also on the Greek state to resolve the issue of recognition.

The revolution of September 3, 1843, by virtue of which Othon's absolutist monarchy was transformed into a constitutional one, created the presuppositions to do so. On November 12, 1843, the Holy Synod submitted a report to the government in which it criticized (a) the removal of the Church of Greece from the Ecumenical Patriarchate's jurisdiction; (b) the appointment of "foreign" prelates; (c) the limitation on the number of bishoprics to ten; (d) the state's neglect of the education of clerics; (e) the dissolution of the monasteries; (f) the activities of the missionaries; and (g) the "desecration" of the institution of marriage. This was the first time the Holy Synod had posed the issue of the 1833 overturn of the status quo so explicitly. In December 1843, the synod drew up a plan for an ecclesiastical statutory law consisting of ten articles. In the first and second articles, it was stipulated that the Church of Greece acknowledged Jesus Christ as its head, and that it was indissolubly related "dogmatically and canonically" to the Great Church of Constantinople, while it was independent at the level of self-governance. The third article mentioned that "decrees and laws" contrary to ecclesiastical institutions were automatically "null and void." Finally, the king (in Article 4) was referred to as the "protector" and "defender" of the church, but not as its "head," as he had been referred to in the Organic (Statutory) Law of 1833.

Thus, paradoxically, just as the first constitution in Greece's political history was being introduced, the Orthodox clergy found the opportunity to restore its lost authority and to impose conditions for the reestablishment of its social hegemony according to the prototype by which the Ecumenical Patriarchate operated in the Ottoman Empire. The work of the Constitutional National Assembly developed into a standoff between the minister of ecclesiastical affairs, Konstantinos Schinas, who supported the positions of the Holy Synod, and former minister Spyridon Trikoupis, who supported the decisions taken in 1833.

In the end, the first two articles of the constitution of 1844 were formulated as follows:

1. The prevailing religion in Greece is that of the Eastern Church . . .
2. The Orthodox Church of Greece, acknowledging our Lord Jesus Christ as its head, is inextricably joined in doctrine with the Great Church in Constantinople and with every other Church of Christ of the same doctrine, like them observing unchanged the holy apostolic and synodic canons and traditions; [but] it is autocephalous, acting independently of every other church in its sovereign rights, and governed by a Holy Synod of Primates.[31]

The royal decree of 1833 was essentially abolished by the second article of the constitution of 1844, since the organization of the church was established on a new basis. Furthermore, in Articles 36 and 42, the king was designated not as the "leader" or "sovereign" of the church, but as its "protector." The entire agenda of demands by the Holy Synod as represented by Konstantinos Schinas at the National Assembly was institutionalized and acquired definitive legal form in the new constitution. Specifically, the reference to the observation of the holy canons opened the way for a normalization of relations with the patriarchate, since it confirmed the spiritual subordination of the Church of Greece to the latter.[32] Although Ioannis Kolettis, the Francophile master of the Greek political stage during the 1840s, with a considerable number of retractions, did not in the end implement at the legislative level the lines indicated by Article 2 of the constitution, it was certain that the situation had changed in favor of Konstantinos Oikonomos and his group. Throughout the 1840s, Oikonomos had developed close ties with Constantinople and the patriarchate, playing an important role in the founding of the Theological School of Halki in 1844 and the corresponding Theological School of the Patriarchate of Jerusalem in 1855.

At the end of the decade, the political presuppositions had been created for the recognition of the Church of Greece by the patriarchate. The pro-French policy followed by Othon called forth a reaction by the British Embassy. Despite the fact that the constitution of 1844 weakened his power, Othon insisted on becoming the main player in the country's rule, and the weaning from the control of British policy entailed a political rapprochement with Russia. This, however, provoked a brief British naval blockade of Piraeus (the prelude for all that would follow during the Crimean War, 1854–56) to prevent any collaboration between Greece and Russia against the Ottoman Empire.

The convergence of Greece and Russia, and the death of Greece's ambassador to Constantinople Iakovos Rizos Neroulos in 1849, provided the chance for a rapprochement with the patriarchate. The Greek state decorated Patriarch Anthimos IV (elected for a second time in 1848),[33] who accepted the award though not the accompanying encyclical from the Holy Synod. The way had been paved: the Holy Synod, with its decision of May 30, 1850, and the Greek government, with a letter to the patriarchate, led the latter to convene a synod in Constantinople to resolve the Greek ecclesiastical question. This was of the greatest importance for the patriarchate: it did not come to sanction the breaking away of the Greek provinces, but with the synod it actually installed the new ecclesiastical regime of Greece.

The synod convened on July 16, 1850, under the presidency of Ecumenical Patriarch Anthimos IV.[34] In its first session, a committee composed of three prelates was formed, and it submitted an outline of the synod's terms—in actuality, a proposal by Konstantinos Typaldos-Iakovatos, Metropolitan of Stavropol and professor at the Theological School of Halki, one of the synod's three prelates. Upon the approval of the terms, the synod decided to recognize Greek autocephaly through a Synodal Tome, the preparation of which was assigned to the committee. At the synod's third session the plan was approved, and on June 29 (the feast-day of the Twelve Apostles), it was read in public by the Ecumenical Patriarch and signed by himself, five former patriarchs of Constantinople, the patriarch of Jerusalem Cyril II, and thirteen prelates.

The initiative to publish the Synodal Tome belonged to Oikonomos and Typaldos-Iakovatos, Metropolitan of Stavropol—i.e., clerics with a strong ecumenical orientation and close Russian ties. The Russian ambassador to Athens, Titov, supported their effort to heal the rift in relations between the patriarchate and the Greek Church. However, while the synod was in session, former patriarchs Gregory VI, Germanos IV, and Anthimos VI had reacted to Anthimos IV's attempt to promote the recognition process. By contrast, the former Patriarch of Constantinople Constantios I, the Patriarch of Jerusalem Cyril II, and all the members of the Patriarchal Holy Synod,[35] were aligned with Anthimos IV. The pro-Russian Gregory VI condemned the entire effort as "concealed Lutheran-Calvinism," since the demand for recognition of the autocephaly by the Ecumenical Patriarchate was made not by representatives of the Greek Church, but the Greek government. Actually, both Gregory VI and Germanos IV insisted on a policy of nonrecognition of autocephaly, in agreement with the basic guidelines of Russian foreign policy from 1833 onward. Conversely, Constantios I, Cyril II, Patriarch Anthimos IV, as well as the patriarchate's Grand Logothete (Chief Secretary) Nikolaos Aristarchis—all individuals who enjoyed good relations with the Russian side, in common with the two former patriarchs—were apparently compelled to accept the new status quo in the wake of coordinated pressure by the Ottoman and Greek governments, the British embassy and its close collaborators such as the princes Stefanos Vogoridis and Konstantinos Karatzas, and the *postelnic* (chamberlain) Dimitrios Fotiadis, and to adjust to the tactics of the Russian embassy in Athens and the mainstays of Russian policy in the Ottoman empire.[36]

In agreement with the Synodal Tome, the Church of Greece was recognized as being autocephalous on condition of its preservation of canonical order—i.e., spiritual subordination to the jurisdiction of the Ecumenical Patriarchate. This would be symbolically shown by the taking of Holy Myrrh, as was the case with all the Eastern Orthodox churches. The Holy Synod, which was to consist of six prelates, would continue as the supreme organ of self-government, but would now have as permanent president the Metropolitan of Athens. In fact, the Greek government formed the Holy Synod with a royal decree on the basis of the seniority of prelates, as the holy canons dictated. But it attempted to maintain a balance, in the belief that the 1833 founding document was not de jure annulled with the signing of the Synodal Tome, since the government did not recognize the Synodal Tome as the founding document of the Greek Holy Synod. The new founding document needed to be voted for by the government itself, which would take into consideration both the Organic Law of 1833 and the Synodal Tome of 1850. The first permanent president of the new Holy Synod was Neophytos Metaxas, Bishop of Attica, who was renamed Bishop of Athens.[37]

The fact that Theoklitos Farmakidis was removed from the position of secretary of the Holy Synod and replaced by his moderate, one-time supporter Misail Apostolidis showed the political will of the government to align itself with the core principles of the Synodal Tome. However, when in 1852 the then-competent minister Stavros Vlachos voted for two laws (the 200th and 201st) on the basis of which the agreements of 1850 would be implemented, both his tone vis-à-vis the Holy Synod as well as the provisions these laws contained deviated from the spirit of the Synodal Tome. As Georgios Mavrokordatos, professor of law at the University of Athens (and a member of Oikonomos's group) pointed out, the majority of provisions in both laws were nothing but a redrafting of those of the royal founding decree of 1833. The government continued to have the right to oversee and intervene in the internal affairs of the Holy Synod, and it had the right to extend the terms of the synod's members, while the role of the royal commissioner continued to be decisive for the validity of meetings. The only essential change was the increase in the number of bishoprics from ten to twenty-four, and their internal differentiation into metropolises (that of Athens, from which the permanent president of the Holy Synod came), archbishoprics (capitals of prefectures, like Corinth), and bishoprics. In any case, despite the fact that the Metropolitan of Athens served as the synod's president, he was in no way considered the leader of the Greek Church (as "archbishop").

Thus, despite the historical compromise between the Greek state and the patriarchate, the Church of Greece continued to be subordinate to the state machine, essentially forming a state mechanism. There was one interesting feature: the state essentially refused to pay clerics a salary, prompting Christians to maintain their spiritual advisers along the model of the Holy Scriptures.

The Nationalization of Religion: The Hybrid Character of National Ideology and the Shadow of Empire

The existence of autocephalous churches was not new in the tradition of the Eastern Orthodox Church. However, this was the first time that their existence was directly connected with that of the rise of modern nationalist movements and the creation of nation-states in the Balkans. The creation of a "national church" constituted something very different from the recognition of "autocephaly" in the old archbishoprics such as those of Cyprus or Ohrid. The founding of a church on the basis of the criterion of nationality would mean the start of the process of splitting the Orthodox *oikoumene*, at least as this was expressed by the Ecumenical Patriarchate. Consequently, the head of what was called the "Orthodox commonwealth,"[38] the patriarchate, would have to acknowledge autocephaly in a church created by metropolises and bishoprics in the former territories of the Ottoman Empire.

This contradiction was expressed most vividly in the conflict between Konstantinos Oikonomos and Theoklitos Farmakidis, which lasted more than twenty years and included accusatory texts and libel on both sides. Its theoretical underpinnings are worth examining, since they indicate the different ways in which the two understood the nation and the church's relationship to it.

Oikonomos focused his critique on the anticanonical nature of the Organic Law of 1833. His critique was motivated not only from the nonrecognition of the Greek Church by the patriarchate, but above all from the "corule" of Christ and the king in the leadership of the church. Thus, despite reformers' declarations about preserving the relationship with the patriarchate at the doctrinal level, the Organic Law in fact created an internal fissure between spiritual (Christ—the archbishop) and governmental (the king—the royal commissioner) competencies.[39] The threat of secularization that Oikonomos brandished was not incidental to his line of reasoning: if someone wanted to found a uniform policy for coreligionists in the Orthodox East that would necessarily include both the patriarchate and Russia, they would have to draw the dividing line with the West.

Oikonomos's followers launched accusations about the "Protestantization" of the Greek Church[40] (accusations that connected Farmakidis's circle and views with the activity of the missionaries of the bible societies, such as Jonas King), while Farmakidis's followers, above all Neophytos Vamvas (another student and supporter of Korais's ideas), intimated in their argumentation that their opponents' position regarding the subjugation of the Greek Church to the Ecumenical Patriarchate implied doubts about the independence of the modern Greek state.[41] Naturally, behind such an accusation was the implication that the defenders of ecumenism were seeking to keep Greece within the Eastern sphere of influence, whether Ottoman or Russian.

Oikonomos considered that Greece should "hitch itself to Russia's chariot," taking advantage of the common bond of Orthodoxy, while Farmakidis believed that Greece should embrace the principles of Western parliamentarianism and constitutionalism. The former aimed at the dissolution of the Ottoman Empire with the help of the Russian army and contributed greatly to the mutation of the *Megali Idea* from a cultural to an irredentist program, while the latter supported reforms both in Greece and in the Ottoman Empire, and sought to rebuild a bipolar system to contain the Slavic threat, particularly after the end of the nineteenth century.

Consequently, the discussion of Greek autocephaly was more complex than some authors would have it, because the feud over the ecclesiastical issue was more than just a recycling of the arguments of these two rival nationalist strategies in nineteenth-century Greece. For apart from the question of the instrumental use of religion by the national ideology, there remained an even more basic issue to resolve: that of the subordination of church to state.

Characteristically, in his feud with Oikonomos, Farmakidis made frequent and laudatory references to the work of Theofan Prokopovič, the man who inspired ecclesiastical reforms in the age of Peter the Great, particularly due to his imposition of the synodic system and the theoretical refinement of the subjugation of the church to the will of the emperor-tsar.[42]

Thus, the opposition of Farmakidis and Oikonomos over Greek autocephaly is wrongly interpreted as a version of the opposition between pro-Western (Koraist) and pro-Russian forces in the newly formed Greek state, since this view does not take into consideration the internal split in Russia between pro- and anti-Westerners already apparent in the eighteenth century.[43]

For Farmakidis, the activity of a church unchecked by the state undermined the very existence of that state.[44] For Oikonomos, on the other hand, keeping its ties with the *genos* (what would be called within the Ottoman framework the *Rum Millet*) was the sole means for the nation to retain its ecumenical characteristics.

Consequently, both versions of Greek nationalist discourse relied on the internal fissure of Russian imperialist discourse, and not necessarily on an opposition that would entail the bipolar opposition West-East.[45] The latter will be deployed only after the end of the Crimean war. Contrary to the views that see the production of nationalist discourse as an unequivocal turn against the imperial past, oftentimes the motifs for the development of imperial nationalism became the model for the reproduction of ideological forms, not only in Greek but in other Balkan nationalisms that represent the nation-state as empire. When the peripheral national movements used the imperial nationalism of the Ottoman, Russian, or Austrian Empires as model, they imagined themselves as newly established "empires." At same time, they initiated a process of Westernization of their societies inspired by then-modern/colonial "empires" of the West, creating interesting hybrid perceptions of what is the "nation." Consequently it should not be considered a weakness on the part of Balkan nationalism and Eastern Europe generally to distinguish between the two types of state: the modern bourgeois state of a Western type, and an obsolete Eastern type of traditional empire. Rather, this was the result of two factors. First, there was a broader interaction between the ideologies of empire in the East with what the West projected onto the East as a distinguishing mark of inferiority, that of religion: however, religion was something that the Eastern empires used as a flag of their own peculiarity, adopting the Western orientalist stereotypes but turning them to the opposite as their advantage.[46] Second, there was a consequent instrumental confrontation with nationalist ideology by the representatives of religion within the empires of the East (as opposed to the classic version of the theory of nationalism, which would have religion as an instrument for the achievement of nationalist-irredentist goals). Thus, for example, if one studies the conflict between pro-Slav and pro-Western forces in Russia, the various mutations of the Ottoman imperial ideology (Ottomanism, Panislamism, Panturkism), and discussions among Greek, Bulgarian, and Turkish nationalists, it is possible to analyze the presuppositions for the emergence of these unconventional ideological hybrids that would decisively influence the course of nationalization of the Balkan peoples both within and outside the Ottoman Empire.[47]

Moreover, if one does not consider the question of the hybrid nature of nationalist ideologies as involving the reconstitution of "nationalist" and "imperialist" elements (concerning the hybrid nature of national identities there can be no doubt), then one cannot interpret the complexity of the nineteenth century except within the purely bipolar schemes of twentieth-century nationalism. For example, the founding of the Greek autocephalous church was the spark that ignited the founding of other nationalized churches in the Balkans. Its recognition by the patriarchate coincided with the rise of Bulgarian nationalism and related demands for the founding of an autonomous Bulgarian national church, or even one independent of the patriarchate. It was thus logical for the radical wing of the Bulgarian nationalist movement to demand from the patriarchate a solution comparable to that provided for Greece in 1850. The patriarchate argued that this would be anticanonical, given that there was no Bulgarian state entity to request autocephaly as there had been in the case of Greece. But the problem was not one of implementing the holy canons; in using this argument, the patriarchate was essentially accepting that the applicant for autocephaly should be a "nation-state" at the same time that it was condemning nationalism. For their part, Bulgarian nationalists, despite having been frequently offered the possibility of a benign compromise through the acceptance of the solution of an exarchate that would mention and be subject to the patriarchate, avoided this solution because the question was not simply one of ecclesiastical independence, but of Bulgarian disengagement from Greek cultural domination in the Balkans, which for the Bulgarians had two basic props: the patriarchate and the Phanariots.

It is debatable whether the patriarchate's 1872 condemnation of the Bulgarian Exarchate as schismatic expressed a religious ecumenism (it is well known that the renunciation of the exarchate as schismatic was accompanied by a famous condemnation on the part of the patriarchate of *ethno-phyletism*—that is, of nationalism as an ideology opposed to the fundamental ideals of Christianity) or was more in line with the growth of Greek nationalism, which in the years to follow would have preferred its rival in Macedonia and Thrace to carry the stigma of being "schismatic."[48] Naturally, both of these a posteriori interpretations, in disconnecting the actual actions of subjects from the Ottoman framework, end up retroactively justifying both sides of this crucial ideological and political conflict.

The first interpretation relies on the theoretical hypothesis of the fundamental "contradiction" between nationalism and Orthodoxy,[49] forgetting that the former attempted to embrace the latter for instrumental reasons, and that the latter also played the game of modernity, contributing to various elements of the modern Greek Enlightenment through its dialogue with the West. The second interpretation has difficulty explaining why, if the patriarchate simply wanted to play the game of Greek nationalism,[50] it made a blanket condemnation of nationalism (including Greek), during a period when the phenomenon was at its nineteenth-century height.[51]

The above views may seem to solve the problem of the interpretation of the 1872 Schism, by selectively employing the trajectory of relations between the Greek autocephalous church and the patriarchate: focusing on the seventeen years that had passed before the former was recognized by the latter would reconfirm the ecumenical orientation of the patriarchate and its willingness to collude with every form of nationalist ideology. However, only two years after the historic compromise of 1850, the term "Helleno-Christianism" (a term inconceivable until that time for the world of the Orthodox *genos*) was introduced into Greek by Spyridon Zambelios. The term represented an internal upgrading of the *Megali Idea*, appearing to incorporate the Ecumenical Patriarchate (or at least, its Orthodox ecumenism) into modern Greek national ideology.

Nonetheless, paradoxically, the world of the patriarchate did not accept (at least until the early twentieth century) modern Greek nationalism's narrative of Byzantium, or the Greek state's strategies for the nationalization of Orthodox populations in the Ottoman Empire. The patriarchate's identification with various versions of Ottoman imperialist discourse (Ottomanism, Panslavism) as well as its desire to avoid dissolving its ties with Russian imperialist discourse produced a new type of ecumenism different from that constructed for it by modern Greek nationalism.[52]

The *Megali Idea* and the Greek Autocephalous Church: From Religious Populism to Religious Reformism

Recognition of the Church of Greece by the patriarchate had both supporters and opponents. Farmakidis would continue his polemic against the Synodal Tome, and to a large degree feel vindicated by Laws 200 and 201, with which the Greek state substantially undermined its spirit. By contrast, one of its most fervid supporters was the monk Christoforos, known as Papoulakos. Under his secular name of Christos Panagiotopoulos, he had led a popular movement that had shaken the rural Peloponnese in the 1850s. Papoulakos began preaching at the age of eighty. Around 1848, he presented himself to the Holy Synod, requesting that he be granted a preacher's license. More specifically, the metropolitans of Athens (Neophytos Metaxas) and Syros-Tinos (Daniel) supported his request, but Bishop Bartholomew of Kalavryta, Bishop Procopius of Oitylos, and Archimandrite Theoklitos Farmakidis, master of ecclesiastical affairs, prevailed, refusing to do so because the applicant did not have the "requisite qualifications and resources." However, the real reasons for denying his request concerned Papoulakos's antiroyalist sermons, which had gathered a motley group of popular audiences that saw in him a defender of their lost aspirations. In 1852, he was arrested as the inciter of an armed insurrection in Lakonia, and was put on trial in the midst of the Crimean War (summer 1853). Due to the support of the now-dissolved "pro-Orthodox" Russophiles, he would be granted amnesty, but led before the Holy Synod, which decided to confine him to Panachrantos Monastery on Andros, where he died eight years later.[53]

The outbreak of the Crimean War significantly altered the political orientations of the Greek state, since Russian policy would lose its mainstays of support. The identification of Othon with Russia would lead to the naval blockade of Piraeus by the British and French fleets (1854–56), and ultimately to the king's expulsion (1862). The gradual turnabout of Russian foreign policy from a defense of the interests of all Orthodox populations in the Ottoman Empire to Panslavism led to a strengthening of British influence that would be expressed with the reign of George I from 1864 and the annexation of the Ionian Islands to the Greek state (and correspondingly, of its archbishoprics to the Church of Greece in 1866).

Papoulakos's movement was inspired by messianic prophecies about the coming of a "blond race" (Russians) and represented a hodge-podge coalition with an anti-Western, antimodernization orientation. It was an early expression of radical populism, whose defeat coincided with the country's broader realignment. The new political environment could not, of course, have tolerated a populist movement with a pro-Russian bent, explaining why the demand for the refounding of the church was replaced by a demand for reforming the church, which in many respects resembled comparable movements of Protestant inspiration. This demand was frequently connected with the new nationalist and irredentist goals of the Greek state. The *Megali Idea* may have been defeated in its first irredentist version (with the end of the Crimean War), and Greece may have more or less passed into the English sphere of influence with the coming of George I, but the goal of annexing new Ottoman territories would remain alive, becoming reinvigorated during the 1870s with the outbreak of the Eastern Crisis.

Early in the 1870s, when the problem of ethnic conflicts in the Balkans became acute as a consequence of the Ottoman state's recognition of the Bulgarian Exarchate, the lower clergy in Greece realized its first significant form of collective organizing through the founding of the association of the Synaxis of Elders. Article 2 of its charter characteristically notes that, "every elder of the free and enslaved Greek race and married deacons of the Eastern Church of Christ may become a member of this association."[54] Thus, the Synaxis was not addressing itself to possible members who were priests in the Greek state only, but also to members of the Orthodox clergy who lived in the territories of the Ottoman Empire, and who were consequently subject to the jurisdiction of the Ecumenical Patriarchate. Accordingly, if until the 1850s the freezing of the Greek state and consequently of the borders of its church to those of 1833 required the recognition of the church by the Ecumenical Patriarchate, after the Crimean War and the transformation of the *Megali Idea* from a program for civilizing the East into an aggressive tool of Greek irredentism, the issue became that of the subordination of the Ecumenical Patriarchate to the pressing needs of Greek nationalism. During the same period, together with the idealizing of Rigas Feraios and Adamantios Korais as the "forefathers" of modern Greek national consciousness, national ideology attempted to embrace the history of the Ecumenical Patriarchate, an institution that up until that time had been identified with the fortunes of the Ottoman state. The constitutive act of this embrace was the ritual burial of the remains of Patriarch Gregory V in 1871, with their transport from Russia fifty years after his death. This had been preceded a decade earlier (1861) by sitting his statue (together with those of Korais and Feraios) in front of the entrance to the University of Athens on the initiative of Archbishop of Athens Misail Apostolidis (1861–62), who also inaugurated the Cathedral of Athens.

Gregory V had been hung by the Ottomans in 1821, not because he supported the Greek revolutionaries, but because he had failed as the leader of the *Rum Millet* to prevent the outbreak of the revolution. Consequently, the transformation of the execution of a patriarch into a patriotic sacrifice, which was constitutive in the founding of the new nation-state, took place at precisely the same moment that the nation-state wanted to subject the world of the patriarchate to a nationalization process.[55]

The founding of the synaxis occurred within the same ideological-political context as the founding of the Association for the Dissemination of Greek Letters (1869) and other similar societies that espoused the irredentist visions of Greek nationalism. In principle, its founding had the approval of Archbishop Theophilus of Athens (1862–73). However, Theophilus (who was already over ninety) withdrew his support in the face of pressure from a group of monks led by Apostolos Makrakis.

The founding of the synaxis had two main objectives: (a) the establishment of Sunday schools, and (b) the improvement of the spiritual and educational state of the secular clergy, since the synaxis was addressed to married, not celibate clergy.[56] Makrakis's group focused its polemic on the second objective—i.e., on the exclusion from society of unmarried clerics, against whom the synaxis would presumably declare war. Probably, however, the real reason for this reaction was the society's first avowed purpose: the establishment of Sunday schools, which, by strengthening (the position of) the vicars, would challenge the primacy of Makrakis and the societies he had founded that specialized in clerical preaching.

Theophilus's renunciation of the synaxis in February 1871 may be considered a victory by the new Papoulakos of Greek spiritual life. However, there were two substantial differences from the popular preacher of the 1850s: first, in contrast to the nearly illiterate monk Papoulakos, Makrakis was highly educated;[57] second, Makrakis preached in the capital of the modern Greek state itself, where he had lived since 1866, rather than in rural areas, as in the case of Papoulakos. Makrakis was, one might say, a representative of bourgeois-philosophical-messianic theology, in contrast with Papoulakos, the representative of a corresponding populist-messianic theology. Makrakis gathered around himself an extensive circle of clerics and lay persons.

In 1876, Makrakis founded the School of the Logos, proclaiming himself a professor of philosophy and the "philosophical sciences." However, his teachings concerning the tripartite nature of man (Body, Mind, Spirit), and his claim that Jesus achieved perfection only at the moment of his baptism in the Jordan (in the presence of all the members of the Holy Trinity) called forth a reaction from the official church. In December 1878, under the presidency of Archbishop Procopius of Athens, the Holy Synod decided to close Makrakis's school, and to condemn his heretical theories (probably without proceeding to excommunication). Makrakis himself was brought to trial in 1879, where he was sentenced to three months in prison. He was released in June of the same year, only to be confined again, this time for eight months. Meanwhile, he had founded (probably the reason why he was imprisoned again) a politically oriented association called Constantine the Great.[58] The object of this organization was to found the Kingdom of God on earth and to put an end to the kingdom of Muhammad through the conquest of Constantinople. He related his messianic visions to prophecies of "Agathangelos" and his own interpretations of the Apocalypse. He sent open letters to his followers from prison, and they proceeded to collect signatures on behalf of his release. Finally, after writing a letter to the minister of justice, Athanasios Petmezas, he was released in 1880; he reestablished his School of the Logos and began to teach there again. The operation of the school, however, was once more interrupted in February 1881, when charges of impiety and heresy were lodged against him. Following a brief term in prison, he was again released, and for the next two decades continued his productive writing activities. In 1905, he died in poverty and isolation on Sifnos, the island of his birth.

The continuous prosecutions alienated those persons, chiefly clerics, with whom Makrakis had been united from the moment he first arrived in Athens. But when the School of the Logos closed for the first time in 1878, in addition to Makrakis himself, the Holy Synod condemned seven of his supporters to exile and confinement in monasteries. In 1883, the latter renounced Makrakis's teachings as erroneous, and the following year they were reinstated by the Holy Synod. One group of those who had broken away from Makrakis, with Konstantinos Dialismas at its head, would create the association Anaplasis, which would also publish the periodical of the same name.

This incident, as with his repeated trials in the late 1870s, was connected with Makrakis's critical stance toward the politics of the Archbishop of Athens at that time, Procopius (1874–89).[59] Unlike his predecessor Theophilus, who in 1867 had recommended Makrakis's just-published newspaper *Logos* as "must reading" for the Orthodox clergy, Procopius was under fire from Makrakis because of his involvement in the Simoniaká scandal in the mid-1870s.[60] More specifically, in 1875, prompted by the filling of three vacant archbishoprics, two government ministers (Ioannis Valasopoulos, minister of ecclesiastical affairs, and Vasileios Nikolopoulos, minister of justice) were bribed by four candidates for the office of archbishop with large monetary payments and other gifts (shares, jewelry) in order to persuade the Holy Synod to elect them to the vacant archbishoprics. The trial opened on January 26, 1876, and finished two months later, on March 31, while Charilaos Trikoupis was prime minister. Testimony was provided by 109 witnesses in all. With one exception, all the accused were found guilty as charged and sentenced: Valasopoulos was sentenced to a prison term of one year, a three-year deprivation of his political rights, and the payment of 56,200 drachmas to the poorhouse; Nikolopoulos was sentenced to a prison term of ten months; and the archbishops were sentenced to a fine equal to twice the amount each had paid as a bribe. The court's decision was conveyed to the Holy Synod so that the case could be dealt with by ecclesiastical law. On April 19, 1876, the synod decided that it did not view these actions as simonist according to the holy canons, but despite this, it placed the archbishops on a three-year suspension from all religious rites. Nikolaos Damalas, a professor of theology who at the time was serving as royal commissioner on the synod, and whose cooperation was required, refused to sign the court's decision. However, the ministry of ecclesiastical affairs again posed the matter to the Holy Synod, and after eighteen months, on October 19, 1877, the synod reconvened and assigned the Bishop of Phocis the task of persuading, in the name of the synod, the three prelates to submit their resignations. Finally, as declared in their related texts, "of their own will and in a desire to put to rest the scandals between church and state,"[61] they resigned on November 18, 1877. Nevertheless, because the Holy Synod under Procopius refused to break away and excommunicate the simonist bishops, Makrakis's clerical followers ceased to invoke the name of the Archbishop of Athens in the Divine Liturgy. The closing of the School of the Logos in 1878 was clearly connected with the scandal.

The Orthodox Church and Civil Society: The Issue of "Para-Ecclesiastical Organizations" and Hybridization of the Public Sphere

If the case of Makrakis is of interest, it is not only for the particular features of a critique leveled against the ecclesiastical hierarchy of the modern Greek state, but because there gathered around Makrakis a circle of laity and clerics who—particularly following his death—would continue to found such associations and societies, which would become known in Greek ecclesiastical history as "para-ecclesiastical organizations."

For example, among Makrakis's fellow travelers, as early as the period of the publication of the periodical *Logos*, were Archimandrite Eusebius Mathopoulos, founder of the Zoe (Life) organization, and his uncle Ierotheos Mathopoulos, later Archbishop of Patra. Eusebius Mathopoulos was among those clerics who, in the wake of the judgment concerning the preferment scandals and his exile to the Monastery of Palaiokastritsa on Corfu, had a falling out with Makrakis. For the next twenty-two years (1884–1906), he preached mostly in provincial cities, without receiving an official appointment by the Holy Synod as vicar or preacher. Nevertheless, his preaching enjoyed the formal approval of the synod.

In 1907, two years after Makrakis's death, Mathopoulos founded the coenobitic "brotherhood," as he called it, of Zoe. The brotherhood would chiefly include young theologians and university students of theology. Its coenobitic nature required its members to practice virginity, poverty, and obedience, just as in regular monastic life. This transfer of the value system of monasticism to the secular sphere, the interpretative approach to the Holy Scriptures along the models of bible societies, and above all the fact that Zoe was formed as a civil body in order to avoid the possibility of the Orthodox clergy (specifically, the Holy Synod) intervening in its internal affairs, led Christos Giannaras to claim that both Zoe as well as the comparable organizations that emerged from it in the twentieth century[62] were Protestant in nature.[63] According to Giannaras, "the Protestant Reformation and extra-ecclesiastical organizations derive from the same raison d'être—namely, the rejection and critique of the ecclesiastical hierarchy."[64] Giannaras considers that Mathopoulos essentially reproduced Makrakis's anticlerical passion, although he acknowledges that the former must have been directly influenced by Protestant texts. However, apart from the fact that Mathopoulos distanced himself from Makrakis precisely because he renounced the latter's attitude toward the higher clergy and Holy Synod, the history of all these para-ecclesiastical organizations[65] shows that not only did they not observe in practice a doubting stance toward the role of the (chiefly, higher) clergy; on the contrary, they were reservoirs from which personnel were drawn for staffing the clerical hierarchy as well as theological and ecclesiastical schools.[66]

According to Şerif Mardin, religion and its representatives played the role of a middleman, the intermediary between the individual and the state.⁶⁷ Legality, knowledge of the law, and education came under the jurisdiction of the body known for its sacred knowledge. The intermediary function was adopted by the Orthodox clergy mainly for the reason of representing the Orthodox population in the Ottoman Empire. This function of the clergy is concerned with the entire extent of "privileges" (about which much has been written in recent years):⁶⁸ control of the educational process, legal transactions, tax collection responsibilities, the civil domain (marriage, divorce, inheritance), and the domain of civil representation before the court. All of these remain vital for the exercise of ecclesiastical authority.

Consequently, the domain that religion occupies (and this can perhaps serve as a general observation for the whole of Eastern and Southeastern Europe) is in fact the intermediate social domain in which the intermediary functions of the clergy are engaged. The intermediate social domain, where the limits of public and private⁶⁹ are found, and where the conditions for the emergence of an autonomous public sphere (what is known as "civil society") and for the formation of an independent economic domain are created, is simultaneously the realm traditionally claimed by the Orthodox clergy in order to propagate its authority.

This is the reason why the clergy does not refrain from, but, on the contrary, recognizes and contributes to the collective organization of the social civil domain: from the moment that it cannot have complete control, as in the case of pro-modernist social formations, it attempts to secure a strong presence in this sphere. Whenever possible, the church inserts itself into these social formations (that is, those formations that cannot exclude the influence of the church), and its involvement creates hybrid conditions. This same church creates organizations, or tolerates their function, but assumes a critical stance when bourgeois (civil) collectivity becomes exclusive, as in the case of the Masonic orders.

According to neo-Orthodox criticism, the functioning of all the para-ecclesiastical organizations is the result of Protestant influence. The existence of these organizations calls into question and provides a substitute for the intermediary role of the clergy in organizing relations between God and the faithful. The Protestant-inspired diffusion of the priesthood to the faithful, however, can only result in the organization of the social domain with a normative model (discipline, work ethics, etc.). The disorganization of the role of the clergy as intermediary between God and the faithful is a necessary condition for ecclesiastical discourse (as civil morality) to rule in the intermediate social domain. This enables the ecclesiastical element to intercede between state and citizen. In this process, the official church not only provides substitutes but contributes enormously.

To be more precise it is not the dominance of the Protestant model within Orthodoxy that is to be preferred but, on the contrary, a reorganization of the sovereign discourse of the church as preferential ally of the state within the borrowed version of the Protestant example. The element of corporate organization is borrowed from one in order to cater to the executive personnel of the other, and to serve as a reservoir of the faithful without ever questioning the intermediary role of the clergy. This role is not abandoned because the church cannot abandon the process of regulating society.

This is the reason why the church naturally does not place itself in civil society, something that the school of Neo-Orthodoxy suppresses. While the system of para-ecclesiastical organizations permit the church to participate in the formation of civil morality, at the same time the church exclusively controls the domain of the religious market. If in fact this movement were a product of a Protestant ethic, it would be receptive to multiple fragmentation and individualization; above all, it would abandon its exclusive position in the marketplace of religious conscience.[70]

The relations between these para-ecclesiastical organizations and the official church, far from being a direct juxtaposition, can be characterized for the entire twentieth century as an exchange of powerful executives, without the former ever challenging the priesthood's intermediary role between the faithful and God. The existence of these organizations was enough to make the area of civil morality autonomous.

Conclusion

It is debatable whether the stance of Makrakis and his descendants was more pro-Western that that of his opponents. When Procopius, with whom Makrakis came into conflict, died in 1889, Germanos Kalligas, formerly the Archbishop of Cephallenia (Kefalonia), ascended to the metropolitan throne of Athens (1889–96). Germanos was the spiritual child of Patriarch of Constantinople Sophronios III (1863–66), who later became patriarch of Alexandria. Sophronios was a fervid supporter of the Tanzimat reforms (which within the Ecumenical Patriarchate meant lay participation in its governance) and a friend of important reformist Ottoman officials such as Âli Paşa and Fuad Paşa.[71] It is no accident that in becoming Archbishop of Athens, Germanos had the unstinting support of another reformist and pro-Western politician, Charilaos Trikoupis,[72] while Germanos had himself exercised control over Makrakis when the latter was preaching in his province without the requisite license from a bishop.[73] Trikoupis's choice of a cosmopolitan prelate such as Germanos, who had passed through Constantinople (seven years at the Theological School of Halki) and Alexandria (as Sophronius's deacon) certainly fell within the spirit of including the church in the process of broader civil transformation. It was no accident that one of the first initiatives of the new Archbishop of Athens was to found the Holy Association (Ιερός Σύνδεσμος) in 1890, essentially the continuation of the failed enterprise of the synaxis under Theophilus, but with significant differences: clerics of all ranks of the priesthood and not only married elders could take part in the Holy Association, while the goals of its founding charter included, in addition to the spiritual and educational improvement of existing clergy, the appropriate preparation of candidates for the priesthood.[74]

Germanos's sudden death on January 18, 1896, brought a cleric with a different political orientation to the metropolitan throne of Athens. This time, in the wake of pressure exerted on the Holy Synod by the government of Theodoros Deligiannis (the great rival of Charilaos Trikoupis, who had been politically eliminated by the bankruptcy of the Greek government in 1893) and the Russian Queen Olga, Procopius II Oikonomidis (1896–1901) would be elected Archbishop of Athens. Procopius was a graduate of the Theological Schools of Athens and Moscow, with obviously close ties to Russia. When elected, he was already a professor at the University of Athens, but did not hold a bishopric; he was still an archimandrite. Therefore, for the first time in the history of the Church of Greece, and despite the strong objections of the Holy Synod, an individual would rise directly to the position of Archbishop of Athens and Archimandrite of the Holy Synod.[75] Procopius ventured to revise the founding charter of the Church of Greece (revoking the status quo of the civil state in the direction of a "mutualism" of church-state relations, exactly as the side represented by Oikonomos had once supported), and to set up an ecclesiastical fund for clerics (an issue directly linked to the still-pending matter of salaries). But, at the same time, he continued to publish the periodical of the Holy Association, just as his predecessor had. His tenure, however, was a brief one, due to the well-known events surrounding the Evangeliká (Gospel

Riots). In 1901, Alexandros Pallis with the consent of the Holy Synod and Theological School (essentially under the supervision and with the approval of Queen Olga) published a translation of the Gospel into demotic Greek, an event that called forth an uprising by University of Athens students. The sad turn taken by this uprising (which included fatalities among its victims) would lead to the resignation of Procopius as well as the Theotokis government. Procopius died the following year.

Theoklitos Minopoulos was elected Procopius's successor as Archbishop of Athens, and his two terms essentially brought the Church of Greece into the twentieth century.[76] His tenure (1902–22) was interrupted for three years (1918–20), when the position of Archbishop of Athens was occupied by his great ideological opponent Meletius Metaxakis, a supporter of the Venizelist camp, who in 1920 would move to the position of Ecumenical Patriarch (the first and only time an Archbishop of Athens became Archbishop of Constantinople), realizing the vision of the Venizelist *Megali Idea*. In contrast, Theoklitos, amid the events of the split between Venizelists and royalists, would publicly excommunicate Venizelos in Constitution Square in 1917. Although it appears he was forced to this action by the Archbishop of Larisa, Arsenius, and royalist conscript officers, he was nonetheless subjected to its consequences, with his dethronement by an ecclesiastical court convened in the summer of that same year following Eleftherios Venizelos's return to Athens (with seven votes in favor and six against).[77] However, in November 1920—that is, after Venizelos's unexpected defeat in the elections following the signing of the Treaty of Sèvres—Theoklitos was reinstated, as the decision by the ecclesiastical court was declared null and void, and Metaxakis was compelled to stand down from the metropolitan throne. One year later (December 1921), he was elected Patriarch of Constantinople.[78]

The nineteenth century's constitutional conflict *between* "civil statists" (such as Farmakidis) and "ecumenists" (such as Oikonomos) became transformed in the twentieth century into a conflict largely *within* the civil statist faction. The conflict between Venizelists and royalists may express the antagonism between two differing versions of Greek nationalism, but neither side (at least at the level of the archbishops of Athens) doubted the subordination of the church to the will of the state's leader. All the archbishops of Athens (not excepting the Russophile Procopius Oikonomidis) were elected with the approval and/or active support of governments. This interdependence of ecclesiastical and political power would lead the church to an involvement in long-term political disputes far removed from the Christian content of its preaching. Through this involvement, noteworthy ideological reversals of nineteenth-century arguments were noted, precisely because they acquired an entirely different content within an altered historical context. To be more precise, they were not "reversals" but rather "espousals" of the positions of those who had been defeated in the nineteenth century—the ecumenists—by representatives of both factions. Thus, for example, the royalist University of Athens professor Christos Androutsos would claim that, "as regards the overall governance of the church, we believe without a doubt that only union with the Ecumenical Patriarchate can preserve the independence of the Church of Greece."[79] On the other hand, the Venizelist Meletius Metaxakis, whose election as Archbishop of Athens was the result of one of the most blatant interventions in the internal affairs of the church, was the first person in the twentieth century to propose a system of reforms by which the church would be released from state control—that is, the model represented by the Ecumenical Patriarchate, which he himself would lead for a brief period. The imperial vision by which the ecumenist wing of the nineteenth century was inspired was a necessary instrument in the various versions assumed by the *Megali Idea*.

The "long nineteenth century" in the history of the Church of Greece came to a close in 1923. The end of the *Megali Idea* and the mutual disdain of Meletius and Theoklitos would bring to the archbishopric of Athens (naturally, with the Venizelists' blessing) Chrysostomos Papadopoulos, a professor in the Theological School and an archimandrite, who became the first prelate to bear the title of Archbishop of Athens and All Greece. The process that had begun in 1833 with the independence of the Greek autocephalous church was completed with the stabilization of its internal hierarchy. Moreover, the voting of a new charter for the Church of Greece that accompanied Papadopoulos's election in 1923 was to bring an especially significant change: the Council of Provincial Bishops was designated the supreme organ of church governance, and it could convene in a body every year without necessarily having the approval of the state. In paradoxical fashion, the ideal of self-governance of the church was brought to fulfillment at the moment of the demise of the *Megali Idea*, when the imperialist visions of the ecumenists who had supported it and its instrumental value during the nineteenth century were no longer of the slightest significance.

One might argue that the history of the Greek autocephalous church in the nineteenth century represented a movement away from the hybrid nature of nationalist ideology toward the hybrid nature of social formation. The Greek Church, having been converted into a state mechanism, would confront the problem of its imperial origins through the clash of modernists and ecumenists. Having gained state legitimacy and a significant degree of control over the formation of the private sphere (with the Patriarchate of Constantinople as its ideal model), the church had a decisive impact on the emergence of civil society in the newly formed state. To be precise, the church, despite its state-mechanism status, did not allow civil society to turn against it. Through ecclesiastical and para-ecclesiastical organizations as well as other coalitions and associations, the church left a heavy imprint on civil society, in addition to reproducing the hegemonic position of the Orthodox clergy, just as had occurred during the Ottoman era. This solution to the problem, the church-state alliance in Greece, served as a model for how political and religious power came to terms with one another in the new era of Balkan nation-states.

List of Archbishops of Athens

Neophytos (Metaxas), 1833–1861
Misail (Michael) (Apostolidis), 1861–1862
Theophilus (Vlachopapadopoulos), 1862–1873
Procopius (Georgiadis), 1874–1889
Germanos (Kalligas), 1889–1896
Procopius (Oikonomidis), 1896–1901
Theoklitos (Minopoulos), 1902–1917 and 1920–1922
Meletius (Metaxakis), 1918–1920

CHAPTER

4

THE SERBIAN ORTHODOX CHURCH

Bojan Aleksov

There are two mutually related issues that require clarification when discussing the history of the Orthodox faith and church among the Serbs during the long nineteenth century. Firstly, although the Serbian Orthodox Church carries the legacy of the Patriarchate of Peć (1346–1463 in medieval Serbia and 1557–1766 in the Ottoman Empire), the Karlovci Metropolitanate (1691–1920 in the Habsburg Empire) and an independent archbishopric established in 1219, its name and present structure date back only to 1920. It was only after the First World War and the creation of the Kingdom of Serbs, Croats, and Slovenes (Yugoslavia from 1929) that the Orthodox Serbs, previously living under six ecclesiastical authorities, united into a single patriarchate and their church took the name by which it is now commonly known. Although united in dogmatic matters, over the previous centuries, these ecclesiastical authorities had developed different practices and administrative systems. Importantly, while Serbs shared some beliefs and customs, local religiosity, morals, and values in the lives of individuals and communities greatly differed.

Secondly, the concept of a monolithic national character of the Orthodox Serbs and their common aspirations for the unification prior to the First World War (and even after it) disregards evidence and ignores the dialectic and dynamic nature of historical processes. Unfortunately, this is a feature of most history writing upon which this chapter is unavoidably based.[1] During the twentieth century the Serbian Orthodox Church came to be considered an inseparable and key part of a timeless and immutable

Serbian national identity. When writing about the church, Serbian historiography tended to view church history as indistinguishable from national history, with both inevitably leading to national liberation and unification.[2] Thus, national consciousness and unity are projected back onto the past of the church when other issues and interests prevailed. As a prominent Serbian clergyman and metropolitan commented regarding the concept of an overarching national principle as recently as the second half of the nineteenth century, "To speak about the national principle in interpreting church canons is sheer anachronism. The national principle only came into being in the middle of this century. The more we look into the past the harder it becomes to find any evidence of it. In the beginnings of our holy church there is no mention about it whatsoever."[3] Taking this tendency into account, this chapter evaluates the position of the Serbs and their church during the nineteenth century from a more nuanced perspective. Following a general introduction, it will provide a separate account for each ecclesiastical authority and identify the main features and conflicts underlying their history preceding their abolition and amalgamation in one entity in 1920. The concluding section will identify some common developments across the lands inhabited by Serbs in the nineteenth century, which fermented the Serbian religious nationalism, a process that was completed in the interwar period.

The nineteenth century in Southeastern Europe began in turmoil due to Napoleonic wars and uprisings against the local Ottoman rulers. During previous centuries Serbs had spread across the western part of the Balkan Peninsula and crossed Sava and Danube into Habsburg central European lands. After two waves of Serbian migration led by church hierarchs (1690 and 1740) away from the Ottoman Empire, there were church structures in both empires. In the Ottoman lands the Sublime Porte nominated its own candidates for Peć (Serbian) patriarchs until 1766, when this patriarchate was abolished. Spiritual authority over the remaining Serbs in the Empire was transferred to the Ecumenical Patriarch of Constantinople and the Phanariots were appointed to former Serbian eparchies (dioceses). The latter remained in notorious collective memory for their extortions from the flock, corruption and lack of contact with the lower clergy, which continued to be exclusively Serbian, uneducated, and unfamiliar with the tenets of Orthodoxy, let alone versed in pastoral care. The influence of the Orthodox spiritual center at Mount Athos waned as its Hilandar Monastery lost its Serbian character and ceased to be a place of learning for Serbian priests. Under these circumstances, the religion of Serbian peasant folk saw the blending of pre-Christian and Islamic traditions with those of Orthodoxy, a necessary and natural process in order to exercise autonomy and use religion to accommodate daily needs.[4] Nevertheless, in comparison to other Balkan peoples, the Serbs were advantageous. There was the opportunity for Serbian priests or monks who wished to engage in learning to cross the Sava or Danube and join their brethren in Hungary, where there was an ecclesiastical jurisdiction, which, for all but formal purposes, was Serbian. The Karlovci Metropolitanate of the Habsburg Empire in particular cherished the legacy of the abolished Peć Patriarchate. Despite imperial restrictions, the Karlovci Church provided a backbone for all future Orthodox ecclesiastical administrations for Serbs in neighboring lands and finally for the creation of the unified Serbian Orthodox Church. The Ottoman legacy, therefore, and especially the all-pervasive influence of the Habsburg domain, determined the history of the church among Serbs in the nineteenth century. The importance of the Habsburg influence also accounts for the order in which various administrations are presented below.

Karlovci Metropolitanate

The Orthodox Metropolitanate of Karlovci (1691/1713–1920) was initially the sole ecclesiastical organization of Orthodox Christians in the Habsburg Monarchy. However, by the nineteenth century its jurisdiction covered only historic Hungary and Croatia as other Habsburg lands acquired their own jurisdictions. Most Orthodox peoples settled in the Habsburg lands in fleeing the Ottoman invasion or some of the failed Habsburg military campaigns to defeat the Ottoman Empire.[5] The foundations of the metropolitanate were laid by the privileges gained from Emperor Leopold I in 1690, 1691 and 1695 following the greatest exodus of Orthodox Serbs from the Ottoman Empire.[6] Leopoldian privileges defined the Serbian ethnic community along the lines of the Ottoman *Rum Millet* (i.e., in confessional terms), and with Orthodox hierarchs as its leaders.[7] The metropolitan (the title of patriarch was reintroduced in 1848) was not only the head of the church but also acted as the leader of the whole Orthodox community and served as intermediary between his flock and the imperial government. Similarly, Orthodox bishops in their dioceses functioned as prefects over the Christian population. In return for their services, bishops and black clergy (monks), from which they were recruited, enjoyed the privileges of landed nobility.[8] These privileges bound the clergy with a tiny stratum of Orthodox merchants, military officers and nobility, creating a confessional community in which the sacral and civil authorities were united and mutually reinforcing.[9] Ethnicity played no role as the Leopoldian privileges were envisioned for the whole Orthodox confessional community. Yet almost all positions of high rank were occupied by the Serbs just as the Greeks dominated the Ecumenical patriarchate under Ottoman rule.[10] Not only were the Greek and Vlach communities of small urban merchants subjected in all matters to the Serbian hierarchs but also the Romanian Orthodox, which made up a majority of the population in Banat and Transylvania, and on the whole were as numerous as the Serbs in the Monarchy.[11] Among Serbian settlers in the Monarchy, those in the Military Border (most of which lies in today's Croatia), the *Grenzer*, enjoyed a special patronage of the emperors and their military but not that of local notables or the Catholic Church. This prompted a centuries-long struggle of the Orthodox *Grenzer* for confirmation of their rights against attempts to bring them into a Union with the Catholic Church.[12] The *Grenzer* were relieved from paying feudal dues, and were allowed a certain degree of autonomy and freedom of religion in return for their military services. Military interests were pivotal in restraining Habsburgs from fully supporting the Catholic Church's engagement in forcing the Orthodox into the Union. However, with the disappearance of the Ottoman threat in the nineteenth century, the services of the *Grenzer* became increasingly redundant until the whole institution of the Military Border was finally abolished in 1881.

Soon after their arrival in the Habsburg lands, the Serbian hierarchs established ties with Russia from where they imported teachers who brought with them a heavy Russian influence in theology, liturgical language, and chant, which were also indicative of their political leanings. Serbs obtained their first taste of higher education at the Kiev Academy, which was firmly in Orthodox ecclesiastical hands yet undergoing strong Western or Latin scholastic influence.[13] By the end of eighteenth century this influence was curtailed by counter-reformation and subsequent reforms by emperors Maria Theresa and Joseph II in the spirit of the Enlightenment.[14] The two imperial *Regulaments* of 1770 and 1777, and the explanatory *Rescript* of 1779, issued to pacify opposition to the first two, established the primacy of Habsburg emperors in Orthodox Church matters, requiring imperial approval and confirmation of all nominations, visitations, excommunications, and other actions performed by the church.[15] In addition, the office of the Imperial Commissar was established, similar to that of the state's *Oberprocurator* in the Russian Church Synod. The new regulations also limited the bishop's power in dioceses by introducing the *Konsistorialsystem* (Catholic-style consistory), which required lay representation in church-governing bodies. Eventually, Theresian and Josephinian reforms not only strengthened imperial control over the Orthodox Church but also decreased its powers by reducing the number of monasteries, monks and religious feasts, and by clearly defining contributions for religious rites. At the same time the Karlovci Metropolitanate acquired a seminary and permission was granted for the first Serb newspaper to appear in Vienna.

These efforts frustrated most clergy but pleased the so-called enlighteners among the Serbs, personified by Dositej Obradović, who, after fleeing the Hopovo Monastery, became the chief proponent of Western education and rationalism.[16] The incipient secular intelligentsia deemed the church hierarchy backward, greedy, selfish, and duplicitous, accusing it of betraying its people and neglecting its basic mission.[17] Travelers' accounts and other surviving testimonies from the late eighteenth and early nineteenth centuries indicate that the education level of the clergy and especially of monks was abysmally low. Nevertheless, boosting a relatively advantageous status over most of their ethnic neighbors thanks to Leopoldian privileges, in possession of a modest school system, political representation and closely linked to the nobility, the Karlovci hierarchy throughout the nineteenth century strove to preserve its status and resisted any change in culture, education, or social relations. A major dispute between the church and reformers erupted when Vuk Karadžić began advocating the use of Serbian vernacular into which he translated the New Testament and devised a new orthography. Karadžić's language and orthography reforms were taken as an attack on the existing Church Slavonic liturgical language and the standing of the church not only as the carrier of the eternal truth but also as the most powerful political and social institution of the Serbs and indeed their representative in the Monarchy.[18] Karadžić's principal adversary was the longest-acting and most noteworthy metropolitan in the nineteenth century, Stefan Stratimirović (1790–1836). Brilliantly educated and in possession of the best library among Serbs at the time, Stratimirović was remembered as a strict, conservative, and authoritarian church leader. He maintained links with the leaders of anti-Ottoman uprising in Serbia, and provided some support for, but stood firm and dogmatic against, any reform attempts that might imperil the church's primacy and monopoly based on dated principles. Nevertheless, threats to the church's real and imagined prestige ensued one after another. Not just Stratimirović but the whole Karlovci hierarchy long refused to acknowledge ethnic distinctions among its flock, thereby discriminating against Romanian believers who in the nineteenth century comprised 40 percent of the Orthodox in Hungary and Transylvania. In 1868, after decades of struggle for the use of the Romanian language, Latin alphabet, and for the appointment of Romanian-born and speaking clerics, the Crown and Hungarian Parliament sanctioned the separation of the Romanian dioceses and the establishment of their own Metropolitanate in Sibiu, headed by Andrieu Şaguna.[19]

The struggle of the Romanians for their own church is illustrative of the magnitude of changes faced by the multiethnic Habsburg Empire at the dawn of the age of nationalism, the first outburst of which came in 1848, when Hungarians demanded democracy and self-rule in their half of the Empire. Without any guarantees that their positions would improve, Habsburg Serbs sided with the emperor in confronting the Hungarians. At their assembly in Sremski Karlovci in 1848, Metropolitan Josif Rajačić was elected Patriarch of the Serbs and as such shared political and military leadership during the one and a half years of bloody revolution and interethnic war.[20] Following the Hungarian defeat, for his services to the throne, Rajačić was appointed administrator of the newly created Serbian Vojvodina albeit with insignificant powers. The Serbs did not get the autonomy they wanted and even the entity called Serbian Vojvodina would soon be abolished. The only rather symbolic benefit of these events was that the emperor confirmed the title of patriarch for Serbian metropolitans.

Invigorated after the Revolution of 1848/49, the Serbian secular intelligentsia began to openly question church domination. On the political level, it focused on the most important institution derived from the Leopoldian privileges, the People's and Church Congress (*Narodno-crkveni sabor*), whose competencies and tasks were drastically reduced in the aforementioned reforms. From the 1860s onwards, a clash evolved regarding which principle the Serbian community should put forward in its struggle to strengthen its political representation and eventual autonomy: the principle of historic rights, as advocated by the church hierarchy and conservatives, or the modern principle of national sovereignty advocated by emerging nationalist liberals led by Svetozar Miletić.[21] The Conservatives were convinced that the social stability, security and rights of all Serbs depended on the church's position. They wanted to install more discipline and emancipate parishes and schools from lay influence, and in these respects, invoked the holiness of the church, its unchangeable Orthodox tradition, and the inherited dignity of the hierarchy (apostolic succession). The Liberals and secular nationalists, on the other hand, claimed that the rights enjoyed by the Serbs had been heavily eroded by the church, and strove to turn the autonomous institutions and, indirectly, the church into instruments of modern politics and nationalism. Lay dominance can be traced from 1864, when the administration of parishes was reformed in accordance with the statute of Protestant churches in Austria. Having acquired a majority in the People's and Church Congress, the Liberals almost fully surrendered administrative organization of Serbian autonomy and the church to elected lay representatives. Gradually the consistorial system of lay participation took hold and by the time the Serbian autonomy was finally abolished in 1912, laymen had a majority in all church bodies with the exception of the Holy Synod.

Serbian autonomy was finally legally regulated with the Hungarian Law of Nationalities in 1868 (Article 9).[22] Although the confirmation required by the Hungarian Parliament clearly reduced the competencies of the autonomy and the Congress that governed it to matters of confession and education, this status was still of extreme importance for a minority ethnic group in times of intensified magyarization. The Karlovci Metropolitanate boasted over seven hundred parishes with churches and other adjacent buildings and twenty-seven monasteries in its seven dioceses. Serbian autonomous institutions at the close of the century included 356 elementary schools, two high schools, four schools for teacher training, three high schools for girls, and one seminary.[23] The Congress also managed the economic affairs of the Church and School Autonomy (*Crkveno-školska autonomija*), whose economic power was guaranteed by the church's large estates of over 130 thousand hectares and charity funds whose value was estimated in 1905 at over 40 million Hungarian forints.[24]

However, during the Dualist period (after the 1867 reform that divided the governing of the monarchy into its Austrian and Hungarian lands), the role of the throne in Orthodox church affairs was replaced by the Hungarian government, which convened the Congress irregularly and usually ignored decisions taken by Serbian representatives instead inaugurating its own. From 1875 to 1908 the Hungarian government sanctioned only one decision of the Serbian Congress. In 1882, in flagrant violation of Congress regulations and Orthodox Church tradition, Emperor Franz Joseph I appointed his own candidate, German Anđelić as patriarch, although he had been heavily defeated in the Electoral Congress in successive ballots. Tight imperial and governmental control over the Karlovci Metropolitanate—as in the appointment of unpopular patriarchs—tended to discredit the hierarchy in the laity's eyes, further encouraging the rise of the anti-clerical Radical Party among Hungarian Serbs (a successor party to Miletić's Liberals).[25] It was a vicious circle whereby the conservatism of the church made its opponents more violently anticlerical, and the violent anticlericalism of its opponents made the church more conservative. The two fractions engaged in protracted disputes within the Congress, which often paralyzed its functioning and contributed to the gradual diminishing of the prerogatives of the Serbian autonomy. The issues at stake were (a) the spiritual jurisdiction over Bosnia and Herzegovina after it was occupied by Austria-Hungary in 1878; (b) the control of great monastic estates after the number of monks drastically declined and estates fell into debt; and (c) the inability of the institutions of the Serbian Church autonomy to maintain Serbian schools, which were in disarray while enrolment oscillated at around only 25 percent.[26] Other problems surfaced within the church alone. Pastoral care was mostly in the hands of white (or married) clergy, who increasingly found themselves in conflict with their superiors. The material position and lack of proper education among married priests weakened their authority and exacerbated their poor pastoral performance. Their sole monetary income (as was the case for priests in all other jurisdictions detailed below) was emoluments paid for rites such as baptism and marriage. At the same time, Karlovci patriarchs enjoyed exorbitant pensions and profited from huge landed estates such as Dalj, which, for example, under Patriarch Georgije Branković, was managed by his son-in-law.[27]

The overall grim and deteriorating position of the Serbs in Hungary in the nineteenth century exacerbated the conflict between the church hierarchy, and Serbian secular elites and political parties. Toward the end of the century, Serbs made up only 5.5 percent of the population of Hungary inclusive of Croatia-Slavonia and only 2.5 percent of inhabitants in Hungary proper. Together with Romanians and the least numerous Ruthenians, they were overrepresented among the rural and agrarian population. Over 80 percent of them were agricultural laborer peasants and 90 percent lived in villages. The few Serbian craftsmen were particularly affected by the advent of industrialization. Their traditional occupations as tanners, wax makers, coppersmiths and the makers of traditional fur and wool clothes and pig skin shoes were destined for extinction in comparison to modern trades usually practiced by German and Hungarian craftsmen. Similarly, the once-powerful, Serbian merchants lost their prestige in the course of the nineteenth century as trade required more investment, new trade roads opened, and bans were lifted allowing other peoples, especially the Jews, to engage in trade. All of these developments contributed to much harsher competition. Furthermore, together with Romanians and Ruthenians, Serbs made up the bulk of Empire's illiterate population. Serbs also showed the highest discrepancy between the percentages of literate men and women, which testifies to the heavily patriarchal character of the Serbian community. The Serbian bourgeoisie and intelligentsia was accordingly the most under-represented among all ethnic elites in the Monarchy.[28] Serbs barely reached one percent of students from Hungary attending foreign universities.[29] Needless to say, all of the above factors—increasing competition, weak elites, land shortage, and lack of job outlets—forced many Serbs to emigrate overseas.[30]

Analyzing the origins of the crisis, several observers at the time blamed the Karlovci hierarchy and stressed it was thoroughly alienated and removed from the vast majority of simple folk.[31] At the same time, being most exposed to outside influences of all lands inhabited by the Serbs, those in the Karlovci Metropolitanate also experienced the most profound transformations of old traditions and institutions, family and kin ties, and underlying religious and moral norms. It is unsurprising that their political elites were the most vocal in demands for reform of the church. Miletić tried to reconcile the liberal demands for democratization of church administration with the Orthodox tradition, claiming for laymen the same rights as those enjoyed by the rulers of Orthodox Empires such as Byzantium or Russia, where the Tsars still governed the church.[32] Besides demand for the laity's control of church affairs, the reformers sought to make the church more "popular" by making the liturgy more comprehensible and attractive, and by addressing the main social questions of the period. Only enlightenment and education, Miletić and his followers believed, combined with the Orthodox faith, would raise the spirit of the nation and place Serbs on equal terms with their neighbors and competitors. Liberals and Radicals accused the hierarchy of all church irregularities and conflicts with lower clergy, blaming it for driving out people from the church because of its insistence on controlling Church and School Autonomy finances.[33] The pro-government stance of the Karlovci leadership was especially targeted. Bishop Gavrilo Zmejanović of Vršac, elected with pressure by the Hungarian government and aspiring to become a patriarch, was reported, for example, as fully participating in magyarization policies, ordering clergy not only to vote but even campaign for Hungarian candidates, suppressing and deposing nationalist priests, teachers and other officials, and duly placing Serbian schools under the full control of local Hungarian authorities.[34]

Yet the final alarm for the hierarchy and clergy was not sounded by the Liberals or Radicals but by the conversion of many Serbs to neo-Protestant Nazarenes, signaling that the Orthodox Church was losing its last dominion—the spiritual realm.[35] The "Nazarene disease," as it was often described, provided the final push for the church's belated but vehement adoption of nationalism. For a long time the hierarchy ignored what the clergy perceived as the new threat, supplying the Liberals with yet another argument in their anticlericalism.[36] But by the end of the century some prominent clerics began to use the Nazarenes to promote an agenda, which consisted of the rejection of liberal reforms and the vision of a Serbian nation united and strengthened only through its bond with the Orthodox faith. The reaction to the Nazarene renegades blended with a mythologized narrative of forced conversions in the past to create the exclusive confessional nationalism of the Serbs. The traditional anti-Catholic theological discourse of the Orthodox Church was revived into concrete anguish. Serbian history in the monarchy was portrayed as nothing more than constant suffering for Serbian nationality and Orthodox faith evident in earlier resistance to the Union. Furthermore, the conversion-threat discourse provided a unique weapon to emphasize and exaggerate the authority and role of the Orthodox Church as the institution of the defense and preservation of a people and their identity from all possible dangers such as secularization or marginalization. Finally, with the appearance of the grassroot lay religious movement later known as *Bogomoljci*, the Serbian clergy found an audience ready to listen and a chance to influence its community.[37] While many priests rejected the *Bogomoljci* from the outset, others tried to channel their religious zeal by applying a set of strategies already used by other churches that were similarly trying to prevent their believers from falling away to other confessions or religious indifference.

As a reaction or in opposition to the appearance and mass spread of the Nazarenes and the Nazarene-inspired *Bogomoljci* movement, the Serbian Church appropriated, adapted, and particularized some of the very strategies of the Protestant and Catholic Churches and forms of piety from folk religion, that it had opposed for a long time. Patriarch Georgije Branković (1890–1907) undertook several important measures to reform the economy and administration of numerous monasteries in Karlovci Metropolitanate as well as to improve the educational level of monks by opening up a monastic school.[38] Order was established in the rather unruly Karlovci Seminary, administration of parishes and eparchies improved, church statistics, press and publishing flourished, and improvements were noticeable in pastoral care.[39] In 1912, with the approval of the Karlovci hierarchy under Patriarch Lukijan Bogdanović, the Hungarian government abolished the Serbian Church and School Autonomy, depriving laymen of any influence. Nevertheless, the Habsburg legacy of self-government and modernization of the Karlovci Metropolitanate in the decades before the autonomy was abolished distinguished this church, its priests and faithful from their brethren in other Serbian regions for a very long time.

Dalmatia

While an Orthodox presence in Dalmatia dates back to medieval times, most Orthodox people settled in the Dalmatian hinterland in the sixteenth and seventeenth century, in some areas even forming the majority of the population over the Catholics.[40] Following the Treaty of Karlovci (1699) and of Požarevac (1718), all of Dalmatia fell under the rule of the Venetian Republic. Strictly Catholic, *la Serenissima* did not envisage confessional arrangements similar to those of the Ottoman and Habsburg Empire. Serbs and other Orthodox were duly placed under the administration of the Archbishopric of Philadelphia, which was a Greek diocese in union with the Catholic Church. Not allowed to have their own hierarchs,

Serbian candidates for priests usually went across the border to be consecrated by bishops in the Ottoman or Habsburg lands. Even bishops were occasionally appointed by neighboring Serbian hierarchs but soon after their return were expelled by the Venetian authorities. Only in 1780, Venice proclaimed religious tolerance and allowed the Serbian Orthodox to have a vicar. Little changed during the first Habsburg possession of Dalmatia (1787–1805) and only the French occupation (1805–14) brought full recognition of the Orthodox Christians. In 1810, by Napoleonic decree, Venijamin Kraljević, a Phanariot bishop who escaped from Bosnia, was appointed the first bishop for the Orthodox Serbs of Dalmatia.

The isolation, religious discrimination, and lack of proper ecclesiastical organization reduced the church life of Dalmatian Serbs to basics. Gerasim Zelić, who was first appointed vicar by the Venetians and then served under the Austrians and French, described a dire lack of priests, schools, church books, and records.[41] In the Montenegrin littoral, Zelić testifies, no priest would leave home without arms. To make matters worse, under Austrian rule the threat of the Union reappeared. Reports conflict upon whether bishop Kraljević himself accepted the Union. In any case four Uniate teachers were brought from Galicia to open a seminary in Šibenik, which provoked an uproar among the people, led by vicar Zelić. Metropolitan Stratimirović intervened with the emperor personally but to no avail. One of the teachers was killed in the uproar, probably plotted in Krka Monastery, for which the plotters of the assassination were duly sentenced and soon Kraljević withdrew to Venice.

The situation settled down after 1828 as the Dalmatian diocese was joined to the Karlovci Metropolitanate and Josif Rajačić was appointed bishop (1829–34). Nevertheless, problems abided as occasionally a priest would join the Union and drag some parishioners along, usually after a conflict with bishops. Bishops were also removed every so often by the authorities. For some time, there were no consistories or other diocesan and parish bodies. It was only under bishops Stefan Knežević (1853–90) and Nikodim Milaš (1890–1910)[42] that the necessary administrative organization was established along the Karlovci model. These two bishops nourished close contact with Belgrade Metropolitan Mihailo, who spearheaded Serbian irredentism abroad, and vociferously engaged in Dalmatian politics.[43] During this period cooperation between Serbs and Croats was replaced by exclusivism and chauvinism. First in Dalmatia and later in Croatia, clergy on both sides actively took part in partisan and nationalist squabbles that seriously undermined the position of South Slavs vis-à-vis Austrian and Hungarian authorities in Vienna and Budapest.

Following the reorganization of the Monarchy in 1873, Dalmatia was extracted from the jurisdiction of the Karlovci Metropolitanate and together with the bishopric of Boka-Kotorska (established in 1870 for the Austrian-controlled Montenegrin littoral) placed alongside Bukovina (inhabited by Orthodox Romanians and Ruthenians) in a rather artificial Bukovina-Dalmatia Metropolitanate. Responsible for the Orthodox in the Austrian half of Austria-Hungary, this ecclesiastical administration merged the opposite borderlands of the Empire, whose bishops had to communicate via interpreters. However, there were tangible benefits for a small church administration. In Dalmatia, the lack of priests was slowly overcome so that by the end of the century around eighty priests cared for around 115,000 Orthodox in 106 parishes. In addition, there were thirty-five monks in three monasteries in Dalmatia and eight in the Montenegrin Littoral. As elsewhere, the church in Dalmatia was not immune to fraudulence, corruption, and even dramatic scandals. The suicide of Dositej Jović, Bishop of Boka-Kotorska, in 1910 was explained by his appropriation of the Serbian autonomous church and school funds. The public accused the Bishop of Zadar, Nikodim Milaš, of the same and he retired.[44] These and other conflicts notwithstanding, the jubilant celebrations in Dalmatia after Serbian victories in the Balkan wars anticipated big changes on the horizon. While centuries of separation left the Orthodox Church in the littoral considerably poor, the long repression as well as recent radicalism of its leaders, made its faithful nationally conscious and eager to unify with their Serbian brethren in Serbia and elsewhere.

Bosnia and Herzegovina

The late eighteenth and early nineteenth century, marked by the decay of the Ottoman Empire and the rule of Phanariot bishops in Bosnia, is considered in some contemporary reports and later historiography as a gloomy period for the Orthodox Church with the Phanariots faring worse than the "Turks."[45] As in Serbia and other lands in the Balkans under the Ottomans, most Christians in Bosnia lived in remote rural areas in patriarchal communities with all but a very rudimentary knowledge of their faith. Over centuries their religious practice had acquired many syncretic features under the influence of Islam.[46] Monastic life had almost died out and almost no new churches were built until the mid-nineteenth century when Tanzimat reforms awoke hopes among the Orthodox for equality. At the same time, some Orthodox communities in towns such as Sarajevo or Mostar saw their economic power increase due to trade links with Orthodox merchants in the Habsburg Empire and beyond. Their prosperity and self-confidence translated into a vivid church life of urban parishes and the almost independent administration of these communities. From the 1850s, there were more consistent efforts to open Orthodox schools and in 1866 the first if short-lived Orthodox seminary opened its doors. When the Ottoman reform era finally reached Bosnia, Sultan Abdul Aziz and his vizier, Mehmed Asim Paşa, even helped financially with the construction of monumental Orthodox churches in Sarajevo and Mostar. The process whereby Christians were awarded new rights was anything but smooth as evident in the incident when the installation of church bells provoked the public outcry of local Muslims whom the Ottoman authorities had to forcibly put under control. At the same time, the movement for an autocephalous Bulgarian Church also influenced Bosnian Serbs themselves to protest against docile Greek bishops accused of amassing personal wealth and neglecting their flock.

The most direct and powerful impetus for the Bosnian Orthodox came from neighboring Serbia, where a series of uprisings against the Ottoman lords took place in the early nineteenth century. The attempt to spread the revolt over the river Drina to Bosnia failed, but the autonomy achieved in Serbia never ceased to radiate over Ottoman-held Bosnia. Liberation seemed to be within easy reach and revolts of Orthodox Christians flared occasionally, often headed by rather destitute village priests. Some clergymen, after attending schools in Serbia or the Habsburg Monarchy, returned to Bosnia and began to set up schools, disseminate books and spread the idea of Serbian national unification. The most noteworthy of them was archimandrite Vaso Pelagić, who was behind the first seminary in Banja Luka. He was not only remembered for his nationalist fury but also for very liberal ideas and a drive to enlighten Bosnian Serb peasants. The Ottoman authorities soon had him arrested and exiled to Asia Minor.[47] Despite moves toward religious equality, the discontent of the mostly landless peasant Christian population in Bosnia continued unabated. The Herzegovina rebellion of 1875 eventually triggered an all-out war against the Ottoman Empire throughout the Balkans and unleashed the better-known Eastern Question crisis (1875–78), which resulted in the Austro-Hungarian occupation of Bosnia and Herzegovina. Serbs initially opposed the occupation and, together with Muslims, fought the new conquerors but soon succumbed to the force of the mighty Empire.

Despite its Catholic bias, the new Christian rule in Bosnia brought great improvements for the Orthodox. One of the most pressing issues for the Habsburg rulers was how to structure and administratively organize and control the Orthodox Church and especially the increasingly nationally conscious and active urban religious communities.[48] There were several options available, none of which foresaw granting the Orthodox self-governance in church affairs or allowing any connection with the church organization of their Serbian brethren in neighboring Serbia and Montenegro. The most logical and historically justifiable option was to join the Bosnia Metropolitanate to the existing Orthodox Church in the Monarchy, that is, the Karlovci Metropolitanate. This was also politically opportune since the emperor and the Hungarian government had full control over its hierarchy. Jointly they blocked all of the actions taken by the Serbian Church and People's assembly, which was, as noted above, dominated throughout this period by nationalist laymen and lower clergy. Indeed, the initial strategy of the Austro-Hungarians was to transfer the Bosnian Orthodox Serbs to Karlovci. Warmly welcomed by the Karlovci hierarchy, the transfer was fiercely rejected by the Serbian nationalists who understood it as the subjugation of Serbian interests. For them the integration of the Orthodox Church in Bosnia into the Karlovci Metropolitanate equaled ceding the fate of Bosnia to the Habsburg Monarchy. Nationalists believed Serbian interests would be better defended by a degree of independence for the Orthodox Church in Bosnia or a continuous link with the Ecumenical Patriarchate, both of which would leave the option of eventual unification of Bosnia with Serbia.

Unification did eventually take place but with a different outcome whereby Habsburg interests and primacy in church matters were secured. As already noted in connection with the Karlovci Metropolitanate, Austro-Hungarian administration in Bosnia strove to dissuade nascent Serbian nationalism by attaining the loyalty of the church leadership and fostering confessional adherence.[49] This policy is well personified by Béni von Kállay, the Habsburg governor of Bosnia for almost a quarter of a century. The cornerstone of his confessional politics was the Convention with the Ecumenical Patriarchate in 1880, which awarded Vienna the right to appoint and remove religious hierarchs and to have full legal and financial authority over them.⁵⁰ In this case the *raison d'état* was more influential than respect for canonicity, in that, the Habsburg Monarch, who was by definition Catholic, obtained the right to appoint Orthodox Metropolitans, who the patriarch in Constantinople only confirmed. The convention with the Ecumenical Patriarchate (then under Patriarch Joachim III) was attained by the regular greasing of palms, as Robin Okey euphemistically puts it, while Austro-Hungarian support for the patriarchate's authority over Christians in the Ottoman Empire against Russian, Bulgarian, Romanian and Serbian pretensions also featured prominently in strictly confident negotiations in Constantinople.⁵¹

Once obtained, the emperor made ample use of his right to decide on church heads or metropolitans in Bosnia. Apart from the first short-lived metropolitan, Emperor Franz Joseph I selected bishops from among the loyal clergy of Hungary and Croatia. Most members of the Orthodox Consistorial or the church's governing body were also imported. They in turn had the authority to appoint, move or punish lower clergy and deal with most day to day affairs. In addition, the government assumed the right to certify priests and teachers in Orthodox schools, against the previous autonomous practices of urban church communities acknowledged by the Statute of the Ecumenical Patriarchate in 1862. The authorities made every effort to make churches part of the state apparatus, providing salaries to bishops and awards to loyal priests and teachers. In order to prevent irregularities, the arbitrary Phanariot tax was replaced by regular taxation, which was fairer but made bishops directly and completely dependent on the state. At the same time, the idea of the occupational authorities was not only to govern religious institutions but also to make them functioning and sustainable in line with its enlightened Absolutism. Once loyalty was achieved, religious institutions were supported and flourished. According to the first census conducted by the new rulers, out of 268 Orthodox parishes many were without a church building although there were as many as 265 priests and eleven monks, a solid number for Bosnia's 352,664 Orthodox Christians. During Austro-Hungarian rule, 236 new churches were built and 91 churches and monasteries reconstructed. In addition, a permanent seminary opened, schools and social life were organized, and from 1887 the metropolitanate had its own press.

Nevertheless, the construction boom and overall development in this period of the Orthodox Church could not dissuade the widespread perception of Catholic domination, which was evident in the mass colonization and employment of Catholics from the rest of the Monarchy and over-proportional state funding for the Catholic Church. Furthermore, only a couple of years after being appointed, the first Orthodox Metropolitan Sava Kosanović was forced to resign when he denounced what he perceived as Catholic proselytism and entered into an open conflict with the Catholic Archbishop Josip Stadler. The reaction of Serbs was immediately translated into the existing matrix of anti-Catholicism, which was already at work in the Karlovci Metropolitanate and Dalmatia and which had been cultivated among the Orthodox at least since the early seventeenth century after often violent attempts of the Roman Curia and Habsburg or Venetian authorities to force them into the Union with the Catholic Church.[52] Worrying signs were not hard to find. In 1894, Pope Leo XIII named Stadler the Apostolic Commissar for fostering the Union in the Balkans and Stadler launched a journal devoted to the issue, appropriately named *Balkan*.

Furthermore, frequent intervention from above caused suspicion among both Orthodox and Muslims, who feared the omnipresent state control despite statistically noticeable benefits for religious life. Von Kállay's authoritarian paternalism reflected the Josephinist legacy in which Habsburg power made its impact personally rather than through bureaucratic forms. Holding back on reforms, using school stipends as political weapons, limiting expenses for schooling, preserving elementary confessional schools and fostering only higher and technical schools, as Okey demonstrates, aggravated the standing of the Monarchy and doubtlessly nurtured radical and nationalist opposition especially among the Bosnian youth.[53] Even the distinct dress code for various confessions inherited from the Ottomans went unchanged throughout the period of Habsburg rule, evidence that confessionalism remained the main tool of social genetics in comparison to half-heartedly introduced modernization. More than anything else, the appointment of docile bishops resulted in rising dissatisfaction among the Orthodox Serbs.

Less than two decades into the occupation, the largest Orthodox urban communities launched a movement for autonomy and began handing out petitions and sending delegations to Vienna. They demanded (a) the right to an assembly without the presence of the authorities; (b) the right to choose their priests and teachers and gain a voice in electing metropolitans; (c) the freedom to manage their funds; and (d) national and cultural rights such as the free use of the national name and the Cyrillic alphabet and the right to establish reading halls, choirs, and other associations. Throughout their struggle the Serbs insisted on their connection with the Ecumenical Patriarchate and on maintaining a link with the Ottoman Empire, hoping that this would prevent annexation and ease their position vis-à-vis the Roman Catholics. In their second memorandum written in 1898, they sought a model of autonomy that foresaw that (a) bishops would be elected by assemblies of priests and laymen and confirmed by the Ecumenical Patriarch claiming the same rights that they enjoyed during the Peć patriarchate; (b) church communities would be in charge of salaries for priests and bishops; (c) priests would maintain church courts and be autonomous in many church issues; (d) church communities would elect priests, which were then confirmed by bishops (metropolitans); and (e) the Orthodox Church in Bosnia would remain part of the Ecumenical Patriarchate. The patriarch, however, rejected this proposal as uncanonical and advised that civic leaders reconcile and find an acceptable solution together with metropolitans. The solution was not reached. Instead members of Serbian urban church communities began a boycott of church services in Sarajevo, Mostar, Livno, and other towns. Thousands refrained from confession and the Eucharist, the baptism of children, and even funerals accompanied by priests, from 1896 until 1905. In Mostar alone, in the course of seven years, there were 438 burials without a church ceremony.[54]

After its protracted refusal, in 1905, the Austro-Hungarian government finally accepted most of the demands and Emperor Franz Joseph I issued the act of Serbian Church autonomy in Bosnia. Church communities were to be governed by assemblies made up of all men of age. They would elect the school and church governing councils, priests and their deputies for diocesan councils and courts. Autonomy was financed by a 10 percent tax that the state collected from all Orthodox Serbs in addition to state support for schools, churches, and priests. The Serbian Orthodox name was reinstated for all communities, courts, and councils. Church communities were also able to maintain a direct link with the patriarchate. Nevertheless, while the new constitution envisaged the right of communities to elect their priests, it stopped short of the right to elect bishops. The emperor continued to use his privilege to choose loyalists as Orthodox hierarchs to the dismay of the people. When, in 1912, Serbian members of the newly established Bosnian assembly condemned in a statement Austro-Hungarian diplomatic reactions to Serbian successes in the First Balkan

War, the Sarajevo Metropolitan Evgenije Letica was the only one to abstain. Some years later, after the First World War was over and the Kingdom of Yugoslavia was created out of the ruins of the Habsburg Monarchy, some of the Habsburg Serb bishops had to resign and hand over their seats to more nationally aware hierarchs in the newly unified Serbian Orthodox Church. Yet national independence and unification of all Serbs into one church organization in the Yugoslav Kingdom also meant the abolition of church autonomy in Bosnia, which maintained hundreds of parishes, 120 primary schools, and two high schools for girls in Mostar and Sarajevo, an active press, and a plethora of cultural associations. Another paradox was that in their own country the Serbs lost their long-fought right to elect their own priests.

Serbia

The modern history of Serbia begins with two uprisings in the early nineteenth century (1804–12 and 1815) that paved the way, first, for its autonomous status within the Ottoman Empire, and then, in 1878, for internationally recognized independence. The rebellion was famously led by mostly illiterate pig merchants, village chieftains, and priests, the only elite in rural Serbia.[55] At first it was hardly more than one in a series of revolts against unruly Ottoman regional lords. Over the years, the close proximity of more nationally conscious Serbs in the Habsburg Empire just across rivers Sava and Danube, and the Napoleonic turmoil in Europe, contributed to the gradual transformation of the uprising into a national liberation struggle. Fervent enemies Karlovci Metropolitan Stratimirović and enlightener Dositej Obradović settled their differences over the need to help their brethren across the rivers. Eventually Dositej Obradović went to Belgrade where he established the first school and became advisor to the leader of the uprising, Karađorđe Petrović, who then appointed him the first Serbian education minister.[56]

Post-Ottoman Serbia was in desperate need of assistance and so was its church. After the Great Migration (1690), the educated clergy almost wholly disappeared from Serbia. The people and lower clergy had hardly any connection to the Phanariot who were usually remembered for wealth-squandering and debt-making.[57] During most of the eighteenth century, monasteries were the only centers of basic learning, and monks served as the chief spiritual care-takers. But monasteries were few and monks were often absent, out collecting alms. Vuk Karadžić left a famous description of the poor state of monastic schools in Serbia in which pupils forgot in summer what they had learnt in winter being forced to mind the livestock of often illiterate and greedy monks.[58] However, Karadžić also pointed out the enormous social importance monasteries played in the life of village flock and described the gatherings in and around monasteries on Sundays and holidays as major social and economic events. A well-disposed Habsburg Serb observer noted that the patriarchal life of the villagers seemed to have no real connection to the churches except for their role as gathering places and fairgrounds on their patron saint day.[59] Karadžić's recording and description of Serbian customs and religion found an echo in Leopold Ranke's seminal *A History of Servia and Servian Revolution*.[60] Ranke was astonished that the village *kneses* (heads) were obliged to keep the churches in good repair and enjoyed the prescriptive right of nominating, from among the monks, the *hegoumens* (abbots)—a privilege without any precedent in the Christian world. Furthermore, Ranke promoted the view of the solid national character of the Serbian Church, determined by the founding of numerous monasteries by Serbian medieval kings, almost all of whom were canonized and venerated by the church. Notwithstanding its firm medieval foundation, some memory of which was preserved in liturgical texts and the celebration of saints, the position of the church changed dramatically during the centuries of the Ottoman rule. After the imposition of Phanariot bishops, the church leadership lost its relevance for the people. Indeed, the hierarchy of the church played a rather minor role in the uprising. On the other hand, many lower Serbian clergy took an active role and fought together with insurgents. One of them, Father Matija Nenadović, achieved the high status of the president of the first provisional government and led negotiations with the Porte. His memoirs provide testimony both of the uprising and of the church in Serbia at the time.[61] In the nascent Serbian state ruled by Prince Miloš Obrenović, the leader of the Second Uprising, the Phanariot leadership was insignificant in his efforts to establish public law, state structures and order, education and culture.[62] The aspirations of bishops, if they were expressed, were castigated by Prince Miloš who did not refrain from slaying priests and even bishops and subjecting the church and clergy to his will.[63]

In the Habsburg Empire at that time, the Serb national consciousness was already fostered by mostly secular activists and intellectuals. There were Serbian presses in Vienna and Budapest, cultural societies, and a growing Serbian literature and historiography. Prince Miloš Obrenović, who eliminated the previous leader Karađorđe, shared his example of establishing close ties with more advanced brethren in Habsburg lands, the so-called Prečani, many of whom he imported to Serbia. When the prince finally managed to acquire autonomy for the Belgrade Metropolitanate from the Ecumenical Patriarchate in 1831, he also assumed the right to select bishops who were then only confirmed by Constantinople. In order to serbianize the Orthodox Church, Prince Miloš got rid of Phanariot bishops and, after the short tenure of local Melentije Pavlović, brought in Metropolitan Peter Jovanović from Hungary.[64] Furthermore, the establishment of a state-sponsored, independent Serbian Church reaffirmed the substitution of Greek by Old Slavonic as the liturgical language, thereby facilitating the redeployment of Orthodoxy as an integral part of Serbian identity. During the rule of Prince Miloš, the practice of state interference in church affairs and the primacy of state interests over canonical principles were firmly established and would remain in place in Serbia until the end of the period observed.[65] The Belgrade Metropolitanate's role was to organize and regulate the life of the people and the church according to the demands of Serbia's rulers or later ruling parties. Implementing their tasks, the metropolitans and consistory also closely emanated Karlovci Metropolitanate policies. Yet unlike its counterpart in the Habsburg Monarchy, the Belgrade Metropolitanate acquired a state-church status in what was becoming an overwhelmingly Serbian and Orthodox country, adding further weight to its role. Surveying the orders of the church authorities, which are preserved for the whole century, it is worth mentioning that the greatest number refers to secular affairs, the most numerous being the imposition of compulsory vaccinations.[66] They are followed by those outlining wedding or burial regulations, providing lists of recruits, maintaining financial records, and reminding state servants to attend church services regularly. Other orders included those banning priests from visiting inns "without particular necessity"; explaining how to make the sign of the cross; and preaching against the use of bad language or weapons at church feasts. Besides administrative regulation, there was a serious need to eradicate the numerous irregularities in religious practice and to achieve uniformity in the church's liturgical and religious outlook. Finally, a considerable number of orders from "higher places" demanded loyalty to and veneration of the royal family, proscribed celebrations of national victories, or, in other ways, tried to instill national consciousness. The measures undertaken were far-reaching and inevitably impacted on education, mores, and the rise of patriotism and loyalty toward the new nation-state.

Urban settlements, previously mostly inhabited by Turks, were serbianized, with Belgrade being the most important. Besides Serbs, many Slavs, Vlachs, and others migrated from the Ottoman and Habsburg territories to Serbia, which was perceived as free and victorious. The tiny educated elite, heavily dominated by Prečani, strove to transform the small state into the Serbian homeland and later the South Slav Piedmont. Once Serbia gained autonomy, Serbian rulers and elites immediately turned to building churches, which was seen as an expression of national activism in the Serbian medieval tradition.[67] During the early days of this sacral construction boom, Karlovci models were replicated. In the eighteenth century, the architecture and painting of these churches abandoned the traditional Byzantine style and leaned toward contemporary European or more precisely Central European artistic trends found in the Habsburg Monarchy.[68] The Cathedral of Belgrade, built in 1841, with its neoclassical style façades and a Baroque bell-tower, became the chief achievement and symbol of this new architectural style. Gradually, Central European views and customs were imposed even upon the traditional burial and death commemoration culture.[69] After a couple of decades, however, the search began for a genuine Serbian style, or for what were believed to be the expressions of the Serbian spirit, sought in artistic styles cherished by the Orthodox Church in its "golden" medieval times.[70]

Nevertheless, the radical transformation of a backward rural country into a modern nation-state proved extremely difficult if not entirely elusive. Whereas in 1846 one priest was in custody of 1,102 people, the number increased by 1874 to more than 1,600, making some of the above tasks delegated to priests unattainable. While the state and Metropolitan Petar Jovanović had already laid the ground for the seminary in 1836, due to lack of funds and cadre, it provided little in terms of a theological education, which was initially to last only one year and was later extended to three. Unsurprisingly, Serbian students who went abroad to study, for example in Halki near Constantinople, could not match their peers and often gave up.[71] For most village priests monasteries remained the only place of learning throughout the century.

The gradual emancipation of the church in Serbia from the Karlovci Metropolitanate became evident when Metropolitan Petar Jovanović was forced to retire and was succeeded by Serbian-born Mihailo Jovanović. One of the first Serbs from the principality to have studied in Russia, Belgrade Metropolitan Mihailo, elected in 1859, was remembered as a tireless national and political activist but a rather weak church administrator.[72] Already in 1862, Metropolitan Mihailo proscribed uniform rules on how to celebrate *Slava* (the Family Patron Saint Day) in a series of attempts to establish *Slava* as the key distinguishing element of Serbian Orthodox identity, which included a journal under the same name later launched in Niš.[73] Furthermore, under Mihailo, the Belgrade Metropolitanate embarked on the introduction of new cults and the veneration and celebration of Serbian saints, most notably Saint Sava. Ever since his death in the thirteenth century, the founder of the Serbian medieval autocephalous church, Prince Rastko Nemanjić or Saint Sava, was celebrated in the church and among the people. The cult of Saint Sava, as we know it today, began to emerge only at the beginning of the nineteenth century, parallel to the liberation struggles of the Serbs, when, according to one church historian, it assumed its new role to "nourish national pride and flame the patriotism and readiness for sacrifice."[74] Over the course of the century, first among Serbs in Hungary and then in Serbia, secular content intermingled with religious celebration and national romanticism shifted the focus from ecclesiastical and religious rites to Enlightenment ideas, the glorification of the medieval past and resistance to foreign culture and oppression. The feast of Saint Sava left the churches where it originated to become a national school holiday, a celebration of the Serbian language and a plea for the unification and liberation of Serbs from foreign domination. The cult was continuously enriched with new content as Saint Sava's preserved hagiographies were unearthed and reinterpreted. After Arsenije Teodorović, in 1807, depicted Saint Sava reconciling his two brothers over their father's relics, Saint Sava's role as unifier became the single most exploited image in the narrative surrounding the cult.[75] National romantic painters first introduced what would later become the much-exploited, figurative representations of the burning of Saint Sava's relics by the Turks, thereby emphasizing Serbian victimhood. The hymn to Saint Sava, the verses of which stress Serbian unity and renewal, was initially sung in Serbian schools in Hungary, and by the middle of the century became an unofficial national anthem. Other elements such as processions from churches to schools, performances in which schoolchildren recited patriotic poems, and a special Saint Sava sermon followed. In

1867, Vladan Đorđević, a medical student in Vienna and a future Serbian prime minister, reported, "Saint Sava is celebrated everywhere, from Pest to Peć (the seat of the Serbian Patriarchate), from Niš and Timok to the Adriatic Sea, in all four countries where Serbian people live torn apart from each other, and even in all countries and cities of Europe where only a few Serbs gather."[76] The veneration of Saint Sava acquired additional significance under the direct influence of Russophiles and Slavophiles, whose chief proponent in Serbia was Metropolitan Mihailo. Whereas the Holy See featured Cyril and Methodius, apostles of Slavs, to strengthen the religious and ecclesiastical adherence of Catholic Slavs and, hopefully, win over those Slavs of the Byzantine rite, the church in Serbia under Metropolitan Mihailo raised the flag of Saint Sava to awaken and assemble Serbs scattered in four countries and under diverse ecclesiastical jurisdictions.[77] After gaining independence in 1878, Serbia was conditioned by Vienna to reject its claims over Bosnia and Herzegovina. Under prince/king Milan Obrenović and the party of the Progressives, Serbia redirected its expansionist campaign to Ottoman Kosovo and Macedonia; one of the most importance auspices under which it was conducted was the Society of Saint Sava, formed in 1886 in Belgrade.[78] At the same time, students of the first Serbian seminary founded in the area under the Ottomans in Prizren, christened their association "Rastko," Saint Sava's secular name, emblematically blurring and superseding the division between the religious and secular under national imperatives.

Following the recognition of Serbia's independence at the congress of Berlin, the Belgrade Metropolitanate attained autocephalous status from the Ecumenical Patriarchate in line with the canonical principle of the Orthodox Church, which sets the ecclesiastical order according to the political one.[79] Nevertheless, the dispute with the Bulgarian Exarchate and the Ecumenical Patriarchate regarding the jurisdiction of Christians in the remaining Ottoman parts of the Balkans, namely Kosovo and Macedonia, intensified toward the end of the nineteenth century.[80] Despite its aspirations and support from Serbian political elites, the Belgrade Metropolitanate under Mihailo and newly established Society of Saint Sava could not compete with the Ecumenical Patriarchate or Bulgarian Exarchate in the struggle for souls in still Ottoman Macedonia as they lacked both funds and educated teachers or priests. The first Serbian bishop was installed in Skopje only in 1902, followed by one in Veles in 1910, whereas the Bulgarian

Exarchate already had seven, claiming the loyalty of two-thirds of the faithful in the respective eparchies. Even smaller was the Serbian share of schools in Macedonia in the period when schools served as the chief tools in this church-state pursuit for Orthodox souls in Ottoman lands that preceded their conquest and division during the Balkan wars.[81]

The only seminary in Belgrade that could have provided priests or teachers, as already noted, offered a very poor education, lacking personnel and discipline.[82] Compulsory school catechetic instruction was deemed doctrinaire, dull, dreary, and unable to inspire moral and religious sentiments.[83] Pastoral care was lacking throughout Serbia. After 1878, the population of Serbia increased tremendously, from less than 1.5 to almost three million before the Balkan wars of 1912–13. The number of priests, however, remained more or less unchanged throughout the period, oscillating around 1,000. In 1909, Serbia had roughly 976 secular parish priests and 109 monks compared to Orthodox Romania, which acquired its independence and autocephalous church at the same period and boasted roughly 1,700 monks, 2,700 nuns, and over 8,000 priests.[84] Even more striking was the small number of monks in Serbia in comparison to other countries, both Catholic and Orthodox during that period. Altogether fifty-three monasteries in Serbia housed ninety-six monks in 1884 and ninety-eight in 1910.[85] Most monasteries had been ruined by high taxes and poor management. Traditional methods of land exploitation and land lending to local peasants could not endure the pressures of a modern economy. Finally, it was widely noted that the monastery elders cared more about their own well-being than about future investment and saving,[86] all of which resulted in monasticism dying a slow death and monastic tonsure reduced to a prerequisite for entering into the church leadership and rank of bishops. The lack of monks was circumvented by an increasing number of widowed priests being turned into monks only to be elected bishops immediately thereafter.

A particularly serious problem was that despite the prohibition of political activities, many priests led the campaigns of nascent political parties, thereby sowing divisions among the people and clergy and actually contributing to indifference toward church and religion. They had, however, a very palpable reason for doing so. Some priests, led by Milan Đurić, himself a parliamentary deputy, struggled to obtain a regular salary from the state budget instead of being forced to charge for their services. They blamed the bishops for not resolving this issue and even demanded their resignation.[87] Moreover, political parties and ideas that attracted Serbian priests and seminarians included clearly secular Socialists. Usually depicted as nationalist hotbeds, Serbian schools became fertile grounds for various other ideas originating in the West, including materialism, atheism, and even anarchism, which appalled Serb visitors from the Habsburg Empire. Famous poet Milica Stojadinović lamented that while she always felt Serbia was her motherland, she feared for its future as destructive, atheist, anticlerical, and antimonarchical ideas took sway.[88]

Despite bans, imprisonment, and the occasional death penalty, the Serbian Nazarenes from Hungary also spread their faith in Serbia.[89] A Scottish philanthropist in Serbia, Frances Mackenzie, indirectly involved his friend and Serbian minister of finance and foreign affairs, Čedomilj Mijatović, in his efforts to protect the Nazarenes from state and church repression.[90] Although Mijatović remained Orthodox until his death and was even featured as a candidate for patriarch, he was continuously accused of being a Nazarene because he sincerely respected and often praised the Nazarenes as true believers. In his book about Serbia and Serbs written for an English language audience, Mijatović even cites them as proof that Serbs "as a race, are not incapable of religious piety."[91] Not surprisingly, Mijatović was remembered as the only religious politician in Serbia in the nineteenth century. Together with Mackenzie he was among the founders of a journal, *Hrišćanski vesnik* (Christian Herald), the aim of which was to reform Serbian religious and moral life, pleading for a free exchange of ideas and opinions.[92] In addition to John Bunyan's *Pilgrim's Progress,* Mijatović translated several works by English Protestant thinkers and preachers and often published his own religious treatises.[93] Nevertheless, his and Mackenzie's ideas and strivings for a religious revival like that of the Nazarenes, the Biblical Society or temperance societies attained little influence or relevance in Serbia.[94]

More successful were the attempts to strengthen the Serbian character of the church. In the overwhelmingly nationalist political atmosphere at the turn of the century, Metropolitan Mihailo was charged in 1895 to head the Committee for the construction of a grandiose church on Belgrade's Vračar Hill, dedicated "to the memory of the greatest Serbian saint, Enlightener and Unifier, Saint Sava." The poor response to the metropolitan's appeal for donations demonstrated not just the poverty of the Serbs at the time but also the lack of a fully developed and widespread national consciousness ready to respond. The general population lacked the cultural homogeneity of a nation, which is, in turn, dependent on a level of literacy and the spread of the printed word.

The dispersal of Serbs was a second major problem in achieving a sense of national unity and attaining national homogeneity. Furthermore, frequent clashes between Serbian secular and religious elites weakened both groups and the national project. As already emphasized, the Serbian state and its rulers, ever since Prince Miloš Obrenović, clearly saw and cherished the church as an integrative force in building the nation and their own authority. However, they went beyond supporting the church, striving to impose strict control and frequently interfering in church life and the canonical order. The most blatant example was the deposition of Belgrade Metropolitan Mihailo, for so long a thorn in the regime's side due to his many political ties with Russia ever since his student days. Moreover, his support for the irredentism of brethren outside Serbia's borders was often beyond state control. Once Prince Milan Obrenović and his government of the Progressives embarked on a clear Austrophile policy, conflict was inevitable. It happened in 1881, over the Taxation Law that the government proposed and the National Assembly adopted and that included taxes on ordination into the priesthood and even monastic tonsure. The metropolitan vociferously opposed this state intrusion in what he defended as holy sacraments (for Orthodox, sacred mysteries). Nevertheless, the government insisted that the Law was passed by the parliament and the particular taxation was necessary because of the abuses of the clergy. Conflict erupted and the king eventually deposed the metropolitan; other bishops, in solidarity, resigned. A new metropolitan was "imported" from Austria-Hungary and a new loyalist uncanonical hierarchy was established. This extraordinary situation lasted until 1889, when King Milan abdicated and Metropolitan Mihailo was allowed to return from exile and reclaim his seat.

Modernizing Progressives were not the only political option available. In fact their pro-Habsburg stance sentenced them to a rather negligent share of Serbian political sympathies. Initiated by the ideas of Svetozar Marković, a self-confessed Socialist, and later modified by Nikola Pašić and his followers, it was the Radical Party that turned into the most powerful, if oppositional, political force in Serbia in the 1880s. Inspired by Russian Slavophiles and Narodniks, the key concern of the Radicals became the destruction of the traditional mode of life by the forces of capitalism. Instead, hope was set in traditional institutions (the extended family, village commune, and so on), which were deemed apt for the creation of a just social order, together with a mystical belief in the particularity of the Russian or Serbian people and their organic development. While Marković remained a firm believer in science and progress, Nikola Pašić, leader of the Radical Party until his death in 1926, adopted from Slavophiles the notion of the superiority of the Orthodox religion as both institution and creed.[95] Influenced by Konstantin Aksakov and other Russian Slavophiles, Pašić praised the Orthodox Church as conciliatory, popular and democratic compared to the hierarchical, expansionist, and absolutist Catholic Church. Pašić and the Radicals came to Orthodoxy via the "West" and criticism thereof in Russia. Nevertheless, they brought a change in the position of the Orthodox Church in Serbia. All previous rulers since liberation saw it only as their political tool, not least because of its potential link to national mobilization. Yet, by the end of the century, Serbia was ruled by the party whose core belief was the special link between Orthodoxy and Serbdom and that strove to make that link immutable and impermeable. At the same time as adopting the idea of nationalism from the West, there was a growing resistance to domestic westernization and modernization. Entering the world market on a big scale as an independent state, Serbia faced enormous problems in modernizing its farming economy, and in the period 1878–1914 experienced a significant decline in per capita output.[96] Fearing the loss of their authority that had been enjoyed in a traditional peasant society, many among the Orthodox clergy also joined the anti-Westernism of the Radical Party. However, in the church, as recent research by Klaus Buchenau has demonstrated, most of the emerging educated theologians chose to associate themselves with secular nationalism and only a minority reflected critically on the rapid social change in Serbia and its ostensibly destructive consequences.[97] Their anti-West interpretation of Orthodox tradition was largely derived from the Russian Orthodox Church and Russian Slavophiles.

Montenegro

As in large rural and mountainous areas of Bosnia and Herzegovina and the Military Border in Croatia, with almost no or a weak literacy tradition and limited contact with the outside world, the remote highlands of Montenegro were naturally the bastions of patriarchal folk religion. The pre-modern belief system of the Montenegrins was defined as essentially Manichean.⁹⁸ Isolated in their villages, the people maintained the tribal and kin structure of life that, besides social organization, acted in place of Christian ethic norms. Writing about religion in Montenegro, Christopher Boehm concluded that the entire formal apparatus of the Eastern Church for maintaining social control appeared to have been relatively ineffectual and tribal community life reigned supreme.⁹⁹ The fear of eternal punishment for committing sins, which lay at the core of Christian belief, was modified by means of a patriarchal society that with the help of pagan rituals established its own survival rules. Prevailing superstition and the norms of a patriarchal society never allowed for a strong influence from the Orthodox or any other church for that matter. Absurdly enough, patriarchal Montenegro has been termed in historiography as a theocracy, a system that presumes the authority of religion. In reality, as Michael Petrovich points out, in Montenegro even the priests were anticlerical. In fact, the clergy and bishop in Montenegro achieved respect only on the battlefield.¹⁰⁰ Dominated by local customs and morals and divided among the clans, the social and institutional role of the church in Montenegrin highlands was almost non-existent, prompting some foreign travelers to conclude that Montenegrins and sometimes Serbs in general have no religion. In reality, the religion they found there was just too remote from their mostly Protestant or sometimes Catholic religious background for it to be recognizable as such.

After the Ottoman invasion and the abolition of the ecclesiastical structures of the medieval Peć Patriarchate, the seat of the Zeta (Montenegro) diocese was transferred to high in the mountains of Cetinje. Real power lay with the squabbling clan chiefs, who variously recognized the authority of the Austrian Empire, the Republic of Venice, the Ottoman Empire or the Cetinje Metropolitan. At the beginning of the eighteenth century, the position of bishops became hereditary and occupied by members of the Petrović-Njegoš clan, although every new bishop had to be confirmed by the assembly of clan chiefs. With the abolition of the Peć Patriarchate in 1766, the Cetinje or Montenegrin diocese was left further isolated and independent.¹⁰¹ Bishop Petar I Petrović Njegoš (1784–1830) obtained consecration in Karlovci, but his successors on the Cetinje throne went to Montenegro's potent ally Russia for consecration and financial aid that reinforced their spiritual and secular powers. During his long and remarkable rule, bishop Petar I strengthened Montenegro by uniting the quarreling clans and suppressing blood vendettas. Petar I also strove to consolidate his own control and introduced the first written laws. Remembered as a brave commander in encounters with the Ottomans, his attempts at liberation and unification of Serbs nonetheless failed. In an exemplary move of nation building, his nephew and successor, Petar II Petrović Njegoš, had him canonized shortly after his death and venerated as Saint Peter of Cetinje. Petar II Petrović or simply Njegoš became the most famous of all the Njegoš bishop rulers, but he is primarily remembered as a poet. Obtaining his education from the leading Habsburg Serb poet and early nationalist Sima Milutinović, Sarajlija Njegoš wrote his magnum opus *The Mountain Wreath* (*Gorski vijenac*) in 1847 as a mighty anthem of the national struggle for liberation and the struggle against evil in general. Dedicated to the liberator of the Serbs, Karađorđe, in a form of poetic drama, it describes the attempt at the beginning of the eighteenth century to wipe out clansmen who converted to Islam, perceived as a threat to the integrity of the Montenegrin Christians. In *The Mountain Wreath*, Orthodox Christianity was conceived as coterminous with Serbdom, and the moral imperative of fulfilling the national mission was reconciled with Christian morality. Its undisputed poetic qualities as well as descriptions of the celebration of the Serbian patron saint (Slava), the dancing of the Serbian round dance (*kolo*), and frequent allusions to the battle of Kosovo soon made it into the Serbian and later Yugoslav national literary canon as a mighty propaganda tool. *The Mountain Wreath* was crowned as the final link in the trajectory of Serbian continuity between the mythical Kosovo battle, centuries of the Ottoman yoke, popular resistance as evident in the oral folk epic, and the nineteenth century liberation struggle. Moreover, Njegoš as a historical figure, bishop and political leader of his people became the emblem of Serbian identity, a literary reification of Serbian culture and spirit, embodying what was later projected as the symbiosis of the church and nation, the key element of the foundation of the Serbian collective self. Celebrated as a hymn to freedom, a glorification of national and human ideals and a rejection of force and tyranny, his poem's troubling plot, which revolves around the alleged massacre of Islamicized Montenegrins, has only recently been questioned.[102]

After Njegoš's death, his successor, Danilo Petrović, decided not to be consecrated a bishop, but, after a short power struggle, became the first secular ruler/prince, which finally transformed Montenegro from a formal theocracy into a secular state. Once devoid of secular powers, the role of Cetinje metropolitans became almost superfluous. Indeed for six years there were none followed by the short-lived tenure of Nikanor Ivanović, which was abruptly terminated by the decision of the new Montenegrin ruler, Prince Nikola Petrović. During this period, attempts were made to set up the first seminary in Cetinje with Russian help although its impact was felt only in the 1880s.

It was only during the three and half decades of Mitrofan Ban's tenure as a metropolitan (1885–1920) that the Orthodox Church in Montenegro finally established institutions and administrative discipline necessary to face the challenges of modern times and state church status.[103] These included the creation and legal constitution of a Holy Synod and Consistory (1904), the establishment of a fund for priests' widows and orphans (1901), and The Law on Parish Priesthood (1909). More than eighty priests came out of the Cetinje Seminary during this period and over forty churches were built or reconstructed. Montenegro's metropolitan was a permanent member of its state council and assembly (1906–14) and also the president of Red Cross. As in Serbia, the church was absolutely submitted to the state, its social role remained weak and folk religiosity prevailed. The church's poor institutional structures and weak links with the people could not be easily strengthened, not even after unification in the Kingdom of Yugoslavia.[104]

Conclusion

Throughout lands inhabited by Serbs and under their various ecclesiastical administrations, the meager development of secular educational systems constituted a major factor accounting for the slow nationalization of the peasantry and their transformation from peasants into Serbs, to paraphrase Eugen Weber.[105] During the nineteenth century, illiteracy was a key obstacle that had to be overcome in order to enact the change from a parochial religious into a secular Serbian identity. By 1866, only 4.2 percent of Serbia's population could read and by 1900 the figure only grew to 17 percent. Lagging behind Greece and Bulgaria in literacy and education, the popularization of the Serbian national program was also slow when compared with the Greek and Bulgarian experience. As late as the Eastern Crisis of 1875–78, regionalism prevailed among Serbia's peasantry, thereby undermining Serbia's war effort.[106] Furthermore, political and ecclesiastical divisions and inherited traditions and interests prolonged and dwindled the nation-building process. The hierarchy of the major "Serbian" ecclesiastical administration, that of the Habsburg Monarchy (including Bosnia and Herzegovina formally under the Ecumenical Patriarchate), remained a hostage to the anachronistic union of throne and altar. Its role in ensuring its flock's political loyalty and emphasis on the religious aspect of ethnic identity conflicted with the more secular model of linguistic nationalism. Churches in Serbia and Montenegro were freed from the imperial legacy but because of their lack of educated clergy became easily manipulated by new secular rulers, which then deteriorated their prestige and ability to reform according to the demands of modern times.

Nevertheless, throughout the areas inhabited by the Serbs, the new notion of the church as the upholder of its people and carrier of its tradition and identity began taking hold. More importantly, new traditions were imagined and created that, via migration, free movement, and a rising level of literacy, spread and spanned across borders and unified the Serbs. Some such included the patron-saint celebration of Slava and the cult of Saint Sava have already been mentioned. Changes affected church music, arts, and all other aspects of religious life. Church singing among Serbs in the nineteenth century transitioned from the medieval monophonic chants that were praised as celestial, angelic hymns to choral polyphony required to fulfill certain artistic tasks.[107] The use of polyphonic harmony first spread under Russian influence but was soon adopted by composers and practitioners from the Habsburg monarchy, most notably Czechs or Serbs who studied in Vienna. This huge transformation affected not only church services but the wider religious, cultural, and social context as it led to a new public, new practitioners (choral or singers' societies), concert halls, composers and conductors, and so on. Romanticism in music meant the search for chants believed to be genuinely Serbian despite similar musical motifs found in all Balkan Orthodox countries.[108]

The Romantic era also brought to the fore the search for the visual resuscitation of the medieval heritage. After some self-taught builders introduced initial changes, the Serbian disciples of Viennese professor Teophil Hansen in the 1880s launched the neo-Byzantine style, which represented a fashionable historicist eclecticism based rather artificially on elements of Byzantine, Islamic, and medieval Romanesque architecture.[109] While introducing a Byzantine ordering of space, the new designs had little to do with Serbian medieval churches. At the same time, the nationalist campaign in the still Ottoman Kosovo and Macedonia, carried out by the Saint Sava Society among others, brought about the (re)discovery of Serbian medieval churches in these areas, notably the church of Gračanica Monastery in Kosovo. The desire to revive the glorious medieval past and furnish Serbia with its own national style in art thus gave birth to the notion of a Serbo-Byzantine style, purportedly a style of architecture dominant in Serbia during the reign of King Milutin at the beginning of the fourteenth century with the Gračanica Church as its archetype.[110] The ascension of this style to the level of an undisputed architectural genre by the end of the nineteenth century in Serbia was clearly underpinned by the dual imperative to celebrate simultaneously both an ancient and an emerging state.[111] Out of all spheres of the arts, church architecture made the most radical break with European trends, which it abandoned for the sake of a revived Serbian-Byzantine style, regarded as a pure manifestation of the Serbian national spirit. The ideology of national regeneration translated into the language of architecture rejected European influences and proclaimed a return to the medieval Serbian golden age. Similarly, the choice to start the construction of a national cathedral in 1895, known as Saint Sava Church, its prominent location and envisaged extensive physical layout indicated, from the beginning, intentions beyond the religious; its dominance and immensity were to impress and accentuate the Piedmontian role of Serbia in the unification of Serbs. This coupling of the secular and religious dimensions set irreversibly the future position of the Saint Sava Church in Belgrade in the visions of national monumentalization advanced by the ecclesiastic hierarchy as well as lay builders of the nation.

Toward the end of the century, the bishops and clergy of Karlovci Metropolitanate in the Habsburg Monarchy also became imbued with the modern political ideology of nationalism, slowly transforming it from an imperial into a national institution. This process finished only after the First World War when the Karlovci Metropolitanate united with various other Orthodox jurisdictions under which the Orthodox Serbs lived in the newly created Serbian Orthodox Church. The pace of changes was faster in the Metropolitanate of Belgrade. In the late nineteenth century, its Metropolitan Mihailo was more of a political than a religious figure. This was common among all newly independent Balkan states where, as a rule, the church came to be seen primarily as a nationalizing and patriotic agent. While the Orthodox in Serbia or Montenegro might not have been considered as ardently religious as their brethren in the Habsburg lands, their leaders, such as Metropolitan Mihailo or Bishop Njegoš, recognized the church's value and magnificent historic legacy for their aspirations. Nevertheless, it was primarily the state and secular elites in Serbia and Montenegro that led the way in rendering the Orthodox Church into an ethnically based national religion using the power of laws, education, and, later, the mass media. The church followed, assuming a national-salvationist self-image and embracing the logic of nationalism. In addition, in all areas examined, the traditional Orthodox hostility to Catholics became imbued with a rather Romantic secular Pan-Slavism and anti-Westernism imported from Russia. The bond between nation and religion among the Serbs (and Croats for that matter) would be finally cemented in interwar Yugoslavia with wide-ranging consequences. The most obvious and tragic were inter-confessional conflicts in the 1940s and then again in the 1990s. While confessional (or religious) differences between Croats and Serbs (and Bosnian Muslims) are indisputable, this chapter has demonstrated how in the Serbian case during the nineteenth century the (Orthodox) religious markers of identity were supplanted by secular and essentially national ones. Not surprisingly in the high age of nationalism during the early twentieth century, political arguments and conflicts among South Slavs have been little concerned with religion except as the expression of national peculiarity.[112] In order to confront these conflicts and their legacy, one needs to begin with the painstaking revision of existing history writing and the commonly held understanding of the bond between nation and religion.

List of Metropolitans and Patriarchs

Karlovci Metropolitanate (Habsburg Monarchy)
Stefan (Statimirović), Metropolitan 1790–1836
Stefan (Stanković), Metropolitan 1837–1841
Josif (Rajačić), Metropolitan 1842–1848, and Patriarch 1848–1861
Samuilo (Maširević), Patriarch 1864–1870
Prokopije (Ivačković), Patriarch 1874–1879
German (Anđelić), Patriarch 1882–1888
Georgije (Branković), Patriarch 1890–1907
Lukijan (Bogdanović), Patriarch 1907–1913

Belgrade Metropolitanate (autonomous from 1831, autocephalous from 1879) (Serbia)
Leontije (Lambrović), 1801–1813
Dionisije II (Popović Nišlija), 1813–1815
Agatangel, 1816–1825
Kirilo, 1826–1827
Antim, 1827–1831
Meletije (Pavlović), 1831–1833
Petar (Jovanović), 1834–1859
Mihailo (Jovanović), 1859–1881; 1889–1898
Teodosije (Mraović), 1883–1889
Inokentije (Pavlović), 1898–1905
Dimitrije (Pavlović), Metropolitan 1905–1920, First Patriarch of the Serbian Orthodox Church 1920–1930

Metropolitanate of Cetinje (Montenegro)
Petar I (Petrović Njegoš), 1784–1830
Petar II (Petrović Njegoš), 1830–1851
Nikanor (Ivanović), 1858–1860
Ilarion (Roganović), 1860–1882
Visarion (Ljubiša), 1882–1884
Mitrofan (Ban), 1885–1920

Orthodox Church in Dalmatia (Dalmatian bishops were initially under the jurisdiction of Karlovci Metropolitanate but were transferred in 1873 to the jurisdiction of the Metropolitanate of Bukovina and Dalmatia)
Venedikt (Kraljević), Bishop 1810–1828
Josif (Rajačić), Bishop 1829–1834
Pantelejmon (Živković), Bishop 1834–1836
Jerotej (Mutibarić), Bishop 1843–1853
Stefan (Knežević), Bishop 1853–1890
Nikodim (Milaš), Bishop 1890–1910
Dimitrije (Branković), Bishop 1910–1920
Eugenie (Hacman), Bishop 1835–1873, Metropolitan 1873; Autocephalous Church after 1873 (Metropolitanate of Bukovina and Dalmatia)
Teofil (Bandella), Metropolitan 1873–1875

Teoctist (Blajevici), Metropolitan 1877–1879
Silvestru (Morariu-Andrievici), Metropolitan 1880–1895
Arcadie (Ciupercovici), Metropolitan 1896–1902
Vladimir (Repta), Metropolitan 1902–1924

Orthodox Church in Bosnia-Herzegovina (Dabar-Bosnia Metropolitanate under the Jurisdiction of Ecumenical Patriarchate)
Venedikt (Kraljević), 1805–1808
Kalinik, 1809–1817
Venijamin, 1817–1835
Amvrosije, 1835–1840
Ignjatije I, 1841–1850
Prokopije, 1851–1853
Dionisije I 1856–1860
Ignjatije II, 1861–1868
Dionisije II Ilić, 1868–1871
Pajsije, 1871–1874
Antim, 1874–1880
Sava (Kosanović), 1881–1885
Đorđe (Nikolajević), 1885–1896
Nikolaj (Mandić), 1896–1907
Evgenije (Letica), 1907–1920

CHAPTER

5

THE ROMANIAN ORTHODOX CHURCH

Lucian N. Leustean

At first glance, the nationalist ideology of the French Revolution seems to have had little impact on the Orthodox Church in Romanian-speaking territories. Romanians were the predominant inhabitants of the principalities of Wallachia and Moldavia and the neighboring territories of Transylvania (including Crișana, Maramureș and Banat), Bukovina, Bessarabia, and Dobrudja. The majority of ethnic Romanians belonged to the Orthodox faith while their communities were at the intersection of geopolitical interests of the Russian, Ottoman, and Habsburg empires.

In 1859 the Principalities of Wallachia and Moldavia (known as the Old Kingdom between 1866 and 1918) united into a single state under the rule of a local prince. The term "Romania" began to be used by the new state in its official documents in 1862. Two years later, the state supported the declaration of a Romanian autocephalous (independent) church that was recognized by the Ecumenical Patriarchate in 1885. As an integrative part of the Orthodox commonwealth, the church was situated between the competing jurisdictions of the Ecumenical Patriarchate and the Russian Orthodox Church, while its declaration of autocephaly followed a pattern in the spread of national churches in Southeastern Europe.

From the Treaty of Kuchuk Kainardji of 1774 to the beginning of the Greek War for Independence in 1821, the Romanian principalities were under the suzerainty of the Ottoman Empire, which had full control of their political and economic affairs. The sultan appointed princes, and the

Porte determined their political and judicial status. The princes were drawn from the "Phanariots," and were directly appointed by the Porte from preponderantly Greek elite rather than the Romanian local elite, the boyars (*boieri*).[1] In each principality, the church was headed by a metropolitan who was under the direct jurisdiction of the Ecumenical Patriarchate.

That religion mattered to local population as a means of social cohesion was suggestively depicted by Anatole de Demidoff, an English traveler in the region in 1837. Arriving in Bucharest, the capital of Wallachia, he claimed that:

> I know of no city in Europe in which it is possible to find more agreeable society, or in which there is a better tone, united with the most charming gaiety. . . . Religion, which is here of the schismatic Greek creed, does not, properly speaking, hold any great empire over the minds of the Wallachian people, but they observe its outward forms, and particularly the austerities of fasting, with scrupulous exactitude. The people are seen to attend divine service with every sign of respect, and the great number of churches existing in Wallachia, bear witness to the ardent zeal with which outward worship is honored.[2]

The Romanian Orthodox Church was a national institution, closely linked to social, economic, and political structures. In most cases, Orthodox hierarchs were appointed from the families of boyars, thus ensuring a close relationship with the state authorities and its policies. As one of the largest landowners in the principalities, the church had a prime role in administrating healthcare and education. Although the majority of the clergy was uneducated, it dispensed both ecclesiastical and civil justice and in many cases worked closely with boyars in local administration.[3] The lower clergy not only contributed directly to the economy but also benefited from tax privileges. Some small villages had an unusually high proportion of clergy in comparison to the overall population. For example, in 1810, Stănislăveşti, a village in the south of Wallachia, was composed of eleven houses and had two priests, five deacons, and three cantors; similarly, the Frăsinet village of nineteen houses had two priests and five deacons.[4] Although these cases were exceptional, they indicate both the economic value of being a member of the clergy and the wider canonical dimension of church jurisdiction.

The special status of the clergy was reflected not only at lower but also at higher levels. Bishops and metropolitans engaged with state policy and in many cases opposition to the authorities led to the loss of a spiritual seat. The metropolitan of each principality worked with the prince and was president of the divan, the gathering of all boyars. He held the right to be the first person to comment on state policy and to make recommendations when the prince was absent. The metropolitan replaced the prince when the principality had no political ruler, such as in the cases of Metropolitan Veniamin Costachi of Moldavia in 1806 and Metropolitan Dositei Filitti of Wallachia, while the bishops of Buzău and Argeş were members of the provisional government during the Russian occupation of the principalities in 1808. The higher clergy had both religious and political prerogatives in relation to foreign powers as evident in their heading of the boyars' delegation to peace negotiation between the Russian and Ottoman empires at Focşani in 1772 and addressing memoranda to the Austrian and Russian governments in 1802.[5]

The primary role of the church in the principalities of Moldavia and Wallachia was paralleled by the national mobilization of Orthodox communities in the neighboring territories that had Romanian inhabitants. Although throughout the region Orthodox communities were incorporated into church structures as part of the Habsburg, Austrian or Russian empires, the nineteenth century was characterized by the leadership's search for political autonomy and the building of a Romanian national identity. The Orthodox communities outside the Old Kingdom maintained relations with the faithful in principalities across the Carpathian Mountains and the Dniester River and sought support in their struggle for political and religious rights.

Orthodoxy and Nationalism before the Unification of Wallachia and Moldavia

Wallachia

At the time of the French Revolution, the Wallachian and Moldavian principalities were engulfed in the Russo-Turkish War of 1787–92. Political instability was reflected in the short periods of rule of Alexandru Moruzi who was appointed prince in both Moldova (1792–93, 1802–6 and 1806–7) and Wallachia (1793–96 and 1799–1801).

Upon his arrival in Wallachia in 1793, Moruzi was welcomed by Bishop Dositei Filitti of Buzău. A few months later Dositei was enthroned metropolitan and held diplomatic positions during the Russo-Turkish War. His leadership was mainly characterized by concern for the number of priests in Wallachia as some clergy were ordained uncanonically. Dositei introduced the requirement for peasants to sign a document indicating their wish to have a priest and that the new priest and his wife were highly esteemed by the local congregation. He ensured that priests began to perform widespread administrative duties by registering births and deaths in their communities and introduced inspectors who reported on the conduct of the clergy. One of the main consequences of his administrative initiatives was better control of non-native monks who visited Wallachia. However, his administrative reform was curtailed in 1801 when Wallachia was occupied by Ottoman troops. Together with a number of boyars he left the principality for Braşov, from where he sent letters to St. Petersburg encouraging Russian military intervention in the Balkans. Five years later, Russian troops occupied Wallachia, retaining control until 1812. Dositei's role in defending both the church and the principality were evident at the time of the Ottoman retreat from Bucharest when he paid a considerable amount of money to have the city spared from destruction. Furthermore, his political leadership was acclaimed in 1808 when, in the absence of an official government, Wallachia was ruled by a regency (*căimăcămie*) in which the metropolitan and the bishops of Buzău and Argeş took part.

Despite having previously had good relations with the Russian government, Dositei was not welcomed by Tsar Alexander I (1801–25) who in 1808 decided that the principalities of Wallachia and Moldavia should have a single metropolitan. An ethnic Romanian, Gavriil Bănulescu-Bodoni, was appointed to this new position. His leadership lasted only until the Russo-Turkish Peace Treaty in 1812 after which he left Moldavia and was appointed Metropolitan of Chişinău and Hotin (1813–21). In 1809, during Gavriil's short ecclesiastical leadership of both principalities, Dositei was deposed and sentenced to a monastery in Moldavia; he managed to escape and went into exile in Braşov. After the signing of the Peace Treaty, the new Wallachian ruler, Ioan Caragea, asked Dositei to return to his ecclesiastical seat in Bucharest, however, he declined due to his age. He remained in Braşov where he died on December 14, 1826, over ninety years old.

The contrast between Dositei's and Gavriil's leaderships is particularly relevant in terms of their understanding of Romanian ethnicity. The appointment of Gavriil Bănulescu-Bodoni, as an ethnic Romanian, represented a shift in imperial Russian policy toward the principalities. Despite being the first Romanian ethnic metropolitan at a time of predominant Phanariot and Greek control, he demonstrated his support for Russian interests in the region. In contrast, Dositei, who was of Greek origin, showed considerable support for the local Orthodox community. His support for the community in Bucharest was visible not only during the Ottoman retreat in 1808 but also in his testament through which he founded the *Filantropia* hospital and a scholarship fund to enable students from Wallachia to study in Western Europe. His testament indicated the slow spread of nationalism in its reference to scholarships for "the support of the nation." During the nineteenth century the fund enabled over 250 Greek and Romanian students to study in the West, many of whom, upon their return, would acquire prime religious and political positions in the principalities.

In 1810 during Dositei's exile in Brașov, the Wallachian Metropolitanate was briefly ruled by Ignatie, an ethnic Greek monk. His lack of knowledge of the Romanian language and a number of financial scandals led some boyars to ask the prince to have him replaced. In 1812 Ignatie was forced to leave and went to Vienna where he worked closely with Ioannis Capodistrias, who in 1827 would become the first head of state of independent Greece.

After Dositei's refusal to return to Bucharest, from 1813 to 1819 Wallachia was ruled by another ethnic Greek, Nectarie, who was previously Bishop of Râmnic. He occupied the metropolitan seat by paying an unusually large amount of money and placed his nephew in his previous position. Under his spiritual leadership he doubled the taxes for clergy, which made him rather unpopular. Nectarie was the last Metropolitan of Wallachia of Greek origin and retained his position until 1819 when, the new ruler, Alexandru Șutu (1818–21) appointed a Romanian, Dionisie Lupu.

The election of Metropolitan Dionisie represented the beginning of a gradual process of removing Greek control of the church. On Dionisie's initiative, the Saint Sava School in Bucharest expelled its Greek teachers and established a school of religious music in the Romanian language. He encouraged Romanian students to study in Western Europe and published the *Efemerida* newspaper written in both Romanian and Greek, following the comparable Greek publication in Vienna that demanded Greek independence.[6] The higher clergy would be appointed from ethnic Romanians, a fact that would increase after the uprising of Tudor Vladimirescu in 1821. Due to political instability during the uprising in Wallachia, Metropolitan Dionisie fled to Brașov and refused to return under the new Prince Grigore Ghica.

Prince Ghica continued the process of consolidating the Romanian hierarchy and appointed as metropolitan another ethnic Romanian, Grigorie Dascălul. Grigorie's appointment followed a rather unusual process, as he was elevated to the highest ecclesiastical office from a mere hierodeacon rather than the traditional custom of selecting one of the bishops of either Râmnic or Buzău.[7] Grigorie retained a considerable influence among the religious and political elite in Wallachia. He was a highly regarded translator of books into Romanian and Greek and during the Russo-Turkish war in 1828–29 he was appointed *căimăcăm*. As was the case for his predecessors, he was not welcomed by the Russian troops that occupied Wallachia and the tsar sent him to Chișinău; however, he managed to return to the Buzău bishopric in 1832 and for a short period of the following year re-occupied the metropolitan seat. He died in 1834, leaving the Wallachian metropolitanate unstable. Until 1840 Wallachia failed to have a metropolitan, the spiritual needs of the Orthodox Church being cared for only by local bishops.

The Russian occupation of the principalities of Wallachia and Moldavia between 1828 and 1834 resulted in the appointment of a single ruler who was president of the two divans. After the succession of a number of presidents of divans, the last president, General Pavel Kisselev (1829–34), finalized the Organic Statute (*Regulamentul Organic*), the first constitutions of Wallachia and Moldavia. The Statute established two legislative bodies titled General Assemblies (*Adunări obșești*) for the principalities (with forty-two deputies in Wallachia and thirty-five in Moldavia) that were composed of boyars and higher member of the clergy. The metropolitans in both principalities retained their prime roles as presidents. The Organic Statute included a section on local Orthodox churches that would gradually lead to closer control of church finances and land ownership. It also made reference to the removal of metropolitans from their seats for either religious or political reasons, in the latter case only at the request of a jury composed of twelve bishops and twelve boyars.[8] The prime impact of the Organic Statute was to modernize the social and political systems in the principalities while ensuring that the Russian and Ottoman empires retained considerable influence.

The uncertainty of the metropolitan seat lasted until June 28, 1840, when the Electoral Collegium (*colegiul electoral*), instituted by the Organic Statute, elected Metropolitan Neofit, who was previously Bishop of Râmnic. Neofit received forty-nine votes out of seventy-six, while Bishop Chesarie of Buzău received twenty-six votes and Bishop Ilarion of Argeș one vote. Neofit's election indicated that the boyars and clergy remained divided toward the Russian presence in the principalities. He largely gained the votes of the Electoral Collegium as in previous years he had maintained close contact with the Russian authorities and was therefore perceived as a stable candidate. On August 6, 1840, Neofit wrote a letter to the tsar informing him of his new ecclesiastical position. Count Nesselrode, in charge of the empire's foreign policy, sent his congratulations and suggested in his reply that the metropolitan's role was to combat the "religious indifference . . . , which had increased in the principalities" and to work closely with the ruler and boyars rather than support the political opposition. Neofit's political stance would soon become public and, despite the advice he had been given, a few months later he wrote a letter to Nesselrode in which he expressed dissatisfaction with Prince Ghica.[9]

Neofit's leadership was relatively stable until 1848, the year of European revolutions, when the nationalist movement in Wallachia was successful in overthrowing the prince. Metropolitan Neofit became president of the new government that, under pressure from the revolutionary movement, accepted a new constitution. With Russian troops approaching Wallachia and an imminent change in political leadership, Neofit remained in Bucharest and denounced the revolution; however, a few days later he was forced to retract and accepted the new constitution. His ambivalent position led to his resignation in 1849 and he died a few months later.

Neofit's pro-Russian stance reflected the conservative position of members of the higher clergy while a significant number of lower clergy supported the nationalist movement as evident on June 9, 1848, during the Islaz proclamation when revolutionaries began their assembly with a prayer by Father Radu Șapcă from Celei. The proclamation, written "in the name of the Romanian people," demanded equal rights for all people and became the basis of the provisional government.[10] The support of the lower clergy for the nationalist movement was also visible during the battle for the defense of Bucharest from Russian troops that aimed to replace the government. In 1848, a priest, Father Ambrozie from Buzău, later nicknamed Popa Tun (Father Gun) would become a nationalist figure of Romanian resistance by ripping out the lit fuse of a gun directed against the masses. After the defeat of the revolutionary movement and the reinstatement of the Organic Statute in Wallachia, Nifon Sevastias, who was previously Bishop of Râmnic, was appointed metropolitan in 1850.

An ethnic Romanian, Metropolitan Nifon would end the fragmentation of metropolitan tenures in Wallachia, retaining one of the longest ecclesiastical leaderships and becoming the first Primate Metropolitan of the unified Principalities of Wallachia and Moldavia.

Moldavia

At the beginning of the nineteenth century, in contrast to Wallachia, Moldavia enjoyed a lengthy period of religious stability. From 1803 until 1846, with the exception of short interruptions between 1808–12 and 1821–23, Metropolitan Veniamin Costachi, ruled the Moldavian Church ensuring steady progress in the development of a national church institution.[11] Veniamin was born into an indigenous boyar family, whose connections helped him to be raised to the position of Bishop of Huşi at the unusually young age of twenty-four. Four years later he was appointed Bishop of Roman, the closest position of ecclesiastical power to that of the metropolitanate seat in Iaşi, the capital of Moldavia. The stability of the ecclesiastical office in the region led to the reorganization of religious education into the Romanian language and education reform. In 1813 Veniamin established a central seminary of theological education in Socola, near Iaşi, where a large number of liturgical books would be published in Romanian.[12] With the implementation of the Organic Statute in both principalities in 1828, Veniamin became president of the General Assembly (*Adunarea obştească*). In Moldavia, the *Statute* also established a Ministry of the Church (*Ministeriu al Bisericii*) under the direct control of the prince. According to the new legislation, bishops were elected from among Romanians thus ensuring a preponderance of locally appointed clergy in the higher ranks.

The significance of the local clergy was evident in the ways in which Veniamin responded to the church's relations with the Catholic minority in Moldavia. He was regarded by the Orthodox faithful as a defender of Orthodoxy and Romanianness by standing against the nomination of a Catholic bishop in the region despite pressure from the Austrian government. Drawing on Article 12 of the Sistova Treaty, which stated tolerance of the Roman Catholic faithful in the principalities, on May 3, 1838, the papal nuncio in Vienna obtained the approval of the Austrian and Moldavian governments to appoint a Catholic bishop; however, he faced Veniamin's strong opposition. Veniamin agreed with the establishment of a Catholic cathedral in Iași on the condition that an apostolic visitor would not be able to visit his clergy and faithful for more than forty consecutive days per year and could not have the title of "bishop." Veniamin's stance was supported by the fact that the Catholic faithful was a small minority (44,317 people with seventy-three churches and two cathedrals at the end of Prince Mihail Sturza's leadership) while the Orthodox numbered 1,356,908, leading him to fear that a foreign bishop may proselytize among the Orthodox congregations.[13]

Veniamin's relations with Prince Sturza became tense in 1835 and increasingly so in the following years leading to the metropolitan's resignation on January 18, 1842.[14] Veniamin's resignation and his departure from Iași demonstrated that the accusations of embezzlement were the product of an internecine battle for political and religious power as the metropolitan was a widely respected figure. The prince feared that his departure could lead to a popular uprising and, on January 28, 1842, decreed a state of emergency forbidding free movement at night. A few days later, Veniamin left the city at night[15] and retired to Slatina Monastery where he died in 1846. The prince's decision to impose the state of emergency indicated that he held control of the church and that any challenge to political authority could lead to the removal of the highest ecclesiastical leader. However, Veniamin did not protest or mobilize the faithful against the prince. It is highly likely that he thought that his resignation under pressure from the prince would be considered uncanonical by the Russian and Ottoman governments and that either Russia would re-appoint him[16] or the Ecumenical Patriarchate would protest against the decision. However, neither happened.

Prince Sturza continued his uncanonical activity in church affairs and, without consulting the Ecumenical Patriarchate, appointed his protégé, Bishop Filaret Beldiman of Apameea, in charge of the metropolitanate's affairs. Faced with a possible split in the church, on April 4, 1842, the

Ecumenical Patriarchate wrote to the prince agreeing with Veniamin's resignation but summoning him to reconsider his ecclesiastical appointment.[17] Bishop Filaret was forced to leave his position, and Meletie Lefter, previously Bishop of Roman, was elected metropolitan in 1844.

Meletie's election by eighty-one votes (his opponent, Bishop Sofronie Miclescu of Huși received twenty-six votes) was agreed by Prince Sturza mainly because it appeared to be the most advantageous for his regime. Meletie was not only older than Sofronie but he also contributed financially to his election. Russia did not protest against the election of the new metropolitan as Veniamin's resignation and the prince's interference in church affairs supported its influence in the Balkans, through which it aimed to bring the Orthodox communities under St. Petersburg's authority. At the time of Meletie's election, Russian clergy traveled throughout Moldavia trying to convince the Moldavian clergy and faithful to sign a petition proposing the unification of the Moldavian Orthodox Church and the Russian Orthodox Church; however, this move did not find popular support.[18]

Despite having a newly elected metropolitan, Prince Sturza's interference in church affairs increased in March 1844 when he appointed Alecu Sturza, his cousin, as the first minister of religious confessions (cults). Prince Sturza established a unified Central House (*Casa Centrală*) in Iași in charge of all financial transactions and properties for all bishoprics and metropolitanates. This decision did not include the "dedicated monasteries" under the control of the holy places in Levant, Mount Athos, Jerusalem, or Sinai, thus fostering dissatisfaction among the local clergy and boyars.

Disappointment with the prince's policy was evident at the time of the 1848 revolution in Moldavia. Although Moldavia did not witness a mass popular national movement against the regime as in Wallachia, Meletie and the clergy signed a memorandum that supported the revolution; however, the impact of the memorandum remained low. A few months later, in 1848, Meletie died during an epidemic of cholera in Iași. In the following year, Prince Sturza was forced to leave the country and went into exile in Paris where he remained until his death.[19] After Meletie left the Bishopric of Roman in 1844 in order to occupy the metropolitan seat in Iași, Prince Sturza appointed Bishop Veniamin Roset in his place. Bishop Veniamin Roset came from a wealthy boyar family, which enabled him to mingle with the top religious and political authorities. At the time of the 1848 revolution, he publicly condemned Prince Sturza and was forced to retire to the Soveja Monastery. In 1849, upon the prince's exile, he returned, declaring his full support for the appointment of the new ruler, Prince Grigore Ghica.

It seemed that Bishop Veniamin held all the cards for a swift election to the metropolitan seat in Iași. In the Moldavian Church tradition, the Bishop of Roman had the primary position in the church after the metropolitan and was the most appropriate successor. Veniamin was confident in his election and even moved some of his possessions from Roman to Iași awaiting official confirmation. However, in the 1851 elections, Prince Ghica favored Sofronie Miclescu from Huși, who not only contributed financially to his election to a greater extent than his opponent but who was also seen as more docile.[20] The election again demonstrated that the prince held the final word on the church leadership. Upon losing the election, Bishop Veniamin returned to the Bishopric of Roman and unexpectedly died a few months later, leaving Sofronie's leadership in Iași unchallenged.[21]

Conflict between bishops regarding the highest position in the church was paralleled at the lower clergy level. In the first years of Sofronie's leadership, the main issue of dispute among the clergy was education. Despite the establishment in 1803 of a central seminary at Socola for training the clergy, many graduates preferred to occupy a position in the boyar's administration rather than be ordained. The lack of trained priests remained an acute issue and decisions toward improving education were also taken at the bishopric level. During his tenure in Roman, Bishop Veniamin Roset established catechetic schools as the first step toward preparing candidates who could study further in the Socola Seminary.[22] The state attempted to homogenize its national policy and in 1849 public education was taken under the responsibility of a newly created Religious Department, which would later become the Ministry of Religious Confessions and Public Instruction.

After its establishment, the Socola Seminary would become not only an influential center for training the clergy but also a center for disseminating ideas on the involvement of the church in supporting Romanian nationalism. In 1843, at the time of ecclesiastical disputes during the reign of Prince Sturza, Bishop Filaret Beldiman appointed Archimandrite Filaret Scriban as rector of the Socola Seminary.[23] Archimandrite Filaret and his brother Archimandrite Neofit, who served at one of the most prestigious churches in Moldavia, the Three Hierarchs Church in Iași, would become active supporters of the unification of the principalities of Moldavia and Wallachia. Both brothers published extensively on unification, and their ideas on Romanian nationalism found an echo among the lower clergy.

In his first years of ecclesiastical leadership, Metropolitan Sofronie publicly rejected the possibility of Romanian unification and favored the conservative boyar party that aimed to bring Prince Mihail Sturza back to Moldavia. The metropolitan's stance had broad ramifications not only from a religious perspective but also because he held the presidency of the elective assembly. Sofronie's sudden change to the cause of unification occurred only after he realized that the unionist party had a high level of support among the clergy and the wider population. He was assured by the French consul in Iași that a unified Principality of Moldavia and Wallachia would not affect his seat.

Support for unification of the two principalities under the leadership of a foreign prince who could ensure the stability of the new state acquired a mystical dimension in the writings of the Scriban brothers. In a pamphlet published in 1856 on "The Unity and Non-unity of Romanian Principalities," Archimandrite Neofit argued that the very word "unity" was closely related to both nationality and religion. In his opinion, "the nation is nothing other than a large family . . . unity is the most important principle for all Christians. . . . A foreign prince [in the united principalities] would not change the religion because the real ruler of emperors and kings is where the real ruler of all people is, in the heart of his servants."[24] By supporting their arguments with political, religious and economic ideas, Neofit suggested that Romanians could be "a strong state surrounded by Slav countries to the north and south"[25] with a particular identity in the Balkans.

A similar argument was put forward by other influential clergy in Moldavia. On June 29, 1856, at public festivities in Huși, in a sermon celebrating Saints Peter and Paul, Archimandrite Melchisedec Ștefănescu, rector of the Huși Seminary, used strong words with a direct impact on the masses, making a connection between the apostolic times and Romanian unity. He pointed out that the church always prayed for the "unity of all. . . . If Romanians are called to unity, it means that they are on the path of the universal progress of humanity . . . [while] those who oppose unification of the principalities are against the will of God, against the idea of progress of humanity and therefore are enemies of both God and people and are only friends of Satan."²⁶ After the unification of the Moldavian and Wallachian principalities, Archimandrite Melchisedec and the Scriban brothers would become hierarchs in the unified Orthodox Church. However, despite their enthusiastic support for the unification cause, the state authorities would not hesitate to marginalize them at the time of wider church reforms.

The clash between those who opposed and those who supported unification of the principalities became a key issue in 1857 on the election of the ad-hoc Divan Assembly. According to the Treaty of Paris, on March 30, 1857, Russia returned the counties, Bolgrad, Cahul, and Ismail back to Moldavia and both principalities were requested to hold ad-hoc assemblies to decide their political future. The population was asked to vote for representatives to these assemblies. The composition of the divans was crucial for winning the unionist cause.

The Porte decided that in addition to the metropolitans and bishops of each principality, the abbots of both dedicated and non-dedicated monasteries and other clergy were also required to elect two lay and two clergy as members of the ad-hoc assemblies. Metropolitan Sofronie's stance in supporting the unionist cause led to conflict with the regency. His unionist position found an echo among the clergy. In a report of March 27, 1857, for example, the archpriest (*protopop*) of the Bacău region claimed that three quarters of the population was in favor of unification and a significant number of the lower clergy joined in spontaneous public demonstrations throughout Moldavia supporting the cause. Although the demonstrations were not publicly instigated by the top clergy, Sofronie was rebuked by the regency for not controlling his flock. In his reply, he claimed that the clergy and the Orthodox faithful, despite holding religious banners and praying for unity, were no more than gatherings of people congratulating the future electors; no disciplinary measures were taken by the church against the clergy joining demonstrations.²⁷ Demonstrations were not only an issue of political concern but also a religious one, as a large number of voices claimed that the solution to political unification would result from ecclesiastical independence.

This was an extremely sensitive point that represented the possibility of declaring the autocephaly of the Moldavian Church from the Ecumenical Patriarchate. On April 19, 1857, the Ecumenical Patriarch Cyril VII wrote a letter to Metropolitan Sofronie in which he condemned his involvement in political disputes, stating that his actions had "grave consequences for the church."²⁸ Sofronie's position provoked the regency to discredit him publicly by publishing accusations against him in Constantinople and distributing leaflets among the clergy and faithful. The leaflets did not produce the expected results, leading the regency to intervene at the Ecumenical Patriarchate with the aim of replacing him. However, due to the protest of the French ambassador in Constantinople, the patriarchate refrained from defrocking Sofronie; according to the Organic Statute in the principalities, only the local boyars and bishops in Moldavia had the authority to convoke a synod that could remove the metropolitan rather than the patriarch.²⁹

Fearing that the unionist cause would prevail at the ad-hoc assembly, the regency decided to remove the names of those clergy who supported unification, claiming that they were not eligible. Their removal, in particular, that of Archimandrite Melchisedec and the Scriban brothers, caused public disruptions and led to protests from both the metropolitan and lower clergy. On July 7, 1857, the elections to the ad-hoc assembly went ahead without the names of the unionist clergy and Sofronie advised the clergy and faithful to abstain from voting. His opposition to the election had an immediate effect. In the following days, he received a large number of complaints from clergy about being intimidated by the state authorities to vote.³⁰ The complaints had a great impact on the path of Romanian nationalism and demonstrated that the church was a prime actor in the political sphere. Under pressure from the great powers, new elections were held, which this time included the names of the unionist clergy.

The new ad-hoc assembly in Moldavia officially opened on September 22, 1857, and lasted until January 2, 1858. During debates, both assemblies in Moldavia and Wallachia requested unification of their principalities into a single state under the leadership of a foreign prince.

On November 4, 1857, the particular stance of the Moldavian Church in supporting unification was enhanced when its ad-hoc assembly decided by seventy-nine votes in favor and no abstentions for the separation of the church from foreign control. A few days later, on December 20, 1857, for the first time in the history of the church, the ad-hoc assembly declared the establishment of an "independent (autocephalic) and orthodox Church of Moldo-Roumania."³¹ The ad-hoc assembly proposed fourteen points for the reorganization of the church, while pointing out that it remained in communion with the "Ecumenical Church of the East." The church should be ruled by a "synodical central authority in Romania for spiritual, canonical as well as disciplinary matters" while "neither the metropolitan nor the bishops of the country can ever or in any way be elected from among foreigners or naturalized [Romanians]."[32]

The declaration of Moldavian autocephaly was only an official document in the debates of the ad-hoc assembly and had no immediate institutional result. It was not paralleled by a similar declaration in the ad-hoc assembly in Wallachia. The decisions of the ad-hoc assemblies were submitted to the great powers, and the declaration of autocephaly was rejected. While France, Great Britain, Russia, Prussia, and Sardinia supported unification of the two principalities, Austria and the Porte objected to it. Despite the failure of the 1857 declaration of autocephaly, ad-hoc discussion and the fourteen points on the church reorganization would become fundamental to the Romanian Orthodox Church after the 1859 unification.

The church continued to support unification, as was evident in the last sitting of the ad-hoc assembly in Moldavia, which ended with religious celebrations and a common declaration addressed to the great powers:

> Before God and man, does this assembly declare that it has only pronounced the great and real wishes of the Romanian nation. It takes God as its witness that at present as always, everywhere and under every circumstance, the inward conviction prevails in the country, that only a plenary and perfect autonomy as stipulated by the capitulations, only the union of the two countries, only a foreign prince placed at the head of them, only a legislative power, and the real representation of all interests of the nation, can assure the national existence of 5,000,000 of Romanians, [to] develop the prosperity of these principalities and satisfy the interests of Europe. . . .
>
> Five million Romanians, with open arms, with eyes fixed on that great center where the fate of their mother country will be decided, await with all confidence that [those] magical words that will render joy and happiness to a whole people, that word that will from one century to another transmit to future generations the names of the benevolent monarchs, that word lastly, which will announce the resurrection of [a] reunited and autonomous Romania.[33]

Orthodoxy and State during the Reign of Prince Cuza[34]

Faced with opposition from Austria and the Porte, the unification of the principalities of Moldavia and Wallachia would result from the political actions of indigenous leaders with the support of the great European powers, in particular France, which saw the new state as a barrier against Russian and Ottoman influence in the Balkans.[35] Following the decisions of the great powers, new ad-hoc assemblies were organized in the principalities with the intention of electing their political leader from the Romanian-born elite rather than a foreign prince.

The ad-hoc assemblies were not officially required to elect two separate leaders, a fact that was perceived by the unionist party in both principalities as the solution to unification. On January 5, 1859, Colonel Alexandru Ioan Cuza, Police Commander of Moldavia and a supporter of the unionist cause, was elected Prince of Moldavia and shortly after, on January 24, 1859, he was also elected ruler of Wallachia.[36] Faced with the decisions of the ad-hoc assemblies and a mass revolt in the principalities, Cuza's election was considered valid by the great powers only during his political leadership rather than as a long-term solution.[37] The deadlock of Cuza's election was resolved on November 20, 1861, when the Ottoman Empire finally accepted the union by issuing "The Firman of Moldavia and Wallachia, concerning the Administrative Organization," but on condition that the unification would cease at the end of Cuza's reign.

When his position was recognized internationally, Cuza sought to strengthen the internal unity of his state. He founded common institutions for both principalities, declared Bucharest as the capital of the country, organized a unified army, and in his speech on December 23, 1861, he was able to state, that, at that moment "Romanian nationality was founded."[38] A few days later, on January 22, 1862, the first Romanian government was set up by Conservative Barbu Catargiu who became prime minister and the term "Romania" began to be used on official documents.[39]

The population of the newly established state was, according to the census of 1859, composed of 3,864,848 people. The data of this census did not indicate the ethnic structure of the population but rather the citizenship of its inhabitants, showing that Romanians were the predominant ethnic group, while the remainder belonged to other European states: 28,136 Austrians, 9,545 Greeks, 3,658 Prussians, 2,823 British, 2,706

Russians, 2,631 Turks, 1,142 French, 167 Italians, and 569 citizens of other states.[40] The religious structure revealed that the population was mainly Orthodox with small Catholic and Jewish communities. Figures from the 1860s show that there was one Orthodox priest for one hundred families; one Orthodox monk for one thousand people; one Orthodox nun for one thousand people; one Orthodox church for 612 people; one Catholic church for 716 people; one Protestant church for 2,408 people; one Armenian Gregorian church for 746 people; one Lipovan church for 1,182 people; one synagogue for 486 people, and one temple for 441 people of other religions.[41] The Orthodox Church had 9,702 priests for its 6,858 churches, while 4,672 monks and 4,078 nuns lived in 173 monasteries. The other religions had the following number of buildings in the country: sixty-three Catholic churches, twelve Protestant churches, eleven Armenian Gregorian churches, seven Lipovan churches, 176 synagogues and three temples of other religions.[42]

Prince Cuza made steady political decisions aimed at imposing better control of the church and at using Orthodoxy to consolidate his regime in both principalities. His first gesture on October 19, 1860, was to transform the Central Houses of the Church in Moldavia and Wallachia into one Financial Department of the state. In this way the state would now collect all financial resources from the Romanian territory.

Cuza's next step in asserting political authority over the church hierarchy was to unify the church from both principalities into one national body taking into account the decisions of the 1857 ad-hoc assembly. Metropolitan Sofronie of Moldavia entered into conflict with Cuza, dissatisfied by the prince's direct control of the church and in particular by the removal of land from the most important Moldavian monasteries, Neamţ, Secul, Agapia, Văratec, Adam, and Verona, which were under the Ministry of Religious Confessions. Prince Cuza's reaction to the metropolitan's opposition was that the political authorities came first. Following the Organic Statute, on February 15, 1861, the government organized a synod composed of twelve bishops who decided that Sofronie should be retired on an annual pension; he died in May that year.[43]

The Orthodox Church was in possession of almost one third of the entire land of Moldavia and a quarter of Wallachia.[44] However, without strong ecclesiastical opposition, on December 17, 1863, Prince Cuza confiscated the land of most "dedicated monasteries," claiming that the revenue belonged to the state and not to a foreign jurisdiction.[45] In addition, he issued a law (*Decretul organic pentru reglementarea schimei monahicești*) on November 30, 1864, aimed at reducing the number of monks in monasteries by making it more difficult to become one as they now needed special approval from the Ministry of Religious Confessions. By restricting the number of monks, Cuza increased his control over those who aspired to become part of the church hierarchy, as according to Orthodox tradition the hierarchy was chosen only from monastic clergy.

Cuza's actions had specific political aims. He made it possible to dispossess the church hierarchy of its vast economic revenue and to control those who wanted to become part of the hierarchical clergy. His laws were officially directed against "dedicated monasteries" and Greek monks who moved to the Romanian Principalities, but in practice also had an effect on the very core of Orthodoxy's organization. The most important effect was that, from then on, officially, Orthodox religious ceremonies could only be held in the Romanian language while the Greek monks were allowed to perform their services in only a few churches.[46] This change indicated that the future role of the Orthodox Church was to promote its mission in society only in the dominant language of the state.

In spring 1865, Cuza gave a prime role to Metropolitan Nifon of Bucharest offering him the title of Primate Metropolitan, and on May 11, 1865, introduced a law that broke with tradition concerning the appointment of bishops and metropolitans in Romania (*Legea pentru numirea de mitropoliți și episcopi eparhioți în România*), enabling him, rather than the church, to make new appointments. The positions of some bishops were empty, and Cuza took advantage of the situation to personally appoint new bishops who supported his political regime and the union of the principalities. Cuza's decisions found support in the Romanian political elite, which saw his actions as a way of consolidating the nation against Greek influence.

Cuza organized the Orthodox Church into two metropolitanates with sees in Bucharest and Iași, and six bishoprics: in Buzău, Argeș and Râmnic in Wallachia and in Roman, Huși and the Lower Danube in Moldavia. With his own people in the church and in order to increase his control of the hierarchy, on December 3, 1864, Cuza introduced a law to establish a synod (*Decretul organic pentru înființarea unei autorități sinodale centrale pentru afacerile religiei române*), the first article of which stated that the Romanian Orthodox Church was independent of the Ecumenical Patriarchate of Constantinople, thus ensuring that all church decisions would require his approval. Cuza's main reason for creating the synod was political, and it would have authority as the official institution dealing with ecclesiastical matters. The first synod of the united Romanian Orthodox Church was held on December 1, 1865, in Bucharest, composed of both metropolitans from Bucharest and Iași, six eparchial bishops (*episcopi eparhioți*), eight vice-bishops (*arhierei*), three deputies from each of the six bishoprics elected from clergy or lay members who had completed theological studies, and two deans of future theological faculties that would be founded in Bucharest and Iași.

An important moment in the opening ceremony of the first synod was the oath that each member had to take in front of the other members. Primate Metropolitan Nifon read the Orthodox Symbol of Faith, and after each paragraph all the members had to declare together "I believe and truly confess," while after kissing the cross and the Gospel, each member had to repeat the same formula again.[47] This oath was purely religious, but it would later acquire a nationalist dimension. After Cuza's regime, at the synods of the Orthodox Church and on the enthronement of new members of the church hierarchy, the required oath was amended to contain both religious and political declarations, representing the allegiance of the church to the Romanian state.

The synods of 1865 and 1867 proposed various changes regarding the discipline and organization of the Orthodox Church in Romania. Most remained only proposals as Cuza endorsed only those that met the state's political interests. The synod's authority was diminished, and, consequently, the bishops refused to meet; the last synod was held in 1869 and was suspended as only four members took part. A clash between the old church hierarchy and the newly appointed bishops supported by the regime arose as two vice-bishops, Neofit Scriban and Ioanichie Evantias, and a priest, Father Păunescu, claimed that the synod was, in fact, a pseudo-synod. In other accusations, these vice-bishops suggested that the synod was completely controlled by Cuza and had nothing to do with real Orthodoxy; that with the synod being composed of bishops appointed by Cuza, the church was not accurately represented; that the president of the synod was Cuza; that the synod intended to change Orthodoxy; and that ordinary people could not participate in the synod's debates.[48] Most of their claims were published in the press but did not have a strong impact on the church as it remained intact and did not split. The vice-bishops and the priest were rejected by the church, lost their positions, and the conflict did not develop further.

Cuza wanted to impose new reforms, such as land and electoral reforms, but his proposals faced opposition from the Conservatives, and were rejected in parliament. For this reason, and following the model of his political hero, Napoleon III, on May 2, 1864, Cuza established a coup d'état that dissolved parliament and asked for a plebiscite that would endorse his political decisions. The plebiscite was held from May 22 to 26, 1864, and was passed with 682,621 votes for, 1,307 against and 70,220 abstentions.[49] According to the new Statute resulting from this plebiscite, the prince became the sole executive authority with the support of a Moderate Body that advised him on his decisions. The Moderate Body was composed of the two metropolitans, all of the bishops, the President of the Court of Cassation and sixty-four members personally appointed by the prince. By electing church hierarchs to the Moderate Body, Cuza suggested that his regime would continue as previously, although it was now authoritarian.

Support of the church hierarchy was also evident in the administrative organization of the plebiscite. The church composed special prayers for the event in which Cuza was portrayed as a defender of Romania whose political actions pleased God: "God, you always looked upon the Romanian nation sending from time to time defenders and leaders and you freed her from the chains of those who wanted to destroy her and erase her from the book of Christian and civilized people . . . and we, like our ancestors, say: God is with us and nobody [will be] against us."[50] In addition, the festivities held in Bucharest on the evening of May 21, 1864, (on the eve of the plebiscite) combined religious and political elements. At the main reception, an ode dedicated to Cuza, inscribed on a large display board, had both a religious and political significance:

> To he who made unity; to he who took [our] wealth from the foreigners' hands; to he who gave land to the peasants; to he who made all Romanians aware of their civilian and political rights; to he who gave free and compulsory education; to he who killed death; to he who built the army; to the defender of nationality; to the protector of justice; to the father of the fatherland; to the ruler of Romanians; Alexandru Ioan I [Cuza]; eternal gratitude.[51]

Both in the prayers and in the ode, Cuza was presented as a special ruler with supreme powers. The ode claimed he was the one "who killed death," making a subtle reference to Christ who, according to Christian doctrine, through his resurrection became the only human being to defeat death. Cuza was thus the providential ruler who united the nation with the church, God, and history. His political acts not only had an impact *hic et nunc* but, moreover, were connected with the history of Orthodox Christianity.

However, Cuza's reign was short, and, faced with the opposition of Conservatives and Radical-Liberals, he was forced to abdicate on February 11, 1866. The interim rulers were Lascăr Catargiu, representative of the Conservatives, General Nicolae Golescu, representative of the Liberals, and Colonel Nicolae Haralambie, representative of the army. The important body lacking from this composition was the church hierarchy, suggesting that even if the church was a representative force in Romania it had not acquired an independent political voice.

In order to avoid the dissolution of the state, which the Ottoman Empire had previously requested would take place after Cuza's regime, Romanian politicians chose Count Philip of Flanders, the brother of King Leopold II of Belgium, as the new ruler. However, afraid of France's opposition, Count Philip declined and, for this reason, the politicians turned to the Hohenzollern-Sigmaringen family. Prince Carol of Hohenzollern-Sigmaringen accepted the throne and on May 10, 1866, was proclaimed Prince of Romania under the name Prince Carol I. The constitution of July 1, 1866, stated in its first article that "The Romanian United Principalities are an indivisible state under the name of Romania," and in this way, the political work achieved by Cuza was continued by Prince Carol I who further strengthened Romanian unity.

Cuza's political and religious reforms had an impact on the future development of church-state relations. He used the financial resources of the church to consolidate his state both politically and economically and to further popular measures such as state education and land reform.[52] By confiscating church land and controlling the Orthodox hierarchy, Cuza acquired a major role in Romanian national consciousness especially after the First World War when the country expanded its territory. He was perceived as an authoritarian ruler who had managed to remove church land from Greek control and to acquire international recognition of the Romanian state. Moreover, his reforms showed that the church could become an important ally in building the Romanian nation-state; power over the church hierarchy gave Cuza overall control of the church and, indirectly, of the Romanian faithful.

Orthodoxy and Politics during the Reign of King Carol I

Political control of Orthodoxy, in its incipient stages during Cuza's regime, acquired more of a nationalist dimension during the reign of Prince Carol I and would gradually increase further during the following decades. Romanian politicians started to employ not only religious elements to propagate the unity of the country but also made increasing connections to the main historical figures of the Romanian principalities, turning them into myths of national unity and identity. Political leaders made reference to popular mythologies that had a religious substratum. The main figures presented in this way in both political and religious discourses were the ruler of Moldavia, Stephen the Great (1457–1504), and the ruler of Wallachia, Michael the Brave (1593–1601). Stephen the Great was presented not only as a victorious ruler who defended his territory from pagan occupation but also as a religious man who enjoyed one of the longest reigns in Romanian history. Building a church after every battle made him both a popular and religious figure. Despite his convoluted personal life, he was widely thought of as a saint.[53] Michael the Brave, who controlled Transylvania and Moldavia, albeit for a few years, and united their territories with Wallachia, was considered a national genius who managed for the first time to unite all provinces that had a Romanian majority. He supported the church and established a bishopric in Alba Iulia for the Romanian population in Transylvania. Both figures combined political with religious elements and, for this reason, were mythologized as examples of the glorious past of Romanians.

From the beginning of Prince Carol I's regime, political leaders employed elements of Romanian national mythology and religion in their political discourse. The telegram sent by Ioan Brătianu, representative of the Romanian government and later prime minister, to Prince Anton of Hohenzollern on April 3, 1866, indicating the decision to appoint Prince Anton's son as the ruler of Romania, suggested that the Romanians were waiting for their ruler as they would a savior: "Five million Romanians are acclaiming as their Suzerain, Prince Carol, the son of your Royal Highness. All temples are open and the voice of the clergy is rising with that of the whole people toward the Eternal Sky, asking for the Chosen One to be blessed and to be made worthy of his ancestors and of the trust the whole nation that relies upon him."[54] Likewise, in his speech on May 11, 1866, after arriving in Bucharest, Prince Carol I used a nationalist and religious discourse. In referring to Stephen the Great and Michael the Brave, he selected two mythologized figures, one from each principality:

> In human destinies there is no more noble duty than to be called to maintain the rights of a nation and to consolidate its liberties. Such an important mission made me immediately leave an independent position, my family and country toward which I was bound with the most sacred laws, in order to follow your appeal. Receiving your election, which put on my head the crowns of Stephen the Great and Michael the Brave, gave me an important responsibility. I hope that with the help of God and with my whole devoutness I shall give my new country a happy existence worthy of its history. Romanians! I am yours with all my heart and soul. You can rely on me at any time as I rely on you.[55]

Prince Carol I was Catholic and, although he was not forced to convert, Article 82 of the 1866 Constitution stated that his children and the future royal rulers of Romania would be brought up in the dominant religion of the state, Orthodoxy. Article 21 of the Constitution referred to the relationship between church and state, asserting that:

> The freedom of conscience is absolute. The liberty of all religious confessions is guaranteed if they do not contravene public order and good custom. The religion of Eastern Orthodoxy is the dominant religion of the Romanian state. The Romanian Orthodox Church is and remains independent of any foreign church, while maintaining unity with the Ecumenical Church of the East regarding its dogma. The spiritual, canonical, and disciplinary affairs of the Romanian Orthodox Church will be regulated by a unique central synod authority, according to a special law. Metropolitans and bishops of the Romanian Orthodox Church will be elected according to a special law.[56]

The political regime continued to favor Orthodoxy as the dominant religion, and Romanian politicians felt the need to explain to other European countries why Romania supported the church and did not convert its population to a different Christian confession. In a letter to the French newspaper *L'Opinion Nationale*, Brătianu suggested that the attachment of the Romanian state to Orthodoxy and not Roman Catholicism was connected to two main points. Firstly, all Orthodox states that had achieved political unity had proclaimed their own national Orthodox Church independent from Constantinople. Brătianu emphasized the role of Orthodoxy in preserving the national identity of Romanians in the past and claimed that the new state had benefited from this religious dimension. Secondly, by preserving Orthodoxy as the state religion, Romania could have a strong political influence in the Balkans among the other Orthodox countries.[57]

The ecclesiastical reform started by Prince Cuza was completed during Prince Carol I's regime. Because the church hierarchy was divided between those appointed before 1859 and those appointed during Cuza's regime, Prince Carol I decided that a law dealing with this matter should be issued with the approval of the Ecumenical Patriarchate, which he personally acquired in 1866 on his visit to the patriarch.[58] Prince Carol I wanted to reinforce the hierarchy's loyalty, and his laws were directed toward ensuring that the church supported his political decisions and national unity. Thus he confirmed that the bishops who had been elected by Prince Cuza would remain in their positions.

Complete control of the church hierarchy was achieved in the law concerning the election of the metropolitans and eparchial bishops (*Legea pentru alegerea mitropoliților și episcopilor eparhioți, cum și a constituirii Sfântului Sinod al Sfintei Biserici Autocefale Ortodoxe Române*) promulgated on December 19, 1872.[59] This law had a number of effects. First, the system of electing the hierarchy changed. The members of the hierarchy were elected by a simple majority in a secret vote of the Electoral Collegium, which included metropolitans, eparchial bishops, appointed vice-bishops and the Orthodox members of parliament (Article 1). Second, the metropolitans would be elected only from bishops and bishops only from the "appointed bishops" (*arhierei titulari*) by the Electoral Collegium and not directly by the Prince (Article 2). The Prince endorsed their election after official confirmation from the Ministry of Religious Confessions (Article 4). Third, the law stated that the highest ecclesiastical office would be the synod, which acquired the title of the Holy Synod; it would be composed of sixteen members including the metropolitans, six bishops and eight vice-bishops, and would meet twice a year (Article 8). Although these measures might appear to have made the church hierarchy more democratically elected, in fact, they created a small circle of people accountable to the regime. The law also raised the possibility of political parties having their own representatives in the church hierarchy by electing their favorite candidates, as the number of members of parliament always surpassed that of the Holy Synod in the Electoral Collegium. The law led to an unstable ecclesiastical life in Romania, and until its modification in 1909 the Orthodox Church was ruled by seven primate metropolitans and seven metropolitan deputies, an instability that would benefit the political regime.[60]

In addition to these provisions, the law had a nationalist dimension. Article 25 stated the establishment of "appointed bishops," which would be elected by "the Holy Synod with the help of the government." These new bishops would not have a bishopric see but would be named after the most important cities in Romania.[61] Their main tasks were to participate in the meetings of the Holy Synod and in the election of the bishops. In this way, the government could guarantee having the majority in the Holy Synod. In addition, as the deposition of a bishop required the agreement of twelve bishops, the government would have complete control in maintaining its support; there would always be at least twelve bishops in the hierarchy who would endorse its position.[62]

Aiming for complete independence from the Ottoman Empire, on May 9, 1877, the government declared Romania an independent state and supported Russia in the Balkan war by invading the northern part of Bulgaria.[63] On May 10, 1877, Prince Carol I addressed the clergy, enlisting support for the government's military efforts. In his speech he reinforced the idea that not only was the Romanian government in conflict with the Ottoman Empire but the whole nation, thereby connecting the church with the people: "In the greatest days of Romania, the clergy was always with the nation, or, to put it better, was the nation itself. It could not be different today when the Romanian nation proclaimed its decision to live its own life, to be the master of its destinies and to be self-governed."[64] With the Russian side winning the war, on February 19, 1878, the Russo-Turkish Treaty of San Stefano marked the official recognition of Romanian independence by the European powers.[65] In order to raise the country's position in the Balkans, Romania declared itself as the Kingdom of Romania and Prince Carol I as its king.

To strengthen its religious position, on March 9, 1882, the Romanian Parliament proposed that the Romanian Orthodox Church have the rank of patriarchate, making it equal to the other patriarchates in Eastern Christianity. Furthermore, in a spiritually symbolic gesture, the Romanian hierarchy officiated a few days later, on March 25, 1882, the celebration of the Holy Myrrh, which represented jurisdictional separation from the Ecumenical Patriarchate. According to church doctrine, only autocephalous churches were entitled to produce myrrh and send it to churches of its jurisdiction. Before 1882, the Romanian Orthodox Church had received myrrh from Constantinople and so, by officiating this ceremony, it *de facto* announced its jurisdictional independence. Thus, after the military victory against Ottoman rule, the church proclaimed its own spiritual victory against Constantinople. On April 25, 1885, by the official *Tomos* of the Ecumenical Patriarch Joachim IV, the actions of the church had King Carol I's support and after intense diplomatic negotiations the Romanian Orthodox Church was finally recognized as an autocephalous church although not yet as a patriarchate.

At the opening of the meeting of the Holy Synod on May 1, 1885, King Carol I signaled the role of the government in gaining the autocephaly of the church and his personal vision of the role of Orthodoxy in Romania. In his opinion, the glory of Romanians was intrinsically linked to Orthodoxy and only by transforming the church into a national institution could the state and church coexist:

> I am happy to announce to your Holy Highnesses that the Secular Autocephaly of the Romanian Orthodox Church received the blessing of His Sanctity Ecumenical Patriarch and that, thus, the position of the Romanian Church is equally defined with the other Autocephalous Orthodox churches, its sisters of the same faith and ritual. This positive result was obtained by the effort of my government, the patriotic support of your Holy Metropolitans and Bishops of the Romanian Church and due to the strong feeling of true Christian brotherhood of His High Sanctity Joachim IV and His Holy Synod. . . . The church, through the defense of which in past centuries Romanians made their glory, was always connected to the destiny of the country. Touched by this historical truth, and knowing the strong faith of the people in their ancient religion, from the first day and during all the time of my reign I have had before my

eyes a permanent aim: the strengthening of the Romanian Church, so that it could be that great state national institution, which the Romanian people could always rely on.[66]

The award of Romanian autocephaly meant that Romanians now had international recognition of their national identity. The process of reaching both religious independence and national unity would be achieved in 1925 when the establishment of Greater Romania would take place together with the creation of the Romanian Orthodox Patriarchate.

The Orthodox Church considered itself at the core of Romanian national identity in contrast with the religion of other ethnic minorities. In a Report of 1882 regarding the relationship between Orthodoxy and other religions in Romania, presented at the meeting of the Holy Synod, Bishop Melchisedec Ștefănescu stated that "the Holy Synod has to do its best from a moral and legal point of view to ensure that the foreign nationalities who live in our country blend with the Romanian nationality, and that they thus become true and complete sons of the Romanian nation."[67] The church saw a political opportunity to engage more actively in the life of the state by claiming that its main priority was to protect Romanian identity from the influence of other religions. As the 1899 census showed, the Romanian Orthodox Church comprised 91.5 percent of the population, with the Jewish population at 4.5 percent and Roman Catholics at 2.5 percent.[68] The church's position toward the Jewish population was supported by the Constitution, which stated in Article 7 that only people of Christian denomination could be landowners. Roman Catholics were seen as a potential threat, as the king was Catholic and their number increased from 45,152 in 1859 to 149,667 in 1899, although still only constituting a small percentage of the population.

Even if the political regime managed to control the church hierarchy with its 1872 law concerning the election of the metropolitans and eparchial bishops, there was a separation between the church leaders and lower clergy. Most Orthodox priests remained poor and uneducated; they memorized their daily religious ceremonials and lived in rural areas with only the material support of their congregations. Prince Cuza's laws, which had deprived the church of its vast land possessions, led the clergy into financial dependence on the budgets of local city halls. Due to these changes, the number of priests dramatically declined. If the 1859 census indicated that there were 9,702 priests in the principalities, in 1904 the

Orthodox Church had only 4,998 priests while the number of monks dropped from 4,672 to 861 and the number of nuns from 4,078 to 2,220.[69]

In an 1888 Report concerning the deplorable material and moral situation of the Romanian clergy, Bishop Melchisedec stated that "the improvement of the priests' situation . . . is a vital element for a nation that wants to consolidates itself. . . . As land would not exist without the sky that gives it light, warmth, air, rain, dew, etc., in the same way a civilized nation would not exist and progress without religion and morality, which are represented by the church and its servants."[70]

Moreover, because the clergy did not receive financial support from the state but from local authorities, it was under permanent political pressure to support the party that promised the most financial assistance. Bishop Melchisedec lamented those priests who supported the wrong candidates: "Pity the priest who worked with the party that lost the elections."[71] Moreover, Bishop Melchisedec argued that without financial support from the state, Orthodoxy faced a dangerous situation. Some priests started to organize associations with a hostile attitude toward the Holy Synod claiming that the hierarchy should be composed only of priests and not bishops. Because the bishops were elected from monks, while priests were married and had families, they argued that the church hierarchy no longer represented them.[72]

The political regime took advantage of the priests' financial crisis in order to use the church, with its strong influence on the masses, as a political tool. A financial solution was promulgated on May 20, 1893, and reworked in 1906 in the law concerning the situation of the Orthodox clergy and theological seminaries (*Legea clerului mirean și a seminariilor*). By paying part of priests' salaries, the state would act as manager of the church, deciding the exact number of priests and churches and limiting the number of those who wanted to become priests. The law had strong political elements. First, the regime indicated that the number of parishes in Romania would be strictly maintained at 368 urban and 3,326 rural (Article 3), no more than twenty church buildings would be constructed each year and these figures could only be changed by law (Article 4). Second, Orthodox priests would gather once a year at pastoral conferences at which they would discuss ecclesiastical matters (Article 19). These conferences, which were later detailed in special regulations on May 5–6, 1910, were used by the state to present its position on political and religious issues.[73] Third, the law indicated that every parish should have a small library that would include "moral-religious, economic and national-historical books." In addition, the Ministry of Religious Confessions would print and send to these libraries sermons written by approved clergy (Article 87). Fourth, each priest had to give to his parish library a copy of each sermon he preached (Article 89), thus enabling the state to monitor his activity more easily.[74]

The law represented the complete and coordinated control of Orthodoxy at the parish level. Primate Metropolitan Iosif opposed discussion of the law at the Holy Synod, arguing that it conflicted with ecclesiastical traditions; as in similar cases, he was soon forced to resign. The law was then promulgated by King Carol I when the Orthodox Church did not have an officially installed Primate Metropolitan.

Total financial management of church possessions by the state was achieved by establishing the House of the Church in Royal Decree No. 255 of January 21, 1902 (*Legea pentru înfiinţarea Casei Bisericii*).[75] The House of the Church was under the direction of the Ministry of Religious Confessions and Education, and oversaw the wealth of every church, monastery, and ecclesiastical establishment in Romania. It offered financial support in paying priests' salaries and conserving church patrimony.

As the 1872 law had allowed the influence of political parties in the election of the church hierarchy, on March 20, 1909, King Carol I decided to change the small circle of those eligible for hierarchical positions. The 1909 revised law introduced two main changes: it created a new institution, titled the Superior Clerical Consistory, and it allowed any Romanian to be chosen as metropolitan or bishop with the condition that they should have been born in Romania and not naturalized (*Legea pentru modificarea Legii sinodale din 1872 şi pentru înfiinţarea Consistorului Superior Bisericesc*). This new institution was composed of all members of the Holy Synod, a professor from the Faculty of Theology in Bucharest, a professor elected from all professors the seminaries, two abbots of monasteries and seventeen priests. The main aim of the Superior Clerical Consistory was to create a "parliament of the clergy united with the Holy Synod."[76] The creation of this forum provoked another crisis within the church led by Bishop Gherasim Saffirin who refused to recognize its authority, and anathematized the Holy Synod and all those who were against his opinion. However, for his views on this matter, and following a now familiar pattern, Bishop Gherasim Saffirin was soon deposed from the church hierarchy.

The 1909 law was widely regarded as too permissive in allowing any Romanian to be a possible candidate for the church hierarchy. Elections proved to be very difficult and lengthy, so on December 18, 1911, the circle of those eligible was again restricted. Thus, metropolitans could be elected only from bishops while bishops could be elected from any member of the Romanian clergy. The state continued to be involved in church elections through the Electoral Collegium, which was composed of members of the Holy Synod, the Superior Clerical Consistory and all Orthodox deputies and senators in parliament.

The 1902 and 1909 laws were significant as they indicated a new phase in the development of the Romanian state. At the beginning of the twentieth century the Romanian Orthodox Church was transformed into a state institution that served the monarchy and the ruling political party. For this reason, political attention shifted not only to controlling the church but also to shaping it into a more viable national institution adaptable to new political situations. In this way, the election of the Primate Metropolitan was meant to reflect both the national unity of Romanians and the possibility that any Romanian citizen would be able to acquire the highest ecclesiastical position in the state. In addition, the establishment of the Superior Clerical Consistory was directed at bringing the interests of the lower clergy closer to the decisions of the church hierarchy. However, the conflict started by Bishop Gherasim Saffirin, the most important clerical dispute since Cuza's period, indicated that state authority would not always be unchallenged.

On the eve of the First World War, when Romania declared its neutrality, various voices attempted to give the church a new role. In a speech given to the opposition Conservative Party on December 3, 1916, Mariu Theodorian-Carada set out the main points of his ideas concerning the "Religious Politics of Romania." He mentioned the opinion of a high-ranking official from the Ministry of Religious Confessions and Education that the church was only an instrument of the state, which held in control the masses and helped the state to bind together various nationalities.[77] Although he did not particularly agree with this official's opinion, his speech showed how widespread the view was regarding state control of the church. In Theodorian-Carada's view, the religious politics of Romania were "very delicate"[78] because only half of the Romanian population lived within Romanian territory while the rest were spread over Transylvania, Bukovina, Bessarabia, and in the Balkans.[79] For this reason, Theodorian-

Carada asked the Conservative Party to promote a form of foreign politics that would lead to the inclusion of all Romanians in one national church. In this way, Romanians who were not living in the Romanian kingdom would be encouraged to retain their national identity.[80]

On October 10, 1914, King Carol I died and because he did not have an heir, the parliament elected his nephew Ferdinand as the next monarch. In 1916 Romania declared war on the Austro-Hungarian Empire and attacked Transylvania with the aim of liberating Romanians living under foreign rule. The attack was unsuccessful, and, in subsequent battles, Romania lost the territory of Wallachia to the German army. During the period of German occupation, the royal family and the Romanian government relocated to Iași. Primate Metropolitan Conon Arămescu-Donici stayed in the capital, and the Germans persuaded him to write a letter to the Romanian soldiers and faithful in Moldavia asking them not to oppose the new authorities. The letter had little effect on the population as the Romanians remained loyal to the monarchy and did not support the occupying forces. As reflected in Mariu Theodorian-Carada's speech, the concern of Romanians living in the Old Kingdom regarding Romanianness was endangered by the lack of unity of the population with large numbers of ethnic Romanians living in the neighboring territories. The territory of Dobrudja was incorporated into the Old Kingdom in 1878 after the Russo-Turkish war and the declaration of Romanian independence.[81]

Orthodoxy and Nationalism in Transylvania, Bukovina, and Bessarabia

By the end of the nineteenth century, around 2,785,000 Romanians lived in Transylvania, (including the adjoining regions of Banat, Crișana and Maramureș), 230,000 in Bukovina and 1,092,000 in Bessarabia.[82] At the crossroads of Hungarian, Austrian, and Russian rule, Romanians retained contact with their compatriots through political and religious institutions.

Transylvania

Transylvania was the most ethnically diverse of all of the provinces. A detailed census of 1850 set out the following ethnic composition: 1,227,276 Romanian; 536,011 Magyar and Szekler; 192,482 Saxon; 78,923 Gypsy;

15,573 Jewish; 7,600 Armenian; 3,743 Slav; and 771 other nationalities.[83] Despite forming the largest ethnic group, Romanians lacked political representation. Since 1437, the nobles of the Magyar, Szekler, and Saxon communities organized themselves into the *Unio trium nationum* (the union of the three "nations") that offered political recognition and enabled them to dominate the Diet, the local government. A distinction needs to be made between the medieval "nation" in the *Unio trium nationum* and the modern interpretation of the "nation." As Keith Hitchins points out, "The idea of nation (*natio*) implied quality rather than quantity; it did not encompass everyone of the same ethnic origin, but only those persons who possessed special rights and immunities. Hence, Magyar, Szekler, and Saxon peasants did not belong to their respective nations. A Romanian *natio* did not exist at all because the Romanians were mainly peasants and thus [. . . were] of low social status and unprivileged."[84] Most nobles belonged to the *Unio trium nationum* and did not welcome the emergence of a Romanian elite. What differentiated Romanians from the other ethnic communities were language and religion: the majority of Romanians were homogenously Orthodox, the Saxons Lutheran, while the Magyars and Szeklers were Calvinist, Unitarian, or Roman Catholic. The uniqueness of Transylvanian ethnic and religious diversity was officially acknowledged by the state that recognized three "nations" (Magyars, Szeklers, and Saxons) and four churches (Lutheran, Calvinist, Unitarian, and the Roman Catholic), at the expense of the Romanian Orthodox population.[85]

In order to achieve recognition as a distinct "nation," in 1700, Bishop Atanasie and many Orthodox clergy in Transylvania accepted union with the Church of Rome. The new church, the Romanian Greek Catholic Church, also known as the Uniate Church, recognized the primacy of the religious jurisdiction of Rome over that of Constantinople. It retained the Byzantine liturgical rite, and incorporated new doctrinal elements from the Roman Catholic Church. In return, it enjoyed similar social rights with the Catholic faithful.

The Greek Catholic Church was officially recognized by the Vienna Court as one of the official religions of Transylvania. The church was embraced by a significant part of the Romanian population, and gradually became a vehicle of national affirmation. Recent archival documents suggest that during the eighteenth century, the Vienna authorities regarded the Greek Catholic Church as the only church of all Romanians while the

Orthodox Church was thought to be the confession of the Greek and Slav population in Brașov and Sibiu. However, this perception contrasted with the situation at the grass root level as many Romanians remained attached to the Orthodox Church.

The Orthodox communities in Transylvania were placed under the jurisdiction of the Serbian Metropolitanate of Karlovci, which oversaw the Orthodox faithful throughout the Empire. In the eighteenth and nineteenth centuries, despite being divided into two churches, the Greek Catholic and the Orthodox, the intellectual and religious elite focused not on religious re-unification but on ensuring that Romanians were recognized as a nation that enjoyed equal political and social rights to those in the *Unio trium nationum*. Political activism took a distinctive religious shape when the Uniate Bishop Inocențiu Micu-Klein took the Romanian cause to Vienna and Rome, and, a few decades later, his ideas were reflected in the 1790–91 publication of the *Supplex libellus Valachorum*. The *Supplex*, written at the time of the French Revolution, was the most important political document of the Romanian elite and proposed historical reasons for the long-standing presence of a "Romanian nation" in Transylvania. It proposed a number of concrete measures that could benefit the Romanian nation, and, although not accepted at the time, they would constantly be put forward during the early nineteenth century, namely economic, social, and political rights for both Orthodox and Uniate populations, proportional representation in local and provincial government, and the use of the Romanian language in local administration. In addition, the *Supplex* proposed the establishment of a national congress under the leadership of the two Uniate and Orthodox bishops of Transylvania to bring together the clergy and local nobles and discuss the means of strengthening a unified Romanian nation.[86]

The publication of the *Supplex* drew criticism from the imperial authorities, with Chancellor Samuel Teleki claiming that the recognition of a Romanian "nation" would fundamentally affect the social and political constitution of Transylvania. However, despite the lack of political recognition, the *Supplex* had a long-lasting effect on both the principality and Vienna. After the death of the Orthodox Bishop Gherasim Adamovici in 1794, the Vienna Court feared national mobilization on religious lines and failed to assign a spiritual leader to the Orthodox Church in Transylvania for nearly two decades. Petitions of both the Transylvanian clergy and the Metropolitanate of Karlovci to assign a bishop were finally listened to in 1810 when Vienna agreed with the setting up of an electoral synod in Turda. The synod, which took place between September 19 and October 1, proposed three candidates (*Protopop* Nicolae Hutovici from Hunedoara, Father Vasile Moga from Sebeș, and Archimandrite Nestor Ioanovici of the Bezdin Monastery) with the emperor having the final word on the appointment. In a surprising decision, despite gaining only thirty-six votes at the electoral synod, as opposed to forty-six for Nicolae Hutovici, the emperor appointed Vasile Moga as the Orthodox Bishop of Transylvania. Moga was the first Romanian bishop in Transylvania for more than one century, since Bishop Atanasie signed the union with Rome in 1700.

One of Moga's first decisions was to move the seat of the Orthodox diocese from Cluj, the capital of the principality that also held the Diet, to Sibiu, thus closer to the cultural and intellectual elite of the Romanian population. Official recognition of his appointment was on the condition of fulfilling nineteen points, which were stated by the local government. The points were received with acrimony by Romanians, who saw in them a step backwards in reaching national recognition. The Diet clearly indicated that Moga had to be aware that his congregation was "tolerated" by the state and not one of the four "recognized" religions; that the Orthodox clergy was not allowed to proselytize among the Uniate faithful; that he was allowed to enter into contact with the clergy in Wallachia and Moldavia; and that he was advised to reduce the number of the Orthodox clergy and retain close contact with the Karlovci Metropolitanate.[87] He also had to write a monthly report to the Diet in Cluj detailing all activities that took place in his diocese. In addition to these points, two were particularly unwelcome by the church. The first, which would become a long-standing issue throughout the nineteenth century, was the introduction of the Magyar language in schools. The second regarded possible proselytism among the Uniate faithful and indirectly affected contact with fellow Romanians. As concrete measures, the Diet insisted that the Orthodox clergy was not allowed to be present when one partner holding a religious wedding was a member of the Uniate Church. Furthermore, in cases when Orthodox believers decided to join the Uniate Church, this process was allowed to take place without restrictions, while Uniate believers who wished to become Orthodox had to attend a six-week course and obtain permission from the local diocese.[88]

Despite the difficulty of following the points, Moga remained faithful to the Romanian cause. In 1812 he established the first theological seminary in Sibiu, which offered six-month training for future clergy, thus ensuring that the local population could provide clergy rather than having them brought in from Wallachia, Moldavia, or Serbia as was the norm until then. Limited financial resources at his disposal meant that his activity was mostly pastoral and did not offer the opportunity to develop the political points included in the *Supplex*. In this regard, he turned to his Uniate counterpart, Bishop Ioan Lemeni, and on a number of occasions, they sent joint petitions to Cluj and Vienna. For example, in 1834, they sent a memorandum to Vienna that repeated the points made by the 1791 *Supplex*, demanding recognition of Romanians as a fourth nation in Transylvania; four years later they approached the Cluj Diet with a similar request, however, without any results.[89] At the time of Moga's death in 1845, the Uniate and the Orthodox churches each attracted around 30 percent of the population in Transylvania with Romanians remaining the dominant ethnic group.[90]

The work of the Uniate and Orthodox faithful would reach a new stage at the time of the 1848 revolution in Transylvania when three leading figures came to symbolize the Romanian cause, namely Simion Bărnuțiu, a former professor of philosophy in Blaj, Andreiu Șaguna, the Orthodox Bishop of Transylvania, and Avram Iancu, the military commander of the Transylvanian troops.[91] With revolutions sweeping the European empires, in 1848 Kossuth Lajos declared the independence of Hungary and included Transylvania in the new state. As a response, on March 24, 1848, Simion Bărnuțiu circulated a Proclamation to Romanians, which was distributed by teachers and clergy among local congregations. The Proclamation demanded the abolition of serfdom and the establishment of a national congress as the authority to decide the organization of the Romanian nation in the new state. Uniate and Orthodox parishes were asked to send two clergy from each deanery and two peasants from each village to a popular assembly in Blaj. The Blaj assembly, which took place on May 14, 1848, and brought together around 40,000 Romanians, was welcomed by the Uniate and Orthodox bishops, and Bărnuțiu gave a speech in which he encouraged national unity.

A particular contribution to the Romanian cause was that of the Orthodox hierarch present at the Blaj assembly, namely Andreiu Șaguna. Șaguna was born into a Macedo-Romanian family in Mișcolț, in northeast Hungary, and was previously an archimandrite and professor at the Vârşeţ Seminary.[92] In 1846, after the Orthodox diocese became vacant, he was appointed general vicar. The following year, the electoral synod proposed his name to Vienna alongside two other candidates, Father Ioan Moga and Father Moise Fulea. In 1848, Şaguna was appointed bishop and ordained in Karlovci. The Blaj assembly occurred exactly at the same time as his return from Karlovci. Together with the Uniate Bishop Ioan Lemeni, the Blaj assembly saw in him a defender of the rights of the Romanian nation and decided that Bishop Şaguna should make use of his ecclesiastical and political contacts in Vienna to lead a Romanian delegation there. The delegation presented sixteen points summarizing the social and political decisions adopted at Blaj.

Strengthening the cause of unity, Blaj became the place of a second assembly in September 1848 with an increased number of representatives at around 60,000 Romanians. The assembly made not only social claims but also stronger political demands and asked for the separation of Transylvania from Hungary. Avram Iancu took charge of a popular army and in 1849 faced military resistance from General Iosif Bem. Despite the suggestion that it was advisable for Romanians and Hungarians to work together against the imperial armies, the Hungarian revolution was defeated in July and August 1849. This cost the lives of around 40,000 Romanian peasants, including around one hundred members of the Orthodox clergy.[93]

Under the new political circumstances, Bishop Şaguna continued the Romanian cause.[94] In 1850 he set up a local synod in charge of church administration and regularly sent memoranda to Vienna. The memoranda shifted from political demands and focused instead on religious issues, asking for the Orthodox diocese to become a metropolitanate. Şaguna provided historical arguments that an Orthodox metropolitanate in Transylvania existed before 1700 and claimed that the re-establishment represented the recognition of a previous organization. Şaguna received a response only in 1860 when Emperor Franz Joseph I offered Transylvania an autonomous position within the Habsburg Empire.[95]

Between October 24 and 26, 1860, Şaguna organized a synod in Sibiu, which brought together representatives of the Orthodox clergy and laymen in Transylvania, and proposed the establishment of a metropolitanate for all Romanian Orthodox faithful in the empire. As Romanians were also part of the Bishopric of Bukovina, Şaguna entered into correspondence with Bishop Eugenie Hacman of Bukovina to convince him of the necessity of a single ecclesiastical structure. As Hacman refused, in 1861 Şaguna published a booklet defending the establishment up of an independent metropolitanate by proposing a national church, which included both clergy and laymen in its administration.[96] Between March 22 and 28, 1864, a new synod in Sibiu gave administrative content to the metropolitanate by proposing 174 measures. In autumn 1864, Şaguna managed to obtain approval of separating his church from the Karlovci Metropolitanate. On December 24, 1864, a date with both religious and personal symbolism, as Christmas Eve and the birthday of Franz Joseph's wife, the emperor signed the establishment of the Orthodox Metropolitanate of Transylvania. The new ecclesiastical structure also included the dioceses of Arad and Caransebeş, which had Romanian populations and which were previously under the jurisdiction of Karlovci.[97]

After the 1867 reorganization of the Empire into the dualist Austro-Hungarian Monarchy, the recognition of the Metropolitanate of Transylvania remained unaltered. In order to maintain stability, between September 28 and October 19, 1868, Şaguna chaired a national congress that brought together ninety participants to decide the structure of the Transylvanian Church. The congress adopted an Organic Statute (*Statutul organic al Bisericii Ortodoxe Române din Transilvania*), which was endorsed by the state on May 28, 1869. The Organic Statute was an innovative document of ecclesiastical administration and reinforced the principle of nationality at the core of the church structure. The document would have a long-standing legacy as it would be adopted by the unified Romanian Orthodox Church in Greater Romania in 1925.[98]

The Organic Statute established two principles at the core of the Transylvanian Church, namely the principle of religious autonomy, which required the church to be separated from the state, and the principle of synodality, which stated that the church was ruled by a synod. While the first was identifiable in relations between other Orthodox churches and states, the principle of synodality, with clergy and laymen working together, was endorsed for the first time in a Romanian province. Since 1850, Şaguna had engaged in correspondence with Bishop Hacman defending the view that the church should be ruled by both clergy and laymen. The Organic Statute inscribed the application of the later principle by stating that laymen were part of the decisional process at both local (parishes and deaneries) and central administrative levels (eparchies). Furthermore, the Organic Statute set up a National Church Congress composed of ninety people (ten clergy and twenty laymen from each diocese), which met every three years and discussed the direction of the church. The metropolitan, the highest religious authority, was elected by a special National Church Congress composed of 120 clergy and laymen (sixty from Sibiu, and thirty each from Arad and Caransebeș). However, despite these new administrative elements, the Organic Statute retained final word on the metropolitan's election for the emperor, which meant that the political authorities were able to interfere in church life. As evident in the election of the next metropolitans, lay representation in church structures also led to an internecine battle for power between the Vienna Court, the Budapest government and the Cluj Diet, all of which wished to see their favored candidate elected.

During his leadership, Șaguna strengthened the Romanian character of the Transylvanian Church. Although a number of intellectuals criticized his Macedo-Romanian origin and his close ties with the Viennese political authorities, which they regarded as an obstacle toward obtaining full political rights, Șaguna remained at the heart of a significant number of cultural and political initiatives with a long-standing impact on the unity of the Romanian nation. Due to his high ecclesiastical position, Șaguna held membership in key administrative and political structures in the empire from which he was able to present the Romanian cause: after 1860 he was a member of the Imperial Senate in Vienna, between 1863 and 1865 a member of the Transylvania's Diet in Sibiu, and, after 1867, a member of the House of Magnates in Budapest, the latter body bringing together all high clergy in Hungary in the Dual Monarchy.

After 1852, he supported a Romanian educational program in his church and organized local schools in all parishes. The result of this campaign was evident at the time of his death in 1873 when more than 800 schools functioned and twenty-five manuals written by clergy circulated in Transylvania. In 1853 he founded a Romanian newspaper in Sibiu, *Telegraful Român* (The Romanian Telegraph), and, in 1861, he was one of the founders of *Asociația transilvană pentru cultura și literatura română—Astra* (The Transylvanian Association for Romanian Culture and Literature—Astra). In addition, although Șaguna was instrumental in setting up an independent church in Transylvania, during his leadership he retained contact with other Orthodox hierarchs in the empire and with those in Wallachia and Moldavia. For example, in 1848, after the bishop's residence and the cathedral were destroyed during an inter-ethnic conflict in Arad, Șaguna supported the local hierarch, Bishop Gherasim Raț, and sent a delegation to Vienna to seek approval to hold a local synod in charge of church affairs. The Arad synod took place on July 23, 1850, and demanded the recognition of the Romanian nation united under a single Romanian metropolitanate. The synod's decision had a limited impact as Bishop Raț died two weeks later.[99]

After Șaguna's death, Bishop Procopie Ivașcovici of Arad was appointed metropolitan. Metropolitan Ivașcovici's leadership was short as a few months later, in 1874, the Synod of the Serbian Patriarchate of Karlovci elected him to the highest hierarchical position. His unusual election from the Romanian Metropolitan of Transylvania to the Serbian Patriarchate seat revealed both the mobility of the Orthodox clergy in the Empire and the role of the political authorities in ecclesiastical elections. In Transylvania, Romanians feared that the new patriarch would aim to bring their church again under the Karlovci's jurisdiction and Ivașcovici agreed to resign and sever his connection with the Transylvanian see. His election to Karlovci was politically motivated, and, a few years later, he entered into conflict with the Budapest government. He was forced to resign in 1880, and died the following year.

After Ivașcovici's resignation, the Transylvanian Church was ruled by Metropolitan Miron Romanul, who, as his predecessor, came from the Bishopric of Arad. His pastoral leadership, which lasted until 1899, was greatly affected by state intervention in education and, in particular, by the 1879 Trefort Law, which stated that all teachers should be able to teach in the Magyar language. The Orthodox hierarchs perceived the new law as a direct attempt at Magyarization at the expense of the Romanian national identity and the following decades witnessed a strong religious activism protecting the language taught in schools. Pressure on the church came in June 1882 when Budapest decided that Magyar was a requisite for teaching in primary schools. In the same year, both the Orthodox and the Uniate metropolitans of Transylvania gave speeches in the House of Magnates in Budapest defending the right of their churches to have schools in Romanian offering many examples of parishes without Hungarian speakers, which had to comply with the new legislation. Anxiety within the church would reach a climax in 1903 when Gyula Wlassics, the minister of religion and education, informed the Orthodox leadership that even the Orthodox Theological Institute in Sibiu did not conform to the 1879 Trefort Law. Tension between the Hungarian government and the Orthodox Metropolitanate would continue until the unification of Transylvania with Greater Romania in 1918.[100]

Metropolitan Ioan Mețianul, who led the church from 1899 until 1916, turned his attention to building the University Theological Institute in Sibiu rather than involving the church in political disputes. His successor, Metropolitan Vasile Mangra, led the Transylvanian Church briefly from 1916 until 1918. He held the office due to his close contact with the Hungarian government and, in rather unusual circumstances for an Orthodox hierarch, on October 1, 1918, died in a hotel in Budapest. A few weeks later, Transylvania would become part of Greater Romania.[101]

Bukovina

In 1774, Bukovina, the northern part of Moldavia, was occupied by Austria, which imposed a military government until 1786 when the province was administratively included in Galicia, which was also under the Austrian rule. In contrast to Transylvania, Bukovina witnessed a significant movement of population, which had a direct impact on its ethnic structure and consequently led to ethnic animosity. In 1774, Romanians represented the majority of the population, numbering around 64,000 out of a total population of 75,000; however, in 1810 they numbered 85 percent and in 1848 dropped to around 55 percent of the population.[102] The largest migrant group was Ruthenian, to the extent that in 1848 Romanians numbered 209,000, Ruthenians around 109,000 while 60,000 belonged to other ethnic groups.[103]

Until 1774 the Romanians of Bukovina were under the religious jurisdiction of the Orthodox Metropolitanate of Moldavia. Under the new political situation, in 1781 Dosoftei Herescu, who had been Bishop of Rădăuți since 1750, moved his residence to Cernăuți. In 1783, Vienna placed his church under the authority of the Serbian Metropolitanate of Karlovci. Ethnic tensions in Bukovina were not only due to the arrival of new migrants but also due to the political control of the Orthodox Church, which owned a significant number of properties in the territory. In 1782, fourteen monasteries and their adjacent properties were taken by the state while, the following year, the state established the Church Fund of Bukovina (*Fondul Bisericesc din Bucovina*) in charge of finance and church properties.[104] The governor oversaw the appointment of the local clergy throughout the province while the emperor appointed the bishop, the highest Orthodox authority.[105]

The state's direct involvement in the administration of the church and a lack of financial resources meant that in the Orthodox Church being unable to engage Romanians in Bukovina in a comparable national movement to that witnessed in Transylvania. Rather than promote a nationalist movement, Bukovina provided a unique model of inter-ethnic relations characterized by inter- and intra- religious tension between Romanians and Ruthenians, the former predominantly Orthodox while the latter were members of either the Ruthenian Uniate Church or the Ruthenian Orthodox Church.[106]

Divergences between Romanians and other ethnic groups were particularly visible in education. In 1778, the government closed the small theological academy at Putna Monastery and opened instead a clerical school at Saint Ilie Monastery near Suceava, which was placed under the Serbian Archdeacon Daniil Vlachovici. Jurisdictional changes and the appointment of a Serbian in charge of the school led to dissatisfaction among Romanians who refused to send their children to study there. In a pastoral letter, Bishop Dosoftei Herescu attempted to alleviate tensions and encouraged Romanians to send their children to the school.[107] The school was later transferred to Cernăuți and would form the basis of a theological institute. However, high costs refrained many Romanians from studying in Cernăuți, and the school was closed between 1818 and 1827.

After Herescu's death in 1789, the Orthodox Church in Bukovina was placed under the leadership of Daniil Vlachovici, who faced pressure from the local government. In 1815, the Catholic Consistory of Lemberg took charge of primary schools in Bukovina, and all teachers were asked to become Catholic. Discontent with this religious affiliation led to the refusal of many Romanians to send their children to school; at the same time, the Orthodox Church was allowed to have only one primary school in Cernăuți. In 1821, this school was transformed into a bilingual German-Romanian school, for both Romanians and Ruthenians; in 1914, it had 224 students, one director, and six teachers who were paid by the Orthodox consistory.[108]

Romanian and Ruthenian relations took on a distinctly religious shape during one of the most controversial leaderships of an Orthodox hierarch in the nineteenth century, namely that of Bishop Eugenie Hacman. Hacman was born into a peasant family in Bucovina, with some sources stating that he was Romanian, others that he was Ruthenian. He studied at the Clerical School where an uncle of his was a professor. He was awarded a scholarship to study in Vienna, and, in 1835, he was appointed the Orthodox bishop in Bukovina. Upon his return to Cernăuți, he seemed to favor both Romanian and Ruthenian communities, and his ambiguous position had an impact on church-state relations in the region.

In 1844, the Vienna Court allowed primary schools to be divided between the Catholic and Orthodox churches, with the Romanian and Ruthenian languages used by the Orthodox communities. The decision encouraged a Romanian nationalist mobilization, and in 1848, Doxache Hurmuzachi, one of the leading Bukovinian boyars, organized a national assembly that brought together around 200 clergy. The assembly demanded that the bishop should be elected by the clergy and laymen rather than nominated by the emperor, and that all Romanians in the Habsburg Empire should organize themselves into a metropolitanate. The assembly set up an Advisory Committee that put pressure on Bishop Hacman to distance himself from a number of Ruthenians who had positions in the church administration. Hacman gave course to the demands and agreed that the Theological Institute in Cernăuți should not only have classes in Latin, Greek, and German as was the use until then but also in Romanian.[109] During the following two years, he seemed to support the nationalist cause and led a number of delegations to Vienna representing the demands of the Romanian community.

Due to the reorganization of the empire, in 1849 Bukovina ceased its administrative links with Galicia and was decreed an autonomous duchy. Hacman, together with the leading provincial aristocracy, was a member of the local committee in charge of drafting the Constitution.[110] After the 1861 electoral law was passed, he was appointed by the emperor as the first chair (*căpitanul țării; Landeshauptmann*) of the Bukovinian Diet, a position he occupied for two years while he was a deputy in the Diet until 1872.[111]

In his new political position, he became more cautious. His ambivalence, which seemed to favor at times either the Romanians or Ruthenians, took a new turn when, in 1860, the emperor decreed the establishment of a Congress in Karlovci for all Orthodox bishops to decide on their jurisdictional organization. If, under the leadership of Bishop Șaguna, the Romanian leadership of Transylvania gathered into a local synod composed of clergy and laymen, Hacman claimed that the clergy should be the only authority to decide on the nature and structure of the church. He entered into correspondence with Șaguna suggesting that laymen should not decide church matters, stating that, "We Bukovinians are not like all Romanians, because some of our brethren are Ruthenians. If we have to choose between Karlovci and Alba Iulia we could not decide between us."[112]

During the Congress in Karlovci, Hacman voted in favor of a Romanian Metropolitanate in Transylvania. However, he refused to bring his church under Șaguna and proposed the establishment of an autocephalous Metropolitanate in Bukovina. The new church would have been under the canonical and dogmatic jurisdiction of a synod composed of all Orthodox bishops in the Empire under the leadership of the Serbian Patriarch. In addition, he proposed that each metropolitanate in the empire should have a local administrative synod composed solely of clergy. Hacman's proposals did not find support among his fellow hierarchs.[113]

In contrast, the Romanian intellectual elite in Bukovina sent two memoranda, to the Vienna Court and to Bishop Hacman, in which they supported the establishment of a united Romanian Church for both Transylvania and Bukovina. Hacman replied in a pastoral letter in which he criticized any attempts to obtain "national-political advantages," claiming that the church should not engage in political disputes. He indicated that "the kingdom of Christ is not in this world [and that . . .] the priesthood does not have anything to do with politics or the spread of nationalism."[114]

The 1867 Constitution that inaugurated the Austro-Hungarian Dualist Monarchy decreed the right of each confession to exercise freely its worship and to be in charge of its own finances. Under the new circumstances, the Karlovci Metropolitanate, directly dependent on Budapest, lost religious authority over Bukovina, which retained close relations with Vienna.

As a result, on January 23, 1873, the Vienna Court approved the establishment of the Metropolitanate of Bukovina and Dalmatia, a supra-ethnic Orthodox structure, divided by a large geographical space, comprised of the Romanians and Ruthenians of Bukovina and the Serbians of the Zara and Cattaro dioceses in Dalmatia.[115] The new metropolitanate proclaimed itself autocephalous with hierarchs meeting annually in Vienna, the capital of the empire, rather than in Cernăuţi. Discussions were held through translators.[116] This structure lasted until the incorporation of Bukovina into Greater Romania in 1918 when the metropolitanate was included into the Romanian Orthodox Church.

The Orthodox hierarchs who succeeded Hacman until 1918 were particularly active in defending education, which was perceived as central to Romanian identity. The 1875 establishment of the University of Cernăuţi included a Faculty of Theology, which regularly held cultural activities supporting Romanian consciousness.[117] Throughout the last decades of the nineteenth century, Romanian-Ruthenian relations remained tense, encouraged at times by the political interests of the Vienna Court.[118] By 1910, the ethnic structure of Bukovina indicated that the number of Ruthenians had slightly surpassed that of Romanians. The majority of both ethnic groups continued to belong to the Orthodox Metropolitanate while attempts to attract either population to Greek Catholicism or Roman Catholicism did not prove successful.[119]

Bessarabia

The Romanian population that lived between the Prut and the Dniester Rivers identified itself as Moldovan in a territory known as Bessarabia. Bessarabia was part of the Principality of Moldavia. However, the Peace Treaty of Bucharest on May 16, 1812, which ended the war between the Russian and the Ottoman empires, included the region into the Russian Empire.[120]

The 1812 Russian occupation did not fundamentally change the structure of the Orthodox Church in Bessarabia. Gavriil Bănulescu-Bodoni, a Romanian, who had been a metropolitan in Moldavia and Wallachia between 1808 and 1812, was appointed Exarch of the Russian Synod. In 1813, he established the Eparchy of Chişinău and Hotin, under the jurisdiction of the St. Petersburg Holy Synod. He selected his metropolitan seat to be in Chişinău, the capital of the province, from where he maintained contact with the local administration and the faithful, as a significant number of the faithful consequently moved across the Moldavian border. A report from Bishop Dimetrie Sulima of Bender and Akkerman to Metropolitan Bănulescu-Bodoni pointed out, for example, that the entire population of Saba village, near Akkerman, fled Bessarabia, except for three or four families.[121]

The spread of nationalist ideas across Europe and the population movement after the Russian occupation led the metropolitan to send a pastoral letter at the end of 1812 in which he encouraged the faithful to remain in Bessarabia. In the letter he supported his plea by stating that, even if Bessarabia was under new authorities, the Russians had decided not to impose serfdom. He told the people that "you will be happy under the Russian rule" as "the high imperial blessing [decided that] you will have a leadership chosen from your people and your language."[122] Local boyars benefited from his personal connections in St. Petersburg, and, under his guidance, they sent three letters to Tsar Alexander I asking for the appointment of a governor selected from the Moldovan population.[123]

Metropolitan Bănulescu-Bodoni took an active stance in the organization of his diocese. In 1813 he set up a spiritual seminary (*seminar duhovnicesc*) for the training of the clergy and in 1823 a spiritual school (*şcoala duhovnicească*) for students who had finished primary school.[124] Although the clergy did not have the financial support of the state, he ensured that each parish had land that was worked by local peasants.[125] In particular, two decisions of Metropolitan Bănulescu-Bodoni had a long-term impact on the life of the church. Firstly, he founded a printing house in Chişinău that published a significant number of religious publications in Romanian, enabling the population to retain its ethnic identity under Russian rule. Secondly, in 1817, he published a New Testament, and two years later the Holy Bible, both in Romanian, under the auspices of the Bessarabian Section of the Russian Biblical Society in St. Petersburg. On the first page the Holy Bible mentioned that the text, in Romanian, was a translation of that previously published in 1795 by the Romanian Greek Catholic Church in Blaj, Transylvania. The metropolitan defended his choice of Romanian translation by arguing that the Transylvanian text was closer to his contemporary language, a decision that also alleviated possible conflict with the Wallachian Church, which used the 1688 Bible published in Bucharest.[126] Most significantly, the metropolitan offered a free copy of the New Testament to new members of the clergy and demanded the purchase of the Holy Bible by all parishes, ensuring thus not only a link with Romanians living in the other principalities but also preserving a common religious and cultural identity in Bessarabia.[127]

From Metropolitan Bănulescu-Bodoni's death in 1821 until the incorporation of Bessarabia in Greater Romania in 1918, the Orthodox Church was ruled by twelve metropolitans, none of whom were Romanian. In

1828 Bessarabia lost its administrative autonomy and was placed under the Novorossiisk government. The eparchy had a constant stream of Russian-appointed hierarchs consolidating imperial policy and submission to the monarchy. The church's status in the life of the local population was endorsed by the construction of the Orthodox Cathedral in Chişinău under the leadership of Metropolitan Dimetrie Sulima (1821–44); the project lasted six years and was inaugurated in 1836.

The church became entangled in conflicting nationalisms promoted by the Moldovan and the Russian communities, and, in 1867, Metropolitan Antonie Sokotov (1858–71) began publishing an official bulletin of the eparchy, *Chişinăuskie eparkhialnye vedomosti* (The Chişinău Eparchial Gazette), with texts in both Russian and Moldovan.[128] The balance between Moldovan and Russian favored the latter when Archbishop Irinarh Popov (1844–58) legislated that all positions in the administration should be occupied by Russians. More significantly, the Moldovan community was affected when Archbishop Pavel Lebedev (1871–82) brought in clergy from outside the province and decided that the official bulletin of the eparchy should be issued only in Russian. In addition, Lebedev closed a number of parish churches, confiscated and destroyed some Moldovan publications, and ordered that all Moldovan churches had to perform religious services in both Moldovan and Russian. His leadership remains controversial, with Moldovan sources placing the number of closed churches at 340.[129]

In 1897, 82 percent of the male population and 96 percent of women in the rural communities were unable to read or write, while the figures for urban centers showed a slight increase to 57 and 78 percent respectively.[130] In a territory in which illiteracy remained high, the preservation of both church services and education in the Moldovan language were prime elements in fostering national cohesion and contact with fellow ethnic citizens living in Greater Romania.[131] The decision to make Russian compulsory in education under the direct supervision of rural parishes led to the closure of an extremely large numbers of schools, from around four hundred with seven thousand pupils in the 1860s to only twenty-three in 1880.[132] The majority of lower clergy in charge of rural parishes were unable to teach Russian. The introduction of the mandatory Russian-taught subjects in the theological seminary in Chişinău in 1840 did little to alleviate this situation.

In addition to the religious tension, jurisdictional changes affected both Romanian and Russian territories following the rewriting of the religious and political map of Southeastern Europe. In 1837, the parishes on the eastern side of the Dniester River were incorporated into the newly established Archdiocese of Odessa and Kherson.[133] Bessarabia's territorial composition changed in 1856 when three southern districts were returned to Moldavia and later became part of the United Principalities of Moldavia and Wallachia, under the jurisdiction of Bishop Melchisedec Ștefănescu. These three districts were re-occupied by the Russian Empire at the end of the 1877–78 Russo-Turkish War.

If officially the church hierarchy reinforced close relations with Russian authorities, the Moldovan lower clergy retained their national identity by organizing themselves in 1899 into a missionary society, *Nașterea lui Hristos* (The Birth of Christ) and in 1904 by founding *Societatea Istorico-Arheologică Bisericească din Basarabia* (The Historical Archaeological Society of Bessarabia), dedicated to the study of church history. Both bodies had the support of the church and were very popular; in 1903 the missionary society published 195,000 copies of its brochure. After the 1905 Russian Revolution, the Moldovan language was allowed to be taught in schools and village priests preached in their language.[134]

The Moldovan printing house in Chișinău, which was closed in 1882 by Metropolitan Serghie Leapidevski (1882–91), was re-opened under the leadership of Metropolitan Vladimir Sinikovski (1904–8). Metropolitan Sinikovski began the publication of church books in Moldovan and encouraged the Frățimea (Brotherhood) Society to publish a church magazine *Luminătorul* (The Light), which issued its first number on January 25, 1908, under the editorial supervision of *Protopop* Constantin Popovici and Hieromonk Gurie Grosu (later Metropolitan of Bessarabia).[135] Metropolitan Sinikovski introduced the Moldovan language into all churches in Chișinău while support for the Moldovan community was probably the reason for his redeployment by the Russian Holy Synod from Chișinău to Novocerkassk.[136]

The church hierarchy faced the nationalist pressure of the lower clergy and the faithful not only through the afore-mentioned Moldovan societies but also through a fundamentalist mass mobilization, known as Inochentism. Between 1909 and 1911, Inochentie, a Moldovan monk at a monastery in Balta, became extremely popular through his sermons proclaiming the age of anti-Christ, the imminent coming of Jesus and the end of the world, and attracted large audiences. Inochentie's exile to an island in the White Sea and his death in 1917 alleviated the constant pilgrimage to hear his sermons and the spread of his beliefs.[137] Although he was officially rejected by the church, Inochentism demonstrated a powerful Moldovan rural mobilization at the expense of the Russian-appointed hierarchy.

The last three metropolitans of the region found themselves torn between allegiance to the Russian Empire and the national mobilization of the predominantly Moldovan population. Although in 1914, Metropolitan Serafim Ciceagov (1908–14) welcomed Tsar Nicolae II and the Royal family to Chișinău,[138] he allowed the publication of sermons in Moldovan and the issuing of two newspapers *Glasul Basarabiei* (The Voice of Bessarabia) and *Cuvânt Moldovenesc* (The Moldovan Word).[139] After the 1917 Revolution, he was appointed Metropolitan of Leningrad; however, he was later forced to retire to a village near Moscow. In 1940, he was arrested by the NKVD and executed. Ciceagov's successor, Metropolitan Platon Rojdestvenski (1914–15) faced a similar fate. He was in charge of the spiritual office only briefly, and after 1917, he went into exile and became in charge of the Russian Church in the United States.

The impact of the 1917 Russian Revolution was evident not only in the political structure of Bessarabia but also in the organization of the church. Between April 19 and 25, 1917, the church hierarchy organized an Extraordinary Assembly of the Clergy and Laymen in the Eparchy of Chișinău, which brought together around two hundred people. The assembly decided that the Orthodox Church in Bessarabia should become "autonomous" while, at the same time, retain its link with the Russian Orthodox Church; in addition, all parishes were allowed to hold services only in the Moldovan language.

The establishment of the Moldovan Diet (*Sfatul Țării*), the executive political body of Bessarabia, led to the declaration of March 27, 1918, of unification with Greater Romania. Metropolitan Anastasie Gribanovski (1915–18), who had initially been proposed to become a member of the Bucharest Holy Synod, left the country and took charge of the Russian Orthodox Church outside Russia (the Karlovci Synod). On June 23, 1918, the Romanian representative, Bishop Nicodim Munteanu of Huși, arrived in Chișinău and took over the church, ensuring its incorporation into the structures of the Romanian Orthodox Church.[140]

Orthodoxy and the "Sacred Unity" of Romanians

The dissolution of the Russian Empire in October 1917, the end of the First World War, and the appeal of Emperor Charles I of Habsburg to his "loyal people" in October 1918 hastened the redefinition of the international system with the creation of the League of Nations and the redrawing of European borders. The Kingdom of Romania found itself in a difficult situation as most of its territory was occupied by German forces. On May 7, 1918, in order to end the war in its country, the Romanian government signed a Peace Treaty with the Central Powers in Bucharest, transforming Romania into an economic satellite of Germany. The signing of the armistice at Compiègne on November 11, 1918, between the Allies and Germany, marking the end of military hostilities would also affect Romania.[141]

On April 9, 1918, the Moldovan Diet in Chișinău decided to unite the Democratic Republic of Bessarabia with Romania, and now, with German forces retreating, the Romanian government felt that there was a unique moment to achieve the national dream: the unification of all Romanians into one state. On November 28, 1918, the Romanian National Council of Bukovina declared its union with Romania, and, on December 1, 1918, over 100,000 people from all parts of Transylvania and Banat attended the Grand National Assembly of Alba Iulia, asking for unification.[142]

During the Paris Peace Conference that followed the end of the First World War, Hungary withdrew its troops from Transylvania; however, in July 1919, its army re-crossed the border and attempted to regain its former territory. Romania's counter-offensive resulted in the defeat of Hungary, and the occupation of Budapest from August until November 1919. Romania promoted its political interests by combining extensive lobbying in the European capitals with military achievements, and, from this position, on December 9, 1919, signed the Peace Treaties of Saint-Germain and Neuilly with Austria and Bulgaria. Shortly thereafter, on December 29, 1919, the Romanian Parliament passed laws ratifying the union of Bukovina, Bessarabia, Transylvania and Banat with Romania. Thus, at the end of 1919, the country had new geographical and population configurations with its territory more than doubled from 138,000 km^2

in 1915 to 295,049 km² in 1918. The 1899 census of the Old Kingdom showed Romania's population was composed of 5,956,690 people; with unification this figure reached around 14.7 million in 1919, and 18,057,028 in 1930.[143]

The Orthodox Church was a leading supporter of Romanian unity and many Romanian clergymen in neighboring territories were members of local assemblies that asked for unification. The position of the church was evident in the composition of the delegation from Transylvania and Banat that went to Bucharest after the assembly of Alba Iulia on December 1, 1918, handing the official proclamation of unification to King Ferdinand and the Romanian government. Bishop Miron Cristea of Caransebeş, who led the four-member delegation, recorded in a letter dated December 5, 1918, to Metropolitan Pimen of Moldavia his thoughts after meeting the king in Bucharest: "We have bowed our motherland to his Majesty King Ferdinand, now the king of all Romanians. The king's eyes were filled with the holy tears of joy. . . . I have lived here the most glorious days in the history of our nation."[144] After territorial unification, on April 23, 1919, the church in Transylvania declared itself to be part of the Holy Synod in Bucharest. On May 28, 1919, at Câmpia Turzii, in a symbolic gesture signifying the unity of Romanians from these new territories with those of the Old Kingdom, the king and government went to the grave of Michael the Brave, the first ruler who, for a short time, had united all Romanian provinces. Bishop Cristea led the religious service of commemoration, and in his speech drew a parallel between King Ferdinand and Michael the Brave:

> The earth of his body [Michael the Brave] is moving today, feeling how Your Majesty, as a good Romanian and Christian, came with your adored Queen and the enthusiasm of all Romanians . . . and the soul of the Great Voivode is happy in the sky seeing that Your Majesty as a second Michael, did not stop your army at Turda . . . but continued victorious until [the river] Tisa, achieving his and our boldest dreams.[145]

Bishop Cristea suggested a direct link between the glorious past of Romanians and the new political situation after unification. King Ferdinand was the first leader chosen by God's providence since Michael the Brave to unite all Romanians while, by claiming that the "soul of the Great Voivode is happy in the sky," the bishop emphasized the idea that past rulers were acting as protectors of the unified Romania's future. The nationalist discourse of Bishop Cristea was continued by King Ferdinand on November 21, 1919, who, in his address at the opening of the first Parliament of Greater Romania, stated: "Today more than ever, the sacred unity of all Romanians who love their country is necessary for the solution of internal and external problems."[146] Thus, the unification of the country achieved a "sacred" character, which it was the "sacred" duty of Romanians to preserve.

The Orthodox Church was perceived by the government as an extremely important part of Romanian national identity in the construction of the state, and it needed to be properly represented in the new political context. Because of collaboration with Germany during the First World War, on December 1, 1919, Primate Metropolitan Arămescu-Donici was forced to resign. On December 29, 1919, only two days after the ratification by parliament of the union of Bukovina, Bessarabia, Transylvania, and Banat with Romania, the Electoral Collegium chose Bishop Miron Cristea as Primate Metropolitan of Romania with 435 votes out of 447.[147] Romanians now not only had a unified country but also a spiritual leader who, coming from a previously occupied territory, represented all of those who before 1918 were under different political authorities. The Primate Metropolitan's position was endorsed by the king who on January 1, 1920, claimed at his official enthronement that "you have the beautiful mission to realize the religious politics of Michael the Brave."[148] As Primate Metropolitan, Miron Cristea continued the tradition of his predecessors in supporting the political regime.[149] On March 11, 1920, the church issued a statement in support of the government, asking the clergy to help the state financially by encouraging the faithful to buy bonds.[150] In this way, the clergy acted as agents of the state, carrying its message directly to the people.

With territorial enlargement, the Orthodox Church reformed its structure. In its reorganization, the church incorporated elements of national identity indicating a special relationship between divinity and Romanian history. This type of discourse that asserted the prime position of national elements would form the basis of the writings of Romanian intellectuals in the 1930s. In a booklet on the "Fundamental Principles for the United Organization of the Romanian Orthodox Church," Primate Metropolitan Cristea pointed out, firstly, that the church should continue to be autocephalous and independent from foreign jurisdiction.[151] Secondly, in his view, the church should be declared the National Church of the Romanian State as the Orthodox faith was part of the Romanian "soul."[152] He suggested renaming some Romanian metropolitanates to make connections with symbolic elements in the country's national history: the Metropolitanate of Bukovina acquired the title "of Suceava" and the Bishopric of Cluj was renamed the "Bishopric of Cluj, Feleac, and Vad" because Stephen the Great had his capital in Suceava and had established a bishopric in Vad.[153] Moreover, Primate Metropolitan Cristea emphasized that the church would always be a "Romanian, national and patriotic church" and "[its] interests would never be in conflict with the purest interests of the state and of the Romanian people."[154] Referring to the position of the clergy, Primate Metropolitan Cristea stated that they should have a stronger position in society and be regarded as equal to civil servants although the structure of the church differed from that of the state administration. In his opinion, "The church is not a democratic institution. It is based on a superior authority, on the corner stone, on Christ. The Christological principle is at the foundation of the church . . . the clergy and bishops should not have fewer rights than their equals in lay, democratic administration."[155] Setting out the role of the church in Romania, the Primate Metropolitan claimed that "the church raises its citizens in faith and morality, in fidelity to the throne and motherland, in patriotism and love, for sacrifice, for the general good, in obedience toward the authorities, in respect toward Constitution and laws, in love of order and fulfillment of all Christian and citizenship virtues; the church exerts charitable acts in asylums, orphanages and other institutes. Finally the church prays for everything and everybody."[156]

In this way, he combined traditional religious values with patriotic duties, referring to "faith and morality" alongside the "motherland," "patriotism," and "obedience toward the authorities." He argued that the church not only had a religious but also a political role to play in society as part of the newly enlarged state.

The king was perceived not only as the elected ruler of Romanians but also as the head of state with divine qualities and his presence at religious ceremonies endorsed the status of the church. The combination of Orthodoxy and politics was particularly evident during Easter when the king blessed the people,[157] and also during the most important religious festivals when students participated in compulsory religious ceremonies.[158] After the First World War, various societies were established with the support of the church. The most important was the National Orthodox

Society of Romanian Women (*Societatea Ortodoxă Națională a Femeilor Române*), whose main purpose was "the development of culture and the education of Romanian children from a national and religious perspective according to patriotic interests."[159] The society campaigned to build a symbolic church, "the Church of the People," dedicated to those who fought in the war;[160] after nineteen years of work, this was achieved at Mărășești, the battlefield of the most dramatic Romanian military resistance.

The climax of Romanian unity was displayed in a combination of religious and political festivities on October 15, 1922, when King Ferdinand was enthroned at Alba Iulia as King of Greater Romania. He was crowned in Transylvania, rather than in the Old Kingdom, in a symbolic gesture of unity with the new territories. In his speech, the king declared that Romania was a nation blessed by God's grace and referred to the enlargement of the country in terms confirming its long temporal significance rather than simply as a result of recent politics:

> Through the grace of God and national will I have inherited the Crown of Romania after the glorious reign of the Founding King [Carol I]. Coming to the throne I asked the Heavens to help the unceasing work that I decided to devote to my beloved country, as a good Romanian and king. The divine grace blessed us and through the strength of the people and the victory of our soldiers gave us the possibility of enlarging the borders of the kingdom and realizing the longing of ancient times of our nation.[161]

The ceremonies represented an orchestrated combination of Orthodox and political messages, using religion to reinforce national politics. Making a connection between "the divine grace" and "the longing of ancient times of our nation," the king suggested that he received the crown with divine help. The church hierarchy endorsed his speech by reiterating the notion of divine participation: "Glory to God in highest heaven, and on earth his peace for men on whom his favor rests. That God blessed his people, his people. Today is the greatest day of joy of Romanians."[162]

"The greatest day of joy" when "God blessed his people" indicated a special relationship between the Orthodox Church and the political regime. Not only was the king sacrosanct but the whole nation was presented as divinely protected, with the enthronement day as the culmination of the "longing" of centuries. The ceremonies combined extensive references to the religious and national past of Romanians, during which the church hierarchs made comparisons with Christ and the Virgin Mary as those who enthroned and protected the monarchy.[163] As the ceremony suggested, the Romanian government and the church hierarchy worked closely together. With the active participation of the church, the government wanted to ensure the support of Romanians from all of the new territories. In this way, the ceremony demonstrated that, despite being imported from a non-Orthodox country, the church had "nativized" the monarch, who had thus acquired divine qualities. The Romanian monarchy was similar in grandeur to that of the Byzantine Empire and the nation was "chosen" by God.

The establishment of Greater Romania represented an important change in the religious composition of the country. The Orthodox Church remained dominant but its faithful dropped from 91.5 percent of the population in 1899 to 72.6 in 1930. The second most important confession in the country was the Greek Catholic Church with 7.9 percent followed by the Roman Catholic Church, which grew from 2.5 in 1899 to 6.8 percent in 1930. Other major religions confessions were the Jewish Community with 4.2 percent, the Reformed Calvinist Church with 3.9 percent and the Lutheran Church with 2.2 percent of the population.[164] The 1923 Constitution declared the Romanian Orthodox Church as the "dominant" church of the state but also offered the Greek Catholic Church an honorific first place among other religions (Article 22).

After 1918, relations between the Orthodox and the Greek Catholics became tense and conflict arose based on the financial and political positions of their churches. The Orthodox hierarchs were concerned that the Greek Catholic Church would attract their faithful to Catholicism. In a book published in Arad in 1923 that presented data from 1910 from Hungarian sources, the author, signed only as "a man of the church," argued that the Roman Catholic Church in Hungary numbered 9,010,305 people, which represented 49.5 percent of all religions in the country. The Roman Catholics possessed 88 percent of the land of all religious confessions representing one land unit for six people. The Greek Catholic Church numbered 1,900,000 people and seven people had one land unit. Other religious confessions were dispersed as follows: the Unitarian Church numbered 74,245 people and seventy-eight people had one land unit; the Reformed Church, 2,603,381 people and eighty-nine people had one unit land; the Lutheran Church, 1,306,384 people and 325 people had one land unit. The Orthodox Church numbered 2,339,979 people, representing 13.1 percent of all religious confessions in Hungary and 115 people had one land unit. However, the Orthodox faithful in Hungary was divided between the Serbian Orthodox Church and the Romanian Orthodox Church. The Serbs numbered 454,431 people and twenty-four people had one land unit, but the Romanians accounted for 1,798,669 people and 1,777 people had one land unit. The author concluded that the huge discrepancy in land possession between the religious confessions was aimed at attracting the Romanian population to Catholicism or to the Greek Catholic Church. Although the author was anonymous, his argument was shared by the Orthodox Church as his findings were published in the church's main journal, *Biserica Ortodoxă Română* (the Romanian Orthodox Church).[165]

Political debates in the Romanian Parliament on the status of religions in Romania led to dissatisfaction among Orthodox hierarchs. The signing of the Concordat with the Vatican in Rome on May 10, 1927, and the new general law of religious confessions in 1928, which offered a better status for other churches and religions, were viewed by Orthodox hierarchs as threats to their spiritual authority. One Orthodox prelate even accused the politicians of being unaware that other religions were in fact "Trojan horses" of other states, which had the political intention of destabilizing the country and obliterating Romanian unity.[166]

The most representative religious dispute in parliamentary debates was between the Greek Catholic Church and the Orthodox Church, with each church claiming that it was the real protector of the Romanian faith.[167] The Greek Catholic Bishop Iuliu Hossu stated in parliament that "We brought [to the people in Transylvania] national awakening by preserving the Latin soul of Romanians . . . [and] unity with Rome was made by faith." The Orthodox reaction was expressed by Bishop Lucian Triteanul who responded rhetorically, "Which faith? Did the Orthodox Church not have the ecumenical faith that was above that of Rome?"[168]

Political leaders were interested in church affairs throughout the interwar period. Political pressure on the church was evident when the Holy Synod agreed to incorporate elements that seemed to modernize it and to offer the country a civilized image in Europe. After attending a Pan-Orthodox Conference in Constantinople in the previous year, on October

1, 1924, the Holy Synod decided to adopt the Julian calendar, maintaining only the date of Easter with other Orthodox countries that had not yet converted.[169] The church hierarchy presented the decision to adopt the new calendar not only as a religious necessity, but also due to the fact that the other Christian confessions celebrated the same festivals but on different days. Consequently people were confused and refused to work on festival days according to both calendars.[170]

The political transformation in the Balkans after the war between Greece and Turkey gave Romania a new position. In 1923, when the Treaty of Lausanne was signed by Greece and Turkey, the Romanian government took advantage of its historical connections with the Ecumenical Patriarchate in Constantinople. During the process of negotiating the treaty, Romania, which enjoyed good relations with both countries, asked Turkey to ensure that the transfer of population stipulated in the treaty would not lead to the abolishment of the Ecumenical Patriarchate.[171] Romania's stance on this cause would soon be rewarded as other Orthodox churches would regard the country as a main protector of its faith. Furthermore, the growing Romanian influence in the Orthodox world was recognized by the 1924 visit of Patriarch Damian of Jerusalem to Bucharest. The patriarch urged the government and the church hierarchy to help financially his churches and monasteries in holy places.

Romania was regarded as one of the most important actors both within and outside the Orthodox commonwealth because it had the largest number of faithful that professed their religion freely. The largest Orthodox Church was the Russian; however, after the October 1917 Revolution it suffered major persecution, while since 1878 the Bulgarian Orthodox Church had been in prolonged conflict with the Ecumenical Patriarchate over its jurisdictional independence. The Romanian government and the church hierarchy took advantage of these international circumstances. A particular opportunity was offered by the fact that in 1925 the Patriarchate of Jerusalem celebrated the 1,600th anniversary of the First Ecumenical Council. There were various voices in the Romanian Orthodox Church and in the parliament claiming that the church should attend the celebrations but in a higher position than that of a simple autocephalous church. In addition, in 1917 the communist authorities in Russia re-established its patriarchate, and in 1920 the Serbians, with a population of only seven million, acted similarly. In order to raise internationally the status of Romanian Orthodoxy, the Holy Synod officially proposed on February 4,

1925, that the Romanian Orthodox Church should acquire the status of patriarchate. By obtaining this title, it would be considered equal to other patriarchate sees and the country's position in the region increased. The proposal was supported by the parliament (*Legea pentru ridicarea scaunului archiepiscopal și metropolitan al Ungrovlahiei, ca primat al României, la rangul de Scaun patriarhal*), which sent a letter to all other Orthodox churches informing them of its decision.

Rather promptly, and recognizing the Romanian government's support of the Ecumenical Patriarchate's place in Constantinople, on July 30, 1925, the Ecumenical Patriarch Basil II gave his *Tomos* of recognition. The religious ceremonies for Patriarch Miron Cristea's enthronement took place on November 1, 1925, and were attended by representatives of other religious confessions in Romania and the patriarchates of Constantinople, Jerusalem, Serbia, Greece, Bulgaria, Poland, and of the Russian diaspora. The patriarch's enthronement mirrored that of the king three years earlier. After King Ferdinand gave the pastoral staff as the symbol of his new authority, Miron Cristea stated that the new mission of the church was to make "our country a model for the state and a blossoming field of all Christian virtues: a Christian, happy Romania."[172] The king showed his close support for the patriarchate and presented his version of national history, referring to the role of the church in the past:

> From the time of the Basarabs and Musats, founders of the country, who established the everlasting Metropolitanates of Wallachia and Moldavia, there was no such glorious page in the history of the Romanian Orthodox Church as that of this year by raising the Primate Metropolitan of Romania to patriarch. National history has proved that for us, Romanians, the nation and religion have always been connected. The church was founded slowly in the shadow of the forests, with the formation of language, of nationality and of the state. The state grew together with the church.[173]

After obtaining Romanian autocephaly the establishment of the Romanian Patriarchate was the most important religious event for the country and represented the climax of the church's support for Romanian nationalism. The king indicated that the church was closely connected with the Romanian language and nationality, and was part of the state's development. According to his view, because of the intrinsic relationship between church, state, nationality, and language, the Romanians were a nation.

His discourse reflected the widespread view that only close cooperation between the religious and political spheres in society could lead to the unity and progress of the Romanian nation.[174]

Conclusion

Located at the crossroads of the Russian, Ottoman, and Austrian empires, Romanian communities shared a similar feature, namely the search for recognition as a nation. Local Orthodox communities that had Wallachian, Moldavian, Transylvanian, and Bukovinian ethnic characters found themselves as part of a Romanian Orthodox Church.

From the first signs of church recognition of the idea of the nation at the beginning of the nineteenth century, when the Wallachian metropolitan left in his will a number of scholarships for "the support of the nation," to the proclamation of the Romanian Orthodox Church as a patriarchate in 1925 following the political unification of all Romanian-speaking territories, the church was gradually influenced by nationalism. Before the 1859 unification of Wallachia and Moldavia, the Orthodox churches in these principalities were in conflict with their Greek-appointed hierarchs and clergy. The church was one of the largest land owners, and a significant proportion of its revenue went to the dedicated monasteries abroad. The building of a national identity across both principalities entailed the mobilization of the local population against the Greek presence and strengthened the national character of the Wallachian and Moldavian Churches. Political unification was soon followed by the integration of religious structures present in both principalities into a unified national Romanian Church.

The national character of the church was achieved through a number of factors that replaced the Wallachian and Moldavian identities with that of a unified Romanian nation. First, the presence of hierarchs in the highest metropolitan seats who felt at ease moving from one diocese to another, demonstrated not only the religious unity of the country but also a common ethnic allegiance. An example of this was Metropolitan Gavriil Bănulescu-Bodoni who briefly ruled not only Wallachia and Moldavia but later moved to Bessarabia. Second, the stability that resulted from hierarchical positions being held for a long period of time in a principality benefited the development of a national identity. For example, when Russian missionaries visited the Moldavian Church under the leadership of Metropolitan Veniamin Costachi, who held one of the longest offices of the church, attempting to bring it under the jurisdiction of the Russian Orthodox Church, they faced the opposition of the local population. Similarly, after Bessarabia was occupied by Russian troops, a significant part of the population decided to emigrate to Moldavia, which prompted the Bessarabian hierarchs to comfort the faithful promising that their new authorities would allow religious and political leaders from "their own people."

The development of a national identity in the Principality of Moldavia led to the first declaration of an "independent (autocephalic) and orthodox Church of Moldo-Roumania" on December 20, 1857, two years before the political unification of Wallachia and Moldavia. The declaration of autocephaly was possible due to close relations between the religious and political fields and would become the model for achieving the independence of the Romanian Orthodox Church.

If in 1859 the first Romanian Prince of the united principalities, Alexandru Ioan Cuza, had to convince the European powers that the populations of Wallachia and Moldavia were one nation, the subsequent monarchical regimes ensured that this united Romanian identity was built on the substratum of the dominant religion. The political use of the Romanian Orthodox Church in the construction of the nation-state was clearly asserted from the first years of the Principalities of Wallachia and Moldavia when Prince Cuza founded a church synod and appointed loyal religious hierarchs. The state needed the church as an ally in its institutional design especially because it supported an ethnic version of the nation before the incorporation of neighboring regions. After the rule of Prince Cuza, politicians understood that by controlling the church hierarchy they would have the support of the church and of the Romanian faithful.

The church played a strong nationalist role not only in the united principalities but also in the neighboring regions. The Romanian population of Transylvania belonged in almost equal proportions to the Orthodox Church and the Greek Catholic Church, both of which were perceived by the local population as indissolubly tied to their national identity. At the 1848 Blaj assemblies, which brought together representatives from throughout Transylvania, both Orthodox and Greek Catholic confessions worked together for the cause of the Romanian nation. By doing so, hierarchs were not attempting religious reunification but sought a common voice to achieve the political recognition of the Romanian nation. In Bukovina, after the Austrian military occupation at the end of the eighteenth century, the identity of the Romanian population was challenged by the growing presence of Ruthenians; however, both Romanians and Ruthenians preserved their ethnic identity on religious lines as part of a unified local Orthodox Church. A similar situation occurred in Bessarabia. After the 1812 incorporation of the region into the Russian Empire, the church preserved the ethnic identity of the local population mainly through education. Mandatory Russian classes imposed by the government had little effect at the grass-root level. The Moldovan lower clergy regarded the preservation of their language and common religion as key elements in retaining links with Romanians living in the Old Kingdom. Despite having Russian-appointed hierarchs, the significance of ethnic mobilization in Bessarabia was evident during the rise of the Inochentist fundamentalist movement that united Moldovan communities.

The fall of the Russian and Austro-Hungarian empires and the redesign of the map of Southeastern Europe led to the establishment of Greater Romania in 1918, which brought together all provinces with a majority Romanian-speaking population. The new state represented a challenge for political and religious leaders as both the church and the regime sought ways of extending their influence in society. The Romanian Orthodox Church followed the Şagunian, Transylvanian, model of church-state relations, which gave laymen a voice in the running of the church. The church became closer to the people however in many cases laymen were politically influenced in the election of a party-favored candidate to an ecclesiastical seat.

Throughout the nineteenth century, Romanians searched for the recognition of their national identity, and for this reason, the nationalism promoted by the church was closely connected to that of the state. The church and the state became engaged in winning the soul of the masses as evident in the discourses of religious and political leaders. By appropriating nationalism to its core, ultimately, the church had a prime voice in the political evolution of the state.

List of Hierarchs and Metropolitans

Wallachia (Metropolitanate of Wallachia or Hungaro-Wallachia)
Dositei (Filitti), 1793–1810
Gavriil (Bănulescu-Bodoni), 1808–1812
Ignatie (Babalos), 1810–1812
Nectarie, 1812–1819
Dionisie (Lupu), 1819–1821
Grigorie (Dascălul), 1823–1829; 1833–1834
Neofit, 1840–1849
Nifon Sevastias, 1850–1875, Primate Metropolitan after 1865
Calinic (Miclescu), Primate Metropolitan 1875–1886
Iosif (Gheorghian), Primate Metropolitan 1886–1893
Ghenadie (Petrescu), Primate Metropolitan 1893–1896
Iosif (Gheorghian), Primate Metropolitan 1896–1909
Athanasie (Mironescu), Primate Metropolitan 1909–1911
Conon (Arămescu-Donici), Primate Metropolitan 1912–1919
Miron (Cristea), Primate Metropolitan 1919–1925, Patriarch 1925–1939

Moldavia (Metropolitanate of Moldavia)
Iacob (Stamati), 1792–1803
Veniamin (Costachi), 1803–1808
Gavriil (Bănulescu-Bodoni), 1808–1812
Veniamin (Costachi), 1812–1821; 1823–1842
Meletie (Lefter), 1844–1848
Sofronie (Miclescu), 1851–1860
Calinic (Miclescu), 1865–1875
Iosif (Naniescu), 1875–1902
Partenie (Clinceni), 1902–1910
Pimen (Georgescu), 1909–1934
Nicodim (Munteanu), 1935–1939, Patriarch 1939–1949

Transylvania (Metropolitanate of Transylvania after 1864)
Gherasim (Adamovici), Bishop 1789–1796 (under the jurisdiction of the Karlovci Metropolitanate)
Vasile (Moga), Bishop 1810–1845 (under the jurisdiction of the Karlovci Metropolitanate)

Andreiu (Şaguna), Bishop 1846–1864, Metropolitan 1864–
1873; Autocephalous Church after 1864
Procopie (Ivaşcovici), Metropolitan 1873–1874
Miron (Romanul), Metropolitan 1874–1898
Ioan (Meţianul), Metropolitan 1898–1916
Vasile (Mangra), Metropolitan 1916–1918

Bukovina (Metropolitanate of Bukovina and Dalmatia after 1873)
Dosoftei (Herescu), Bishop of Rădăuţi 1750–1783 (under the jurisdiction of the Metropolitanate of Moldavia), Bishop of Bukovina 1783–1789 (under the jurisdiction of the Karlovci Metropolitanate)
Daniil (Vlahovici), Bishop 1789–1822 (under the jurisdiction of the Karlovci Metropolitanate)
Isaia (Baloşescu), Bishop 1823–1834 (under the jurisdiction of the Karlovci Metropolitanate)
Eugenie (Hacman), Bishop 1835–1873, Metropolitan 1873; Autocephalous Church after 1873
Teofil (Bandella), Metropolitan 1873–1875
Teoctist (Blajevici), Metropolitan 1877–1879
Silvestru (Morariu-Andrievici), Metropolitan 1880–1895
Arcadie (Ciupercovici), Metropolitan 1896–1902
Vladimir (Repta), Metropolitan 1902–1924

Bessarabia (Eparchy of Chişinău and Hotin under the jurisdiction of the Russian Orthodox Church)
Gavriil (Bănulescu-Bodoni), 1813–1821
Dimitrie (Sulima), 1821–1844
Irinarh (Popov) 1844–1858
Antonie (Sokotov), 1858–1871
Pavel (Lebedev), 1871–1882
Serghie (Leapidevski), 1882–1891
Isakie (Polokenski), 1891–1892
Neofit (Nevodcikov), 1892–1898
Iacov (Peatnitki), 1898–1904
Vladimir (Sinikovski), 1904–1908
Serafim (Ciceagov), 1908–1914

Platon (Rojdestvenski), 1914–1915
Anastasie (Gribanovski), 1915–1918

Dobrudja (Bishopric of Lower Danube under the jurisdiction of the Metropolitanate of Moldavia)
Melchisedec (Ștefănescu), Bishop 1864–1879
Iosif (Gheorghian), Bishop 1879–1886
Partenie (Clinceni), Bishop 1886–1902
Pimen (Georgescu), Bishop 1902–1909
Nifon (Niculescu), Bishop 1909–1922

CHAPTER

6

THE BULGARIAN ORTHODOX CHURCH

Daniela Kalkandjieva

The Bulgarian Orthodox Church is one of a number of Southeastern European churches that played a significant role in the formation of the country's national identity. The relationship of the Bulgarian Church with nationalism in the Ottoman period differs from that of the other Orthodox churches in the Balkans. This specificity was an outcome of the delayed institutional establishment of the Bulgarian Church, which was founded in 1870 as an exarchate, by a special decree of the Ottoman sultan. Until then Bulgarians were under the jurisdiction of the Patriarchate of Constantinople—a canonical institution that fully corresponded to their Orthodox faith, but was not their national church. This was at the time when the Serbian and the Romanian Churches were already established. In this sense, the advent of nationalism and its early development in the Bulgarian lands was not assisted by a national church institution as it was elsewhere. The absence of such a body in Bulgarian society before 1870 raises questions about the forces that promoted the ethno-religious nationalism of the Bulgarian Orthodox Church demonstrated after the Liberation of Bulgaria (1878). In a search for answers to these questions, this chapter focuses on the ways in which religion and ethnicity gave shape to the agencies of nationalism in pre-1870 Bulgarian society.

The Bulgarian case needs some preliminary clarifications concerning the term "Bulgarian Orthodox Church," which is widely used in Bulgarian historiography as a notion that de facto embraces several historical entities: the Bulgarian archbishopric (870–927);[1] the Bulgarian Patriarchate (927–1018) of which the headquarters, initially situated in Preslav, were moved to Ohrid on the eve of the Byzantine conquest of the First Bulgarian State (1018); the Patriarchate of Tûrnovo (1235–1393),[2] abolished at the end of the fourteenth century; the Bulgarian Exarchate (1870–1953) and the present day Patriarchate of Bulgaria proclaimed in May 1953.[3] All of these religious bodies are regarded as consecutive successors of the one Bulgarian Orthodox Church. This approach stems from their historical development, closely linked to that of the Bulgarian people, its culture and language as well as political history of the country.[4] At the same time, this approach neglects the ruptures in history, thereby impeding critical analysis of these bodies. To this list of church structures, Bulgarian historiography adds the Archbishopric of Ohrid that was joined to the Second Bulgarian State as a second Orthodox church, next to the Patriarchate of Tûrnovo, by Tsar Ivan Asen II (1218–41).[5]

Although the adjective "Orthodox" in the discussed term correctly describes the present-day national church, it hides potential problems. Sometimes it is applied to the church history of Bulgaria without distinguishing between the original theological meaning of the concept of Orthodoxy and the post-1054 notion of Orthodoxy as an anti-Catholic and even as an anti-western Christian denomination. In such accounts, the name "Bulgarian Orthodox Church" implies that Bulgarians have always been anti-Catholic and anti-western. This approach enhances the ethno-religious orientation of Bulgarian nationalism and colors all non-Orthodox religious communities negatively.

The adjective "Bulgarian" also provokes concerns, especially among theologians. According to Orthodox ecclesiology, canonical churches are organized on a territorial principle, rather than that of *ethno-phyletism*. Therefore, names such as Bulgarian or Greek Orthodox Church incite sharp criticism among many Orthodox ecclesiologists, who would prefer the term "the Orthodox Church in Bulgaria" or "the Orthodox Church in Greece." This position is not shared by historians who cannot neglect the fact that names such as "the Bulgarian Orthodox Church" have been recorded in archival sources and so reflect past realities. This divergence between the theological and historiographical approaches to the name of one or another Orthodox Church often flares up in heated debates between the representatives of the two disciplines. To avoid this type of misunderstanding, the analysis in this chapter is limited to the sphere of the historiographical debate on the Bulgarian Orthodox Church and nationalism in the nineteenth century, in other words, debates in which the church is largely discussed as a historical institution.

Bulgarians as Part of the *Rum Millet*, 1393–1870: A Nation without Its Own Church

During the fourteenth century the Second Bulgarian State[6] experienced political instability that brought about its split into new political entities, mainly comprising the Kingdom of Tûrnovo and the Kingdom of Vidin. Soon afterwards the territorial jurisdiction of the Patriarchate of Tûrnovo was reduced to the borders of the corresponding kingdom, while the rulers of the other successor states of the Bulgarian Empire moved under that of the Patriarchate of Constantinople. Some western areas, previously controlled by the Bulgarian tsars, came under the rule of the Serbian kings and were subordinated to the Patriarchate of Ipek (or Peć in Serbian), while others were under the jurisdiction of the Archbishopric of Ohrid.[7] This political and ecclesiastical decomposition of the Bulgarian lands predetermined their destiny over the following centuries and facilitated their conquest by the Ottomans, who in 1393, took over the Kingdom of Tûrnovo and, three years later, that of Vidin. At the same time the Patriarchate of Tûrnovo, whose canonical authority had already diminished, lost its autocephalous status and soon disappeared from the ecclesiastical map of the Orthodox world.[8] Its flock was subordinated to the Great Church of Constantinople, which began to install its own bishops in the dioceses of the former Patriarchate of Tûrnovo. Thus, researchers have identified only a few Orthodox bishops of Bulgarian origin acting during the period from the beginning of the fifteenth century to the Crimean War (1853–56).[9] The introduction of a hierarchy of Greek origin in the Bulgarian lands had a two-fold effect on the local religious culture. It dealt a blow to the Bulgarian religious elite, while, at the same time, it changed the religious culture of Orthodox Bulgarians. The difficulty of communication between the Bulgarians and their foreign churchmen, who often did not speak the language of the flock and conducted the liturgy in Greek, made the former more attentive to the ritualistic rather than the theological aspects of Orthodoxy. Meanwhile, the other Orthodox nationalities in the Ottoman Empire were in a relatively better situation in being able to preserve both their native Orthodox hierarchy and their church institutions: Wallachians and Moldavians enjoyed the internal autonomy of their principalities as well as that of their metropolitanates, Greeks relied on the Patriarchate of Constantinople, while Serbs (although with some interruptions) came under the Patriarchate of Ipek.[10]

The *Rum Millet* system, introduced by the Ottomans in the conquered lands, radically changed the socio-religious status of Bulgarians. Together with the Greeks, Serbs and all other nationalities who belonged to Orthodoxy, they were included in the *Rum Millet* in which the Patriarch of Constantinople was recognized as the head of all Orthodox subjects of the sultan. Jews and Armenians were organized in their own *millets* on religious grounds.[11] As part of the ethnically divergent *Rum Millet*, Bulgarians experienced a process that may be defined as proto-secularization. The new Muslim rulers did away with the church-state unity that characterized the Balkan Orthodox states before their conquest and changed the nature of the Orthodox Church. Appointed as the leader of the Orthodox population in the Ottoman Empire, the Patriarch of Constantinople functioned not only as its religious supervisor but was also burdened by a series of secular duties. Under the Ottomans he became "a lay administrator, obliged to organize law-courts and fiscal services and to give directives on secular politics."[12] He was responsible for the loyalty of the Orthodox believers, ensuring that they respected "the Sultan's authority and abstained from disorders."[13] As a reward he was allowed to keep many of the privileges of the patriarchs of Constantinople from the Byzantine period. He was also able to plead for his adherents at the Sublime Porte. Meanwhile the new tasks of the Great Church of Constantinople required the appointment of laymen in administration, all of whom, however, had to be masters of Greek language and literacy. As a result, the non-Greek nationalities were de facto excluded from the religious and secular government of affairs of the *Rum Millet*. In the case of Bulgarians, who had neither their own church institution nor another body uniting them as a separate nationality, this situation brought about a shortage of a well-educated and experienced ecclesiastical and administrative elite.[14] From such a perspective, any statements concerning a nationalistic role of the Bulgarian Orthodox Church before the establishment of the exarchate in 1870 are highly questionable.

Thus, Bulgarian society lacked an institutional center of power that could coordinate its transformation into a modern nation when the ideas of modern nationalism penetrated the Balkans. The absence of its own church institution is the most pertinent feature that distinguishes early

Bulgarian nationalism from that of Greek, Serb, and Romanian. Its advance was additionally delayed by the social structure of Bulgarians. Studies on the first half of the nineteenth century reveal a tiny level of intelligentsia; researchers have registered for this period only nine Bulgarians with diplomas in medicine[15] and sixty-four teachers.[16] Insignificantly small was the number of Bulgarians who succeeded in being appointed to higher levels in the Ottoman administration.[17] In many cases, the same persons were listed in several groups, as physicians also worked as teachers or publishers and state officials as teachers and vice versa. According to estimates, over 60 percent of Bulgarian intelligentsia came from the families of craftsmen and retail tradesmen, about 30 percent from those of priests, teachers or artisans, while the rest were of peasant origin.[18] The level of literacy was correspondingly extremely low, estimated at 3.3 percent in 1880[19] when about 80 percent of the Bulgarian population was rural.[20]

Despite these adverse conditions, the seeds of the Bulgarian national awakening can be traced in the works of eighteenth century writers such as Christophor Zhefarovich, Father Spiridon of Gabrovo, and Father Paisii of Hiledar. Their texts developed an image of Bulgarians as a nation different from that of the other Orthodox people living under Ottoman rule by evoking memories of the glorious past when Bulgarians had their own state and church.[21] Exceptionally influential was the manuscript *Istoriya Slavyano-Bolgarskaya* (Slavonic-Bulgarian History) written by Father Paisii of Hiledar in 1762 and reproduced in hundreds of handwritten and printed copies in the period before the Liberation of Bulgaria (1878). Compared to his contemporary historiographers, he was the first author to define both the Ottoman Empire and the Patriarchate of Constantinople as the main enemies of the Bulgarians. At the same time, although Father Paisii regarded the Ottomans as the main obstacle on the road to political liberation, he considered the Patriarchate of Constantinople as a greater evil because it employed the Orthodox faith as a means of destruction of the national consciousness of his compatriots. According to Father Paisii, the patriarchate not only assisted in the subjection of Orthodox Bulgarians to the Ottomans, but endangered their existence as a separate nation with its own language and history by imposing the Greek liturgy in their churches and teaching their children only in Greek. He recognized that the high quality of the schools run by the patriarchate offered better prospects to their graduates for social and economic prosperity, but warned that the most frequent result of this education was a hellenization of the non-Greek pupils, which he considered dangerous for the formation of a Bulgarian national elite.

Among the most important factors that assisted in the survival of the self-consciousness of Bulgarians as a separate *narodnost,* or community of people united by their common language, ethnic origin, folk traditions, historical memories, and faith, were the Bulgarian monasteries. Although they were under the jurisdiction of the Patriarchate of Constantinople, their brotherhoods succeeded in preserving the liturgy in Church Slavonic.[22] These monasteries became the major centers of veneration of saints such as Saint Ivan of Rila and Saint Petka of Tûrnovo, who enjoyed great popularity among Bulgarians. By transmitting the lives of the saints from one generation to another through the cycle of religious feasts and commemorations, these monasteries protected the Bulgarian nationality from extinction. They also contributed to the self-consciousness of a Bulgarian identity through the scrupulous work of their monks who spent their lives copying medieval Bulgarian manuscripts, recording the historical experiences of their compatriots and maintaining "cell schools" where children learnt the Cyrillic alphabet, liturgical texts in Church Slavonic, and elementary mathematics.

In this way, the veneration of Bulgarian saints, the cell schools, the writings of Bulgarian monks, and the partially preserved Slavonic liturgy became major factors that kept alive the national memory of Bulgarians despite the absence of their own church institution or native Orthodox hierarchy. Petûr Nikov, one of the leading Bulgarian historians from the interwar period, suggested a conditional use of the term "the Bulgarian Orthodox Church" when referring to the period before 1870. According to Nikov, the term concerns only the community of Orthodox Bulgarians united by their common faith, language, Slavonic liturgy, veneration of Bulgarian saints, and the practicing of their folk traditions.[23] In the 1970s, Bulgarian communist historiography returned to this view and developed the thesis that the Bulgarian monasteries played an important role in the Ottoman age by preserving the national consciousness of Bulgarians.[24]

More recently, Svetlana Ivanova, a Bulgarian historian of the Ottoman period, has offered a new analysis of the pre-1870 status of Bulgarians in the Ottoman Empire, revealing that, despite their lack of official recognition as a separate nation, Bulgarians were distinguished as an ethnic group.[25] She points out that tax-registers from the seventeenth and the eighteenth century listed taxpayers from different towns and villages not only according to their faith but also by their ethnicity. In these documents, Bulgarians were mentioned on an equal footing with Serbs, Greeks, and other nationalities. These facts indicate that the Sublime Porte had no special policy aimed at the assimilation of Bulgarians. Moreover, by mentioning the ethnic status of Bulgarians, the Ottoman registers respected and retained their sense of belonging to a specific nationality.[26] Ivanova also suggests a link between the survival of national consciousness and the Ottoman system of government. By permitting a high number of laymen in the religious councils at both the parochial and diocesan levels, the Sublime Porte de facto guaranteed the participation of Bulgarians especially in the councils organized in their villages.[27] In the eighteenth century, an intensified migration of Bulgarians to the cities enabled them to become the majority in the eparchial councils too, thus ending their Greek dominance.

It was not only the Ottoman authorities but also the Patriarchate of Constantinople itself that recognized the ethnicity of Bulgarians in the period before the advent of nationalism. In a 1688 letter, the Patriarch of Constantinople appealed to the juvenile tsars of Russia Ivan and Peter (the future Peter the Great), to support the fight of the other Christian states against the Ottomans. In his letter, the patriarch mentioned Bulgarians as one of the Orthodox nations in the Balkans that had to be liberated together with the Orthodox Serbs, Wallachians, Moldovans, and Greeks.[28] The Russian ambassadors to Constantinople also distinguished Bulgarians from the other Balkan nationalities, one of whom, in 1735 reported to the government in St. Petersburg the willingness of Bulgarians and their Orthodox neighbors to support a new war against the Ottoman Empire.[29]

All of these facts demonstrate that the Bulgarian Revival was not a single act but a lengthy and complex process that brought about the restoration of the Bulgarian Church and state institutions in the late nineteenth century. One of the most studied aspects of the Bulgarian Revival is the National Church Movement (*tsŭrkovno-natsionalno dvizhenie*) (also known as the Bulgarian Church Movement) (1820–70), which determined the evolution of the national consciousness of modern Bulgarians by linking their sense of nationhood with the idea of church independence. Its sources and features will be discussed in three stages.

The Bulgarian Movement for a Native Hierarchy, 1820–1856

The first stage of the Bulgarian Church Movement was not inspired by an idea of establishing a national church, but by the appeal of having a native hierarchy. The movement emerged under the influence of a complex set of factors. The preserved ethnic identity of Bulgarians conditioned the rise of nationalism, but was not the only cause for it. To a great extent, its development on Bulgarian soil was influenced by the earlier advent of nationalism in neighboring Balkan lands. The uprisings of Serbs (1804 and 1815) and of Greeks and Romanians (1821) gave the impetus to Bulgarians to fight for their own political liberation from Ottoman rule, as did the Russian-Turkish wars in 1806–12, 1828–29 and 1853–56, when many Bulgarians joined the Russian army as volunteers. Meanwhile, the European revolutions of 1848 did not seem to have a direct impact on the Bulgarian national revival.[30] According to historiography, the Church Movement of Bulgarians was strongly influenced by the attempts of their Orthodox neighbors to establish state churches (as took place in the Kingdom of Greece in 1833) or to secure the independence of their existing ones (as was achieved by the autonomous rulers of Serbia after 1830 and of Romania after 1859). These developments shook the authority of the Patriarchate of Constantinople as the Ottoman institution responsible for the *Rum Millet* and incited Bulgarians to raise their own demands for a native hierarchy and Slavonic liturgy.[31]

The attempts of the Ottoman Empire to modernize itself through a series of reforms during the Tanzimat Age (1839–76) also facilitated the Bulgarian Revival. Communications in the Balkan provinces of the Empire were improved through the first railways, a system of new roads and bridges, and the introduction of telegraph services. The infrastructure of the main cities was developed by paving streets, opening hospitals, and developing public services.[32] These projects stimulated advances in industry, manufacturing, and trade. They also motivated many Bulgarians to move from the villages to the cities, a process that expanded the role of craftsmen and tradesmen in the local guilds and laid the grounds for a national petit bourgeoisie. The growing contribution of this new social class to the taxes levied by the Patriarchate of Constantinople on the Orthodox subjects of the sultan made its members sensitive to the ways in which their money was used. Under the influence of nationalism, Bulgarian craftsmen and tradesmen preferred to invest their income in the development of a network of modern schools where their children would be taught in their mother tongue and in the appointment of a native clergy able to serve the Slavonic liturgy. However, they were confronted by a different reality in which their taxes were used by the Patriarchate of Constantinople to support its own Greek hierarchy and to promote a Greek education and liturgy. Consequently, the Bulgarians rejected this policy and accused the patriarchate of attempting to hellenize them.[33]

This financial issue became of special importance for Bulgarians, whose church taxes increased between 1820 and 1870 due to a sharp decline in the income of the Patriarchate of Constantinople after the 1821 Greek uprising and soon afterwards when it lost control over its eparchies in the rebellious provinces, which constituted the free Greek Kingdom (1832). The union of Wallachia and Moldova into a single Romanian state in 1859 and the church reforms of Prince Alexandru Ioan Cuza in the 1860s delivered another blow to the financial resources of the Great Church of Constantinople[34] and Orthodox Bulgarians became its main taxpayers. Relations between the Bulgarians and the Great Church of Constantinople deteriorated as the patriarchal leadership tried to strengthen its control over the Bulgarian eparchies by promoting the idea of Great Greece (*Megali Idea*) and launching a systematic policy aimed at a hellenization of Bulgarians by banning the Slavonic liturgy and fighting the spread of Bulgarian schools and education. Meanwhile, the increased financial burden of higher taxes motivated Bulgarians to fight against the ecclesiastical monopoly of Constantinople. As a result, early Bulgarian nationalism was built on opposition to Greek dominance.

During the first stage of the Church Movement (1820–56) all dioceses in which Bulgarians were in the majority, were caught up in remonstrations against the local Greek bishops who were accused of the misuse of finances, corruption, and anti-Bulgarian activities, leading the laypeople en masse to demand the replacement of the culpable churchmen by Bulgarians whom they could trust.[35] The driving force of these protests was the Bulgarian guilds, the societies of craftsmen and tradesmen. Forming the most active economic class of Bulgarian society in the nineteenth century, this national petit bourgeoisie was very critical of the arbitrary increase of church taxes by the Patriarchate of Constantinople and wanted to know how its money was spent. With significant material, financial and human resources at their disposal these guilds became the main social force to challenge the Patriarchate of Constantinople. In addition, being located in the cities and connected through their business contacts, these guilds created a kind of national network able to influence the decisions of the Ottoman authorities.[36]

Another important player in the Church Movement was the Bulgarian Orthodox diaspora, whose contribution remains under-researched. Particularly important for the national Church Movement were the initiatives of the Bulgarian community in Odessa. One of its most influential personalities was Vasil Aprilov, who, in 1835, sponsored the establishment of the first modern Bulgarian school in Gabrovo, the city of his birth, where his compatriots were able to educate their children in accordance with the principles of modern learning and in their mother tongue. Aprilov also invested money in printing and distributing books on Bulgarian history and advised his compatriots living in the Ottoman Empire to fight for native bishops who would care more about the education and improvement of the Bulgarian youth. According to Aprilov, the Bulgarians had to cease paying taxes to the Patriarchate of Constantinople and to start utilizing the economized resources for the prosperity of their own nation.[37] In 1837, the leaders of the Bulgarian community in Odessa succeeded in persuading St. Petersburg to allow Bulgarian boys from the Ottoman territories to study in the Russian ecclesiastical seminaries and academies and in the following year, the Russian emperor gave stipends to three Orthodox Bulgarians to study theology. This practice assisted in the efforts of Bulgarians to free its future church elite from the hellenizing influence of the schools of the patriarchate in Constantinople.[38] Some of these Russian graduates dedicated their time to the research of medieval Bulgarian Church history. They included the founder of modern Bulgarian historiography, Professor Marin Drinov, who worked mainly in Russia,[39] and Father Natanail, who became the first Metropolitan of Ohrid (1872–78) appointed by the Bulgarian Exarchate that was set up in 1870.[40] During the Crimean War (1853–56) another representative of the Bulgarian diaspora in Russia, Nikola Palauzov, published selected medieval documents on the restoration of the Bulgarian Patriarchate by Tsar Ivan Asen II in 1235. By presenting academic arguments in favor of Bulgarian demands for ecclesiastical independence, these works helped to surmount the negative attitude of Russia and of her church leadership to the attempts to establish a Bulgarian Church that prevailed until the 1860s.[41]

A major problem for the Bulgarian Church Movement before the Crimean War (1853–56) was a lack of native bishops and metropolitans, and so the fight for a native hierarchy was initiated and run mostly by laymen. During the first stage of the national Church Movement, the Patriarchate of Constantinople turned aside all requests for the consecration of Bulgarian bishops. Meanwhile, in July 1845, on behalf of all Orthodox Bulgarians, two Bulgarian monks, Neofit Bozveli and Ilarion Makariopolski, who were recognized by their Orthodox compatriots as national church leaders, submitted a memorandum to the Sublime Porte. It included a request for control over the patriarchate's financial debts, the introduction of fixed salaries for its episcopate,[42] the appointment of bishops of Bulgarian origin for the dioceses where Bulgarians prevailed over the rest of the local Orthodox population, the appointment of three Bulgarian hierarchs as members of the Holy Synod in Constantinople, guarantees for the right of Bulgarians to elect and change their hierarchs without the patriarchate's intervention and without the sole permission of the Sublime Porte, as well as the appointment of four Bulgarian representatives at the Sublime Porte who would act as national negotiators.[43]

This initiative ended with the arrest of fathers Neofit Bozveli and Ilarion Makariopolski, who were sent in exile to the Holy Mount of Athos where the former died in 1848, while the latter was released five years later. Their arrest was made by the Ottoman authorities in response to a request by the Patriarchate of Constantinople and the intervention of Russia. The former needed its Bulgarian flock as a main source of income, while the latter considered the memorandum a threat to the unity of the Orthodox population in the Ottoman Empire, which it regarded as a major guarantee for its control over the Straits. St. Petersburg was able to exert additional pressure over the Sublime Porte thanks to its status as protector of the *Rum Millet*, obtained by the Russian emperor after his victory over the Ottomans in 1829. Therefore, when the patriarchate asked the Sublime Porte to arrest the Bulgarian monks Neofit and Ilarion as enemies of Russia, its request was satisfied.[44]

The failure of the memorandum made clear that the solution of the Bulgarian Church question should be sought in Constantinople and so the laymen leadership of the national Church Movement concentrated its efforts on turning this city into the center of its struggles. This plan was realized with the support of the twenty-four Bulgarian guilds in the Ottoman capital city, which gave the necessary financial, material, and moral support. In 1848 the Bulgarian community in Constantinople received permission from the Sublime Porte to build its own church where to serve the liturgy in Church Slavonic. A year later, it established a Bulgarian parish that took the lead of the national Church Movement.[45] In this way, the very notion of the parish was changed. If, within the *Rum Millet* system, the parish was a territorial unit, bringing together believers from the same confession regardless of their ethnicity, the Bulgarian parish in Constantinople was something new. Linked with the idea of nationhood, it became both an expression and a tool of the revived national self-consciousness of Orthodox Bulgarians.

Toward a Nation-Made Church, 1856–1860

The Crimean War (1853–56) changed the course of the Bulgarian Church Movement in many ways as it entered a new stage that bound its development with the fight of the Great Powers for influence over the Balkans and the Middle East. The defeat of Russia diminished her exclusive rights as a guardian of Eastern Orthodoxy in the Ottoman Empire, guaranteed by the Treaty of Kuchuk Kainarji (1774) and confirmed by that of Edirne (1829). It undermined the ability of St. Petersburg to utilize the confessional unity of the Orthodox population in the Balkans for its own political ends, while increasing the influence of the Western Great Powers and Western Christianity in the region. This new international situation had a two-fold effect on the Bulgarian Church Movement. On the one hand, Russia was not strong enough to defend the monopoly of the Patriarchate of Constantinople over the Orthodox Bulgarians, who received a real chance to regain independence of their church. On the other hand, the domination of Orthodoxy as the traditional faith of Bulgarians was shaken by the Protestant and Catholic missions that were allowed to spread their activities in the region.[46] This development burdened the solution of the Bulgarian Church question with the old rivalry between the Orthodox East and the Catholic West. In this way, the Bulgarian fight for church independence from the Patriarchate of Constantinople exceeded its national and canonical dimensions and became an issue of transnational and interdenominational significance.

In domestic terms, the Crimean War assisted in the solution of the Bulgarian Church question by changing the overall political climate of the Ottoman Empire. In 1856, the sultan issued the *Hatt-i Humayun*, a decree that introduced the principle of national self-identification and proclaimed the equality of all nationalities inhabiting his Empire. It allowed a transformation of the old *Rum Millet* system, from confessional to national grounds, thus assisting the progress of Bulgarian nationalism.[47] The newly granted rights made it possible for Bulgarians to establish their own national, municipal, and village councils responsible for their local self-government without the consent of the Church of Constantinople. According to the *Hatt-i Humayun*, the permission of the Ottoman authorities was enough for their creation. Therefore, once registered, the Bulgarian councils for local self-government began to act independently from the patriarchate. These new councils were also beneficial for the Sublime Porte in securing the regular levy of taxes, observance of the law, and public order in the Bulgarian areas. At the same time, they undermined the grounds on which the Patriarchate of Constantinople claimed the right to administrate Orthodox Bulgarians and to collect church taxes from them. All of this put under question the belonging of Bulgarians to the *Rum Millet* and the idea of a Bulgarian *millet* came into existence. With their own bodies of self-government, Bulgarians received the opportunity to run their local schools and parochial churches independently from the Patriarchate of Constantinople. Now they were free to appoint not only teachers but also parochial priests. Only purely religious issues such as the consecrations of bishops and the ordaining of priests remained the patriarchate's prerogative.[48] The new municipal and village councils had also the right to solve family issues such as wedding contracts, testaments, and property transfer as well as to observe the community's morale.[49] As a result, the patriarchate lost the means to impede the drive of Bulgarians to teach their children in their native language and to use the Slavonic liturgy in their parishes. Nevertheless, until the schism of 1872, it was able to control the number of higher and ordinary clerics of Bulgarian origin.

The adoption of the *Hatt-i Humayun* changed the aims of the Bulgarian Church Movement[50] as previous demands for a native hierarchy were expanded by a plea for church autonomy. In 1856, upon its establishment, the Bulgarian municipal council in Constantinople went to the sultan with a petition to grant limited national autonomy to his 6,400,000 Bulgarian subjects.[51] It requested the appointment of two native Bulgarians, one of whom would deal with the church affairs of his Orthodox compatriots with the other responsible for civil matters.[52] Although this appeal was rejected, its authors were not persecuted, and their example was followed by that of other Bulgarian municipalities, which dispatched similar requests to the Sublime Porte. In addition, the major municipalities elected special representatives who were sent to Constantinople with the task of working to establish an autonomous Bulgarian Church. During a short period of time, over sixty delegates arrived in Constantinople where they set up a kind of parliament at the local Bulgarian municipality. The slow advance of the church question did not allow most of them to stay in the city until the ultimate solution of the problem. Therefore, those who had to return home authorized representatives of the Bulgarian guilds in Constantinople to act temporary as their deputies.[53] For the first time since the end of the fourteenth century, Bulgarians had their own institutional center of power, which would coordinate their struggles for church autonomy and national emancipation over the following years.

In the first decade after the Crimean War, the local councils in the Bulgarian provinces of the Ottoman Empire recognized the Council in Constantinople as their central authority. In parallel, they ceased to pay taxes to the Patriarchate of Constantinople but continued to collect money from their communities, which was spent on their own schools and churches. In many places the local Greek bishops were removed, and the Greek liturgy was replaced by that in Slavonic. In this regard, the ecclesiastical structure of the Bulgarian lands, established by the Patriarchate of Constantinople and consisting of metropolitan sees with their subjected bishoprics and parishes, served as a pattern for the newly created network of Bulgarian municipal and village councils. Therefore, the role of these councils in the national Church Movement was established in correspondence with that structure (i.e., those in the metropolitan cities occupied leading positions), while those in towns and villages were secondary.[54] The weight of a city in the Ottoman administrative system was also taken into account. As a result, the Bulgarian municipalities in Tûrnovo and Plovdiv, where the two major metropolitan sees were situated, became regional centers coordinating the national Church Movement in the northern and southern Bulgarian lands respectively.

After the 1856 defeat of Russia in the Crimean War, the Ottoman state became the major arbiter in the Bulgarian-Greek Church conflict. In 1858 it invited the Patriarchate of Constantinople to convoke an ecclesiastical council with the task of solving the conflict. Bulgarians used the forum to give greater publicity to their major demands: the replacement of the old diocesan hierarchs imposed by the Patriarchate of Constantinople with new ones, elected by their flock; for all higher clerics to be fluent in

Bulgarian; and the introduction of fixed salaries as a guarantee against corruption.[55] These demands indicate that Bulgarians were not so much concerned with the ethnic origin of their bishops, but with their ability to speak their language. Priority was also given to the rights of believers to participate in the election of their hierarchs and to control the ways in which the higher clergy used church taxes. As a result, St. Petersburg had to change its attitude to the Bulgarian Church question. Although Russia continued to resist the establishment of independent Orthodox churches in the Ottoman Empire, her diplomats were ordered to persuade the Patriarchate of Constantinople to reduce the taxes levied from Bulgarians, to appoint native bishops, and to allow the Slavonic liturgy.[56] The Great Church, however, did not take this advice and made only minimal concessions. Only four Bulgarians were allowed to take part in the ecclesiastical council, which was attended by forty-one Greek deputies. The fact that the Bulgarians were represented by laymen also doomed their cause to failure.[57]

Despite the negative results of the 1858 council, it marked an important moment in shaping the idea of the Bulgarian Church and nation. Its decisions were not signed by the Bulgarian participants who protested against the suppression of the church freedoms of their compatriots by the Patriarchate of Constantinople, a situation that could be traced throughout history. Their major argument was the 1767 abolishment of the Archbishopric of Ohrid. Two years later, one of the Bulgarian deputies to the 1858 council, Nikoli Minchoglu from Tûrnovo, issued a petition asking for the restoration of that Archbishopric together with the Bulgarian Patriarchate of Tûrnovo, which had been destroyed at the end of the fourteenth century. He referred to both churches as Bulgarian bodies.[58]

To a great extent, this approach was developed under the influence of the *Slavonic-Bulgarian History*, written by Father Paisii in 1762.[59] By becoming the most widely read and republished account of Bulgarian history, this book spread the thesis of its author that the Patriarchate of Tûrnovo and the Archbishopric of Ohrid were Bulgarian Churches.[60] These views were also represented in nineteenth century Russian historiography, according to which, in the period 1185–1767, the Archbishopric of Ohrid was a continuation of the autocephalous church of the First Bulgarian Kingdom destroyed by the Byzantine Emperor Basil II in 1018.[61] A Russian church historian pointed to the fact that even after the abolishment of the Archbishopric of Ohrid in 1767, the sultan's decrees for the appointment of the patriarchs of Constantinople listed the dioceses of the former Archbishopric separately from the other dioceses of the same patriarchate.[62] This study presented a full account of the ethnic composition of the former dioceses of the Archbishopric of Ohrid in the second half of the nineteenth century, most of which were dominated by Bulgarians.[63]

Under the influence of Father Paisii, the leaders of the Bulgarian Church Movement drew the imaginary borders of their future church in a way that encompassed the dioceses of the old churches of Tûrnovo and Ohrid, both destroyed by Constantinople.[64] These ecclesiastical borders became the most important markers of the territory of the modern Bulgarian nation. In the mid-nineteenth century this view was enhanced by the zealous support that the national Church Movement received not only from the present day territory of Bulgaria but also from the non-Greek Orthodox population inhabiting the Macedonian eparchies of the Patriarchate of Constantinople.[65] No less important is the fact that the very idea of the establishment of a national Bulgarian Church became the major driving force that was able to mobilize all Orthodox Bulgarians, including those in the Macedonian eparchies, while the references to the medieval Patriarchate of Tûrnovo and the Archbishopric of Ohrid were mostly used as arguments for the achievement of this common goal. As a result, Bulgarian nationalism became closely linked with the territorial dimensions of that imagined Bulgarian Church, and, after the establishment of the Bulgarian Exarchate (1870), with its physical borders.

Father Paisii was especially influential in determining the anti-Greek character of the Bulgarian Church Movement. Although he argued that the Ottoman conquest had destroyed the medieval Bulgarian statehood, he launched his primary attack against the Church of Constantinople. He accused the latter of depriving Bulgarians of their "church freedoms" through the abolishment of the Patriarchate of Tûrnovo and the Archbishopric of Ohrid.[66] A century later, this view was widely adopted by Bulgarian society. In a popular pamphlet, Georgi Rakovski, one of the political leaders of the Bulgarian Revival, wrote that the Patriarchate of Constantinople had persuaded the Ottomans to abolish the Bulgarian Church in pursuit of achieving the long-standing dreams of the Byzantine rulers to do away with the Bulgarian people. In his *Slavonic-Bulgarian History*, however, Father Paisii did not limit his attacks to the Greek hierarchy. Especially powerful was his criticism of those of his compatriots who were ashamed to call themselves Bulgarians, and preferred to speak and write in Greek. He condemned them for taking part in the crimes of the Patriarchate of Constantinople against their own nation.

In the late 1850s, the anti-Greek zeal of the Bulgarian Church Movement went so far that some Bulgarians were ready to compromise with the religion of their forefathers and to enter in union with the Roman Pope. The first such act took place in 1858, when the Orthodox population of Kukush, a town in Macedonia, removed the Greek bishop by force and asked the patriarchate to appoint in his place the Bulgarian monk Partenii Zografski.[67] When their request was declined, many Bulgarians joined the Catholic mission, which had been established in Thessaloniki in the second half of the eighteenth century.[68] This behavior alarmed both the patriarchate and the Russian Embassy in Constantinople. The former immediately consecrated Ilarion Makariopolski and offered him the position of Bishop of Kukush. Although he did not agree to take the position, Ilarion visited the town and pacified his compatriots, many of whom he persuaded to return to Orthodoxy. Soon afterward, the patriarchate consecrated Partenii Zografski and sent him to Kukush, thus fulfilling the original wish of the local people.[69]

The consecration of a few Bulgarian bishops,[70] however, did not satisfy the lay leaders of the national Church Movement, who now pleaded for ecclesiastical independence from Constantinople. Many of them, being graduates of Hellenistic universities, seminaries and schools, had developed their views under the influence of such great Greek enlighteners as Adamantios Korais. This group of learned Bulgarians was familiar with his arguments for the establishment of a separate Greek Church, which had developed after the Greek uprising (1821), namely the moral corruption and degradation of the Patriarchate of Constantinople.[71] According to his thesis, the Orthodox clergy in the Kingdom of Greece should not recognize the Patriarch of Constantinople as the head of their church, because, as an appointee of an infidel ruler, this hierarch served a foreign oppressive regime. Korais considered that the Orthodox Church in free Greece had to be governed independently from Constantinople by a synod of locally elected clerics and laymen. He also insisted that the clergy had to be well educated and to work for the enhancement of democracy, equality, and brotherhood in society.[72] These ideas were developed by his disciple, Theoklitos Farmakidis, who justified the right of the

Kingdom of Greece to have its own autocephalous church. In his view, autocephaly was another dimension of the political sovereignty of the young Greek state. On these grounds, he did not consider it necessary to ask for the consent of the Patriarchate of Constantinople for the accomplishment of this act in 1833.[73] This link between church and state independence in free Greece had a long-term effect on the modern Bulgarian concept of the relationship between church and state. At the same time, having no state of their own, Bulgarians applied the Greek example in reverse by fighting for the establishment of their own church as an institution that would lay the grounds of their future state. In other words, they used the church institution as a means of national emancipation while being part of the Ottoman Empire.

On April 3, 1860, under pressure from his flock, Bishop Ilarion Makariopolski omitted the name of the Patriarch of Constantinople from the Easter liturgy and declared the establishment of an independent Bulgarian Church, after which the believers sang a song dedicated to the sultan, an act that was aimed at preventing the patriarchate from presenting their behavior as a rebellion against the Ottoman state.[74] This event, known in Bulgarian historiography as the Easter Action (*Velikdenska aktsiya*), irritated the Russian ambassador who claimed that the Bulgarians had declared the Ottoman ruler as the head of their church.[75] The song, however, reassured the Sublime Porte of the loyalty of its Bulgarian subjects, and it did not launch any repressive measures against them. Under these conditions, Bulgarians living in the countryside followed the example of their compatriots in Constantinople and began to esteem Ilarion Makariopolski as their church leader. If the lay Bulgarians had no doubts about the rightfulness of the Easter Action, Bishop Ilarion had reservations about its canonicity and instructed one of his priests to mention the name of the Patriarch of Constantinople in the morning prayers when the church was not full of worshipers. When his congregation learned about the order, the more zealous antagonists of the patriarchate found the priest and beat him up. Afterward, they went to the bishop's office and warned him to keep the national cause. Having no other choice, Ilarion Makariopolski obeyed his compatriots but asked them to protect him from the patriarchate. He conducted his first liturgy after Easter on April 24 only after receiving their written guarantees. Once again he omitted the name of the Patriarch of Constantinople. The latter responded immediately by condemning this behavior as an act of disobedience and requested the Sublime Porte to be allowed to punish Ilarion Makariopolski according to canon law. The Ottoman authorities, however, remained silent.[76]

This attitude of the authorities gave courage to three other Orthodox hierarchs to break with the Great Church of Constantinople and to declare their support for the Easter Action. All of them administrated dioceses ethnically dominated by Bulgarians, but only Avksentii of Veles was of Bulgarian origin. The second was the Albanian Metropolitan Paisii of Plovdiv, who had been in conflict with the patriarchal see in Constantinople, while he third, Gedeon of Sofia, was of Greek origin and was forced by his flock to mention the name of Ilarion Makariopolski as head of their church. However, he soon changed his position and returned under Constantinople's jurisdiction.[77] Seeing the growing support of the Easter Action, the leaders of the Bulgarian Church Movement in Constantinople set up a special body for the government of ecclesiastical affairs that included the hierarchs Ilarion and Avksentii and three laymen.

Although the Ottoman authorities did not persecute the self-declared Bulgarian Church, they did not recognize it officially, thus deepening the gap between the two Orthodox nations, Bulgarian and Greek. In October 1860, the Sublime Porte invited the former to pay its respects to the newly elected Patriarch Joachim II of Constantinople. The leaders of the Bulgarian Church Movement, however, disobeyed because such an act would contradict the Easter Action. In response, on February 24, 1861, the patriarchate convoked a church council that condemned the Bulgarian defiance. Attended by nine former and current patriarchs of Constantinople and twenty-seven metropolitans (three of whom were of Bulgarian origin), this forum deprived Bishop Ilarion Makariopolski and his supporters, metropolitans Avksentii of Veles and Paisii of Plovdiv, of their Episcopal dignity and sentenced them to exile.[78] At the same time, it made some concessions to the rebellious Bulgarians and consecrated as bishops two of their archimandrites, Panaret and Antim.[79] The first was immediately appointed as Metropolitan of Plovdiv, while Antim became Metropolitan of Vidin in 1867. Owing their elevation to the patriarchate, these Bulgarian hierarchs initially abstained from the national Church Movement, while their lay compatriots did not go back on the Easter Action but continued to fight for the recognition of the Bulgarian Church.

The Fight for the Recognition of the Bulgarian Church, 1860–1870

Losing its religious leadership, the Bulgarian Church Movement was once again in the hands of laymen, some of whom, headed by the layman Dragan Tsankov, looked for an alternative solution to the Bulgarian Church question by signing a union with the Holy See. In March 1861, several Bulgarian deputies visited the Roman Pope who appointed their fellow Archimandrite Josif Sokolski as the Exarch of the United Bulgarians. The fast growth of the new church clashed with the policy of St. Petersburg of keeping the unity of the Orthodox nations in the Balkans. The Russian Embassy in Constantinople swiftly organized the kidnapping of Sokolski who, at the beginning of June 1861, was held captive in the Kiev Pechersk Lavra.[80] Over the following months, Russian diplomats succeeded in drawing other influential personalities away from his church and many United Bulgarians returned to Orthodoxy. At the same time, the Russian embassy in Constantinople persuaded the leaders of the Bulgarian Church Movement who remained loyal to Orthodoxy to drop their previous demands for ecclesiastical independence and to replace them with a request for changes in the government of the Patriarchate of Constantinople. Thus, they called for the introduction of proportional representation of Orthodox Bulgarians at all levels of church administration. In a special petition to the Sublime Porte, Bulgarians expressed their will to participate in the election of the Patriarch of Constantinople in accordance with their number. They also wanted half the members of the patriarchate's synod to be Bulgarians, to have their own hierarch responsible for Bulgarian religious and national affairs whose work would be supervised by a board of laymen and clerics, and to elect their own bishops who would have fixed salaries.[81] These requests, however, were again turned down by the Patriarchate of Constantinople.

The intensification of the Bulgarian Church Movement at the beginning of the 1860s did not go unnoticed by Russia. Its synod changed its attitude to the Patriarchate of Constantinople and began to exert pressure over it to make concessions to the Orthodox Bulgarians. The influential Metropolitan Filaret of Moscow even advised the Patriarch of Constantinople to expand the rights of the Metropolitan of Tûrnovo by granting him the status of "Exarch of Bulgaria." In August 1861, Metropolitan Filaret criticized the double standards of the Greek hierarchy in Constantinople who rejected the national principle as an argument for the establishment of a new Orthodox Church, while making use of it in their own interests. Filaret argued that the Bulgarian demands had to be heard because the Pentecostal presence of the Holy Spirit justified the right of different nationalities to confess their faith in their own languages.[82]

Correspondingly, the government in St. Petersburg took a more favorable stand on the Bulgarian question. In 1862, its ambassador to Constantinople, Prince Alexey Lobanov-Rostovski, reported that the Bulgarians began to regard church autonomy as the first step to political independence. In his view, Russia had to make a clear choice between supporting Bulgarian demands for a national church and continuing its policy of guarding the unity of the Balkan Orthodox people under the jurisdiction of Constantinople. At the same time, he admitted that in both cases she was going to lose: both its control over the Bulgarians and over the Patriarchate of Constantinople.[83] In 1864, the new Russian ambassador, Count Nikolay Ignatieff, persuaded St. Petersburg to change its attitude to the Bulgarian Church question. Although Russia continued to look for a compromise between the patriarchate and the Bulgarians, she stopped rejecting the right of the latter to have church autonomy with a native hierarchy and Slavonic liturgy.

Within the framework of its new policy, St. Petersburg made use of its network of consulates established in the Bulgarian lands after the Crimean War to persuade Bulgarians that "Orthodoxy is the only faith that corresponds to the spiritual needs of the Slavonic tribes and that the retreat from it meant the death sentence of the Bulgarian people."[84] The Russian Consul in Plovdiv protested against the use of the ethnonym "Bulgarian" in the names of village councils of Bulgarian Muslims and Bulgarian Catholics, and the Ottoman authorities refused to register them as such.[85] In order to preserve her influence over the Orthodox majority of Bulgarians, Russia enhanced the notion of their nation as one that was Slavic in blood, Bulgarian in language and Orthodox in faith. The Russian government also took measures against the spread of Catholicism and Protestantism among Orthodox Bulgarians. It regularly provided stipends for Bulgarians to study in Russia, offered financial support for publishing pro-Russian newspapers and books in their lands and even worked for the physical elimination of those Bulgarians who endangered her interests in the Balkans.[86] All of these measures assisted in the development of ethnoreligious nationalism in nineteenth-century Bulgarian society and alienated its non-Orthodox members.

The Russian policy on the Bulgarian Church question, however, failed to recognize the importance of economic motives that took a central place in the conflict with the Patriarchate of Constantinople. Bulgarians refused to pay its financial debts, arguing that there was a lack of clarity about their origins.[87] According to estimates made in 1864, the amount of money that had been levied by the patriarchate since 1770 was enough to pay of the maintenance of 1,492 schools for Bulgarian children to study in their mother tongue.[88] This resistance undermined the social power of the Greek hierarchy and the Patriarchate of Constantinople referred to the Ottoman authorities with a request to assist its efforts to collect the church taxes by force. The intervention of the latter, however, provoked open clashes between state officials and the Bulgarian population in many places,[89] thus increasing the danger of transforming the Bulgarian-Greek Church conflict into a political one.

In order to prevent such a development, in 1864, the Sublime Porte invited the Great Church of Constantinople to convoke a new church council, attended by the acting as well as many former patriarchs of Constantinople, Alexandria, Antioch, and Jerusalem. As at the previous councils, the Bulgarian deputies were a minority. This time their group consisted of one layman, Gavril Krastevich, and metropolitans Panaret of Plovdiv, Antim of Preslav, and Dorotheos of Sofia, all of whom were known for their loyalty to the Patriarchate of Constantinople. With such a disposition, this council was not able to offer an adequate solution to the Bulgarian question, as was the result of the next council, convoked in April 1866, attended by only one Bulgarian metropolitan and one layman. Meanwhile, to reduce discontent among Orthodox Bulgarians, in September 1864 the Sublime Porte released the exiled hierarchs Ilarion and Avksentii. As a result of the protests of the Patriarchate of Constantinople, however, they were banned from serving liturgies in the Bulgarian parochial church in Constantinople. Under these circumstances, they went to live in Ortakoy, another district of the city, where the Bulgarian Church Movement established its headquarters.[90]

The fight of the Bulgarian laymen gathered strength in all territories where they formed the majority. The Greek priests were dismissed and replaced by native clergy, an initiative, however, which revealed a shortage of Bulgarian priests. The problem was partly overcome by an expansion of priestly duties, in that one Bulgarian cleric had to serve in several parishes. When possible, priests were imported from other dioceses. In some places, the local councils of self-government required their teachers also to become priests. Usually they were sent to Bucharest or Tûrnovo to take ordination.[91] This shortage of ordinary clergy was not the only serious problem faced by Orthodox Bulgarians. A no less serious problem was the lack of canonical legitimacy of the self-proclaimed Bulgarian Church. Without such a status it was not able to produce the Holy Myrrh (the Chrism) necessary for conducting the liturgy and sacraments. Therefore, the disobedient Bulgarians began to dilute the Holy Myrrh they had with olive oil in order to have sufficient reserves until their church question was resolved.[92]

In 1867, the Greek rebellion on the island of Crete shook the position of the Patriarchate of Constantinople in the Ottoman Empire and made its hierarchy more amenable to the Bulgarian demands. On request from St. Petersburg, Patriarch Gregory VI gave the Russian Ambassador Count Nikolay Ignatieff a draft project for a Bulgarian autonomous church, headed by a metropolitan with the title of "Exarch." The future church, however, was planned to include only the dioceses in north Bulgaria, situated between the Danube River and the Balkan Range. The proposal was immediately rejected by the Bulgarians as disrespectful of their rights as a separate nation and destructive for their national unity.[93] They also criticized the silence about the financial autonomy of their future church from the patriarchate. Finally the coincidence of this act of Gregory VI with the hundredth anniversary of the abolishment of the Archbishopric of Ohrid added fuel to the Bulgarian-Greek Church conflict. In his turn, Stoyan Chomakov, who represented the Orthodox Bulgarians from the Plovdiv diocese at the Bulgarian municipal council in Constantinople, sent a petition to the Sublime Porte that required the restoration of that Archbishopric "on the grounds of canon law, history and the principle of freedom of consciousness."[94]

At the same time, Bulgarians advanced their own project about their future church, which was issued in two slightly different versions. Both drafts foresaw a full internal autonomy of their church, according to which the Patriarchate of Constantinople would only have the right to approve the future Bulgarian supreme hierarch, while the Bulgarian bishops would take their offices with the approval of the Ottoman authorities. The new church would have the right to prepare its own statutes, which would be entered in force after their approval by the Sublime Porte, that is by a civic administrative act instead by the canonical blessing of the Patriarchate of

Constantinople. The same projects also required the mandatory knowledge of the Bulgarian language for the entire clergy. Native Greeks were allowed to serve only in parishes and areas with a Greek population. All Bulgarian priests had to be elected by their flock, while bishops would be elected by the Bulgarian Synod. The same documents located the see of the future head of the Bulgarian Church in Constantinople (i.e., in the city prescribed by canon law for the Patriarch of Constantinople).

These drafts were supported not only by the lay leaders of the Church Movement but also by the three bishops, Ilarion Makariopolski, Paisii of Plovdiv and Panaret of Plovdiv, previously declared as schismatics by the patriarchate. In 1868, the Bulgarian city and village councils in Macedonia also expressed their support for these projects and recognized the Bulgarian parochial church in Constantinople as their institutional center. The growth of the national Church Movement did not leave any hope among the supporters of the patriarchate that they would be able to preserve their metropolitan sees if they did not take the side of the Bulgarian majority. As a result, three more hierarchs of Bulgarian origin joined the rebellious church. Dorotheos of Sofia, Antim of Vidin and Ilarion of Lovech went to Constantinople and settled at the "St. Stefan" Bulgarian Church. On December 16, 1868, together with Panaret of Plovdiv, they sent a letter to the Patriarch of Constantinople declaring that they no longer recognized him as their supervisor and that they were joining the Bulgarian Church.[95] They also established a national Church council, of which the full right members became not only the rest of the Bulgarian episcopate but also the lay leaders of the national Church Movement. This new body referred to the Sublime Porte with a request to recognize its church. Thus, the nation-made church was born. Its legal and canonical legitimatization followed in the schedule of Bulgarian nationalism.

The Institutionalization of the Bulgarian Church in the Ottoman Empire, 1870–1878

The participation of six Orthodox hierarchs in the Bulgarian Church council established in Constantinople reinforced the positions of the clergy at the expense of the laity, while also allowing Bulgarians to refer to canon law when insisting on full independence from the Patriarchate of Constantinople. The increased number of hierarchs supporting the Bulgarian Church met the requirement of the minimum number of diocesan bishops necessary for the establishment of an autocephalous Orthodox Church.[96] This state of affairs gave greater self-confidence to the Bulgarian hierarchs despite their treatment as schismatics by the Patriarchate of Constantinople. In January 1869, they sent a petition to the Sublime Porte repeating the demands for a national church. According to them, the separation of the Bulgarian Church from the Patriarchate of Constantinople did not violate church canons. They supported their position with arguments from the history of Orthodoxy and particularly from the experience of Russians, Georgians, Armenians, and Goths.[97] In their view, the unity of the Orthodox Church was a unity of faith that cannot be limited to an institutionalized form of subjection to the Patriarchate of Constantinople. On these grounds they concluded that the Bulgarian Church question was not only ecclesiastical but also national, and thus it had to be solved by the secular authorities (i.e., by the Sublime Porte). The Bulgarian Church council in Constantinople also refuted the claims of the patriarchate that only an ecumenical council had the right to solve the matter.[98]

In response, the Great Church of Constantinople invited the other autocephalous Orthodox churches to send their representatives to a special church council, convoked with the task of stopping the Bulgarian schismatics. Neither the autocephalous Russian Orthodox Church nor the hierarchs of the Serbian and the Romanian Orthodox Churches, however, responded to this appeal.[99] In this regard, it is important to emphasize that in 1869 the latter two churches were not autocephalous but autonomous bodies that continued to be formally subjected to Constantinople jurisdiction. The advance of Serbian and Romanian nationalism, however, set their Orthodox hierarchies and communities against the Patriarchate of Constantinople. They regarded the latter as an Ottoman institution and a promoter of Greek nationalism rather than as a truly religious body defending Orthodoxy.[100] The moral support received from their non-Greek co-believers gave a new impetus to the Bulgarians to appeal to the Orthodox world and, on February 25, 1869, their hierarchs issued another petition. This time they supported their request for an independent Bulgarian Church with documentary evidence about the role of the Patriarchate of Constantinople in the abolition of the Patriarchate of Tûrnovo and the Archbishopric of Ohrid. In addition, they made reference to the protests of the Montenegrin Bishop Sava against the Constantinople Act of 1776.[101]

Within the Ottoman Empire, there was an important secular aspect that needs to be taken into account in regards to recognition of the Bulgarian Church. The resolution of the Bulgarian Church question was impossible without the consent of the Ottoman authorities. In the summer of 1869, the Sublime Porte appointed a Bulgarian-Greek commission on each side of which were three laymen. The Bulgarian participants, Gavril Krastevich, Ivancho Peychovich, and Georgi Stoyanov, insisted that the territorial jurisdiction of their new church had to include the dioceses of the former Patriarchate of Tûrnovo and the Archbishopric of Ohrid.[102] This request was rejected by the Patriarch of Constantinople who considered that a lay commission had no competence to deal with such a canonical issue. For their part, the Bulgarians evaded the attempts of the Russian Ambassador Count Nikolay Igantieff to persuade them to make concessions to the Greek party.[103] Under these circumstances, administrative recognition of the Bulgarian Church by the Sublime Porte was the only way to preserve the loyalty of its Bulgarian subjects.

Finally, the Sublime Porte took the resolution of the Bulgarian Church question in its hands. On February 28, 1870, the Grand Vezir Âli Paşa invited representatives of the above-mentioned Bulgarian-Greek commission and handed them the decree for the establishment of the Bulgarian Exarchate.[104] It seems that the Ottoman authorities had carefully premeditated this act as its announcement preceded by only a couple of days the celebration of the millennium of the Bulgarian Archbishopric (March 4, 870) by Bulgarians.[105] It also coincided with the first anniversary of the 1869 appeal of their hierarchy to the Orthodox world to support their separation from the Patriarchate of Constantinople. Finally, the sultan's decree was issued on the eve of the Feast of Orthodoxy (the Sunday of Orthodoxy) when Eastern Christianity celebrated its ninth century victory over iconoclasm.

Russia was not prepared for this move by the Sublime Porte.[106] Her ambassador to Constantinople made an immediate statement that the sultan's decree had to be changed in case of disapproval by the Patriarchate of Constantinople.[107] He seems to have used his contact with leaders of the Bulgarian Church Movement to suppress the association made by their compatriots between the millennium of their church and the sultan's decree. Nevertheless, on March 1, 1870, after the liturgy in the Bulgarian parochial temple in Constantinople, Bishop Ilarion Makariopolski expressed the gratitude of the Orthodox Bulgarians for the granted religious freedom. In his speech the hierarch compared the establishment of the exarchate to a fruit of the seed sown during the Easter Action of April 3, 1860.[108] At the same time, one of the secular leaders of the movement, Petko Slaveykov,[109] suggested that the celebration of the millennium of the Bulgarian Church, scheduled for March 3, should be moved to May 11, the feast of the Slavonic brothers St. Cyril and St. Methodius.[110] Although his idea was rejected, the different interpretations of the decree for the establishment of the exarchate weakened the image of the sultan as a just ruler who restored the Bulgarian Church.

The political goals pursued by the Sublime Porte in establishing the Bulgarian Exarchate can also be seen with regard to the absence of any Orthodox clergy during the meeting of the grand vezir with the Bulgarian-Greek commission on February 28. This absence was not simply a way of avoiding new clashes between Bulgarians and Greeks, but an attempt to make the impression that the Ottoman authorities refrained from intervention in the religious affairs of the Orthodox Church.[111] In fact, the sultan's decree was such an intervention as it imposed changes on the structure of the Patriarchate of Constantinople and set up the Bulgarian Exarchate as an autonomous body within its canonical territory. The other aim of the decree was to demonstrate an equal treatment of both Bulgarians and Greeks. However, in reality, it created a knot of ecclesiastical, ethnic, and political contradictions between these Orthodox nations that impeded Russian plans to use their common faith for the ends of its own policy in the Balkans.

In fact, the sultan's decree did not guarantee the full independence of Orthodox Bulgarians from the Patriarchate of Constantinople. At the same time, it was neither a restoration of the Archbishopric of Ohrid, as hinted at in the association with its millennium, nor of their medieval Patriarchate of Tûrnovo. Instead, this act established a new entity, the Bulgarian Exarchate (i.e., an institution without a clear meaning in Orthodox ecclesiology). The term "exarch" has been used in different ways throughout the history of Orthodox Christianity.[112] It could be an envoy of the Patriarch of Constantinople sent with a particular task to a place situated within his own canonical territory or outside it. Sometimes such exarchs were appointed as administrators of areas consisting of one or more dioceses. In all cases, however, their appointment was as a privilege of the patriarch, who had the canonical right to dismiss them and to abolish their offices. In this sense, the existence of the Bulgarian Exarchate as an institution, which had been created with the consent of the sultan, depended on the loyalty of its hierarchy, clergy, and laity to the Ottoman state. Meanwhile, the resistance of the Patriarchate of Constantinople to recognize the new church would bring Bulgarians closer to their Muslim rulers rather than to the Orthodox Greeks or Russians.

Despite these complications, the secular leaders of the Bulgarian Church Movement were satisfied by the result. In political terms, they regarded the sultan's decree for the establishment of their exarchate as a guarantee for their national autonomy within the Ottoman Empire and considered it as the first "Magna harta liberatum" of Bulgarians.[113] In religious terms, the act gave an internal autonomy to the Bulgarian Church, while limiting the rights of the Patriarch of Constantinople to approve the appointment of the hierarch elected by Bulgarians as their Exarch. The decree also mapped the borders of the modern Bulgarian nation by including in the territory of the new exarchate most dioceses that used to belong to the medieval Patriarchate of Tûrnovo and several others that were formerly situated under the jurisdictions of the Archbishopric of Ohrid and the Patriarchate of Ipek at the time of their abolition (1766–67).[114] Moreover, Article 10 of the decree gave an opportunity for the Bulgarians in the Orthodox eparchies in Macedonia to join the new church body on condition that two thirds of the population voted for such a change in special referendums. As a result, most dioceses of the former Archbishopric of Ohrid joined the Bulgarian Exarchate. In 1873, the population of the dioceses of Skopje and Ohrid voted for the union with the exarchate, while after 1878 the dioceses of Debar, Bitolja, Strumitza, and Nevrokop (the present city of Gotse Delchev in Bulgaria) followed suit.[115]

The decree of February 28, 1870, however, did not mean the immediate establishment of the exarchate. In addition to its territorial expansion, the new Church needed to work out its statutes, which also had to be recognized by the Ottoman authorities. For this purpose, on March 8, thirty-nine of the most distinguished representatives of the Bulgarian leadership in Constantinople elected ten laymen, who, together with the five Bulgarian metropolitans,[116] established a provisional synod. Its duties were to represent the new Church until the election of its Exarch, to elaborate its statutes and to convoke a people's council for its approval. The latter was convoked on February 23, 1871, and was again dominated by laity. It consisted of five metropolitans, three archimandrites, five priests, and thirty-eight laymen. On May 14, the Church-People's Council (*Tsûrkovno-naroden sŭbor*) adopted the Statutes of the Bulgarian Exarchate, which, however only came into force in July 1873, when the Sublime Porte finally gave its official approval for their use.[117] Similarly, the Ottoman state intervened in the promotion of the Bulgarian exarchs. Although the Church-People's Council in 1871 elected Metropolitan Ilarion of Lovech as the head of their new Church, under pressure from the Ottoman authorities, he refused to take office.[118] The next round of elections was won by Metropolitan Antim of Vidin, who became the first Bulgarian Exarch. During the uprising of his compatriots in April 1876, however, he was forced to resign. In his place, the Sublime Porte appointed Metropolitan Josif of Lovech but did it in violation of the statutes of the Bulgarian Church, which required the new exarch to be elected by its flock.

The appointment of Exarch Antim and the legal recognition of his religious organization offered only a partial solution to the Bulgarian Church question. From a purely ecclesiastical perspective, the exarchate was not able to become a proper Church without the canonical recognition of the Orthodox world. After centuries of existence under the jurisdiction of the Patriarchate of Constantinople, Bulgarians needed its blessing in order to justify their separation and the establishment of a new Church. The patriarchate, however, had no interest in supporting such a development. Facing the disapproval of the Russian Synod and the Patriarchate of Jerusalem, as well as that of the autonomous churches of Serbia and Romania, it had to look for formal arguments to justify its resistance to Bulgarian Church independence. Its plan was facilitated by the decision of Bulgarians to establish the headquarters of their exarchate in Constantinople, the city reserved by canon law for the see of the Ecumenical Patriarch. The lack of any restrictions in the Sultan's Decree of 1870 concerning the location of their Exarch allowed Bulgarians to infringe canons in favor of their national interests. They made use of the Ottoman *Rum Millet* system, which turned the leaders of the religious communities also into their lay administrators. Therefore, they located the see of their exarch in Constantinople, next to the Sublime Porte and the embassies of the Great Powers, where he would effectively be able to prevent any acts of the Patriarchate of Constantinople that may violate the religious as well as the national rights and freedoms of his Bulgarian *millet*. This decision had a negative effect on the canonical status of the young Bulgarian Church and gave theological arguments to the Patriarchate of Constantinople to declare a schism over its episcopate and laity on September 16, 1872.[119]

The effect of this was much stronger than the accusations of *ethno-phyletism* emphasized by Greek nationalist propaganda in the previous years. At first, however, Bulgarians did not feel adversely affected by the declaration of the schism. In their view, this act set them free from the chains of the "Greek Patriarch." Until the restoration of the Bulgarian state, they did not experience the most negative consequence of the schism, which would be their isolation from the rest of the Orthodox world.[120]

The Exarchate and Nationalism after the Liberation of Bulgaria, 1878–1908

The Russo-Turkish war (1877–78) and the establishment of the Principality of Bulgaria (1878) introduced the new state institution of the Bulgarian Exarchate as a factor in the development of Bulgarian nationalism. Until 1908, however, the lack of full political sovereignty of the principality diminished its impact on this process.[121] Therefore, in the period 1878 to 1908, Bulgarian nationalism was a shared responsibility between the exarchate and the newly liberated state, which advance was complicated by the crash of the hopes of Bulgarians that their state territory would overlap with that of their exarchate in agreement with the preliminary peace treaty signed by the representatives of the Russian emperor and the sultan in San Stefano on March 3, 1878. According to this act, the borders of the future state de facto coincided with those of the exarchate (i.e., the state contained all Bulgarian eparchies, including those in Macedonia). The project was wholeheartedly supported by Bulgarians who began to refer to this entity as San Stefano Bulgaria (*Sanstefanska Bûlgariya*). A few months later, however, this arrangement was revised by the Great Powers. In July, their congress in Berlin divided the territory of San Stefano Bulgaria into three parts. The first was situated between the Danube River and the Balkan Range and included the region of Sofia. Under the name of the Principality of Bulgaria it became a dependent state that paid annual tribute to the Ottoman Empire. The second part consisted of the exarchate's dioceses of Plovdiv and Sliven that were organized in an autonomous province named Southern Rumelia. The third part included the exarchate's eparchies in Macedonia and Edirne Thrace, which were returned to their pre-1878 status.

The Berlin decision provoked sharp protests among Bulgarians, because it divided their nation and made their liberation partial and conditional. This situation turned the restoration of San Stefano Bulgaria into a national ideal, determining the policy of all Bulgarian governments until the end of World War II. In the summer of 1878 Bulgarians had limited resources to achieve that goal, one of which was the recently established Principality of Bulgaria with its limited state sovereignty, while the other was the exarchate. Its existence as an institution uniting the Orthodox Bulgarians in the principality, Southern Rumelia, and Turkey was also put under question. This state of affairs was additionally complicated because during the Russo-Turkish War, Exarch Josif and his metropolitans from Macedonia sought asylum in Plovdiv.

Despite the disparate situation Bulgarians made the first step toward the restoration of the San Stefano ideal during the national assembly convoked in 1879 in the city of Tûrnovo, the medieval Bulgarian capital before the Ottoman conquest. The task of the assembly was to elaborate and adopt the Constitution of the Principality of Bulgaria, according to Article 39 of which "the Bulgarian State, being an inseparable part of the Bulgarian Church territory, in the sphere of ecclesiastical matters is subordinated to the Holy Synod—the supreme power of the Bulgarian Church, without regard to where this synod is situated."[122] In this way, the Tûrnovo Constitution recognized the difference between the territory of the Principality of Bulgaria, established by the Treaty of Berlin (1878), and that of the exarchate, which almost overlapped with the borders of San Stefano Bulgaria, thus conditioning the future expansion of the former toward the latter. The authors of the quoted constitutional text also took into consideration the lack of clarity regarding the future government of the Bulgarian Church. When the Constitution was adopted, it was not clear whether Exarch Josif would be allowed by the Sublime Porte to resume his see in Constantinople. At the same time, such a development hid some threats for the principality because the Sublime Porte could use its right to appoint and remove the exarch as a means of intervening in the domestic affairs of the young Bulgarian state. To avoid such threats, Article 39 did not define the Exarch, but the Holy Synod (i.e., a collective body that did not depend on the sultan as the bearer of supreme power in the Bulgarian Church). In 1883, the Bulgarian government adopted a special version of the exarchate's Statutes, the Adapted Statues, which were applied only within the territory of that state. In this way, the synod of Bulgarian metropolitans in Sofia became independent from the sultan but came under the control of the Bulgarian state, while the Exarch's Office in Constantinople preserved its dependence on the Sublime Porte—a status that allowed it to take care of the affairs of Orthodox Bulgarians, inhabiting the dioceses in Southern Rumelia,[123] Macedonia and Edirne Thrace.

In the first decades after the Berlin decision the restoration of San Stefano Bulgaria made slow but steady progress. In January 1880, Bulgarian Exarch Josif succeeded in returning to Constantinople, although it took several years before he received official recognition from the Sublime Porte as administrator of Orthodox Bulgarians in Macedonia and Edirne Thrace.[124] In the 1880s, his efforts to restore the network of Bulgarian schools in Macedonia and Edirne Thrace were more successful than those in the ecclesiastical sphere, where his attempts to appoint Bulgarian bishops in the Macedonian dioceses were impeded by the combined resistance of Russian, Greek, and Serbian diplomacy.[125] Meanwhile, the School Department, established at the Exarch's Office in Constantinople, revived the network of Bulgarian schools and in 1883 the exarchate was in charge of 237 Bulgarian schools, 351 teachers and 16,068 students in Macedonia and Edirne Thrace.[126] As a result of the efforts in the sphere of education, on the eve of the Balkan Wars (1912–13), the number of Bulgarian schools in these provinces had grown to 1,373 with 2,266 teachers and 78,854 students.[127]

The above-mentioned activities in the Ottoman territories were supported by Bulgarian governments, which began to lend regular financial support to the exarchate at the beginning of the 1880s.[128] In 1885, the successful Reunion of the Principality of Bulgaria with Southern Rumelia gave a new impetus to the activities of the exarchate in the Ottoman Empire. The following year, the principality removed another obstacle to its policy of strengthening the position of the exarchate in Macedonia. The government in Sofia broke its relations with Russia, whose diplomats tried to restore the unity of Orthodoxy in the Balkans by making concessions to Greeks and Serbs at the expense of Bulgarian interests in Macedonia. This shift in Bulgarian foreign policy changed the attitude of the Sublime Porte to the exarchate. In 1890, the former officially approved the appointment of Bulgarian metropolitans in Ohrid and Skopje, in 1894 in Veles and Nevrokop, and in 1897 in Bitolja, Debar, and Strumitsa. By resolving the issue of its Macedonian hierarchs, the office of Exarch Josif in Constantinople became the main institution working for the preservation of the national consciousness of Orthodox Bulgarians in the Ottoman Empire. This task was mainly accomplished by two types of activities. The first was in the secular sphere of education and consisted of measures for the development and maintenance of a network of national schools, while the second concerned the institutional organization of the Bulgarian Church structures in Turkey and the defense of the Slavonic liturgy. In this way, by 1912, the Exarch's Office in Constantinople was in charge of seven metropolitans, 1,310 priests, 1,331 parochial churches, 234 chapels, and seventy-three monasteries, situated in Ottoman territories.[129] It seemed that the exarchate was the main tool for restoring San Stefano Bulgaria.

In 1908, however, the partnership of church and state in promoting Bulgarian national unity by means of the exarchate was undermined. On September 22, Bulgaria was proclaimed as an independent kingdom. Its recognition by the Great Powers increased the self-confidence of the government in Sofia and gave priority to the state over the church in the pursuit of the San Stefano dream. The new political status of the country provoked its secular leaders to abandon the old policy for a peaceful restoration of San Stefano Bulgaria, in which the leading role was played by the exarchate, and to make plans for a military solution. The losses of Bulgaria in the Balkan Wars (1912–13) and World War I (1914–18), however, ruined the achievements of Exarch Josif and his administration in Macedonia. In 1913, he returned to Bulgaria where he died two years later. Only a small part of his dioceses in Macedonia and Edirne Thrace were joined to Bulgaria, while the rest were divided between Greece and Serbia. The exarch's see formally preserved its location in Constantinople but lost its previous meaning as an institutional center of Orthodox Bulgarians in Macedonia and Edirne Thrace. In addition, the Bulgarian state and church lost Southern Dobrudja, which was given to Romania after World War I. The war defeats and the failure of the Bulgarian government to defend the interests of its people opened a new stage in the development of Bulgarian nationalism in the interwar period.

Bulgarians tried once again to achieve their San Stefano dream during World War II, when Southern Dobrudja was returned to Bulgaria with the consent of Hitler and Stalin in 1940. The following April, after becoming a partner of Nazi Germany, Bulgaria installed its military, civil, and church offices in the territories of Vardar Macedonia and Aegean Thrace. Facing another national catastrophe in September 1944, both the Bulgarian state and its Orthodox church withdrew their officials and clergy from the occupied territories of Greece and Serbia. In January

1945, the Bulgarian Exarchate made the decision to move its headquarters finally from Istanbul to Sofia, where the see of the newly elected Exarch Stefan was now located. It also agreed to give up its claims over the former Bulgarian eparchies situated outside the borders of post-war Bulgaria.[130] A month later, on February 22, the Patriarchate of Constantinople abolished the schism with the Bulgarian Church that had lasted almost seventy-three years. In this way, the Bulgarian Orthodox Church was released from its nationalism, conditioned by the San Stefano dream. In ecclesiastical terms, it became a canonical church, recognized as a proper Orthodox body by the entire Orthodox world. As a result, the anti-Greek phase of Bulgarian nationalism came to an end. Its ecclesiastically motivated irredentism also became history. Meanwhile the establishment of the communist regime provoked a shift in Bulgarian nationalism that gave priority to anti-Turkish and anti-western sentiments.

Conclusion

The rise of nationalism in the Bulgarian lands was stimulated by its earlier advance in the neighboring Greek and Serbian nations. It was also inspired by memories of past independence of the medieval Bulgarian states and churches. At the same time, Bulgarian nationalism differed from that of the Orthodox Greeks, Serbs, and Romanians by its "bottom up" approach and lack of an institutional center during its initial phase. To a great extent, its major characteristics were shaped in the course of the Bulgarian Church Movement (1820–70). The most profound feature of early Bulgarian nationalism was its anti-Greek zeal, which started with demands for a national hierarchy, the Slavonic liturgy and Bulgarian schools, aimed at preserving the cultural identity of Bulgarians as a separate nationality within the *Rum Millet*. In the mid-nineteenth century, however, Bulgarian nationalism entered a new stage, in which the notion of national emancipation was no longer limited to the cultural identity of Bulgarians but was expanded by an understanding of economic and ecclesiastical independence as a condition of national rights and freedoms.

At the same time, Bulgarian nationalism appeared to be theologically weak because of the centuries-long absence of a national hierarchy and its own church institution. The fight of Bulgarians against the Patriarchate of Constantinople was initiated and led by laymen, while clergy, especially the episcopate, adopted real power only in the 1870s, after the establishment of the Bulgarian Exarchate. In their search for national emancipation, Bulgarians were not afraid of entering into a union with the Catholic Church or of living in schism with the Orthodox world if this status preserved their language and national identity. Moreover, the leaders of the national Church Movement did not abstain from joint acts with the Ottoman authorities in order to achieve their ultimate goal of an independent Bulgarian Church. No less notable is the fact that the educational activities of the Bulgarian Exarchate in the period 1872 to 1913, were concentrated on the establishment and sustenance of schools that were not ecclesiastical or religious, but secular (i.e. maintained by municipalities and the state), and aimed at preserving the national consciousness of the Bulgarian youth. In this sense, it is possible to conclude that in the nineteenth-century Bulgarian nationalism revealed a high degree of pragmatism by giving priority to nationality over Orthodoxy in the resolution of the church question.

Another specific feature of nineteenth century Bulgarian nationalism is its emphasis on church independence, characterized by a selective approach to Orthodoxy that distinguishes between its theological and ecclesiastical aspects and thus can be defined as "ecclesiastical nationalism." In general, Bulgarian nationalism affirms the historical belonging of Bulgarians to the teaching and rituals of Eastern Orthodox Christianity, but rejects church jurisdictions that might infringe upon national interests. As a result, Bulgarians were ready to unite with the Roman Pope, if he promised to preserve their Orthodox rites. In pursuit of national church independence, they went so far to break canon law, to enter into open conflict with the same-faith churches such as the Patriarchate of Constantinople and the Russian Synod, and to accept a schismatic status that isolated them from the rest of the Orthodox world for over seventy years. At the same time, they did not mind that their exarchate was established by a non-Christian and even non-Orthodox ruler as it granted them the opportunity to have an institutional center able to guarantee their integrity within the lands they considered their national territory.

After 1878, tied to the dream of San Stefano Bulgaria, the exarchate concentrated its efforts on the dioceses that remained in the Ottoman Empire and on keeping Bulgarian nationalism within the spheres of cultural and national identity. The growing role of the free Bulgarian state in the development of nationalism brought about its politicization and, between the two world wars, turned the Bulgarian Church into a hostage of the militaristic plans for the restoration of San Stefano Bulgaria. In 1945, by moving its headquarters from Istanbul to Sofia and giving up any pretensions over the dioceses in Macedonia, the Bulgarian Exarchate wiped out the opportunity to justify any territorial claims of Bulgaria toward its neighbors on ecclesiastical grounds. In this way, the complicated relationship between the Bulgarian Orthodox Church and nationalism was redirected toward the domestic affairs of the country. At the same time, Bulgarian nationalism lost its ecclesiological orientation and anti-Greek zeal.

List of the Hierarchs of the Bulgarian Exarchate (1870–1878)[131]

Exarch Antim (1816–1888)
    1861—Consecrated bishop
    1865—Rector of the Halki School of the Patriarchate of Constantinople
    1867—Appointed by the Patriarchate of Constantinople as Metropolitan of Vidin
    1868—Joined the Bulgarian Church Movement
    1872—Became the first Bulgarian Exarch

Exarch Josif (1840–1915)
    1876—Consecrated bishop and appointed as the exarchate's Metropolitan of Lovech
    1877—Appointed Bulgarian Exarch

Metropolitan Ilarion of Kyustendil (1800–1884)
    1849—Consecrated bishop
    1852—Appointed Metropolitan of Lovech by the Patriarchate of Constantinople
    1868—Joined the Bulgarian Church Movement
    1870–1872—Exarchate's Metropolitan of Lovech
    1872–1884—Exarchate's Metropolitan of Kyustendil

Metropolitan Ilarion of Tûrnovo (1812–1875)
    1858—Consecrated bishop (Ilarion Makariopolski)
    1872–1875—Exarchate's Metropolitan of Tûrnovo

Metropolitan Dorotheos of Skopje (early nineteenth century—1875)
  1853—Consecrated as bishop and appointed Metropolitan of Vratsa
  1860—Appointed Metropolitan of Sofia
  1872–1874—Exarchate's Metropolitan of Skopje
  1874—Resigned

Metropolitan Paisii of Plovdiv (1810–1872)
  1853—Consecrated bishop
  1853–1858—Metropolitan of Smirna (Izmir)
  1858–1860—Metropolitan of Plovdiv
  1860—Dismissed and sent into exile by the Patriarchate of Constantinople
  1868—Joined the Bulgarian Church Movement

Metropolitan Panaret of Plovdiv (1805–1883)
  1851—Consecrated bishop and appointed Metropolitan of Xanti (Greece)
  1861—Appointed Metropolitan of Plovdiv
  1868—Joined the Bulgarian Church Movement
  1870–1883—Exarchate's Metropolitan of Plovdiv

Metropolitan Avksentii (1789–1865)
  1831—Consecrated bishop
  1837—Appointed Metropolitan of Herzegovina
  1848—Appointed Metropolitan of Veles
  1851—Administrator of the diocese of Kyustendil

Metropolitan Partenii of Nish (1818–1876)
  1859—Consecrated Bishop Polyanski (in Kukush)
  1867–1874—Metropolitan of Nish
  1870–1874—Exarchate's Metropolitan of Nish
  1874—Resigned

Metropolitans Appointed by the Bulgarian Exarchate (1870–1878)

1870[132]

Metropolitan Genadii of Veles
Metropolitan Partenii of Nish

1872

Metropolitan Dorotheos of Skopje
Metropolitan Ilarion of Lovech[133]
Metropolitan Ilarion of Tûrnovo
Metropolitan Grigorii of Russe
Metropolitan Meletii of Sofia
Metropolitan Natanail of Ohrid
Metropolitan Simeon of Varna
Metropolitan Victor of Nish

1873

Metropolitan Averkii of Vratsa
Metropolitan Serafim of Sliven

1874

Metropolitan Ilarion of Kyustendil

1875

Metropolitan Kiril of Skopje

1876

Metropolitan Josif of Lovech

Bishops Consecrated by Hierarchs of the Bulgarian Exarchate (1870–1878)

1870—Bishop Serafim
1872—Bishops Victor, Meletii, Kiril, Simeon
1873—Bishop Averkii, Gervasii, Kliment, Dionisii
1875—Bishop Sinesii
1876—Bishop Josif

Postscript

Lucian N. Leustean

This volume's analysis of Orthodox Christianity and nationalism in nineteenth-century Southeastern Europe has demonstrated how Orthodox churches have been indissolubly tied to the concept of the nation. The legacy of the relationship between Orthodox Christianity and nationalism has been visible in the following areas:

First, the beginning of the twentieth century saw fully fledged national churches in Greece, Serbia, and Romania, each of which played an important role in shaping the religious, social and political lives of their own states. Although churches in these countries lost significant revenue due to the process of land and estate secularization, they remained prime societal actors. In contrast, the Bulgarian Church continued to have its headquarters in Constantinople (Istanbul after the fall of the Ottoman Empire) and the hierarchs were refused access to the Court. The Bulgarian Orthodox Church was officially recognized as an autocephalous church only in 1945, and, in 1953, was raised to the rank of patriarchate.

Second, the dissolution of the Ottoman, Austrian, and Russian empires and the recognition of the newly established nation-states in Southeastern Europe found support in the national character of their Orthodox churches. Political leaders were crowned in Orthodox cathedrals as embodying the past glories of the nation and summing up the climax of national unification.

Third, during the interwar period, Southeastern Europe found Orthodox churches in need of reshaping their jurisdictional status. Bucharest, the new capital, became the religious and political center of all Romanians from the Old Kingdom, Transylvania, Bukovina, and Bessarabia; Athens brought together the Greek population after the Lausanne Treaty; and Belgrade supported a unified Serbian Orthodox Church for the previously scattered communities in Serbia, Montenegro, Dalmatia, and Bosnia-Herzegovina.

Fourth, national identity and Orthodoxy were invoked at times of political crisis, as evident during the world wars and, later, during the communist atheist period. By being deeply rooted at the national level, Orthodox churches were ultimately able to survive years of persecution. Thus, in Bulgaria and Romania, communism developed a distinctly national character, due in part to the recognition by the regimes that the national identity of the churches could be of benefit to them in maintaining national cohesion.

Fifth, from the perspective of international religious diplomacy, the Ecumenical Patriarchate and the Moscow Patriarchate saw their influence in Southeastern Europe redefined. Both patriarchates would work closely with the newly established national churches in the region.

Sixth, the end of the nineteenth century and the beginning of the twentieth century showed the rise of diasporic Orthodox churches, mainly in Western Europe, the American continent, and Australia. These churches retained contact with those in Southeastern Europe; however, questions arose on the link between Orthodoxy and the concept of the nation in these new communities. The national character of these churches decreased while second and third generations of the faithful did not see themselves as belonging to a Bulgarian, Greek, Romanian, or Serbian Church, favoring instead the establishment of local Orthodox churches.

Seventh, and perhaps most significantly, the legacy of nineteenth-century nationalism has been perceived at the dawn of the twenty-first century in the rise of new Orthodox churches claiming to be the product and defender of their nations. The Macedonian Orthodox Church, situated at the religious confluence of the Greek, Bulgarian, and Serbian Orthodox Churches, proclaimed its autocephaly in 1967. Although the last census in 2002 revealed that more than a million people claimed to be Orthodox, the Macedonian Orthodox Church is still not officially recognized within the Orthodox commonwealth; the Orthodox Church in Montenegro is in a similar situation. Furthermore, outside Southeastern Europe, the dissolution of the Soviet Union led to new Orthodox communities aspiring to the rank of a national church. Despite these new communities, in defending the status and integrity of the Orthodox commonwealth, Orthodox churches still regard the 1872 Ecumenical Patriarchate's condemnation of *ethno-phyletism* as the norm to follow.

Nationalism was to stay deeply situated within Orthodox Christianity throughout the twentieth and the beginning of the twenty-first centuries, affecting the ways in which the clergy and the faithful perceived their national and religious affiliation both at home and in diaspora. From a theological view, only a small number of Orthodox scholars addressed the issue of nationalism, and when they did so, could not escape the historical and political boundaries in which their churches were entangled. Leading scholars of this period have criticized the concept of a national church, while others have welcomed it, even suggesting that nations and national churches are not only historical products but are instituted by God. This debate continues today.

NOTES

1. Orthodox Christianity and Nationalism: An Introduction
Lucian N. Leustean

1. My translation. "Cuvântul rostit de către părintele Neofit Scriban, în vechea catedrală a Moldovei în ziua de 5 (17) ianuarie 1859, Iași publicat în *Steaua Dunărei*, no 6, January 10, 1859" [The Speech of Father Neofit Scriban in the Old Cathedral of Moldavia on 5 (17) January 1859, Iași, published in *The Danube's Star*, no 6, January 10, 1859] in Academia Română. Publicațiunile Fondului Princesa Alina Știrbei, *Acte și Documente relative la Istoria Renascerei României publicate de Dimitrie A. Sturdza și J. J. Skupiewski* [Acts and Documents Regarding the History of Romania Published by Dimitrie A. Sturdza and J. J. Skupiewski], vol. 8, 1858–59 (Bucharest: Institutul de Arte Grafice Carol Göbl, 1900), 338–39.

2. For the history of Greece, see Charles A. Frazee, *The Orthodox Church and Independent Greece, 1821–1852* (Cambridge: Cambridge University Press, 1969); Richard Clogg, *A Concise History of Greece* (Cambridge: Cambridge University Press, 1992); Douglas Dakin, *The Unification of Greece, 1770–1923* (London: Benn, 1972); and Peter Mackridge, *Language and National Identity in Greece, 1766–1976* (Oxford: Oxford University Press, 2009).

3. For the history of Serbia, see Paul Pavlovich, *The History of the Serbian Orthodox Church* (Toronto: Serbian Heritage Books, 1989); Pedro Ramet, ed., *Eastern Christianity and Politics in the Twentieth Century* (Durham, N.C.: Duke University Press, 1988); Thomas Bremer, *Ekklesiale Struktur und Ekklesiologie in der Serbischen Orthodoxen Kirche im 19. und 20. Jahrhundert* (Würzburg: Augustinus Verlag, 1992); Branimir Anzulovic, *Heavenly Serbia: From Myth to Genocide* (London: Hurst, 1999); Tim Judah, *The Serbs: History, Myth and the Destruction*

of Yugoslavia (New Haven, Conn.: Yale University Press, 2000); Vjekoslav Perica, *Balkan Idols: Religion and Nationalism in Yugoslav States* (Oxford: Oxford University Press, 2002); Thomas Bremer, *Ekklesiale Struktur und Ekklesiologie in der Serbischen Orthodoxen Kirche im 19. und 20. Jahrhundert* (Würzburg: Augustinus Verlag, 1992); and Klaus Buchenau, *Auf russischen Spuren. Orthodoxe Antiwestler in Serbien, 1850–1945* (Wiesbaden: Harrassowitz, 2011).

4. For the history of Romania, see Daniel Chirot, *Social Change in a Peripheral Society: The Creation of a Balkan Colony* (New York: Academic Press, 1976); Gerald J. Bobango, *The Emergence of the Romanian National State* (Boulder, Colo.: East European Mongraphs; distributed by Columbia University Press, 1979); Barbara Jelavich, *Russia and the Formation of the Romanian National State, 1821–1878* (Cambridge: Cambridge University Press, 1984); Paul E. Michelson, *Conflict and Crisis: Romanian Political Development, 1861–1871* (New York: Garland, 1987); Keith Hitchins, *Rumania, 1866–1947* (Oxford: Clarendon Press, 1994); Keith Hitchins, *The Romanians, 1774–1866* (Oxford: Clarendon Press, 1996); Lucian Boia, *History and Myth in Romanian Consciousness* (Budapest, Central European University Press, 2001); and Sorin Mitu, *National Identity of Romanians in Transylvania* (Budapest: Central European University Press, 2001).

5. For the history of Bulgaria, see Carsten Riis, *Religion, Politics, and Historiography in Bulgaria* (Boulder, Colo.: East European Mongraphs; distributed by Columbia University Press, 2002); James Lindsay Hopkins, *The Bulgarian Orthodox Church: A Socio-Historical Analysis of the Evolving Relationship between Church, Nation and State in Bulgaria* (Boulder, Colo.: East European Monographs; distributed by Columbia University Press, 2009); Richard J. Crampton, *A Concise History of Bulgaria* (Cambridge: Cambridge University Press, 1996); and Thomas A. Meininger, *The Formation of a Nationalist Bulgarian Intelligentsia, 1835–1878* (New York: Garland, 1987).

6. Eric J. Hobsbawm, *Nations and Nationalism since 1780: Programme, Myth, Reality* (Cambridge: Cambridge University Press, 1990).

7. Elie Kedourie, *Nationalism* (London: Hutchinson, 1960), 9.

8. Émile Durkheim, *The Elementary Forms of the Religious Life*, trans. by J. Swain (London: Allen and Unwin, 1915), 214.

9. Grigorios D. Papathomas, *Le Patriarcat Oecumenique de Constantinople (y compris la Politeia monastique du Mont Athos) dans l'Europe unie* (Katerini: Editions Epektasis, 1998), 705.

10. Henri Grégoire, "The Byzantine Church" in *Byzantium. An Introduction to East Roman Civilization*, ed. Norman H. Bayner and H. St. L. B. Moss (Oxford: Clarendon Press, 1948), 127. For the history and spirituality of Orthodox Christianity, see also Jaroslav Pelikan, *The Christian Tradition. A History of the*

Development of Doctrine, vol. 2: *The Spirit of Eastern Christendom (600–1700)* (Chicago: The University of Chicago Press, 1974); John Meyendorff, *Byzantine Theology: Historical Trends and Doctrinal Themes* (New York: Fordham University Press, 1974); John Meyendorff, *The Byzantine Legacy in the Orthodox Christianity* (Crestwood, NY: St. Vladimir's Seminary Press, 1982); Timothy Ware, *The Orthodox Church* (London: Penguin Books, 1997); J. M. Hussey, *The Orthodox Church in the Byzantine Empire* (Oxford: Oxford University Press, 2004); Aristotle Papanikolaou, *Being with God: Trinity, Apophaticism, and Divine-Human Communion* (Notre Dame: Notre Dame University Press, 2006); John Anthony McGuckin, *The Orthodox Church: An Introduction to Its History, Doctrine, and Spiritual Culture* (Oxford: Wiley-Blackwell, 2008).

11. John Breuilly, *Nationalism and the State* (Manchester: Manchester University Press, 1993).

12. Paschalis M. Kitromilides, "The Legacy of the French Revolution: Orthodoxy and Nationalism" in *The Cambridge History of Christianity*, ed. Michael Angold (Cambridge: Cambridge University Press, 2006), 229. See also Paschalis M. Kitromilides, "Imagined Communities and the Origins of the National Question in the Balkans," *European History Quarterly* 19 (1989): 149–92; Paschalis M. Kitromilides, "Balkan Mentality. History, Legend, Imagination," *Nations and Nationalism* 2 (1996): 163–91.

13. Benedict Anderson, *Imagined Communities: Reflections on the Origins and Spread of Nationalism* (London: Verso, 1983); John A. Armstrong, *Nations before Nationalism* (Chapel Hill: The University of North Carolina Press, 1982).

14. Steven Runciman, *The Great Church in Captivity. A Study of the Patriarchate of Constantinople from the Eve of the Turkish Conquest to the Greek War of Independence* (Cambridge: Cambridge University Press, 1968); Paschalis M. Kitromilides, "Imagined Communities and the Origins of the National Question in the Balkans," *European History Quarterly* 19, no. 2 (1989): 149–92; Paschalis M. Kitromilides, *Enlightenment, Nationalism, Orthodoxy: Studies in the Culture and Political Thought of South-East Europe* (Aldershot: Variorum, 1994).

15. Anthony D. Smith, *Nationalism. Theory, Ideology, History* (Cambridge: Polity, 2001), 33. See also Anthony D. Smith, *The Ethnic Origins of Nations* (Oxford: Blackwell, 1986) and Adrian Hastings, *The Construction of Nationhood: Ethnicity, Religion and Nationalism* (Cambridge: Cambridge University Press, 1997).

16. John Hutchinson, "Ethnicity and Modern Nations," *Ethnic and Racial Studies* 23, no. 4 (2000): 661.

17. Walter Kolarz, *Myths and Realities in Eastern Europe* (London: Lindsay Drummond, 1946), 222.

18. Anthony D. Smith, *Chosen People: Sacred Sources of National Identity* (Oxford: Oxford University Press, 2003), 201–4.

19. Smith, *Nationalism. Theory, Ideology, History*, 51

20. Apostolic Canon 34 states that "The bishops of every nation (*ethnos*) must acknowledge him who is first among them and account him as their head, and do nothing of consequence without his consent; but each may do those things only which concern his own parish, and the country places which belong to it. But neither let him (who is the first) do anything without the consent of all; for so there will be unanimity, and God will be glorified through the Lord in the Holy Spirit." Translated in Lucian Turcescu, "Dumitru Stăniloae (1903–1993)" in *The Teachings of Modern Orthodox Christianity on Law, Politics, and Human Nature*, ed. John Witte Jr. and Frank S. Alexander (New York: Columbia University Press, 2007), 295–342.

21. Ibid.

22. Gennadius Scholarius, "Contre les Juifs" in *Ouvres Completes*, vol. 3 (Paris, n.p., 1928–36), 252 quoted in Steven Runciman, *The Last Byzantine Renaissance* (Cambridge: Cambridge University Press, 1970), 22. Runciman also states that "It is to be remarked that though he repudiates the name of Hellene he calls the Imperial City not New Rome or Constantinople, but by its old Hellenic name."

2. The Ecumenical Patriarchate
Paschalis M. Kitromilides

1. Paschalis M. Kitromilides, "Orthodoxy and the West: Reformation to Enlightenment," in *Eastern Christianity*, ed. Michael Angold, vol. 5 of *The Cambridge History of Christianity* (Cambridge: Cambridge University Press, 2006), 202–9.

2. These prelates included the Patriarch of Constantinople Cyril VI, metropolitans of Ephesus, Meletios and Dionysios, Metropolitan Ignatius of Hungro-Wallachia, Metropolitan Dorotheos of Adrianople and Archbishop Kyprianos of Cyprus. On Korais's appraisal, see Προλεγόμενα στους αρχαίους Έλληνες συγγραφείς [Prolegomena to Ancient Greek Authors], vol. 1 (Athens: National Bank Cultural Foundation 1984), 502, 555–56, 561–62.

3. Manuel Gedeon, Ιστορία των του Χριστού πενήτων [History of Christian Paupers], vol. 1, ed. Ph. Iliou (Athens: National Bank Cultural Foundation, 2010), 289.

4. Ibid., 290.

5. Paschalis M. Kitromilides, "The Orthodox Church in Modern State Formation in South-Eastern Europe" in *Ottomans into Europeans. State and Institu-*

tion Building in South Eastern Europe, ed. Alina Mungiu-Pippidi and Wim Van Meurs (London: Hurst, 2010), 31–50.

6. Robert O. Crummey, "Eastern Orthodoxy in Russia and Ukraine in the Age of the Counter-Reformation" in *Eastern Christianity*, ed. Angold, 305–6. See also Borys A. Gudziak, *Crisis and Reform: The Kyievan Metropolitanate, the Patriarchate of Constantinople and the Genesis of the Union of Brest* (Cambridge, Mass.: Harvard University Press, 1998), 168–87.

7. For details, see Paschalis M. Kitromilides, "The Legacy of the French Revolution: Orthodoxy and Nationalism," in *Eastern Christianity*, ed. Angold, 233–40.

8. Constantios I in 1833, Anthimos IV in 1852, Sophronios III in 1866, Joachim III in 1879 and 1882.

9. Maximos of Sardis, *The Ecumenical Patriarchate in the Orthodox Church* (Thessaloniki: Patriarchikon Hidryma Paterikōn Meletōn, 1976), 303–9. See also Paschalis M. Kitromilides, "The Ecumenical Patriarchate and the 'National Centre,'" *An Orthodox Commonwealth*, Study No. 13 (Aldershot: Ashgate/Variorum, 2007).

10. Kitromilides, "The Legacy of the French Revolution," in *Eastern Christianity*, ed. Angold, 240–44. Orthodox attitudes to the Bulgarian question, involving a sharp critique of both Bulgarian but especially Greek nationalism and their impact in the church as incompatible with the catholicity of Orthodoxy, are recorded in a work published anonymously by Manuel Gedeon at the time under the title Μία σελίς εκ της ιστορίας της συγχρόνου εκκλησίας. Σκέψεις ενός ορθοδόξου [A Page from the History of the Contemporary Church. Reflections of an Orthodox] (Athens: n.p., 1874).

11. Gedeon, Ιστορία, vol. 1, 228–30.

12. On the method of composing the synod, see ibid., 230–31.

13. Philaretos Vapheidis, Εκκλησιαστική Ιστορία [Ecclesiastical History], vol. 3, 1453–1908 (Alexandria: n.p., 1928), 230–31.

14. Ibid., 226–40, and Gedeon, Ιστορία, vol. 1, 101–20. The complete text of the "General Regulations" in Οι κανονισμοί των Ορθόδοξων ελληνικών κοινοτήτων του οθωμανικού κράτους και της διασποράς [The Charters of Orthodox Greek Communities of the Ottoman State and the Diaspora], ed. Ch. K. Papastathis (Thessaloniki: Kyriakidis Bros, 1984), 78–110. The complex story of the application of the reforms in the governance of the Orthodox community is told in detail by Dimitris Stamatopoulos, Μεταρρύθμιση και εκκοσμίκευση: προς μια ανασύνθεση της ιστορίας του Οικουμενικού Πατριαρχείου τον 19ο αιώνα [Reform and Secularization: Toward a Reconstruction of the History of the Ecumenical Patriarchate in the Nineteenth Century] (Athens: Alexandreia, 2003).

15. For extensive discussion, see Stamatopoulos, Μεταρρύθμιση.

16. Gedeon, Ιστορία, vol. 2, 232–36. On the interplay of the politics of the Greek Orthodox community with the Bulgarian question, see Stamatopoulos, Μεταρρύθμιση, 113–16, 310–16, 339–44.

17. Paschalis M. Kitromilides, "Imagined Communities and the Origins of the National Question in the Balkans," *European History Quarterly* 19, no. 2 (1989): 183–85.

18. For details, see Paschalis M. Kitromilides, "Greek Irredentism in Asia Minor and in Cyprus," *Middle Eastern Studies* 26 (1990): 3–17, and Paschalis M. Kitromilides, "Byzantine Twilight or Belated Enlightenment in Asia Minor?," *Byzantine Asia Minor* (Athens: n.p., 1998), 433–46. Both studies reprinted in *An Orthodox Commonwealth...*, 2007. On the significance of the association movement, see George A. Vassiadis, *The Syllogos Movement of Constantinople and Ottoman Greek Education 1861–1923* (Athens: Center for Asia Minor Studies, 2007).

19. Benedict Englezakis, *Studies on the History of the Church of Cyprus, 4th–20th Centuries* (Aldershot: Variorum, 1995): 257–78.

20. This was noted by contemporary observers who admired the patriarch's ecumenical outlook. See the comments by the Anglican clergyman Adrian Fortescue in Claude Delaval Cobham, *The Patriarchs of Constantinople* (Cambridge: Cambridge University Press, 1911), 39–40. See also F. Cayré, "Joachim III, Patriarche Grec de Constantinople, 1834–1912," *Echos d'Orient* 16 (1913), 61–67, 163–72, 322–30, 431–43.

21. Paschalis M. Kitromilides, "The End of Empire, Greece's Asia Minor Catastrophe and the Ecumenical Patriarchate," Δελτίο Κέντρου Μικρασιατικών Σπουδών [Bulletin of the Center for Asia Minor Studies] 17 (2011), 29–42.

22. On the status of the Ecumenical Patriarchate in Ottoman system, see for the early period Elizabeth Zachariadou, "The Great Church in Captivity, 1453–1586" in *Eastern Christianity*, ed. Angold, 169–86, and on the subsequent three centuries, see P. Konortas, Οθωμανικές θεωρήσεις για το Οικουμενικό Πατριαρχείο [Ottoman Perspectives on the Ecumenical Patriarchate] (Athens: Alexandreia, 1998), esp. 298–361.

23. Kitromilides, "Orthodoxy and the West," in *Eastern Christianity*, ed. Angold, 206–9.

24. M. I. Gedeon, Πατριαρχικοί πίνακες [Patriarchal Lists], ed. N. L. Phoropoulos (Athens, n.p., 1996), 602.

25. Ibid., 600.

26. N. Gr. Zacharopoulos, Γρηγόριος Ε΄. Σαφής έκφρασις της εκκλησιαστικής πολιτικής επί Τουρκοκρατίας [Gregory V.: A Clear Expression of Ecclesiastical Politics under Ottoman Rule] (Thessaloniki: n.p., 1974).

27. See, for example, Το Αρχείον του Σμύρνης Χρυσοστόμου [The Archive of Chrysostom of Smyrna], vol. 3, ed. Al. Alexandris (Athens: n.p., 2000), 138.

28. See Letter by G. Krestidis, January 1, 1852, Gennadeion Library, Athens, Mousouros Archive, IX, 1.

29. Synopsis of the provisions of the Hatt-i Humayun, Vapheidis, Εκκλησιαστική ιστορία, vol. 3, 19–20. The complete text is in C. K. Papastathis, Οι κανονισμοί, 21–26.

30. Selim Deringil, *The Well-Protected Domains. Ideology and the Legitimation of Power in the Ottoman Empire 1876–1909* (London: Tauris, 1998), 44–50.

31. Ibid., 133.

32. Şerif Mardin, *The Genesis of Young Ottoman Thought: A Study in the Modernization of Turkish Political Ideas* (Princeton, N.J.: Princeton University Press, 1962).

33. Gedeon, Πατριαρχικοί πίνακες, 626–28.

3. The Orthodox Church of Greece
Dimitris Stamatopoulos

1. For a history of the first decades of the Greek autocephalous church, see Charles A. Frazee, *The Orthodox Church and Independent Greece, 1821–1852* (Cambridge: Cambridge University Press, 1969).

2. Dimitris Stamatopoulos, "Ecumenical Ideology in the Orthodox *Millet* (19th–20th Centuries)" in *Economy and Society on Both Shores of the Aegean*, ed. Lorans Tanatar Baruh, Vangelis Kechriotis (Athens: Alpha Bank Historical Archives, 2010), 201–47.

3. The Russian influence was mainly exerted within the Orthodox clerical hierarchy in the environment of the Ecumenical Patriarchate, where the pro-Russian wing was always strong and effective in the promotion of patriarchs controlled by the Russian embassy. For the crucial issue of what the "pro-Russian" or "pro-Western" identities meant for the members of the High Orthodox clergy, see Dimitrios Stamatopoulos, Μεταρρύθμιση και Εκκοσμίκευση: προς μια Ανασύνθεση της Ιστορίας του Οικουμενικού Πατριαρχείου τον 19° Αιώνα, [Reform and Secularization: Toward a Reconstruction of the History of the Ecumenical Patriarchate] (Athens: Alexandreia, 2003), 367–70. A Greek autocephalous church dependent on the policy and incorporated into the climate of the Ecumenical Patriarchate would increase the possibilities of the empowerment of the Russian party and its supporters in Greece, especially at the beginning of the 1830s when the Ottoman Empire improved its relations with Moscow signing the Treaty of Hünkâr İskelesi (July 8, 1833, seventeen days before the proclamation of Greek autocephaly on July 25).

4. The reforms of Peter the Great already foresaw in the early eighteenth century that the "head" of the church was to be considered the ruler, while yielding ecclesiastical authority to the operation of a "Standing Holy Synod," naturally

with the goal of weakening the head of the Russian Church, the patriarch (each successive Metropolitan of Moscow). In the past, it had often been shown that the latter was a potential pole of authority unchecked by central rule, especially when joined with the aristocratic class of the boyars. Each of these elements was repeated, one by one, in the case of the Greek autocephalous church. For the Russian Standing Holy Synod, see Simon Dixon, "The Russian Orthodox Church in Imperial Russia 1721–1917" in *Eastern Christianity*, ed. Michael Angold, vol 5 of *The Cambridge History of Christianity* (Cambridge: Cambridge University Press, 2006), 325–47, especially 326–27.

5. In referring to "imperial nationalism," I have in mind not only Russian or Ottoman nationalism but also that of the Western colonial empires.

6. When Othon came to Greece in 1833, he was only seventeen years old; for this reason he was placed under the supervision of a regency. Othon's reign falls into three periods: (a) the years of regency (1832–35); (b) the years of absolute monarchy (1835–43); and (c) the years of constitutional monarchy (1843–62). The Bavarian advisors were arrayed in a regency council headed by Count Josef Ludwig von Armansperg, who was president of the privy council and the first representative (or prime minister) of the newly created Greek government. Other members of the regency/council included Karl von Abel and Georg Ludwig von Maurer, with whom von Armansperg frequently clashed. Although Maurer remained in Greece for only six months, he was responsible for both the foundation of the Greek autocephalous church and the establishment of the legislation of the newly formed state. After the king attained his majority in 1835, von Armansperg was made arch-secretary; he was called arch-chancellor by the Greek press.

7. Zina Markova, *Bâlgarskata Ekzarhija, 1870–1879* [The Bulgarian Exarchate 1870–1879] (Sofia: B.A.N, 1989); James Lindsay Hopkins, *The Bulgarian Orthodox Church: A Socio-Historical Analysis of the Evolving Relationship between Church, Nation and State in Bulgaria* (Boulder, Colo.: East European Monographs; distributed by Columbia University Press, 2009). For a critical reflection on the recent bibliography on the Bulgarian Schism, see Dimitris Stamatopoulos, "The Splitting of the Orthodox *Millet* as a Secularizing Process: The Clerical-Lay Assembly of the Bulgarian Exarchate (Istanbul 1871)" in *Griechische Kultur in Südosteuropa in der Neuzeit. Beiträge zum Symposium in memoriam Gunnar Hering* (Wien, 16–18 Dezember 2004), ed. Maria M. Stassinopoulou and Ioannis Zelepos (Vienna: Verlag der Österreichischen Akademie der Wissenschaften, 2008); and Dimitrios Stamatopoulos, "The Bulgarian Schism Revisited," *Modern Greek Studies Yearbook* 24/25 (2008–9): 105–25.

8. Chrysostomos Papadopoulos, Αι Ορθόδοξαι Εκκλησίαι Σερβίας και Ρουμανίας [The Orthodox Churches of Serbia and Romania] (Jerusalem: Editions of the

Holy Fraternity of the Holy Sepulchre, 1923). For the history of the Serbian Church, see Paul Pavlovich, *The History of the Serbian Orthodox Church* (Toronto: Serbian Heritage Books, 1989).

9. On this critical issue, see the addendum by Paschalis Kitromilidis in the Greek edition of his dissertation, Paschalis Kitromilidis, *Modern Greek Enlightenment: The Political and Social Ideas* (Athens: MIET, 1996).

10. There were six metropolises in the Peloponnese at the beginning of the eighteenth century: Corinth, Monemvasia, Old Patra, Lakedaimonia (Sparta), Christianoupolis, Argos, and Navplion. Later, in the early nineteenth century, there was a massive promotion of bishoprics or archbishoprics to metropolises, see Chrysostomos Papadopoulos, Ιστορία της Εκκλησίας της Ελλάδος (Athens: n.p., 1920), 16. Specifically, the liberated metropolises and bishoprics totaled: (a) twenty-six in the Peloponnese; (b) twelve in Central Greece, and (c) ten in the Aegean islands; see Theoklitos Stragkas, Εκκλησίας Ελλάδος Ιστορία 1817–1967 [History of the Church of Greece], vol. 1 (Athens: n.p., 1969), 2–3.

11. Konidaris's view is in contrast to that of Chrysostomos Papadopoulos, who believed that Capodistrias would come to an understanding with the patriarchate; see Gerasimos I. Konidaris, Σταθμοί Εκκλησιαστικής Πολιτικής εν Ελλάδι από του Καποδιστρίου μέχρι σήμερον [Watersheds of Ecclesiastical Policy from Capodistrias to the Present] (Athens: n.p., 1971), 57.

12. In any case, in his first letter, Capodistrias clearly referred to the "Orthodox Church of the New State." Chrysostomos Papadopoulos, Ιστορία, 45.

13. Dionysios Thereianos, Αδαμάντιος Κοραής [Adamantios Korais], vol. 3 (Trieste: Publishing House of Austro-Hungarian Lloyds, 1889–90), 143. See also Paschalis M. Kitromilidis, "The Orthodox Church in Modern State Formation in South-East Europe," in *Ottomans into Europeans: State and Institution Building in South-East Europe*, ed. Alina Mungiu-Pippidi and Wim van Meurs (New York: Columbia University Press, 2010), which includes the eight articles of Korais for Greek autocephaly in English translation.

14. On Korais's life and work, see the recent edition of Paschalis M. Kitromilides ed., *Adamantios Korais and the European Enlightenment* (Oxford: Voltaire Foundation, 2010).

15. However, as regards the paternity of the plan, Farmakidis would relate that, "Mr. Maurer, while he brags a great deal in his work on Greece about this brilliant structure, does not condescend to mention anything about all those who contributed to a greater or lesser degree in its construction." See Theoklitos Farmakidis, Απολογία [Apology] (Athens: ek tou typografeiou Aggelou Aggelidi, 1840), 18–22.

16. Theoklitos Farmakidis, Ο Συνοδικός Τόμος ή περί Αληθείας [The Synodal Tome or About the Truth] (Athens: ek tou typografeiou Nikolaou Aggelidi, 1852), 5–7.

17. Here of course the counter-argument was that Peter the Great, following the abolition of the patriarchate and the establishment of the Standing Holy Synod, asked Patriarch Jeremiah III (1716–26, 1732–33) to ratify the changes, which took place in 1723. Kallinikos Delikanis, *Τα εν τοις κώδιξι του Πατριαρχικού αρχειοφυλακείου σωζόμενα επίσημα εκκλησιαστικά έγγραφα τα αφορώντα τας σχέσεις του Οικουμενικού Πατριαρχείου προς τας εκκλησίας Ρωσσίας, Βλαχίας και Μολδαβίας, Σερβίας, Αχριδών και Πεκίου, 1564–1863* [The Official Preserved Ecclesiastical Documents of the Ecumenical Patriarchate's Archive Regarding the Relations of the Ecumenical Patriarchate with the Churches of Russia, Wallachia and Moldavia, Serbia, Ohrid and Peć, 1564–1863], vol. 3 (Constantinople: ek tou Patriarchikou Typografeiou), 234–36.

18. Papadopoulos, *Ιστορία*, 105–107, where there is a comparison of Articles 10, 14, and 18 of the Organic Law with the corresponding Articles 38, 76, and 64 of the Bavarian Consistorium.

19. Papadopoulos, *Ιστορία*, 106.

20. John Anthony Petropoulos, *Politics and Statecraft in the Kingdom of Greece, 1833–1843* (Princeton, N.J.: Princeton University Press, 1968).

21. Efraim Karsh, *Empires of the Sand: The Struggle for Mastery in the Middle East* (Cambridge, Mass.: Harvard University Press, 2001), 35.

22. Both Farmakidis and Maurer believed that the fall of the previous patriarch, Constantios I, in 1834 was due to the fact that he was prepared to accept the proclamation of (Greek) Autocephaly. However, his fall was more likely due to the fact that he had been accused by Pertev Paşa of being a "Russophile"; Constantios himself was the author of pamphlets in which he criticized the founding document of the Greek Holy Synod. In a note he had written in a codex of the archive of the patriarchate, he characterized the new church not only as "schismatic" but also "heretical," see Ivan I. Sokolov, *Konstantinopolskaja cerkov v 19veka. Oput istoriceskovo izsledovanija* [History of the Church of Constantinople in the Nineteenth Century. An Attempt at a Historical Study], vol. 1, doctoral dissertation, Saint Petersburg, 1904, 527, and he himself viewed as suspect the fact that in Article 1 of the royal decree, there was mention of the "Apostolic" and not the "One Holy and Catholic" Church.

23. Papadopoulos, *Ιστορία*, 124.

24. Ibid., 125.

25. Ibid.

26. For example, one of the regents, Armansberg, married his two daughters (who were Catholic) in 1835 to the two sons of Prince Kantakouzinos (who were Orthodox); the wedding hierology occurred on the same day and at the same hour for both weddings, in one case with a Catholic performing the ceremony and in the other with an Orthodox priest; see Papadopoulos, *Ιστορία*, 131–32. En passant, during this period the same problem erupted with vehemence in the

Ionian Islands, which were under British occupation, but whose metropolitans were subject directly to the patriarchate, which intervened. The reaction of Gregory VI (inter alia) to the overthrow of the holy canons on impediments to marriage led to the British embassy's intervention, and to the pro-Russian patriarch's removal from the patriarchal throne in 1840.

27. K. Dyovouniotis, "Η κατά το 1834 διάλυσις των Μοναστηρίων εν τη ελευθέρα Ελλάδι" [The Dissolution of the Monasteries in Independent Greece in 1834], Ιερός Σύνδεσμος [Holy League], 1908, nos. 84, 85.

28. The women's convents were all dissolved with only three exceptions. The minimum number of nuns for a monastery to continue to operate was thirty, otherwise it was dissolved; see Konstantinos Oikonomos, Τα σωζόμενα εκκλησιαστικά συγγράμματα του Κωνσταντίνου πρεσβυτέρου και οικονόμου του εξ Οικονόμων [The Preserved Ecclesiastical Writings of Konstantinos Presbyter and Steward of the Stewards], vol. 2 (Athens: Typois Ph. Karampinou, 1862–66), 236–38.

29. Theofilos Kaïris, the founder of and teacher at the school that bore his name in Andros, his homeland, developed a philosophy ("theosophy") inspired by the teachings of the French Deists. For this reason he was exiled by the Greek state to Skiathos, and his teachings were condemned by the Patriarchate of Constantinople in 1839; see Dimitrios Paschalis, Θεόφιλος Καΐρης [Theofilos Kaïris] (Athens: Typografeio Estia, 1928).

30. Papadopoulos, Ιστορία, 298.

31. G. K. Zinopoulos, Ελληνική νομοθεσία από του 1833 μέχρι του 1860, [Greek Legislation from 1833 to 1860], vol. 1 (Athens: Ek tou typografeiou Ioannou Aggelopoulou, 1860), 15.

32. As Chrysostomos Papadopoulos has characteristically put it: "The canons form the ecclesiastical founding charter for the Holy Orthodox Church," Papadopoulos, Ιστορία, 317. Naturally, the problem of possible conflicts on occasion between the holy canons and the provisions of the constitution remained unresolved. Since the latter laid the basis for the validity of the holy canons, there was nothing to compel the church to bow to the will of the state or a political ruler.

33. Following Anthimos VI's removal in October 1848, Anthimos IV (Vamvakis) returned to the patriarchal throne. But in contrast with his first period as patriarch (and also with what Gedeon believed—namely, that Aristarchis's influence continued under Vamvakis), the reelection of Anthimos IV had been promoted by Ioannis Psycharis, the bey of Chios, see Stamatopoulos, Μεταρρύθμιση και εκκοσμίκευση, 44–46.

34. See Κώδιξ ιερός περιέχον τα πρακτικά της Αγίας και Μεγάλης Συνόδου της συγκροτηθείσης εν Κωνσταντινουπόλει επί του παναγιωτάτου Οικουμενικού πατριάρχου Ανθίμου του Βυζαντίου, περί της εν Ελλάδι Ορθοδόξου Εκκλησίας [Holy Code that Contains the Proceedings of the Holy and Great Synod Taken

Place in Constantinople during the Age of the Ecumenical Patriarch Anthimos Vyzantios, about the Orthodox Church of Greece] (Constantinople: Publishing House of the Ecumenical Patriarchate, 1850). On the same subject, see Papadopoulos, Ιστορία, 70; Chrysostomos Papadopoulos, Η Εκκλησία της Ελλάδος επί τη 1900 επετείω της ιδρύσεως αυτής υπό του Αποστόλου Παύλου [The Church of Greece on the 1900th Anniversary of Its Establishment by Apostle Paul] (Athens: Theologia, 1951), 138–48; and Evlogios Κουρίλας, Πατριαρχική Ιστορία, [Patriarchal History], vol. 1 (Athens: n.p., 1951), 111. See also Frazee, *The Orthodox Church*, 171.

35. The metropolitans of Caesarea, Herakleia, Nicomedia, Ephesus, Derkoi, and probably, Cyzicus.

36. G. Metallinos, Ελλαδικού αυτοκεφάλου παραλειπόμενα, [*Paralipomena of the Greek Autocephalous Church*] (Athens: Domos, 1989), 193–95, 208, 216–17, 395, 401–3, 415.

37. His secular name was Nikolaos Metaxas. Born in 1762, he was a cleric, fighter in the Revolution of 1821, and the first Metropolitan of Athens. In 1792 he was ordained a deacon at the Penteli Monastery, where he also served as a teacher. In 1803, he was ordained the Bishop of Talantion, and started his abundant and significant national activity. During the revolution, he played an active role, leading the struggle to liberate the province of Atalante and assisting Athanasios Diakos in Alamana. He took part in the First National Assembly, as well as in subsequent assemblies, and was present at all the efforts of the administration to reform ecclesiastical affairs. In 1833, he was named Bishop of Athens, and in 1850, following the publication of the Synodal Tome by the Ecumenical Patriarchate, he was appointed the first and permanent president of the Holy Synod of the Church of Greece and named Metropolitan of Athens, an office he held until his death. He came into conflict with King Othon over the management of ecclesiastical and monastic property.

38. Paschalis M. Kitromilidis, "Από την Ορθόδοξη Κοινοπολιτεία στις Εθνικές Κοινότητες: το πολιτικό περιεχόμενο των ελληνορωσικών πνευματικών σχέσεων κατά την Τουρκοκρατία" [From the Orthodox Commonwealth to the National Communities: The Political Content of Greek-Russian Spiritual Relations during the Ottoman Domination], in Χίλια Χρόνια Ελληνισμού—Ρωσίας [One Thousand Years of Hellenism—Russia Relations] (Athens: Gnosi, 1993), 139–65.

39. Oikonomos, Τα σωζόμενα εκκλησιαστικά συγγράμματα, vol. 3.

40. Oikonomos would characteristically call Farmakidis an "arch-pastor"; see Oikonomos, Τα σωζόμενα εκκλησιαστικά συγγράμματα, vol. 3, 24.

41. According to Vamvas, the supporters of Oikonomos wanted "the provinces of Greece to become once more provinces of the sultan via the Patriarchate of Constantinople . . . for Greece to once more become the sultan's handmaid,

and for exarchs, tyrannical commands, spies, disturbances of the common peace, perverters of public education to be sent [to Greece] from Byzantium." See Neofytos Vamvas, Αντεπίκρισις εις την υπό του Πρεσβυτέρου και Οικονόμου Κωνσταντίνου του εξ Οικονόμων Επίκρισιν [A Counter-Criticism against the Criticism of the Presbyter and Steward (*oikonomos*) Konstantinos of the Family of Oikonomon] (Athens: ek tou typografeiou Aggelou Aggelidi, 1839), 12–13.

42. Farmakidis's references to "Russian theologians" or specifically to Prokopovič were often ambiguous, but they always aimed to expose Oikonomos. Theoklitos Farmakidis, Ο Ψευδώνυμος Γερμανός [Pseudonymous Germanos] (Athens: ek tis typografias Aggelou Aggelidou, 1838), 26. He attempted to reprimand them for their views on the sacraments (for example, on baptism, for which they also accepted the Catholic version of sprinkling [aspersion]), and therefore Oikonomos was wrong to trust them. Other times (Οικονόμος ο εξ Οικονόμων: ή περί όρκου, Athens, 1849, 26–27), they were right to accept forms of political oaths (Farmakidis supported oath-taking in courts; Oikonomos did not), and thus Oikonomos was erring in not taking them into consideration. But the common denominator in Prokopovič's views generally was the subordination of the church to the will of the state, and this could not but move Farmakidis to respond.

43. Here we may recall that Peter the Great's reforms actually had a "Western" source of inspiration: the Anglican Church as it was organized as early as the age of Henry VIII.

44. "When infants play, they often build palaces; the moment they are finished, they straightaway tear them down. Who could believe that the Greek nation would do what foolish infants do? In July 1833 they built a splendid edifice and were praised by all thoughtful men, Greek and non-Greek. And now, after seventeen years they have demolished that splendid and magnificent edifice. . . . This act was a great political sin, and if another one of its ilk is repeated, it will be enough to bring Greece once more under the rule of the Ottoman sultan."; see Theoklitos Farmakidis, Ο Συνοδικός Τόμος ή περί Αληθείας [The Synodal Tome or Concerning the Truth] (Athens: Typois Nikolaou Angelidou, 1852), 1. Worth noting in the above quote is the paternalistic disposition of a Balkan modernizer, who confronts the nation as a "child" requiring guidance and special training.

45. We could argue that the individual who endeavored in the nineteenth century to develop a discourse against the East, with the goal of including the Greek state and its corresponding national identity in the West, was the "national" historiographer Konstantinos Paparrigopoulos.

46. Dimitrios Stamatopoulos, "From the Vyzantism of K. Leont'ev to the Vyzantinism of I. I. Sokolov: The Byzantine Orthodox East as Motif of the Russian Orientalism," in *Byzance dans l'Europe du Sud-Est aux epoques moderne et contemporaine*, Mondes méditerranéens et balkaniques, ed. Olivier Delouis, Anne Courderc, Petre Guran (Athens: École française d'Athènes, 2013), 321–40.

47. Dimitrios Stamatopoulos, *Το Βυζάντιο μετά το Έθνος: το πρόβλημα της συνέχειας στις Βαλκανικές ιστοριογραφίες*, [Byzantium after the Nation: The Problem of Continuity in Balkan Historiographies] (Athens: Alexandreia, 2009).

48. Consequently, the condemnation of the supporters of the Bulgarian Exarchate by the patriarchate appeared to acquire a twin (and contradictory) character: for important leading groups in the patriarchate, the condemnation was one of *ethno-phyletism* (i.e., nationalism), and consequently concerned not only the Bulgarian Exarchate, but every other attempt to break away from the unified Orthodox flock of the patriarchate on the basis of the criterion of nationality, including Greek nationality. For Greek nationalism and its supporters in Constantinople (chiefly, the circle of nationalists around the newspaper Νεολόγος, published by Stavros Voutyras), the Schism needed to be understood as a harsh response to the ambitions of the Bulgarians for control of Macedonia and Thrace; see Stamatopoulos, *Μεταρρύθμιση και εκκοσμίκευση*.

49. This "contradiction" between nationalism and Orthodoxy was introduced by Paschalis Kitromilidis in a now-famous article (1989), the first attempt to apply Benedict Anderson's model of "imagined communities" to Balkan nationalisms; see Paschalis M. Kitromilides, "'Imagined Communities' and the Origins of the National Question in the Balkans," *European History Quarterly* 19, no. 2 (1989): 149–92. The article was unquestionably pioneering for its time, and characteristic of a theoretical movement that had built conceptual bipolar oppositions on the basis of which it understood the process of nationalization of nineteenth-century Greek Orthodox populations: Athens/Constantinople, nation-state/empire, nationalism/religion. Subsequent studies have shown that this relationship was more complex, though they have rarely managed to proposal a theoretical framework to convincingly replace the bipolar oppositions of earlier historiography.

50. See, for example, the case of Paraskevas Matalas, *Έθνος και Ορθοδοξία: οι περιπέτειες μιας σχέσης* [Nation and Orthodoxy: Adventures of a Relationship] (Athens: Crete University Press, 2002), who attacks an easy target (the presumed "contradiction" between Orthodoxy and nationalism) in order to claim that the patriarchate was nothing but a tool of Greek foreign policy. This, however, was a position of Bulgarian (and Romanian) nationalism in the nineteenth century: the adoption of the rival nationalist arguments can be interpreted as a critical assessment of the arguments of Greek national historiography. However, it is difficult to reduce the complexity of the Ottoman environment to positions, such as that the announcement of the Schism by the patriarchate constituted a manifestation of Greek nationalism: neither the approach employing contradiction nor that concerning the dominance of Greek nationalism take account of the hybrid nature of identities and ideologies in the nineteenth century or more importantly of the ability of the Orthodox clergy to employ instrumentally ideological for-

mations of "ecumenism" or "nationalism" as required by circumstances in order to reproduce its own hegemony under new conditions. On this issue, see Dimitrios Stamatopoulos, "Ο Μ. Γεδεών και η επαναδιοργάνωση του οικουμενιστικού μοντέλου" [M. Gedeon and the Re-Negotiation of the Model of Ecumenism], in *Τα Άφθονα Σχήματα του Παρελθόντος: ζητήσεις της πολιτισμικής ιστορίας και της θεωρίας της λογοτεχνίας, Πρακτικά Επιστημονικής Συνάντησης* [In Memoriam of Alkis Aggelou. Multiple Schemas of the Past: Quests in Cultural History and Theory of Literature. Conference Proceedings], ed. M. A. Aggelou (Thessaloniki: University Studio Press, 2004), 377–87.

51. The problem of *a posteriori* interpretations concerns not only the hybrid nature of nationalist ideology in the nineteenth century, but also the weakness of such interpretations in explaining the conflicting nature of the actions of individual and collective subjects, in other words to solve the problem of hegemony. For example, if one wanted to interpret the above-noted contradictions, he would need to describe *grosso modo* the political rivalry over control of the patriarchate during the decade preceding the Schism. The most important political group that influenced developments within the patriarchate during this period was that of the bankers, under the leadership of Georgios Zarifis and Christakis Zografos and the patriarchs through whom it was politically expressed—namely, Joachim II (1860–63, 1873–78) and Joachim III (1878–84, 1901–12). When it lost control of the patriarchate in 1863, this group began to oppose the rival patriarchs, and on the basis of the Bulgarian question driving them to extreme policies against the Bulgarian side, even when they had advanced to moderate pronouncements in order to ascend to the patriarchal throne. In order to regain control of the patriarchate, they had to pursue not only politics but social hegemony, something they achieved by playing a leading role in the founding of associations. This meant that the dominance of the bankers' group within the *Rum Millet* reflected not only its "independent" imposition against its rivals in the patriarchate (chiefly the Neo-Phanariot families that had emerged after the end of the 1821 War of Independence), but at the same time, by virtue of its dynamic infiltration into the area of social influence, an alternative, but essentially the only possible strategy for control of Greek Ottomans against those who were "Greek-centered" (i.e., radical nationalists). At the same time they were adopting the arguments of the nationalists (e.g., the termination of the Schism in the summer of 1872), and were making the preeminence of the views of irredentist nationalism prohibitive. This, as it is now clear, had consequences not only in Constantinople but in the provinces, where the Greek state was carrying out (rather belatedly) the "struggle on behalf of all" against the Bulgarian nationalists. This is also the reason why sooner or later the old Neo-Phanariot families adjusted to the decisions of this group: the new way in which they processed the reproduction of control of the Greek Ottomans (bourgeoisie and Neo-Phanariots)

repressed the processes of nationalization of Greek Orthodox populations in the Empire. Even if the Bulgarian issue and the solution afforded by the Schism gave the Greek state greater possibilities for interventionism in the organization of mechanisms for the production of nationalist discourse, this was not sufficient for a definitive resolution of issues involving the choice of national identities. See extensively for these problems, Stamatopoulos, Μεταρρύθμιση και Εκκοσμίκευση. Finally and for the same reason, the leadership of the Greek kingdom, with the pro-Western Trikoupis at its head, realized that the "ecumenical" model represented by Joachim III was not a simple variant of a nationalist strategy, but included Ottomanism in an organic manner and, paradoxically and simultaneously, a political rapprochement with Russia. If the former had occurred, then the Greek embassy and its allies in Constantinople would not have been so slow to restore him to the patriarchal throne. See Evangelos Kofos, "Patriarch Joachim III (1878–1884) and the Irredentist Policy of the Greek State," *Journal of Modern Greek Studies* 4, no. 2 (1986): 107–20.

52. It is especially interesting that this insistence of promoting the "ecumenist" nature of the patriarchate against the nationalist demands of the other Balkan peoples who questioned its dominance resembles the demand by Turkish historiographers who wanted to defend the political model of the Ottoman Empire as presumably tolerant of other religions and multicultural, in contrast to the "bad" nationalisms that had dissolved it. "Ecumenism" and "Empire" had the same opponents (the Balkan nationalisms), not only at the historical and political, but at the historiographic level.

53. Theoni Stathopoulou, Το κίνημα του Παπουλάκου: οι πολιτικές, κοινωνικές και θρησκευτικές διαστάσεις του [The Movement of Papoulakos: Political, Social and Religious Dimensions], unpublished PhD diss., Panteion University, Athens, 1991.

54. Andreas Nanakis, Εκκλησία Εθναρχούσα και Εθνική: μέσα από τη Σύναξη των Πρεσβυτέρων και τον Ιερό Σύνδεσμο της Εκκλησίας της Ελλάδος (1870–1922), [Church *Millet* and National: Through the "Synaxis of Presbyters" and the "Holy Association" of the Church of Greece (1870–1922)] (Thessaloniki: Vanias Publications, 2007), 17.

55. Haris Exertzoglou, "Πολιτικές τελετουργίες στην νεότερη Ελλάδα. Η μετακομιδή των οστών του Γρηγορίου Ε΄και η πεντηκονταετηρίδα της Ελληνικής Επανάστασης," [Political Rituals in Modern Greece: The Transferring of Grigorios V's Bones and the Fiftieth Anniversary of the Greek Revolution], Μνήμων [Mnemon] 23 (2001): 153–82. On the conflicting interpretations of Grigorios V's act, see Nikos Zacharopoulos, Γρηγόριος Ε΄ σαφής έκφρασις της εκκλησιαστικής πολιτικής επί τουρκοκρατίας, [Grigorios V: A Distinct Expression of Ecclesiastical Policy under Ottoman Domination] (Thessaloniki: n.p., 1974), where the issue of relations between the Ecumenical Patriarch and Otto-

man authority was radically posed for the first time; the response of conservative national historiography may be found in Tasos Gritsopoulos, "Παρατηρήσεις επί μιας νέας μελέτης περί του πατριάρχου Κωνσταντινουπόλεως Γρηγορίου Ε΄," [Remarks on a New Study about Patriarch Grigorios V of Constantinople], *Μνημοσύνη* [Mnemosyne] 6 (1976–77): 299–332: and "Ο πατριαρχικός αφορισμός κατά Υψηλάντη και το πραγματικόν αυτού νόημα" [The Patriarchal Excommunication of Ypsilantis and its Real Meaning], *Μνημοσύνη* [Mnemosyne] 14 (1998–2000): 3–32.

56. The income from the society, like the equity invested capital, would come from members' contributions, "fifty cents each week, until the fulfilment of the time for his pension," plus a one-time fee of five drachms upon enrollment. Any cleric who interrupted payment was crossed off the membership list, but the money he had contributed remained to enrich the society. Nanakis, *Εκκλησία Εθναρχούσα*, 71.

57. He was not only familiar with Patristics and ancient Greek philosophy, but Western philosophy as well. While residing in Paris (1862–64), where he worked as a private tutor, he studied Western philosophy from Descartes to Hegel.

58. After this political association also failed, Makrakis founded a comparable one in 1901 called "Plato." In each instance, the founding of these associations was a vehicle for Makrakis's involvement in politics. Nevertheless, although he stood for election as a candidate for parliament four times, he was never elected. In addition, he founded two religious associations under the names of "John the Baptist" (1877) and "John the Theologian" (1884) at the beginning and end of the period in which his relations with the Holy Synod as well as the state had become frayed. Christos Giannaras, *Ορθοδοξία και Δύση στη Νεώτερη Ελλάδα* [Orthodoxy and West in Modern Greece] (Athens: Domos, 1992), 361.

59. It is very interesting that after Theophilus's death in 1873, the Holy Synod at its meeting on July 28, 1873, proceeded to elect the Archbishop of Corfu Antonius Chariatis to the office of Archbishop of Athens. However, the Greek state did not confirm the election, and Antonius resigned, given that he had been viewed as a "blind tool of the Slavs" and adherent of Pan-Slavism. Nanakis, *Εκκλησία Εθναρχούσα*, 122–23.

60. Apart from the "*Simoniaká*," for over twenty years Makrakis's polemic was aimed at the operation of Masonic lodges in Greece. Many of his works were devoted to this subject.

61. Nanakis, *Εκκλησία Εθναρχούσα*, 122–23.

62. The most famous splitting of "Zoe" led to the founding of "Sotiras" (Savior), an association of theologians, closely connected with the Palace's circles.

63. Giannaras, *Ορθοδοξία και Δύση*, 362–90. See also page 391, which states that "It would not be an exaggeration to claim that the phenomenon of

extra-ecclesiastical organizations was the most decisive stage in the historical elaboration of the alienation of modern Hellenism."

64. Giannaras, Ορθοδοξία και Δύση, 362–90.

65. Giannaras's choice of the term "extra-ecclesiastical" is not accidental as long as he believes that the Orthodoxy must be absolutely alien from these types of ecclesiastical institutions. However "para-ecclesiastical" seems to better render their organizational dimension.

66. I believe that the issue of these organizations is directly connected with that of the emergence of civil society in Southeastern Europe. Dimitris Stamatopoulos, "The 'Return' of Religious and Historiographic Discourse: Church and Civil Society in Southeastern Europe (19th–20th Centuries)," *Journal for the Study of Religions and Ideologies* 8 (2004): 64–75.

67. Şerif Mardin, "Civil Society and Islam," in *Civil Society: Theory, History, Comparison*, ed. John A. Hall (Cambridge: Polity Press, 1995), 292–93. In fact, and particularly in the case of Islam, which in contrast to most branches of Christianity is characterized by the lack of a classical priesthood, the capacity of the *ulema* is enmeshed as lawmakers/legislators of secular authority, of the teacher, of the judge.

68. On this issue, see Benjamin Braude, "The Foundation Myths of the *Millet* System," in *Christians and Jews in the Ottoman Empire: The Function of a Plural Society*, vol. 1, ed. Benjamin Braude and Bernard Lewis (New York: Homes & Meier, 1985), 69–88; Halil Inalcik, "The Status of the Greek Orthodox Patriarch under the Ottomans," *Turkica* 21–23 (1991): 407–36.

69. Here one could investigate the historic lack of social radicalism in Orthodoxy in contrast to the practice of the Roman Catholic clergy in social movements (e.g., Latin America). Social radicalism requires the experience of distinguishing public from private and the incorporation of the church in the latter even if this happens in the form of a self-regulating organization.

70. On this issue, see Rodney Stark and William Sims Bainbridge, *The Future of Religion. Secularization, Revival and Cult Formation* (Berkeley: University of California Press, 1985).

71. Stamatopoulos, Μεταρρύθμιση και Εκκοσμίκευση, 229–72.

72. Vasileios Atesis, "Τα περί την εκλογήν του Αρχιεπισκόπου Κεφαλληνίας Γερμανού Καλλιγά, ως μητροπολίτου Αθηνών (5 Ιουλίου 1889)" [On the Election of the Archbishop Germanos Kalligas of Cephallenia as Metropolitan of Athens (July 5, 1889)], Αρχείον Εκκλησιαστικού και Κανονικού Δικαίου [Archive of the Ecclesiastical and Canonical Law] 6, no. 1 (1951): 17–25.

73. More specifically, he had published a pamphlet entitled Ομιλία κατά των διαταραξάντων την Εκκλησία, Kefalonia, 1886, where inter alia he related: "This new heresy-leader is on the pretext of human salvation seeking human rather than divine glory. . . . This ostensibly pious apostle, unrestrainedly abus-

ing kings and governments, prelates and priests and society and generally all things human and divine, is pursuing MP positions and worldly offices; upon failing to obtain what he longs for, he resorts to bringing about divisiveness in society through his impious teachings." Cited by Nanakis, Εκκλησία Εθναρχούσα, 106.

74. Ο Κανονισμός του εκκλησιαστικού συλλόγου "Ιερός Σύνδεσμος," [The Regulation of the Ecclesiastical society "Holy Association"] (Athens: n.p., 1890). Here it is worth mentioning that the education of the clergy in the nineteenth century was being carried out by the Theological School of Athens (founded in 1837), the Rizarios School (founded in 1844), and the three seminaries, founded in 1856 in Chalkida, Tripoli, and Syros. After the Ionian Islands were united with Greece (1864), a seminary was established on Corfu, and correspondingly in Larissa (1884) following the annexation of Thessaly. However, during the 1890s the seminaries had closed, and one of the main demands on the "Holy Association's" political agenda was that these schools begin operating again.

75. This same phenomenon would be repeated only twice in the twentieth century: in 1923, with the election of Chrysostomos Papadopoulos, and in 1967 (during the Junta), with the election of Ieronymos Kotsonis. Like Procopius Oikonomidis, both of these men were professors in the Theological School.

76. From the standpoint of ecclesiastical governance, it could be argued that the most important development during Theoklitos's first term comprised the two laws voted by the Mavromichalis government in 1909 (immediately after the Goudi coup)—namely, "περί Γενικού Εκκλησιαστικού Ταμείου και διοικήσεως Μοναστηρίων" [On the General Ecclesiastical Fund and the Governance of Monasteries] and "περί ενοριακών ναών και της περιουσίας αυτών, περί προσόντων εφημερίων και μισθοδοσίας αυτών" [On Parish Churches and their Property, the Qualifications of Parish Priests and their Salaries], which came into effect in 1910. The former law endeavored to provide a solution to the problem of payment of the clergy, while the second made the Churches independent legal entities with their own property, from which the clergy who conducted divine services had to be paid a salary. Nanakis, Εκκλησία Εθναρχούσα, 168–69.

77. Georgios Th. Mavrogordatos, Εθνικός Διχασμός και Μαζική Οργάνωση: οι επίστρατοι του 1916 [National Split and Mass Organization: The Conscripts of the 1916] (Athens: Alexandreia Publications, 1996), 107.

78. Georgios Stragkas, Εκκλησίας Ελλάδος ιστορία εξ αψευδών πηγών (1817–1967) [History of the Church of Greece from Truthful Sources (1817–1967)], vol. 2 (Athens: n.p., 1970), 929–61.

79. Christos Androutsos, Εκκλησία και Πολιτεία εξ απόψεως ορθοδόξου, [Church and Polity from an Orthodox Perspective] (Thessaloniki: Rigopoulos Publications, 1964), 112.

4. The Serbian Orthodox Church
Bojan Aleksov

1. Some of the general works used in preparing this chapter are Sima Ćirković et al., *Istorija srpskog naroda* I–VI [History of the Serbian People I–VI] (Belgrade: Srpska književna zadruga 1981–85); Đoko Slijepčević, *Istorija Srpske pravoslavne crkve I–III* [History of the Serbian Orthodox Church I–III], 2nd ed, (Belgrade: Bigz, 1992); *Azbučnik Srpske Pravoslavne Crkve po Radoslavu Grujiću* [ABC of the Serbian Orthodox Church according to Radoslav Grujić] (Belgrade: Beogradski izdavačko-grafički zavod, 1993); Predrag Puzović, *Kratka istorija Srpske pravoslavne crkve* [Short History of the Serbian Orthodox Church] (Kragujevac: Kalenić, 2000); Čedomir Marjanović, *Istorija srpske crkve* [History of the Serbian Church] (Belgrade: Ars libri, 2001); Radomir Milošević, *Srpska pravoslavna crkva u vremenu i prostoru* [The Serbian Orthodox Church in Time and Space] (Smederevo: Narodna biblioteka, 2009). I have used archival material of the Archive of Karlovci Metropolitanate (AMK) and Archive of Serbia (AS), period church and secular press as well as monographs on specific topics.

2. As this chapter was going to press, a comparable interpretation of Serbian Church history and its link to nationalism was offered in Bratislav Pantelić, "Memories of a Time Forgotten: The Myth of the Perennial Nation," *Nations and Nationalism* 17, no. 2 (2011): 443–64.

3. *Poslanica Nikodimu Milašu* [Letter to Nikodim Milaš] (Pančevo: n.p.: 1884), 5. The author signed as Bosanski popo was most probably Rev. Đorđe Nikolajević, the dean of the Sarajevo Seminary and future metropolitan. He was referring to disputes over church jurisdiction in Bosnia and Herzegovina after annexation by the Habsburg Monarchy.

4. Anthony Giddens, *Profiles and Critiques in Social Theory* (Berkeley: University of California Press, 1982), 37–39, as interpreted by Peter T. Alter in "Nineteenth-Century Serbian Popular Religion: The *Millet* System and Syncretism," *Serbian Studies* 9, no. 1–2 (1995): 88–103.

5. See Dušan Popović, *Velika seoba Srba 1690* [Great Migration of Serbs 1690] (Belgrade: Kultura, 1954).

6. There is no recent history of the Karlovci Metropolitanate. However, it features in all volumes on Serbian Church history mentioned above as well as in Vasilije Krestić, *History of the Serbs in Croatia and Slavonija 1848–1914*, trans. Margot and Boško Milosavljević (Belgrade: Beogradski izdavačko-grafički zavod, 1997). Some early attempts include Emile Picot (Stevan Pavlović), *Les Serbes de Hongrie* (Prague: Grégr & Dattel, 1873) and Alois Hudal, *Die serbisch-orthodoxe Nationalkirche* (Graz and Leipzig: n.p., 1922).

7. For the Serbian Church under the Ottomans and their *Rum Millet* system, see László Hadrovics, *Le peuple serbe et son église sous la domination turque* (Paris: Les Presses Universitaires de France, 1947).

8. For estates of the metropolitanate, see Slavko Gavrilović, "Daljsko vlastelinstvo karlovačke Mitropolije u XVIII veku" [Dalj Estate of the Karlovci Metropolitanate in the Eighteenth Century] and "Daljsko vlastelinstvo karlovačke Mitropolije (od kraja XVIII veka do revolucije 1848–1849)" [Dalj Estate of the Karlovci Metropolitanate from the End of the Eighteenth Century to the 1848–1849 Revolution], *Zbornik Matice srpske za društvene nauke* [Matica Srpska Almanac for Social Sciences] 46 and 47 (1967).

9. See Traian Stoianovich, "The Conquering Balkan Orthodox Merchant," *Journal of Economic History* 20, no. 2 (1960): 234–313.

10. The Serbian hierarchs refused to appoint Romanians, claiming there were no satisfactory candidates. This attitude is reminiscent of the arrogance of the Ottoman Greeks who looked down upon the other Balkan peoples as dull and ignorant country bumpkins or *kondrokephalai* (wooden-heads or blockheads) as recorded by J. H. A. Ubicini, *Letters on Turkey II* (London: John Murray, 1856), 173.

11. For Vlachs or Aromanians, see Victor A. Friedman, "The Vlah Minority in Macedonia: Language, Identity, Dialectology, and Standardization" in *Selected Papers in Slavic, Balkan, and Balkan Studies*, ed. Juhani Nuoluoto et al., *Slavica Helsingiensa: 21* (Helsinki: University of Helsinki, 2001), 26–50, which focuses on the Vlachs of Macedonia but summarizes the origins and history of the Vlachs. More details are in Tom Winnifrith, *The Vlachs: The History of a Balkan People* (London: Duckworth, 1987) and *Shattered Eagles, Balkan Fragments* (London: Duckworth, 1995). Romanians inhabited Transylvania and Banat throughout the period these regions formed part of the medieval Kingdom of Hungary, Ottoman Empire, and finally Habsburg Empire.

12. For *Grenzer* and Union attempts, see Gunther Rothenberg, *The Austrian Military Border in Croatia, 1522–1747* (Urbana: University of Illinois Press, 1960) and *The Military Border in Croatia, 1740–1881* (Chicago: University of Chicago Press, 1966); Johann Schwicker, *Politische Geschichte der Serben in Ungarn* (Budapest: L. Aigner, 1880); and Bojan Aleksov, "The 'Union' as a Seed of Dissension between Serbs and Croats" in *Konfessionelle Identität und Nationsbildung. Die griechisch-katholischen Kirchen in Ostmittel- und Südosteuropa im 19. und 20. Jahrhundert*, ed. Hans-Christian Maner and Norbert Spannenberger (Stuttgart: Franz Steiner Verlag, Forschungen zur Geschichte und Kultur des östlichen Mitteleuropa, 2007), 211–23.

13. From 1721 to 1762 at least 28 Serbs attended this academy and thus made the most numerous foreign student group. See Nikola Radojčić, "Kijevska akademija i Srbi" [The Kiev Academy and the Serbs] in *Srpski književni glasnik* [Serbian Literary Herald] 31 (1913).

14. In the Habsburg Empire, at least since the Counter-Reformation, a specific sort of Clericalism played an important role, usually described as sinister.

On the one hand, most changes in the religious sphere undertaken during the reign of Maria Theresa and Joseph II and later associated with *Josephinismus* such as legal equality, religious toleration and rational government were in the secularizing spirit of the Enlightenment. At the same time, the state's control over the church was reinforced so that the Catholic and, to a similar extent, other recognized churches, including the Orthodox, remained key institutions in governing people, both in controlling them and providing for their welfare. In addition, religious allegiance and ecclesiastical organization were often abused for political and economic purposes; hierarchies were appointed and kept in close touch with the throne in order to exercise influence on their flock whereby domination, intrigue and corruption abided. Moreover, a distinct attitude to non-Catholic minorities was established, described by Okey as a confessionalising approach, with the tendency to recognize their religious rather than ethnic aspects of their identity. The emperor remained the protector of the Catholic Church possessing and using the veto right in church matters including the election of Popes. Furthermore, leaning on the structures of the Catholic Church stood at the core of the monarchy's foreign policy. The Holy See also profited from Habsburg patronage as in the case of Bosnia, as demonstrated below, where it hoped the Habsburg occupation could secure Bosnia as a jumping board for the Catholic mission among South Slavs. See Robin Okey, "State, Church and Nation in the Serbo-Croat Speaking Lands of the Habsburg Monarchy, 1850–1914" in *Religion, State and Ethnic Groups. Comparative Studies on Governments and Non-Dominant Ethnic Groups in Europe*, ed. Donald Kerr (Dartmouth, N.H.: European Science Foundation and University Press, 1992), 51–78.

15. For the impact of Theresian and Josephinian reforms on the Karlovci Metropolitanate, see Mita Kostić, *Dositej Obradović u istoriskoj perspektivi XVIII i XIX veka* [Dositej Obradović from the Historical Perspective of the Eighteenth and Nineteenth Centuries] (Belgrade: Naučna knjiga, 1952) and *Grof Koler kao kulturnoprosvetni reformator* [Count Coller as Cultural and Educational Reformer] (Belgrade: Srpska Kraljevska Akademija, 1932).

16. *The life and adventures of Dimitrije Obradović, who as a monk was given the name Dositej, written and published by himself*, trans., ed., and with an introduction by George Rapall Noyes (Berkeley: University of California Press, 1953) is the translation of Dositej's autobiography containing the most important contextual information.

17. The first conflict between the secular intelligentsia and church hierarchs took place at the Serbian People's and Church Congress in Timişoara in 1790. See Slavko Gavrilović and Nikola Petrović, eds., *Temišvarski sabor 1790* [Timişoara Congress in 1790] (Novi Sad and Sremski Karlovci: Institut za izučavanje istorije, and Vojvodine: Arhiv Vojvodine, 1972).

18. For more on Karadžić and his conflict with the Karlovci hierarchy, see Miodrag Popović, *Vuk Stef. Karadžić* (Belgrade: Nolit, 1964) and Wilson Duncan, *The Life and Times of Vuk Stefanovic Karadzic, 1787–1864: Literacy, Literature, and National Independence in Serbia* (Ann Arbor: Michigan Slavic Publications, 1986).

19. For the Romanian struggle for ecclesiastical emancipation, see Keith Hitchins, *Orthodoxy and Nationality: Andreiu Şaguna and the Rumanians of Transylvania 1846–1873* (Cambridge, Mass: Harvard University Press, 1977).

20. Gordana Petković, *Patrijarh Josif Rajačić (1785–1861)* [Patriarch Josif Rajačić (1785–1861)] (Belgrade: Zavod za izdavanje udžbenika, 2009).

21. For the role of the church in the early stages of Serbian nationalism, see Emanuel Turczynski *Konfession und Nation. Zur Fruhgeschichte der serbischen und rumanishchen Nationsbildung*, (Dusseldorf: Schwann, 1976); Philip Adler, "Nation and Nationalism among the Serbs of Hungary, 1790–1870," *East European Quarterly* 13 (1979): 271–85 and Gale Stokes, "Church and Class in Early Balkan Nationalism," *East European Quarterly* 13 (1979): 259–27.

22. Regulation of the Church and School Autonomy for Serbs in Hungary was followed by a special law adopted in the Croatian Assembly in 1887, which had powers regarding the interior affairs of Croatia, then part of the Kingdom of Hungary.

23. "Karlovačka mitropolija" [Karlovci Metropolitanate] in *Azbučnik Srpske Pravoslavne Crkve* [ABC of the Serbian Orthodox Church] and Arpad Lebl, "Privredna politika Sabora" [Economic Policy of the Congress] in *Godišnjak filozofskog fakulteta u Novom Sadu* [Annual of the Philosophy Faculty Novi Sad] 13, no. 1–2 (1970).

24. By that time the Hungarian forint or Austrian florin (Austro-Hungarian gulden) were already replaced by krone/korona as part of the introduction of the gold standard.

25. For Serbian Radicals in Hungary, see Lazar Rakić, *Radikalna stranka u Vojvodini do početka XX veka* [The Radical Party in Vojvodina until the Beginning of the XX Century] (Novi Sad: Istraživanja 3, 1974). The leader of the Serbian Radical Party in Hungary and a prolific author, Jaša Tomić was the most vocal opponent of the hierarchy and clergy, which he disdained and held responsible for the decline, poor faith and morals of the people. Among many of his anticlerical works *Karlovačka Mitropolija i Hrišćanstvo* [The Karlovci Metropolitanate and Christianity] (Novi Sad: Štamp. S. Miletića, 1913) stands out.

26. Vladimir Radašin, *Srpska autonomna školska uprava u Karlovačkoj mitropoliji 1867–1912* [The Serbian Autonomous School Administration in the Karlovci Metropolitanate 1867–1912] (Novi Sad: Matica srpska, 1987).

27. Dušan N. Petrović, *Patrijarh Georgije Branković (1890–1907)* [Patriarch Georgije Branković (1890–1907)] (Sremski Karlovci: Srpska pravoslavna bogoslovija

Svetog Arsenija I Sremca, 2005), 28. When Patriarch Prokopije Ivačković resigned in 1879, he was awarded a 24,000 forint annual pension, compared to 800 earned by a doctor or 1,100 by a professor at the Karlovci High School at the time. See Mladen Leskovac, *Zmajev bečki dnevnik* [Vienna Diary of Jovan Jovanović Zmaj] (Novi Sad: Matica srpska, 1983): 24–25.

28. Horst Haselsteiner, "O profesionalnoj, obrazovnoj i socijalnoj strukturi u Ugarskog početkom XX veka s posebnim osvrtom na Srbe" [in original "Zur Berufsgliederung, Bildungs-und Sozialstruktur in Ungarn am Beginn des 20. Jahrhunders unter besonderer Berücksichitgung der Serben," On Professional, Educational and Social Structure in Hungary at the Beginning of the Twentieth Century with Special Regard on Serbs] in *Kulturno-politicki pokret naroda Habsburske monarhije u XIX veku* [Cultural and Political Movements of the Peoples of the Habsburg Monarchy in the Nineteenth Century] (Novi Sad: Matica srpska, 1983). The statistics come from 1910 when Serbs composed 5.3 percent of the population of Hungary including Croatia.

29. László Szögi, *Ungarländische Studenten an den Deutschen Universitäten und Hochschulen 1789–1919* (Budapest: ELTE, 2001): 55–58.

30. Michael Pupin, *From Immigrant to Inventor* (New York: Charles Scribner's Sons, 1960) is the memoir of one of the most famous of these immigrants.

31. Đorđe Natošević, *Za što naš narod u Austriji propada?* [Why Are Our People in Austria in a State of Decay?] (Novi Sad: n.p., 1866) or Josif Podgradski, *Otvorena knjiga dru Svetozaru Miletiću u Vac via Pest. O žalosnom stanju narodno-crkvenog života kod Srba* [Open Letter to Dr. Svetozar Miletić in Vac via Pest. about the Sad State of the Serbian Peoples and Religious Life] (Novi Sad: n.p., 1871).

32. For Miletić, see Nikola Petrović, *Svetozar Miletić* (Belgrade: Nolit, 1958).

33. This was a golden age of anti-clericalism throughout Europe, very much related to the hardening of the position of its principal adversary, the church, as best exemplified by the progress of ultramontanism in the Catholic Church. See René Rémond, "Anticlericalism: Some Reflections by Way of Introduction," *European Studies Review* 13 (1983): 121–26. In Greece, similarly, criticism of the church related neither to its monopoly of spiritual authority, nor to a questioning of its doctrines but toward what might be called the "practical" conduct of its representatives and what was seen as its privileged position. See Roger Just, "Anti-Clericism and National Identity: Attitudes toward the Orthodox Church in Greece" in *Vernacular Christianity: Essays in the Social Anthropology of Religion Presented to Godrey Lienhardt*, ed. Wendy James and Douglas H. Johnson (Oxford: JASO, 1988), 15–30.

34. Quoted in Vasilije Đ. Krestić, "Pismo Mite Klicina Milanu Đ. Milićeviću" [A Letter of Mita Klicin to Milan Đ. Milićević] in *Zbornik Matice sprske za istoriju* [Matica Srpska Almanac for History] 49 (1994): 152–54.

35. On the changes in the Karlovci metropolitanate as a result of the Nazarenes, see Bojan Aleksov, *Religious Dissent in the Age of Modernization and Nationalism: Nazarenes in Hungary and Serbia 1850–1914*, Balkanologische Veröffentlichungen, vol. 43, (Wiesbaden: Harrassowitz Verlag, 2006). For the ecclesiological and theological turn that followed, see Thomas Bremer, *Ekklesiale Struktur und Ekklesiologie in der Serbischen Orthodoxen Kirche im 19. und 20. Jahrhundert* (Würzburg: Augustinus Verlag, 1992).

36. Archive of Karlovci Metropolitanate Fond A, 1881–108, 1882–167, 1886–538, 1897–347, 1897–408.

37. *Bogomoljci* (*Bogomolytsy*) was variously translated in English as God-worshippers, God-prayers and Devotionalists.

38. Petrović, *Patrijarh Georgije*, 53–103. See also Gordana Petković, *Patrijarh Georgije Branković (1830–1907)* (Novi Sad: Muzej grada, 2007). Monastic school turned out to be a cumbersome if not fully vain task as only a handful of monks remained and were too busy with the economic maintenance and survival of the large estates of which they were in charge to improve their education.

39. For more on the Karlovci Seminary, see Nikola Gavrilović, *Karlovačka Bogoslovija (1794–1920)* [The Karlovci Seminary (1794–1920)] (Sremski Karlovci: Srpska pravoslavna bogoslovija Svetog Arsenija, 1984). For the Karlovci Metropolitanate press, see Triva Militar, *Štamparstvo u Vojvodini* [Publishing in Vojvodina] (Novi Sad: Štamparsko i izdavačko D. D, 1940). The Karlovci Metropolitanate regularly published its schematism and many parish priests published detailed surveys of their own parishes. These publications then facilitated pastoral care while today they represent invaluable historical evidence.

40. Mile Bogović, *Katolička crkva i pravoslavlje u Dalmaciji za vrijeme mletačke vladavine* [The Catholic Church and Orthodoxy in Dalmatia during Venetian Rule] (Zagreb: Kršćanska sadašnjost, 1982 and 1993); Marko Jačov, *Venecija i Srbi u Dalmaciji u XVIII veku* [Venice and Serbs in Dalmatia in the Eighteenth Century] (Belgrade: lstorijski institut, 1984); Nikodim Milaš, *Pravoslavna Dalmacija* [Orthodox Dalmatia] (Belgrade: Sfairos, 1989; first edition in 1901).

41. *Žitije Gerasima Zelića I–III* [The Life of Gerasim Zelić] (Belgrade: Srpska književna zadruga, 1897, 1898, 1900).

42. Nikodim Milaš was the best educated of all the Serbian hierarchs in the nineteenth century. Prolific historian and writer he is remembered as author of many editions of church canons.

43. Lujo Bakotić, *Srbi u Dalmaciji od pada Mletačke republike do ujedinjenja* [The Serbs in Dalmatia from the Fall of Venice until Unification] (Belgrade: Geca Kon, 1938).

44. "Dalmacija" in *Vesnik srpske crkve* [Serbian Church Herald] 1 (1912): 93.

45. Sources are listed in Svetislav Davidović, *Srpska pravoslavna crkva u Bosni i Hercegovini (od 960 do 1930 god.)* [The Serbian Orthodox Church in Bosnia and Herzegovina from 960 to 1930] (Sarajevo: n.p., 1991) and Slijepčević, *Istorija*, 454–73. Among Phanariot bishops in addition to Greeks there were a couple of Bulgarians. See Nedeljko Radosavljević, *Šest portreta pravoslavnih mitropolita 1766–1891* [Six Portraits of Orthodox Metropolitans 1766–1891] (Belgrade: Istorijski Institute SANU, 2010).

46. Alter, "Nineteenth-Century Serbian Popular Religion"; Milenko Filipović, "Folk Religion among the Orthodox Population in Eastern Yugoslavia," *Harvard Slavic Studies* 2 (1954): 359–75; and Davidović, *Srpska pravoslavna*.

47. Risto Besarović, *Vaso Pelagić* (Sarajevo: Svjetlost, 1969); and Slavko Mićanović, "Predgovor" [Foreword] to Vaso Pelagić, *Izabrana djela I–III* [Selected Works I–III] (Sarajevo: Veselin Masleša, 1971): 5–21. Being awarded the highest monastic rank of archimandrite at the age of only 28, Pelagić had the chance of a brilliant ecclesiastic career. Yet after he escaped from internment, he caused embarrassment and unease for the authorities albeit now among his own people and in his own church. Once settled in Serbia Pelagić lessened his nationalist zeal and instead turned to preaching social and class emancipation. He helped organize artisans' and workers' societies, was among the founders of the Belgrade newspaper *Socijal-Demokrat* and became the most vocal advocate of socialism, materialist views on the development of nature, and atheism. Because of his relentless criticism of the church, Pelagić was defrocked and excommunicated by Belgrade Metropolitan Mihailo in 1895 in an inquisition-style ceremony performed in Belgrade Cathedral in 1895.

48. For churches in Bosnia and Herzegovina under the Habsburgs, see Petar Vrankić, *Religion und Politik in Bosnien und der Herzegowina* (1878–1918) (Paderborn: Schöningh, 1998). The Serbian Orthodox Church produced its own volume on this period, *Spomenica povodom osamdesetogodišnjice okupacije Bosne i Hercegovine (1878–1958)* [On the Eightieth Anniversary of the Occupation of Bosnia and Hercegovina (1878–1958)] (Belgrade: Srboštampa, 1959). More generally on Habsburg rule of Bosnia, see Srećko M. Džaja, *Bosnien-Herzegowina in der österreichisch-ungarischen Epoche (1878–1918) Die Intelligentsia zwischen Tradition und Ideologie* (Munich: R. Oldenbourg Verlag, 1994) and Robin Okey, *Taming Balkan Nationalism. The Habsburg "Civilizing Mission" in Bosnia 1878–1914* (Oxford: Oxford University Press, 2007).

49. Ubicini, *Letters on Turkey II*.

50. Bojan Aleksov, "Habsburg 'Colonial Experiment' in Bosnia and Herzegovina Revisited" in *Schnittstellen: Gesellschaft, Nation, Konflikt und Erinnerung in Südosteuropa. Festschrift für Holm Sundhaussen zum 65. Geburtstag*, ed. Stefan Troebst and Ulf Brunnbauer, Südosteuropäische Arbeiten, vol. 133 (Munich: R. Oldenbourg Verlag, 2007): 201–16.

51. Robin Okey, "A Trio of Hungarian Balkanists: Béni Kállay, István Burián and Lajos Thallóczy in the Age of High Nationalism," *The Slavonic and East European Review* 80, no. 2 (2002): 234–66.

52. Aleksov, "The 'Union.'"

53. Robin Okey, "Education and Modernisation in a Multi-Ethnic Society: Bosnia, 1850–1918" in *Schooling, Educational Policy and Ethnic Identity*, ed. J. J. Tomiak (New York: European Science Foundation and University Press, 1991), 319–41.

54. Božo Madžar, *Pokret Srba Bosne i Hercegovine za vjersko-prosvjetnu autonomiju Bosne i Hercegovine* [The Movement of Serbs of Bosnia and Hercegovina for Religious and Educational Autonomy] (Sarajevo: Veselin Masleša, 1982), 219–22.

55. One of the most notable ones, Father Matija Nenadović, left his memoirs full of vivid descriptions of the beginning of the modern Serbian state and society. See *The Memoirs of Prota Matija Nenadović*, ed. and trans. by Lovett F. Edwards (Oxford: Clarendon Press, 1969).

56. Dositej is said to have come to Serbia in August 1807 on the day of the Transfiguration. One of the laudatory speeches after his death exclaimed: "Dositej came to Serbia and Serbia transfigured." Quoted in Andra Gavrilović, *Dositije u Srbiji 1807–1911* [Dositej in Serbia 1807–1811] (Belgrade: n.p., 1902).

57. This is the general opinion of the historiography often based on contemporary travel accounts such as Oto Dubislav pl. Pirh, *Putovanje po Srbiji u godini 1829* (Belgrade: Prosveta, 1983), 22–23. In the original *Reise in Serbien im Spätherbst 1829, von Otto v. Pirsh* (Berlin, 1830), first edition in Serbian (Belgrade, 1900). Recent research, however, paints a more complex and dynamic picture as illustrated by the study of lives of Ecumenical Patriarchate hierarchs in Serbia and Bosnia in this period. See Nedeljko Radosavljević, *Šest portreta* and *Pravoslavna crkva u Belgradeskom pašaluku, 1766–1831 (uprava Vaseljenske patrijaršije)* [The Orthodox Church in the Belgrade Pashaluk, 1766–1831 (The Administration of the Ecumenical Patriarchate)] (Belgrade: Istorijski institut, 2007).

58. Translated in Duncan Wilson, *The Life and Times of Vuk Stefanović Karadžić 1787–1864* (Oxford University Press, 1970; reprinted Ann Arbor: University of Michigan Press, 1986), 18–20.

59. Joakim Vujić, *Putešestvije po Serbiji* [Travel in Serbia] (Gornji Milanovac: Lio, 1999; first published in Buda, 1828). Travelers were puzzled by the absence of church towers in villages in Serbia, many of which had no churches. See Franz Sherer, *Bilder aus dem serbischen Volks- und Familienleben* (Neusatz: n.p., 1882), 64 and 142–72.

60. Leopold von Ranke, *A History of Servia and the Servian Revolution*, trans. Mrs. Alexander Kerr (New York: Da Capo Press, 1973; reprint from London,

1848). For a recent synthesis of popular religion in Serbia, see Radmila Radić, *Narodna verovanja, religija i spiritizam u sprskom društvu 19. i u prvoj polovini 20. veka* [Popular Beliefs, Religion and Spiritism in the Serbian Society of the Nineteenth and the First Half of the Twentieth Century] (Belgrade: Institut za noviju istoriju Srbije, 2009).

61. *Memoirs of Prota Matija Nenadović*, ed. and trans. Edwards.

62. Dragan Novaković, *Državno zakonodavstvo o pravoslavnoj crkvi u Srbiji od 1804. do 1914. godine* [State Legislation of the Orthodox Church in Serbia 1804–1914] (Belgrade: Pravoslavni bogoslovski fakultet Univerziteta u Belgradeu, 2010).

63. Ranke describes the slaying of Bishop Nikšić in 1816 in *A History of Servia*, 334–35.

64. Victor Roudometof, "Invented Traditions, Symbolic Boundaries, and National Identity in Southeastern Europe: Greece and Serbia in Comparative Historical Perspective (1830–1880)" in *East European Quarterly* 32, no. 4 (1998): 445.

65. These were the features of all laws regulating the church in Serbia that were passed in 1836 (1847) 1862, 1882, and 1890. See Novaković, *Državno zakonodavstvo*.

66. See Zoran Ranković and Miroslav Lazić, eds., *Uredbe i propisi Mitropolije Belgradeske 1835–1856 1893* [Regulations and Directives of Belgrade Metropolitanate 1835–1856] (Požarevac: Eparhija braničevska, 2010); Zoran Ranković and Miroslav Lazić, eds., *Uredbe i propisi Mitropolije Belgradeske 1857–1876 1893* [Regulations and Directives of Belgrade Metropolitanate 1835–1876] (Požarevac: Eparhija braničevska, 2010); Zoran Ranković and Miroslav Lazić, eds., *Uredbe i propisi Mitropolije Belgradeske 1877–1893* [Regulations and Directives of Belgrade Metropolitanate 1835–1893] (Požarevac: Eparhija braničevska, 2011).

67. Miroslav Lazić, "Ktitori i priložnici u srpskoj kulturi 19. i početkom 20. vek" [Maecenas and Contributors in the Serbian Culture in the Nineteenth and Early Twentieth Century] in *Privatni život kod Srba u devetnaestom veku* [Private Life among Serbs in Nineteenth Century], ed. Ana Stolić and Nenad Makuljević (Belgrade: Clio, 2006), 611–59.

68. Miodrag Jovanović, *Srpsko crkveno graditeljstvo i slikarstvo novijeg doba* [Serbian Modern Church Architecture and Painting] (Belgrade and Kragujevac: Kalenić, 1987), 53.

69. Igor Borozan, "Kultura smrti u srpskoj građanskoj kulturi 19. i prvim decenijama 20. Veka" [The Culture of Death in Serbian Bourgeois Culture of the Nineteenth and Early Twentieth Century] in *Privatni život*, ed. Stolić and Makuljević, 889–983.

70. Nenad Makuljević, *Umetnost i nacionalna ideja u XIX veku: sistem evropske i srpske vizuelne kulture u službi nacije* [Art and National Idea in the Nine-

teenth Century: European and Serbian Visual Culture in the Service of the Nation] (Belgrade: Zavod za udžbenike i nastavna sredstva, 2006).

71. Radić, *Narodna verovanja*, 82.

72. Dimitrije Stefanović, ed., *Život i delo Mitropolita Mihaila (1826–1898)* [The Life and Deeds of Metropolitan Mihailo (1826–1898)] (Belgrade: Srpska Akademija Nauka i Umetnosti, 2008).

73. Bojan Jovanović, "Krsna slava" [Patron Saint] in *Privatni život*, ed. Stolić and Makuljević, 610.

74. See Radoslav Grujić, "Kult Sv. Save u Karlovačkoj mitropoliji XVIII i XIX veka" [The Cult of Saint Sava in the Karlovci Metropolitanate in the Eighteenth and Nineteenth Centuries], in *Bogoslovlje* 10, no. 2–3 (1935): 143.

75. The image appeared on the fresco in the church of the Assumption of Virgin Mary in Zemun. See Dejan Medaković, "Istorijske osnove ikonografije sv. Save u XVIII veku" [Historical Foundations of the Iconography of Saint Sava in the Eighteenth Century] in *Sava Nemanjić—Sveti Sava—istorija i predanje*, ed. Jovan Babić, Dimitrije Blagojević, et al. [Sava Nemanjić—Sveti Sava—History and Tradition] (Belgrade: SANU, 1979), 400.

76. *Matica* [Matica], vol. 2 (Novi Sad: n.p., 1867), 495, quoted in Grujić, "Kult Sv. Save u Karlovačkoj mitropoliji XVIII i XIX veka."

77. Geert van Dartel, *Ćirilometodska ideja i Svetosavlje* [The Cyrillo-Methodian Idea and Svetosavlje] (Zagreb: Kršćanska sadašnjost, 1984) is the pioneering attempt to describe the interactions of these two competing ideologies. See also Ljubomir Durković-Jakšić, *Kult slovenskih apostola Ćirila i Metodija kod Srba* [The Cult of Cyril and Methodius, Apostles of the Slavs, among the Serbs] (Belgrade: Sveti Sinod SPC, 1986).

78. For the activities of the Saint Sava Association in Kosovo and Macedonia, see Đorđe Mikić, "Delatnost Društva Sv. Save na Kosovu (1886–1912)" [Activities of St. Sava Society in Kosovo (1886–1912)] in *Naša prošlost* [Our Past] (Kraljevo: n.p., 1975), 61–87; Jovan Hadži-Vasiljević, *Spomenica Društva Sv. Save 1886–1936* [St. Sava Society Memorial 1886–1936] (Belgrade: Društvo Sv. Save, 1936).

79. *Nezavisnost Srpske crkve proglašena 1879 godine* [The Acquisition of Autocephalous Status by the Serbian Church in 1879] (Belgrade: n.p., 1880) contains all relevant documents.

80. Athanasios Angelopoulos, "Relations between the Ecumenical Patriarchate and the Church of Serbia during the Period 1885–1912," *Balkan Studies* 13, no. 1 (1972): 119–27.

81. By 1886, Greek institutions maintained 836 schools, enrolling 45,000 students in Macedonia. In addition, they were running theaters, presses, and musical and gymnastic societies. Bulgarians were influential at the time and had

a solid state budget to finance over 800 schools and close to 30,000 students plus those in secondary schools and teaching colleges. Serbia, on the other hand, by 1900 had opened only 217 schools with around 9,000 students. See Andrew Rossos, *Macedonia and the Macedonians: A History* (Stanford: Hoover Institution Press, 2008), 72–78.

82. *Sveštenstvo i manastiri u Srbiji iz putnih beležaka jednog bogoslova* [The Clergy and Monasteries in Serbia from Travel Notes of a Seminarist] (Belgrade: n.p., 1892), 11.

83. Jos. V. Stojanović, "Hrišćanski katihisis pravoslavne crkve za učenike niže gimnasije i realke" [Christian Catechism for High School Students] and "Crkveno Obredoslovlje za učenike srednjih škola" [Liturgical Manual for High School Students] in *Nastavnik* [Teacher] 8 (1897): 74–79 and 121–23.

84. For Romanian figures, see *Romania. Handbooks Prepared under the Direction of the Historical Section of the Foreign Office. No. 23* (London: H.M.S.O., 1920), 57. For Serbia, see S. M. Veselinovitch, "Religion" in *Servia by the Servians*, ed. Alfred Stead (London: Heinemann, 1909), 155. The number of clergy in Romania was at its lowest since the ecclesiastical reform of 1864 abolished the privileges of the church and left it in destitution.

85. Holm Sundhaussen, *Historische Statistik Serbiens 1834–1914* (Munich: R. Oldenbourg Verlag,1989), 595.

86. "Govor na skupštini našoj o kaluđerima" [Speech on the Assembly regarding Monks] in *Pravoslavlje* [Orthodoxy] 1 (1871): 532–34. Also see *Sveštenstvo i manastiri u Srbiji*, 21.

87. It is a topic of every issue of *Vesnik Srpske Crkve*; see, for example, the report from the XVI Assembly of Priests, held on August 1905, in *Vesnik Srpske Crkve* 11 (1905): 1028–42.

88. Aleksa Ivić, *Arhivska građa o jugoslovenskim književnim i kulturnim radnicima, Vol. 4, 1723–1887* [Archival Sources on Yugoslav Literary and Cultural Figures, vol. 4, 1723–1887] (Belgrade: Srpska Kraljevska Akademija, 1935), 411–12.

89. Đoko Slijepčević, *Nazareni u Srbiji do 1914. godine* [Nazarenes in Serbia until 1914] (Belgrade: Jugoistok, 1943) provides a detailed account based on documentation of the Ministry of Education and Church in AS.

90. Count Chedomille Mijatovich, *The Memoirs of a Balkan Diplomatist* (London: Cassel and Company, 1917), 204.

91. Chedo Mijatovich, *Servia and the Servians* (London: Sir Isaac Pitman & Sons, 1908), 52.

92. Branko Cisarž, *Jedan vek periodične štampe Srpske pravoslavne crkve* [A Century of Publication of the Serbian Orthodox Church Press] (Belgrade: Sveti arhijerejski sinod, 1986), 61.

93. Slobodan G. Marković, "Grof Čedomilj Mijatović—protestantski duh medu Srbima" [Count Čedomilj Mijatović—Protestant Spirit among the Serbs]

in *Liberalna misao u Srbiji. Prilozi istoriji liberalizma od kraja XVIII do sredine XX veka* [Liberal Thought in Serbia. Contributions to the History of Liberalism from the End of the Eighteenth to Mid-Twentieth Century], ed. Jovica Trkulja and Dragoljub Popovic (Belgrade: CUPS and Fridrich Naumann Stiftung, 2001), 247–80.

94. See more in Petar Kuzmič, *Vuk-Daničićevo Sveto pismo i Biblijska društva* [Vuk-Daničić Translation of the Bible and Biblical Societies] (Zagreb: Kršćanska sadašnjost, 1983).

95. For a recent English language evaluation of the Radicals and their ideas, see Augusta Dimou, *Entangled Paths towards Modernity* (Budapest: CEU Press, 2009), especially 113–18.

96. Michael Palairet, *The Balkan Economies c.1800–1914* (Cambridge: Cambridge University Press, 1997).

97. Klaus Buchenau, *Auf russischen Spuren. Orthodoxe Antiwestler in Serbien, 1850–1945* (Wiesbaden: Harrassowitz, 2011).

98. Michael B. Petrovich, introduction to Milovan Djilas, *Njegoš* (New York: Harcourt, Brace & World, 1966), 23.

99. Christopher Boehm, *Montenegrin Social Organization and Values* (New York: AMS Press, 1983), 89.

100. Petrovich, introduction to Milovan Djilas, *Njegoš*, xx.

101. This later caused many controversies and some people in Montenegro in recent years have opposed the Serbian Orthodox Church asking for an autocephalous church.

102. Andrew Baruch Wachtel, "How to Use a Classic: Petar Petrović Njegoš in the Twentieth Century" in *Ideologies and National Identities: The Case of Twentieth-Century Southeastern Europe*, ed. John Lampe and Mark Mazower (Budapest: CEU Press, 2004), 131–53, discusses the trajectory of Njegoš as a national poet. For a less critical but extensive biography, see Djilas, *Njegoš*.

103. M. Pavle, "Voštanica na grobu Mitropolita Mitrofana" [Speech at the Grave of Metropolitan Mitrofan], http://stari.mitropolija.me/aktuelno/svedocenja/mpavle-mitrofan_ban_l.html (accessed February 8, 2013).

104. During Communist rule (1945–90), Montenegro experienced almost an eradication of the (Serbian Orthodox) Church, incomparable with that in any other region of Yugoslavia.

105. Eugen Weber, *Peasants into Frenchmen: the Modernization of Rural France, 1870–1914* (London: Chatto and Windus, 1979).

106. When, following the Bosnian insurrection of 1875, the Serbian Parliament considered going to war against the Ottoman Empire, a peasant deputy reportedly protested by saying: "If we wrench Bosnia, my own field will not become any larger." Quoted in Dimitrije Đorđević, "The Serbian Peasant in the 1876 War" in *War and Society in East Central Europe*, vol. 17: *Insurrections, Wars, and*

the Eastern Crisis in the 1870s, ed. B. K. Kiraly and G. Stokes (Boulder, Colo: Social Science Monographs, 1985), 309–11.

107. Ivana Perković-Radak, *Od anđeoskog pojanja do horske umetnosti: srpska horska crkvena muzika u periodu romantizma, (do1914.godine)* [From Angelic Chanting to Art of Choir Singing: Serbian Choir Church Music in the Age of Romanticism, until 1914] (Belgrade: Fakultet muzičke umetnosti, 2008).

108. In Serbia this new genre of church music was defined and personified in the works of Stevan Stojanović Mokranjac. See Jelena Milojković-Djurić, "The Roles of Jovan Skerlic, Steven Mokranjac, and Paja Jovanovic in Serbian Cultural History, 1900–1914," *Slavic Review* 47, no. 4 (1988): 687–701, and *Tradition and Avant-Garde: Literature and Art in Serbian Culture, 1900–1918* (Boulder, Colo.: East European Monographs; distributed by Columbia University Press, 1988).

109. Pavle Vasić, "Crkvena umetnost kod Srba u XVIII i XIX veku" [Serbian Church Art in the Eighteenth and Nineteenth Centuries] in *Srpska Pravoslavna Crkva 1219—1969* [Serbian Orthodox Church 1219–1969] (Belgrade: Sveti Arijerejski Sinod SPC, 1969), 349. On Hansen and its school, see also Jovanović, *Srpsko crkveno*, 109–30.

110. Slobodan Ćurčić, *Gračanica: King Milutin's Church and Its Place in Late Byzantine Architecture* (University Park: Pennsylvania State University Press, 1979).

111. The Serbian King Petar also opted for the Serbo-Byzantine style in the competition for the Royal Family Mausoleum Church that ran parallel to that for Saint Sava Church. Miodrag Jovanović, *Oplenac* (Topola: Centar za kulturu Dušan Petrov, 1989), 27.

112. This was first noted by R. W. Seton-Watson who referred to a certain similarity between their relationship and that of the English to the Irish. Hugh and Christopher Seton-Watson, *The Making of a New Europe. R. W. Seton-Watson and the last years of Austria-Hungary* (Seattle: University of Washington Press, 1981), 57.

5. The Romanian Orthodox Church
Lucian N. Leustean

1. Keith Hitchins, *The Romanians, 1774–1866* (Oxford: Clarendon Press, 1996), 5.

2. M. Anatole de Demidoff, *Travels in Southern Russia and the Crimea; Through Hungary, Wallachia & Moldavia during the Year 1837*, vol. 2 (London: John Mitchell, Royal Library, 1853), 159, 188. For more on Western travelers to Wallachia and Moldavia, see Mihaela Grancea, "Western Travellers on the Romanians Religiosity (1683–1789)" in *Church and Society in Central and Eastern Europe*, ed. Maria Crăciun and Ovidiu Ghitta (Cluj-Napoca: European Studies Foundation Publishing House, 1998), 400–412; Mihaela Grancea, *Călători*

străini prin Principatele Dunărene, Transilvania și Banat (1683–1789). Identitate și alteritate [Foreign Travelers through the Danubian Principalities, Transylvania and Banat (1683–1789). Identity and Alterity] (Sibiu: Editura Universitară "Lucian Blaga"); Ileana Căzan and Danela Bușă, eds., *Orașul românesc și lumea rurală: realități locale și percepții europene la sfârșitul secolului al XVIII-lea și începutul celui de al XIX-lea* [Romanian City and the Rural World: Local Reality and European Perceptions at the End of the Eighteenth Century and the Beginning of the Nineteenth Century] (Brăila: Editura Istros, 2004); Edward Daniel Clark, *Travels in Various Countries of Europe, Asia and Africa*, 6 vols. (London: T. Cadell & W. Davies, 1810–23); Leyon Pierce Balthasar von Campenhausen, *Travels through Several Provinces of the Russian Empire; with an Historical Account of the Zaporog Cossacks, and of Bessarabia, Moldavia, Wallachia, and the Crimea* (London: Printed for R. Phillips, 1808); William Wilkinson, *An Account of the Principalities of Wallachia and Moldavia* (London: Longman, Hurst, Orme, Rees, Brown, 1820); Reverend Robert Walsh, *Narrative of a Journey from Constantinople to England* (London: Frederick Westley and A. H. Davis / Edinburgh: John Boyd / Dublin: Westley and Tyrrel, 1828); G. Waddington, *The Present Condition and Prospects of the Greek, or Oriental Church* (London: n.p., 1829); John Paget, *Hungary and Transylvania; with Remarks on Their Condition, Social, Political and Economical. With Numerous Illustrations from Sketches by Mr Hering*, 2 vols. (London: John Murray, 1839); Felicia Skene, *Wayfaring Sketches among the Greeks and the Turks and on the Shores of the Danube* (London: n.p., 1849); Mary Adelaide Walker, *Eastern Life and Scenery with Excursions in Asia Minor, Mythilene, Crete and Roumania*, 2 vols. (London: Chapman and Hall, 1866); Major E.C. Johnson, *On the Track of the Crescent—Erratic Notes from the Piraeus to Pesth* (London: Hurst and Blackett, 1885); Thomas Allom, *Constantinople and the Scenery of the Seven Churches of Asia Minor. Illustrated*, 2 vols. (London: Fisher, Son & Co., 1850). I am grateful to Dr. Alex Drace-Francis for providing these sources.

3. Hitchins, *The Romanians, 1774–1866*, 36–43.

4. N. Stoicescu, "Regimul fiscal al preoților din Țara Românească și Moldova până la Regulamentul Organic" [The Fiscal Regime of the Clergy in Wallachia and Moldavia until the Organic Statute], *Biserica Ortodoxă Română* (henceforth BOR) [The Romanian Orthodox Church] 3–4 (1971): 335–54.

5. Hitchins, *The Romanians, 1774–1866*, 36–43.

6. Mircea Păcurariu, *Istoria Bisericii Ortodoxe Române* [The History of the Romanian Orthodox Church], vol. 3 (Bucharest: IBMBOR, 1981).

7. Nicolae M. Popescu, "Viața și faptele părintelui Grigorie Dascalul mitropolitul Țării Românești" [The Life and Activities of Father Metropolitan Grigorie Dascalul of Wallachia], *BOR* 52, no. 5–6 (1934): 289–305.

8. For church-state relations in Wallachia and Moldavia, see Sever Buzan, "Regulamentele Organice și însemnatatea lor pentru dezvoltarea organizației

Bisericii Ortodoxe Române" [The Organic Statutes and their Significance for the Development of the Structure of the Romanian Orthodox Church], *Studii Teologice* [Theological Studies] 8, no. 5–6 (1956): 363–75; Ioan V. Coverca, "Legiuri bisericești cu privire la cler in veacul XIX până la Cuza Voda" [Canon Law Regarding the Clergy in the Nineteenth Century until Prince Cuza], *BOR* 78, no. 5–6 (1960): 496–509; Mircea Nișcoveanu, "Biserica Ortodoxă din Moldova și Patriarhia Ecumenică" [The Orthodox Church in Moldavia and the Ecumenical Patriarchate], *Mitropolia Moldovei și Sucevei* [Metropolitanate of Moldavia and Suceava] 52, no. 9–12 (1976): 662–76; Paul Brusanowski, *Stat și biserică în Vechea Românie între 1821–1925* [State and Church in Old Romania between 1821 and 1925] (Cluj-Napoca: Presa Universitară Clujeană, 2010).

9. Ioan C. Filitti, *Domniile Române sub Regulamentul Organic, 1834–1848* [Romanian Regimes under the Organic Statute, 1834–1848] (Bucharest: Librariile Socec & C. Sfetea, 1915), 131–33.

10. Ibid., 418–19.

11. For more on Metropolitan Veniamin Costache, see Teodor N. Manolache, "Bibliografia mitropolitului Veniamin Costache" [The Biography of Metropolitan Veniamin Costache], *BOR* 64, no. 10–12 (1946): 545–600; Nicolae Iorga, *Viața și faptele mitropolitului Moldovei Veniamin Costache* [The Life and Activities of Metropolitan Veniamin Costache of Moldavia] (Bucharest: n.p., 1904); Mihai Manuca, "Mitropolitul Veniamin Costache" [Metropolitan Veniamin Costache], *BOR* 86, no. 1–2 (1968): 165–81.

12. Constantin Mosor, "Biserica Moldovei în timpul domniei lui Mihail Sturdza (1834–1849)" [The Church of Moldavia during Mihail Sturza's Reign] *BOR*, no. 5–6 (1971): 593–605.

13. Filitti, *Domniile Române*, 514–15.

14. The conflict centered on financial issues as the prince intended to bring a number of highly productive monastery properties under state control. Veniamin agreed to exchange some church land in Bukovina for that in Moldavia. Under pressure from an anonymous letter that accused him of embezzlement, he resigned. Ioan C. Filitti argued that Prince Sturza may have written the letter to remind Veniamin that a previous metropolitan, Iacob, who had been in a similar financial position, was stabbed.

15. Filitti, *Domniile Române*, 517–18.

16. Ibid.

17. Mosor, "Biserica Moldovei"; Melchisedec Ștefănescu, *Cronica Romanului și a Episcopiei de Roman* [The Chronicle of Roman and the Bishopric of Roman], vol. 2 (Bucharest: n.p., 1875), 200.

18. Filitti, *Domniile Române*, 530.

19. Nicolae Dobrescu, *Studii de Istoria Bisericii Române Contimporane. Istoria Bisericii din România (1850–1895)* [Studies of the History of the Contemporary

Romanian Orthodox Church. The History of the Church in Romania (1850–1895)] (Bucharest: Tipografia "Bukarester Tagblatt," 1905), 34–37.

20. Constantin Erbiceanu, a church historian, wrote in 1903 that Sofronie paid a large amount of money in order to buy his metropolitan seat.

21. Dobrescu, *Studii*, 23.

22. Ibid.

23. *Albina românească* [The Romanian Bee Newspaper] (1843), 33, quoted in Mosor, "Biserica Moldovei."

24. The full text is available in *Acte și documente relative la Istoria Rensacerei României publicate de Ghenadie Petrescu, Dimitrie A. Sturdza și Dimitrie C. Sturdza* [Acts and Documents regarding the History of Romania Published by Ghenadie Petrescu, Dimitrie A. Sturdza and Dimitrie C. Sturdza], vol. 3 (Bucharest: Institutul de Arte Grafice Carol Göbl, 1889): 1–7 [henceforth, *Acte și documente*].

25. Ibid.

26. The full text is available in *Acte și documente*, 620–27.

27. "Răspunsul Mitropolitului Sofronie Miclescu către Caimacamul Vogoride" [The Answer of Metropolitan Sofronie Miclescu to Caimacam Vogoride], April 14, 1857, in *Acte și documente*, 433.

28. "Scrisoarea patriarhului Constantinopolui Ciril către Mitropolia Moldovei" [The Letter of the Ecumenical Patriarch Cyril to the Metropolitanate of Moldavia], April 19, 1857, in *Acte și documente*, 465.

29. Dobrescu, *Studii*, 82–83.

30. "Declarația archimandritului Neofit Arbore și iconomului Vasile Arbore" [The Declaration of Archimandrite Neofit Arbore and Vasile Arbore], July 7, 1857, in *Acte și documente*, 158–59.

31. The text in the original English translation uses "Rouman/Roumania" for "Romanian/Romania." The full debates of the ad-hoc assemblies were published in *Acte și documente* and a summary was translated into English in *The National Wishes of Moldavia and Wallachia pronounced by the Divans ad hoc Assembled at Jassy and Bucarest in Accordance with the Treaty of Paris. Official Extracts of the Protocols of the Moldavian Divan from no1 to 32 Inclusive, also the "Memorandum" of the Wallachian Divan Explanatory of the Four Wishes of the Nation, with Its Annexed Capitulations with the Ottoman Empire, second improved and enlarged edition, Introduction "To the Reader" signed by An Englishman* (Brussels: J. van Buggenhoudt, 1858), 109–11.

32. *The National Wishes of Moldavia and Wallachia*, 65–66. See also J. C. Bratiano, *Memoire sur la Situation de la Moldo-Valachie depuis Le Traite de Paris* (Paris: Czech A Franck, 1857), which contains the text of the Treaty of Paris.

33. *The National Wishes of Moldavia and Wallachia*, 118–19.

34. The following two subchapters draw on Lucian N. Leustean, "The Political Control of Orthodoxy in the Construction of the Romanian State, 1859–1918," *European History Quarterly* 37, no. 1 (2007): 60–81.

35. *L'Empereur Napoléon III et Les Principautés Roumaines* (Paris: E. Dentu, 1858); *La Question d'Orient et la Nation Roumaine* (Paris: Librairie du Luxembourg, 1867).

36. T. W. Riker, *The Making of Roumania. A Study of an International Problem, 1856–1866* (London: Oxford University Press, 1931), 348–49.

37. *Le Protectorat du Czar ou La Roumanie et la Roussie. Nouveaux documents sur la situation européenne* (Paris: Au Comptoir des Imprimeurs-Unis, 1850); M. T. Cidharold, *La Turquie et les Principautés Danubiennes* (Paris: E. Dentu, 1857); *L'Autriche et le Prince Roumain* (Paris: E. Dentu, 1859).

38. Dan Berindei, Elisabeta Oprescu, Valeriu Stan, *Documente privind domnia lui Alexandru Ioan Cuza: 1859–1861* [Documents Regarding the Reign of Alexandru Ioan Cuza: 1859–1861], vol. 1 (Bucharest: Editura Academiei, 1989).

39. Hitchins, *The Romanians, 1774–1866*, 297.

40. Commission Princière de la Roumanie a l'Exposition universelle de Paris en 1867, *Notice sur la Roumanie principalement au point de vue de son économie rurale industrielle et commerciale avec une carte de la Principauté de Roumanie* (Paris: Librairie A. Franck, 1867), 17.

41. Ibid., 19.

42. Ibid., 18.

43. Dobrescu, *Studii*, 34–37.

44. R. W. Seton-Watson, *A History of the Roumanians: from Roman Times to the Completion of Unity* (Cambridge: The University Press, 1934), 306–7.

45. His decision was approved by the national assembly with a vote of 93 for and 3 against on December 25, 1863. Hitchins, *The Romanians, 1774–1866*, 313. The Orthodox Church had around seventy dedicated monasteries; *Quelques mots sur la sécularisation des biens conventuels en Roumanie* (Paris: E. Dentu, 1864), 29. See also *La France. Le Prince Couza et la Liberté en Orient* (Paris: Chez les Principaux Librairies, 1864) and *Quelques mots sur la sécularisation des biens conventuels en Roumanie* (Paris: E. Dentu, 1864).

46. Ministerul Cultelor și Instrucțiunii, 7.

47. Stelian Izvoranu, "Sinoadele de sub Regimul lui Cuza Vodă. Importanța lor pentru viața bisericească" [The Synods during the Reign of Cuza. Their Importance for Church Life], *BOR* 7–8 (1960): 658–82.

48. Ibid., 675.

49. Paul E. Michelson, *Conflict and Crisis: Romanian Political Development, 1861–1871* (New York: Garland, 1987).

50. *Plebiscitulŭ Poporului Românu* [The Census of the Romanian People] (Bucharest: Typografia Cesar Boliac, 1864), 12–13.

51. Ibid., 25.

52. Cuza started a national educational program aimed at reducing the level of illiteracy and at offering more land to the peasants. However, the impact of these laws was limited as at the end of the nineteenth century around 78 percent of Romanians were still illiterate.

53. Stephen the Great was sanctified by the Romanian Orthodox Church in 1992.

54. *1866–1896. Trei-deci de ani de domnie ai Regelui Carol I. Cuvântări și acte* [1866–1896. Thirty Years of the Reign of King Carol I. Speeches and Documents], vol. 1 (Bucharest: Institutul de Arte Grafice Carol Göbl, 1897), 1.

55. Ibid., 88–89.

56. "Constituția din 1866" [The 1866 Constitution] in *Monitorul—Jurnal Oficial al României*, no. 142 from June 1, 1866.

57. J. C. Bratiano, *La question religieuse en Roumanie. Lettre a Monsieur le Directeur de l'Opinion Nationale* (Paris: Librairie du Luxembourg, 1866).

58. Nicolae Iorga, *Istoria Bisericii Românești și a vieții religioase a Românilor* [The History of the Romanian Church and of the Religious Life of Romanians], vol. 1 (Vălenii-de-Munte: Tipografia "Neamul Românesc," 1908), 313.

59. *Monitorul Oficial*, no. 280, from December 19, 1872.

60. Nifon (1850–75); Calinic Miclescu (1875–86); Iosif Gheorghian (1886–93); Ghenadie Petrescu (1893–96); Iosif Gheorghian (1896–1909); Athanasie Mironescu (1909–11); Conon Arămescu-Donici (1912–19). During the period when there was no Primate Metropolitan, the church was ruled by the following metropolitan deputies: Inochentie Moisiu Ploieșteanul (August–November 1886); Gherasim Timuș Pitești (April–May 1893); Iosif Naniescu, Gherasim Timuș and Partenie Clinceni (May–December 1896); Teodosie Atanasiu Ploieșteanul (July 1911–February 1912); Platon Ciosu Ploieșteanul (January–December 1919).

61. Ploieșteanul for the Metropolitanate of Wallachia; Craioveanul for the Bishopric of Râmnic; Râmniceanul for the Bishopric of Buzău; Piteșteanul for the Bishopric of Argeș; Botoșăneanul for the Metropolitanate of Moldavia; Bacăoanul for the Bishopric of Roman; Bârlădeanul for the Bishopric of Huși; Gălățianul for the Bishopric of Dunărea de Jos. See Chiru C. Costescu, *Colecțiune de legi, regulamente, acte, deciziuni, circulări, instrucțiuni, formulare și programe privitoare la Biserică, culte, cler, învățământ religios, bunuri bisericești, etc.* [Collection of Laws, Regulations, Documents, Decisions, Circular Letters, Instructions, Forms and Programs] (Bucharest: Institutul de Arte Grafice C. Sfetea, 1916), 42.

62. Administrația Casei Bisericii, *Biserica Ortodoxă și Cultele Străine din Regatul României* [The Orthodox Church and Foreign Confessions in the Romanian Kingdom] (Bucharest: Institutul de Arte Grafice Carol Göbl, 1904), 148.

63. Frederick Kellogg, *The Road to Romanian Independence*, West Lafayette, Ind.: Purdue University, 1995; Barbara Jelavich, *Russia and the Formation of the Romanian National State, 1821–1878*, Cambridge: Cambridge University Press, 1984; Charles and Barbara Jelavich, *The Establishment of the Balkan National States, 1804–1920*, Seattle: University of Washington Press, 1977.

64. *1866–1896. Trei-deci*, 415.

65. Dennis P. Hupchick, *The Balkans from Constantinople to Communism* (New York: Palgrave, 2002), 265.

66. Ministerul Cultelor și al Instucțiunii Publice, *Acte privitoare la autocefalia Bisericei Ortodoxe a României* [Documents on the Autocephaly of the Orthodox Church of Romania] (Bucharest: Tipografia Cărților Bisericești, 1885), 3–4.

67. Episcopul de Roman Melchisedek, *Raportu despre relațiunile bisericesci ale clerului orthodoxu românu cu creștinii eterodoxi seu de alt ritu și cu necredincioșii carii trăiesc în Regatul Românu* [Report on the Clerical Relations of the Romanian Orthodox Clergy with Heterodox Christians or Other Confessions and with Non-believers Who Live in the Romanian Kingdom] (Bucharest: Tipografia Cărților Bisericești, 1882.)

68. *Recensământul Populațiunei din Decembrie 1899* [Census of the Population in December 1899] (Bucharest: Eminescu, 1905).

69. Ministère de l'Agriculture, de l'Industrie, du Commerce et des Domaines, *La Roumanie. 1866–1906* (Bucharest: Imprimerie Socec, 1907), 111.

70. Melchisedec Episcopul Romanului, *Memoriu despre starea preoților din România și despre posițiunea lor morală și materială* [Report on the Clergy's Situation in Romania and on its Moral and Material Situation] (Bucharest: Tipografia Cărților Bisericești, 1888), 9.

71. Ibid., 13.

72. Ibid., 14.

73. Mihai Constandache, "Măsuri noi de organizare în Biserica Ortodoxă Română la începutul veacului al XX-lea" [New Measures in the Organization of the Romanian Orthodox Church at the beginning of the Twentieth Century], *BOR* 40 (1965): 765.

74. The revised law was published in *Regulament pentru punerea în aplicare a Legei asupra clerului mirean și seminariilor sancționată prin înaltul decret regal no 869 din 25 februarie 1906* [Regulations for the Implementation of the Law of the Clergy and Seminaries Approved by the High Royal Decree No. 869 of February 25, 1906] (Bucharest: Imprimeria Statului, 1909); Administrația Cassei Bisericii, *Regulamentul Legii Clerului Mirean și Seminariilor* [Regulations of the Law of the Clergy and Seminaries] (Bucharest: Tipografia Cărților Bisericești, 1914).

75. Ministerul Cultelor și Instrucțiunii, *Casa Bisericii 1902–1919* [The House of the Church 1902–1919] (Bucharest: Tipografia Cărților Bisericești, 1920).

76. Păcurariu, *Istoria Bisericii Ortodoxe Române*, 142.

77. M. *Theodorian-Carada, Politica Religioasă a României. Conferință ținute la Cercul de studii al Partidului Conservator, în ziua de 3 decembrie 1916* [The Religious Politics of Romania. Conference Held at the Center for Studies of the Conservative Party on December 3, 1916] (Bucharest: Tipografia "Cooperativa," 1916), 7.

78. Ibid., 8.

79. Ibid., 17.

80. Mariu Theodorian-Carada gave the example of some Armenians who left Romania to enlist in the Russian war and suggested that this happened because they did not feel that Romania was their own country. Ibid., 21.

81. In 1857, under the jurisdiction of the Metropolitanate of Moldavia, a consistory was established in Ismail for Romanians living in the districts on the eastern side of the Prut River. In 1864 the consistory was transformed into the Bishopric of Lower Danube. In 1878 the Bishopric moved its headquarters to Galați and extended its jurisdiction to include Romanians living in Dobrujda. In addition to the Bishopric of Lower Danube, the Metropolitanate of Drystra (Silistra) and the Metropolitanate of Proilavia (Brăila), both of the Ecumenical Patriarchate, had Romanians among their faithful.

82. Hitchins, *Rumania, 1866–1947*, 211.

83. Eduard A. Bielz, *Handbuch der Landeskunde Siebenbürgens* (Hermannstadt: S. Filtsch, 1857), 159–60.

84. Hitchins, *The Romanians, 1774–1866*, 199.

85. Since the sixteenth century, Protestant Churches had equal rights to the Roman Catholic Church. Keith Hitchins, *A Nation Discovered: Romanian Intellectuals in Transylvania and the Idea of Nation, 1700–1848* (Bucharest: The Encyclopedic Publishing House, 1999), 12.

86. Keith Hitchins, *The Rumanian National Movement in Transylvania, 1780–1849* (Cambridge, Mass.: Harvard University Press, 1969), 119.

87. Ibid., 140–45.

88. Păcurariu, *Istoria Bisericii Ortodoxe Române*, 65–75.

89. Ibid.

90. The 1850 census of Transylvania revealed a total population of 2,062,379 divided into 648,410 Greek Catholic, 638,017 Orthodox, 295,790 Protestant Helvetic Confession, 219,721 Roman Catholics, 198,851 Protestant Ausburg Confession, 46,016 Unitarian and 15,574 Jewish confession. Bielz, *Handbuch*, 162.

91. Hitchins, *The Rumanian National Movement*, 220.

92. For a detailed biography, see Johann Schneider, *Der Hermannstädter Metropolit Andrei von Șaguna. Reform und Erneuerung der Orthodoxen Kirche in Siebenbürgen und Ungarn nach 1848*, Studia Transylvanica (Cologne: Böhlau Verlag, 2005).

93. Păcurariu, *Istoria Bisericii Ortodoxe Române*, 348–68.

94. After the 1848/49 revolution, Transylvania was a province directly dependent on the Vienna Court and ruled by a governor in Sibiu: General Ludwig Wohlgemuth (1849–51), Prince Karl von Schwarzenberg (1851–58), and General Friedrich Lichtenstein (1858–60).

95. Transylvania was ruled by a civil government under the leadership of Count Imre Mikó, provisional governor (1860–61) who was succeeded by Louis Folliot de Crenneville (1861–67). The capital was moved from Sibiu to Cluj.

96. Andreiu Șaguna, *Anthorismos, sau deslușire compărătivă asupra broșurei "Dorințele drept credinciosului Cleru din Bucovina în privința organisărei canonice a diecezei, și a ierarchicei sale referințe în Organismulu bisericei ortodocse din Austria"* [Anthorimos, or Comparative Treatise of the Brochure "The Wishes of the Blessed Clergy in Bukovina Regarding the Canonical Organization of the Diocese, and Its Hierarchical Reference within the Orthodox Church in Austria"] (Sibiu: Tipografia diecesană, 1861).

97. The Bishopric of Arad was established in 1706 and the Bishopric of Caransebeș in 1865. The Arad region had a population of 557,880 and the Caransebeș 336,361. Data from Magaret G. Dampier, *History of the Orthodox Church in Austria-Hungary* (London: Rivingtons, 1905), 69.

98. Paul Brusanowski argues that although the Transylvanian Church had not publicly declared autocephaly, preferring instead to term of "coordinated to the Serbian metropolitanate," it acted as an autocephalous church thoughout the nineteenth century. This volume supports this view and indicates that autocephaly was enjoyed not only by the Metropolitanate of Transylvania but also by the Metropolitanate of Bukovina and Dalmatia. Brusanowski quotes Metropolitan Nicolae Bălan who stated in the Holy Synod of February 4, 1925, when the Romanian Orthodox Church was raised to the rank of patriarchate, that "With the exception of the Bessarabian Archbishopric . . . [the Churches] of Transylvania and Bukovina entered into Romanian unity as autocephalous Churches." Paul Brusanowski, *Reforma Constituțională din Biserica Ortodoxă a Transilvaniei între 1850–1925* [The Constitutional Reform in the Orthodox Church of Transylvania between 1850 and 1925] (Cluj: Presa Universitară Clujeană, 2007), 118–20.

99. Șaguna asked for financial support from Wallachia and Moldavia for the reconstruction of around forty churches that were burned during the 1848/49 revolution. Păcurariu, *Istoria Bisericii Ortodoxe Române*, 77–86 and 92–112.

100. Hitchins gives Hungarian sources on education in Transylvania indicating that, in 1880, 5.7 percent of the population had knowledge of the Magyar language. The percentage increased to 8.7 in 1900 and 12.7 in 1910. Keith Hitchins, *A Nation Affirmed: The Romanian National Movement in Transylvania, 1860–1914* (Bucharest: The Encyclopaedic Publishing House, 1999), 220.

101. Păcurariu, *Istoria Bisericii Ortodoxe Române*, 195–207; Mircea Păcurariu, *The Policy of the Hungarian State Concerning the Romanian Church in Transylvania under the Dual Monarchy, 1867–1918* (Bucharest: The Bible and Mission Institute of the Romanian Orthodox Church, 1986).

102. In 1810, Bukovina had around 150,000 Romanians and 48,000 non-Romanians. In 1774, the Jewish population numbered 526 people; in 1848 it represented around 11,600. Hitchins, *The Romanians, 1774–1866*, 226. For the Jewish presence in Bukovina, see Daniel Hrenciuc, *Dilemele conviețuirii: Evreii în Bucovina (1774–1939)* [Dilemma of Co-Habitation: The Jews in Bukovina (1774–1939)] (Iași: TipoMoldova, 2010).

103. Hitchins, *The Romanians, 1774–1866*, 226.

104. I. Nistor, *Istoria Fondului Bisericesc din Bucovina* [The History of the Church Fund of Bukovina] (Cernăuți: Editura Glasul Bucovinei, 1921), 32.

105. Ibid., 227.

106. For differences between the Ruthenian Uniate and Orthodox Churches, see Barbara Skinner, *The Western Front of the Eastern Church. Uniate and Orthodox Conflict in 18th-Century Poland, Ukraine, Belarus, and Russia* (DeKalb: Northern Illinois University Press, 2009); John-Paul Himka, *Religion and Nationality in Western Ukraine. The Greek Catholic Church and the Ruthenian National Movement in Galicia, 1867–1900* (Montreal: McGill-Queen's University Press, 1999); Timothy Snyder, *The Reconstruction of Nations. Poland, Ukraine, Lithuania, Belarus, 1569–1999* (New Haven, Conn.: Yale University Press, 2003), 106–8.

107. I. Nistor, *Istoria bisericii din Bucovina și a rostului ei național-cultural în viața românilor bucovineni* [The History of the Church in Bukovina and its National-Cultural Role in the Life of Bukovinian Romanians] (Bucharest: Institutul de Arte Grafice Carol Göbl, 1916), 27–28.

108. Ibid., 39

109. Ibid., 66

110. Mihai-Ștefan Ceaușu, *Parlamentarism, partide și elita politică în Bucovina Habsburgică (1848–1918). Contribuții la istoria parlamentarismului în spațiul central-est european* [Parliamentarism, Parties and Political Elite in Habsburg Bukovina. Contributions to the History of Parliamentarism in Central-East European Region] (Iași: Junimea, 2004), 75

111. Ibid., 108 and 486.

112. Nistor, *Istoria bisericii din Bucovina*, 81.

113. Ibid., 84–85.

114. Ibid., 89.

115. The establishment of the Metropolitanate of Bukovina and Dalmatia was not welcomed by the Churches in the other Romanian provinces. Metropolitan Calinic Miclescu of Moldavia and Suceava sent an official protest to his government claiming jurisdiction in Bukovina. Nistor, *Istoria bisericii din Bucovina*, 115.

116. Ibid., 113.

117. Ion Căpreanu, *Bucovina: Istorie și cultură românească (1775–1918)* [Bukovina: Romanian History and Culture] (Iași: Editura Moldova, 1995), 68

118. Ibid., 112

119. Data in 1910 shows that 273,254 spoke Romanian; 305,101 Ruthenian; 168,851 German; 102,919 Yiddish; 36,210 Polish; 10,391 Hungarian; 1,005 Czech; 81 Slovenian; 36 Italian. See I. Nistor, *Românii și rutenii din Bucovina. Studiu istoric și statistic* [Romanians and Ruthenians in Bukovina: Historical and Statistical Study] (Bucharest: Librăriile Socec & Comp, 1914), 1. In 1910 the religious structure of Bukovina counted: 547,603 Orthodox; 341 Armenian; 3,232 Lippovenian; 98,565 Roman Catholics; 26,182 Greek Catholics; 657 Armenian Catholics; 14 Old Catholics; 20,029 Evangelical Augustine; 484 Evangelical Helvetics; 2 Other religious confessions; 102,919 Jewish; 8 Muslim; 62 Without religion. Nistor, *Istoria bisericii din Bucovina*, 196.

120. The census of 1817 revealed that 86 percent of inhabitants (419,420 out of 482,630) were Moldavians, 6.5 percent (30,000) were Ukrainians and 4.2 percent (19,130) were Jews. In 1897, 56 percent (1,092,000 out of 1,935,412) were Moldavians, 18.9 percent Ukrainians and Russians and 11.7 percent Jews. Hitchins, *Rumania, 1866–1947*, 239–40.

121. *Facts and Comments Concerning Bessarabia, 1812–1940. Compiled by a Group of Romanian Press Correspondents* (London: George Allen and Unwin Ltd, 1941), 40.

122. Ion Varta, "Politica de deznaționalizare și mișcarea națională a românilor basarabeni sub ocupație țaristă (1812–1918)" [The Politics of Denationalization and the National Movement of Romanian Bessarabian under Tsarist Occupation (1812–1918)] in *200 Ani din Istoria Românilor dintre Prut și Nistru* [200 Years of the History of Romanians between Prut and Dniester Rivers], ed. Ioan Aurel-Pop and Ioan Scurtu (Chișinău and Bucharest: Fundația Culturală Magazin Istoric. Grupul Editorial Litera, 2012), 71.

123. Ibid., 72.

124. Ion Nistor, *Istoria Basarabiei. Ediție și studiu bio-biobliografic de Stelian Neagoe* [The History of Bessarabia. Edition and Bio-Biographical Study by Stelian Neagoe] (Bucharest: Humanitas, 1991), 228.

125. Ibid., 229.

126. Boris Buzilă, *Din istoria vieții bisericești din Basarabia (1812–1918; 1918–1944)* [Church History in Bessarabia (1812–1918; 1918–1944)] (Bucharest: Editura Fundației Culturale Române and Chișinău: Intreprinderea Editorial-Polografică Știința, 1996), 38–39.

127. Ștefan Ciobanu, *Cultura românească în Basarabia sub stăpânirea rusă* [Romanian Culture in Bessarabia under Russian Occupation] (Chișinău: Editura "Asociației Uniunea Culturală Bisericească din Chișinău," 1923), 50.

128. Buzilă, *Din istoria vieții bisericești*, 38–39.
129. Nistor, *Istoria Basarabiei*, 237.
130. *Facts and Comments Concerning Bessarabia, 1812–1940*, 50.
131. The 1897 census revealed the following ethnic structure according to maternal language (in percentage). Rural population: 5.1 Russian; 20.3 Ukrainian; 0.3 Polish; 5.6 Bulgarian; 53.5 Moldovan; 3.5 German; 0.07 Greek; under 0 Armenian; 0.5 Gypsy; 7.2 Jewish; 3.4 Turkish; 0.3 other language; Urban population: 26.4 Russian; 15.7 Ukrainian; 2 Polish; 3.9 Bulgarian; 14.1 Moldovan; 0.7 German; 0.4 Greek; 0.4 Armenian; 0.1 Gypsy; 37.1 Jewish; 0.6 other languages. Dinu Postarencu, *Contribuții la istoria modernă a Basarabiei* [Contributions to the Modern History of Bessarabia] (Chișinău: Tipografia Centrală, 2009), 59–60.
132. Hitchins, *Rumania, 1866–1947*, 244–45.
133. Nistor, *Istoria Basarabiei*, 232.
134. Hitchins, *Rumania, 1866–1947*, 246–47.
135. Nistor, *Istoria Basarabiei*, 237.
136. Buzilă, *Din istoria vieții bisericești*, 38–39.
137. Hitchins, *Rumania, 1866–1947*, 246–47.
138. In 1997 he was canonized by the Russian Orthodox Church.
139. Varta, "Politica de deznaționalizare," 97.
140. Buzilă, *Din istoria vieții bisericești*, 81–82.
141. Glenn E. Torrey, *Romania and World War I: A Collection of Studies* (Iași and Portland: Center for Romanian Studies, 1998); Costică Prodan and Dumitru Preda, *The Romanian Army during the First World War* (Bucharest: Univers Enciclopedic, 1998).
142. R. W. Seton-Watson, *A History of the Roumanians: From Roman Times to the Completion of Unity* (Cambridge: The University Press, 1934), 521–54.
143. Academia Română, *Istoria Românilor, România întregită (1918–1940)* [The History of Romanians, United Romania (1918–1940)], vol. 8 (Bucharest: Editura Enciclopedică, 2003), 31.
144. The Central National Historical Archives, Bucharest (henceforth ANIC), Fond Miron Cristea, Dossier 2.
145. Ilie Sandru and Valentin Borda, *Un nume pentru istorie—Patriarhul Elie Miron Cristea* [A Name for History—Patriarch Elie Miron Cristea] (Târgu-Mureș: Cartea de Editură "Petru Maior," 1998), 127–28.
146. Ioan Scurtu, Constantin Mocanu, Doina Smârcea, *Documente privind istoria României între anii 1918–1944* [Documents of Romanian History from 1918 to 1944] (Bucharest: Editura Didactică și Pedagogică, 1995), 38–39.
147. Sandru and Borda, *Un nume pentru istorie*, 130.
148. Ibid., 133.
149. Antonie Plămădeală, *Contribuții istorice privind perioada 1918–1939: Elie Miron Cristea, documente, însemnări și corespondențe* [Historical Contributions

on the 1918–1939 Period: Elie Miron Cristea, Documents, Notes and Correspondence] (Sibiu: Tiparul Tipografiei Eparhiale, 1987).

150. ANIC, Fond Miron Cristea. Dossier 3.

151. Miron Cristea, *Principii Fundamentale pentru Organizarea Unitară a Bisericii Ortodoxe Române* [Fundamental Principles for the United Organization of the Romanian Orthodox Church] (Bucharest: Tipografia Cărților Bisericești, 1920), 3.

152. Ibid., 4.

153. Ibid., 6.

154. Ibid., 11.

155. Ibid., 20.

156. Ibid., 14.

157. Philip Martineau, *Roumania and Her Rulers* (London: Stanley Paul & Co., 1927), 107–8.

158. American Committee on the Rights of Religious Minorities, *Roumania. Ten Years After* (Boston: The Beacon Press, 1928), 96.

159. Article 5 of *Regulamentul general al Societății Ortodoxe Naționale a Femeilor Române* [General Regulations of the National Orthodox Society of Romanian Women] (Bucharest: Tipografia Albina, 1943).

160. Pimen, Mitropolitul Moldovei, *Mărășești, locul biruinței cu biserica neamului* [Mărășești, the Place of Victory with the Church of the People] (Neamț: Tipografia Monastirei Neamțu, 1924).

161. Scurtu, *Documente privind istoria*, 53–54.

162. ANIC, Fond Miron Cristea, Dossier 3.

163. Ibid.

164. *Recensământul Populațiunei din Decembrie 1899* [Census of the Population of December 1899] (Bucharest: Eminescu, 1905); Institutul Central de Statistică, *Recensământul General al Populației României din 29 decembrie 1930, publicat de Dr. Sabin Manuilă* [General Census of the Population of Romania of December 29, 1930, published by Dr. Sabin Manuilă], vols. 2–4 (Bucharest: Monitorul Oficial, Imprimeria Națională).

165. Un om al bisericii [A Man of the Church], *Papism și Ortodoxism în Ardeal sau Porfiră și cunună de spini. Studiu statistic bisericesc*, [Papism and Orthodoxism in Transylvania or Porphyry and Thorn Wreath. A Study of Clerical Statistics], Arad: Tiparul tipografiei diecesane, 95 pages in I. Mihălcescu, "Cronica internă" [Internal Chronicle], *BOR* 7 (1923): 535–39.

166. Arhiereu Grig. L. Botoșăneanu, "Biserica Ortodoxă Română și celelalte confesiuni" [The Romanian Orthodox Church and Other Confessions], *BOR* 6 (1928): 487.

167. Nicolae Bălan, *Biserica neamului și drepturile ei. Discurs rostit la discuția generală asupra proiectului de lege a cultelor, în ședința dela 27 martie 1928, a*

senatului român [The Church of the People and Its Rights. Speech Presented at the General Discussion on the Proposed Law of Religious Confessions, at the Meeting on March 27, 1928, at the Romanian Senate] (Sibiu: Tiparul Tipografiei Arhidiecezane, 1928).

168. "Spicuiri în cuvântările dela Senat despre Legea Cultelor" [Quotations from Senate Speeches on the Law of Religious Confessions], *BOR* 5 (1928): 459–61.

169. The new calendar led to a split in the church and the creation of a small fraction, the Orthodox Believers of Old Rite, which continued to preserve the old calendar. The state supported the Orthodox Church and persecuted the leaders of the Old Rite who were seen as challenging the state's interests.

170. "Cronica bisericească" [Ecclesiastical Chronicle], *BOR* 1 (1924): 33.

171. Academia Română, *Istoria Românilor*, vol. 8, 210.

172. "Cronica Bisericească. Investitura Patriarhului României" [Ecclesiastical Chronicle. The Enthronement of the Romanian Patriarch], *BOR* 11 (1925): 703–4.

173. Ibid., 704–5.

174. A general report in 1935 of the Romanian Patriarchate revealed that 12,375,850 people (3,432,541 families) declared themselves Orthodox. The church was structured at the local level into 8,474 parishes; there were 820 urban and 7,654 rural parishes in charge of 10,740 church buildings. The Orthodox clergy numbered 8,542 priests, 7,868 of which received salaries from the state, 380 salaries from private funding, 188 were retired while 106 priests were without state salary. The composition of the clergy showed that most of them had only elementary theological education. Only 76 priests had doctoral degrees in theology, 1,446 had university degrees, while 3,287 had completed seven or eight years in a seminary and 537 only four years. In addition, the priests were helped by 10,452 cantors; 9,166 received state support and 1,268 private funding. "Rapoarte generale pe anii 1932–1935 către Cogresul Național Bisericesc din 14 octombrie 1935" [General Reports on 1932–35 to the National Clerical Congress from October 14, 1935], *BOR* 1–2 (1936): 23–25.

6. The Bulgarian Orthodox Church
Daniela Kalkandjieva

1. Despite debates in Bulgarian historiography, the year 927 has been widely accepted as the date when the patriarchal dignity of the medieval Bulgarian Church was proclaimed. This date is given on the website of the Bulgarian Patriarchate, http://bg-patriarshia.bg/ (accessed February 8, 2013).

2. In fact, the Bulgarian Church was restored upon the liberation of Bulgaria from Byzantine rule in 1187, but due to the Union of the Bulgarian Church

with the Roman Pope signed in 1204; this interim period is omitted by Orthodox historians. The Union was denounced in 1235 when the Bulgarian Church was recognized as patriarchate by the council of the ancient Orthodox Churches in Lampsak. The year 1393 marks the fall of the Bulgarian Kingdom of Tûrnovo, while the exact date of the abolishment of the Patriarchate of Tûrnovo remains an open question for historians.

3. The recognition of the patriarchal dignity of the Bulgarian Orthodox Church by all Orthodox Churches, however, took some time and was only confirmed in 1961.

4. As with the Bulgarian Orthodox Church, the notion of the Bulgarian state embraces several political entities known under the name Bulgaria throughout the centuries—i.e., their three kingdoms (681–1018, 1187–1396 and 1878–1946) and one republic (since 1946)

5. The Bulgarian character of the Archbishopric of Ohrid was advanced in 1672 by Father Paisii of Hilendar in his *Istoriya Slavyanobolgarskaya* [Slavonic-Bulgarian History]. Over following centuries it was developed by Bulgarian and Russian Church historians. The most elaborate study on the Archbishopric of Ohrid was made between the two world wars by Ivan Snegarov, *Istoriya na Ohridskata Arhiepiskopiya* [History of the Archbishopric of Ohrid], 2 vols., 1st ed., vol. 1, Sofia: 1924; vol. 2, Sofia: 1932 (Sofia: Akademichno izdatelstvo "Prof. Marin Drinov," 1995).

6. The terms "First," "Second" and "Third Bulgarian State" are adopted by modern Bulgarian historiography to signify three political entities with the same name that existed consecutively on the present territory of Bulgaria since 680.

7. Although the Archbishopric of Ohrid was integrated into the Bulgarian Empire in the 1230s, its dioceses were not subjected to the Patriarchate of Tûrnovo. Ivan Snegarov, *Istoriya na Ohridskata Arhiepiskopiya* [History of the Archbishopric of Ohrid], vol. 1 (Sofia: Akademichno izdatelstvo "Prof. Marin Drinov," 1995), 88–161. More recently, the changes in the ecclesiastical geography of the Bulgarian lands have been studied by Olga Todorova, *Pravoslavnata tsûrkva i bûlgarite, XV–XVIII vek* [Orthodox Church and Bulgarians, XV–XVIII Centuries] (Sofia: Akademichno izdatelstvo "Prof. Marin Drinov," 1997), 64–92.

8. In August 1394, the Patriarch of Constantinople appointed the former Metropolitan of Moldavia Jeremiah as head of the church of Tûrnovo but with limited rights. The new hierarch had no independent competence to appoint bishops for the dioceses of his church. Until today it remains unclear when and how the Patriarchate of Tûrnovo was abolished. Todorova, *Pravoslavnata tsûrkva*, 38–40.

9. Olga Todorova presents a list of Slavonic bishops who had their tenures in the Bulgarian lands from the beginning of the fifteenth century to the mid-nineteenth century. In most cases, their ethnic origin remains unknown (i.e.,

they could be Bulgarians, but also Serbs). See Todorova, *Pravoslavnata tsûrkva*, 151–54. Pierre Voillery lists the names of twelve metropolitans of Bulgarian origin acting in the period from 1800 to 1878. Most of them took up office in the period from the Crimean War (1853–56) to the establishment of the Bulgarian Exarchate (1870), while five did so after 1870. P. Voillery, *Mezhdu dva svyata: Bûlgarite v Rumeliya, XVIII–XIX* [Between Two Worlds: Bulgarians in Rumelia, Eighteenth–Nineteenth Centuries], trans. M. Petrova, V. Lazarova, et al. (Sofia: KAMA, 2005), 191–92.

10. Upon their Ottoman conquest, the Serbs, as the Bulgarians before them, lost their state and church. In the second half of the sixteenth century, however, the Grand Vezier Mehmet Sokolovich, who was of Serbian origin, restored the Patriarchate of Ipek and appointed his brother as its patriarch.

11. The Catholic Church avoided relations with the Sublime Porte on a *Rum Millet* basis, but used different types of legitimatization such as international contracts. Roma tribes were also outside the *Rum Millet* system. In their case the Ottoman Empire referred to the ethnic principle. Svetlana Ivanova, "Predi da se rodi bûlgarskiaya milet" [Before the Birth of the Bulgarian *Millet*] in *Dûrzhava & Tsûrkva—Tsûrkva & Dûrzhava v bûlgarskata istoriya* [State and Church—Church and State in Bulgarian History] (Sofia: Universitetsko izdatelstvo "Sv. Kliment Ohridski," 2006), 146–50.

12. Steven Runciman, *The Orthodox Churches and the Secular State* (Oxford: Oxford University Press and Auckland University Press, 1970), 29.

13. Runciman, *The Great Church in Captivity* (Cambridge, Mass.: Cambridge University Press, 1968), 175.

14. Rumyana Radkova, *Bûlgarskata inteligentsiya prez Vûzrazhdaneto* [The Bulgarian Intelligentsia during the Revival] (Sofia: Nauka i izkustvo, 1986); Todorova, *Pravoslavnata tsûrkva*; Voillery, *Mezhdu dva svyata: Bûlgarite v Rumeliya, XVIII–XIX*.

15. Radkova, *Bûlgarskata inteligentsiya*, 256.

16. Ibid., 240–49.

17. Ibid., 259–70.

18. Ibid., 284.

19. Rumyana Preshlenova, *Po pûtishtata na evropeizma: Visheto obrazovanie v Avstro-Ungariya i bûlgarite* [On their Way to Europeanism: Higher Education in Austro-Hungary and Bulgarians] (Sofia: Paradigma, 2008), 93.

20. Nikolai Genchev, *Socialno-psihologicheski tipove v bûlgarskata istoriya* [The Social and Psychological Typology of Bulgarian People throughout History] (Sofia: DI "Septemvri," 1987), 68.

21. Dimitûr Angelov, *Neugasvashto samosûznanie: Bûlgarskata narodnost prez vekovete* [Immortal Self-Consciousness: Bulgarian Nationhood throughout Centuries] (Sofia: BAN, 1991), 159.

22. Church-Slavonic was codified as a liturgical language in the 1650s. It was created through the reforms of Patriarch Nikon of Moscow who unified the liturgical texts used by his church until then. Many such books were imported to the Balkans by Orthodox hierarchs and monks who often made trips to Moscow begging its tsars for material and moral support.

23. Petûr Nikov, *Vûzrazhdane na bûlgarskiya narod: Tsûrkovno-natsionalni borbi i postizheniya* [The Revival of Bulgarian People: Church-Nation Struggles and Achievements], 1st ed. in 1929 (Sofia: Izdatelstvo "Prof. Marin Drinov," 2008), 45.

24. Georgi Neshev, "Pravoslavnite institutsii prez XV–XVIII v." [The Orthodox Institutions in the Fifteenth–Eighteenth Centuries] in *Pravoslavieto v Bûlgariya* [Orthodoxy in Bulgaria], 151.

25. Ivanova, "Predi da se rodi bûlgarskiaya milet," 150–53.

26. Generally, researchers do not discuss whether the mentioned Ottoman policy concerned only the Orthodox Bulgarians or also those who converted to Islam. More specific is the case of the Bulgarian Catholics, who constituted a separate, relatively small religious community. Their nationality was respected by both the Roman Pope and the Sublime Porte until the Chiprovtsy Uprising (1688) when the latter destroyed the Catholic dioceses in the Bulgarian lands. The history of the Roman Catholic Bulgarians under Ottoman rule is studied by Nikola Milev, *Katolishkata propaganda v Bûlgariya prez VII vek. Istorichesko izsledvane i priliozheniya* [Catholic Propaganda in the Seventeenth Century] (Sofia: Pridvorna pechatnitsa, 1914); Svilen Stanimirov, *Politicheskata deynost na bûlgarite-katolitsi prez 30-te/70-te godini na XVII vek: Kûm istoriyata na bûlgarskata antiosmanska sûprotiva* [The Political Activities of the Bulgarian Catholics in the 1630s–1670s: Concerning the History of Bulgarian Anti-Ottoman Resistance] (Sofia: Nauka i izkustvo, 1988).

27. Ivanova, "Predi da se rodi bûlgarskiaya milet," 171–75.

28. The text of the letter was published by Vladimir Teplov, *Greko-Bolgarskii tserkovnyi vopros po neizdannym istochnikam* [A Study on the Greek-Bulgarian Church Question, Based on Unpublished Sources] (St. Petersburg: Imperskaya Akademiya Nauk, 1889), 24.

29. Ibid., 25–26.

30. Zina Markova, *Bûlgarskata Ekzarkhiya, 1870–1879* [The Bulgarian Exarchate, 1870–1879] (Sofia: BAN, 1989), 19.

31. Nadya Danova, "Razrivût mezhdu grûtskite vûzrozhdentsi i Tsarigradskata patriarshiya" [The Break between the Greek National Leaders and the Patriarchate of Constantinople], *Izvestiya na Balgarskoto istorichesko druzhestvo* [Proceedings of the Bulgarian Historical Society] 27 (1970): 61–62.

32. Zvi Keren, "The Actions and Contribution of Mithat Pasha to the City of Ruschuk as the First Vali of Tuna Vilaayet-i" in *Istoriyata i knigite kato priyatelstvo* [History and Books as Friendship] (Sofia: IK "Gutenberg," 2007), 365–67.

33. Nikov, *Vûzrazhdane na bûlgarskiya narod*, 51–54.

34. Andreas Liberatos, "Vselenskata patriarshiya, natsionalismût i bûlgarskiya tsûrkoven vûpors (1856–1872)" [The Ecumenical Patriarchate, Nationalism and the Bulgarian Church Question (1856–1872)] in *Religiya i tsûrkva v Bûlgariya* [Religion and Church in Bulgaria] (Sofia: IK "Gutenberg," 1999), 131–32.

35. One of the best reviews of these struggles was carried out by Petûr Nikov. Nikov, *Vûzrazhdane na bûlgarskiya narod*, 61–113.

36. Nikov, *Vûzrazhdane na bûlgarskiya narod*, 70.

37. Letter from Vasil Aprilov to his compatriots written in Odessa on May 1, 1845. Published in Vasil Aprilov, *Sûchineniya* [Works] (Sofia: Biblioteka Vûzrozhdenska Knizhnina, 1968), 352–57.

38. Daniela Kalkandjieva, "The Higher Theological Education of Bulgarian Orthodox Clergy (19th–20th Centuries)," *Studia Universtitatis Petru Maior. Historia* 5 (2005): 229–30.

39. Marin Drinov, "Bolgare i Konstantinopol'skaya patriarkhiya" [Bulgarians and the Patriarchate of Constantinople], *Beseda* [journal "Talks"] 4 (1871): 324–59; Ibid. "Istoricheski pregled na Bûlgarskata tsûrkva ot samoto y nachalo do dnes" [Historical Review of the Bulgarian Church from Beginning until Today] (Vienna: n.p., 1869) in *Trudove na M. S. Drinov* [Reprinted Works by M. S. Drinov] (Sofia: Dûrzhavna pechatnitsa, 1911).

40. Father Natanail defended a dissertation on the medieval Bulgarian Church in the Kiev ecclesiastical academy in 1851. Nikov, *Vûzrazhdane na bûlgarskiya narod*, 120.

41. Ibid.

42. The request for fixed salaries was aimed at avoiding an arbitrary increase of church taxes, which was a common practice of the Patriarchate of Constantinople.

43. Nikov, *Vûzrazhdane na bûlgarskiya narod*, 87.

44. Ibid., 91.

45. Ibid., 112.

46. The number of Bulgarians belonging to Latin rite Catholicism in the Ottoman Empire was quite insignificant, especially after the Chiprovtsi Uprising (1688). Organized by the local Catholic hierarchy, its suppression ended with a mass exodus of Bulgarian Catholics to the Habsburg Empire, while the Catholic Church succeeded in restoring its position in the Bulgarian lands only in the second half of the nineteenth century, thanks to its missions and the Union signed with Bulgarians in 1861.

47. Ivanova, "Predi da se rodi bûlgarskiaya milet," 138.

48. The episcopate of the Patriarchate of Constantinople continued to ordain Bulgarian priests but their appointment and salaries depended directly on their Bulgarian parishioners who were also able to fire the priests, if they did not meet their requirements.

49. Daniela Kalkandjieva, "The Bulgarian Orthodox Church and the 'Ethics of Capitalism,'" *Social Compass* 57, no. 1 (2010): 85.

50. According to Petûr Nikov, in the first half of the nineteenth century the idea of an autonomous state prevailed in Bulgarian society, but after the *Hatt-i Humayun* it was replaced with the idea of church autonomy. Nikov, *Vûzrazhdane na bûlgarskiya narod*, 119.

51. Ivan Snegarov, "Bûlgarskite tsûrkovno-natsionalni borbi" [The Bulgarian National-Church Struggles], *Rodina* [Motherland] 3 (1940): 86.

52. Nikov, *Vûzrazhdane na bûlgarskiya narod*, 119–20.

53. Ibid., 204.

54. Ibid., 224–51.

55. Ibid., 143.

56. Ibid., 173–74.

57. Ibid., 143.

58. Ibid., 145.

59. Father Paisii was born in 1722 in the eparchy of Samokov, which was then under the jurisdiction of the Patriarchate of Ipek and was abolished by the Church of Constantinople in 1766. Evgenii Golubinskii, *Kratkii ocherk istorii pravoslavknykh tserkvey Bolgarskoy, Serbskoy i Rumynskoy ili Moldo-Valashkoy* [Short Histories of the Bulgarian, Serbian or Moldavian-Wallachian Orthodox Churches] (Moscow: Universitetskaya tipografiya, 1871), 149.

60. In 1861, during one of the most extreme moments of the struggles for a national church one of the leaders of the Bulgarian Revival, Georgi S. Rakovski, published a study, in which he referred to the Archbishopric of Ohrid as Bulgarian. Rakovski, "Razgovor o balgarskomu sveshtenomu voprosu" [Conversation about the Bulgarian religious question] in *Sûchineniya* [Works], vol. 3 (Sofia: Bûlgarski pisatel, 1984), 259–73. The same thesis was supported with detailed historical analysis by the founder of modern Bulgarian historiography in his monograph *Istoricheski pregled na bûlgarskata tsûrkva ot samoto i nachalo do dnes* [Historical Review of the Bulgarian Church from Beginning until Today] (Vienna: n.p., 1869), 125–39.

61. Golubinskii, 107–15. Marin Drinov, "Bolgare i Konstantinopol'skaya patriarkhiya" [Bulgarians and the Patriarchate of Constantinople], *Beseda* [Talks] 4 (1871): 324–59.

62. Golubinskii, *Kratkii ocherk istorii*, 118.

63. Ibid., 153–54.

64. In 1843, Konstantin Fotinov, one of the fathers of the Bulgarian Revival, presented his view on the ethnic borders of his people in *Obshtoe zemleopisanie* [General Geography], published in an edition of 2,795 copies. According to Fotinov, Bulgarians numbered about five million people, who inhabited the territories of Misia (present day North Bulgaria), Thrace and Macedonia. There was

also a considerable Bulgarian diaspora in Asia Minor, Russia, Wallachia, Moldavia and other European countries. Zdravka Konstantinova, *Dûrzhavnost predi dûrzhavata* [State Culture Preceding the State Establishment] (Sofia: Universitetsko izdatelstvo "Sv. Kliment Ohriski," 2002), 151.

65. Contemporary Bulgarian and Macedonian historiographies differ in their assessment of the national character of this population. The first defines it as Bulgarian, while the later as Macedonian.

66. Rakovski, "Razgovor o balgarskomu sveshtenomu voprosu," 260.

67. Contemporary Macedonian historians define Bishop Partenii Zografski, who was born in the territory of present day FYR of Macedonia, as *domoroden* (i.e., locally born). According to Jovan Belchovski, the term "Bulgarians" that was used in the original texts of the historical sources actually meant "Macedonians." Jovan Belchovski, *Avtokefalnosta na Makedonskata pravoslavna tsrkva* [The Autocephaly of the Macedonian Orthodox Church] (Skopje: Nova kniga, 1990), 92–93.

68. Kiril, Patriarch of Bulgaria, *Prinos kûm uniyatstvoto v Makedoniya sled Osvoboditelnata voyna (1879–1895)* [Contribution to the Uniatism in Macedonia after the Liberation War (1879–1895)] (Sofia: Sinodalno izdatelstvo, 1968), 197.

69. Yanko Dimov, *Ne si pravi kumir (Izh. 20:4)* [You Shall Not Make for Yourself an Idol (Exodus 20:4)] (Sofia: BO Inzhenering i serviz, 1992), 55. Nikov, *Vûzrazhdane na bûlgarskiya narod*, 138.

70. On the basis of publications by Bulgarian authors, the list of bishops of Bulgarian origin consecrated by the Patriarchate of Constantinople during the Bulgarian Church Movement (1820–1870) includes: Avksentii in the diocese of Veles (consecrated in 1831); Ilarion in the diocese of Lovech (consecrated in 1850); Panaret in the diocese of Plovdiv (consecrated in 1851); Dorotei in the diocese of Vratsa (consecrated in 1853); Venedikt in the diocese of Bitolya (consecrated in 1854); Ilarion Makariopoloski (consecrated in 1858); Partenii Zografski (consecrated in 1858); and five more bishops consecrated in the 1860s: Ignatii in the diocese of Kyustendil; Antim in the diocese of Preslav; Paisii in the diocese of Skopje; Genadii in the diocese of Veles and Vasilii in the diocese of Ankhialo. Not all of them were appointed as diocesan metropolitans. See Dimov, *Ne si pravi kumir*; Vera Boneva, *Bûlgarskoto tsûrkovno-natsionalno dvizhenie, 1856–1870* [The Bulgarian National Church Movement, 1856–1870] (Veliko Tûrnovo: Za bukvite, 2010), 1083–96.

71. Danova, "Razrivût mezhdu grûtskite vûzrozhdentsi i Tsarigradskata patriarshiya," 60.

72. Quotation from the introduction to a volume of works of Aristotle written by Amandios Korais in Paris in 1821. Danova, 51.

73. Ibid., 55–56.

74. The song was published in the newspaper *Bûlgariya* [Bulgaria] on April 9, 1860. Moreover, the editor appealed to his compatriots in the countryside to sing

this song in all parishes where Bulgarians declared their break with the Patriarchate of Constantinople. Boneva, *Bûlgarskoto tsûrkovno-natsionalno dvizhenie*, 221.

75. Document No. 135 "Letter of the Ambassador Lobanov-Rostovski to Nayden Gerov, April 11, 1860, Constantinople" in *Arkhiv na Nayden Gerov* [Nayden Gerov's Archive], ed. Mikhail G. Popruzhenko, vol. 1 (Sofia: Dûrzhavna pechatnitsa, 1931), 130.

76. Boneva, *Bûlgarskoto tsûrkovno-natsionalno dvizhenie*, 225–28.

77. Snegarov, "Bûlgarskite tsûrkovno-natsionalni borbi," 90.

78. Ibid.

79. Nikov, *Vûzrazhdane na bûlgarskiya narod*, 192–201.

80. Daniela Kalkandjieva, "Katolitsizmût v bûlgarskite zemi i zalezût na Osmanskata imperiya prez vtorata polovina na XIX vek" [Catholicism in the Bulgarian Lands and the Decline of the Ottoman Empire in the Second Half of the Nineteenth Century], *Rodina* [Motherland] 1–2 (1997): 166–86. St. Stanimirov, "Iz zhivota i dejnostta na Josif Sokolksi" [Notes on the Life and Activities of Josif Sokolski], *Izvestiya na istoricheskoto druzhestvo* [Review of the Bulgarian Historical Society] 6 (1924): 148–62.

81. Snegarov, "Bûlgarskite tsûrkovno-natsionalni borbi," 91.

82. Nikov, *Vûzrazhdane na bûlgarskiya narod*, 178.

83. Ibid., 179.

84. Archive of the Bulgarian Revival at the National Library "St. Cyril and St. Methodius," Sofia, (henceforth, NBKM-BIA), fund 113 [Nikolay Palauzov's Fund], a.e. [archival unit] 67, 134.

85. Such cases are presented in documents published in *Arkhiv na Nayden Gerov*, Vol. 1, Document No. 461 "Letter from Nayden Gerov to Count N. Ignatieff, Plovdiv, December 15, 1869," 519; Document No. 432 "Letter from Nayden Gerov to Count N. Ignatieff, Plovdiv, April 2, 1869," 488–89.

86. Kalkandjieva, "Katolitsizmût v bûlgarskite zemi," 174–83.

87. Snegarov, "Bûlgarskite tsûrkovno-natsionalni borbi," 87.

88. "Druga smetka" [Different Accounts], *Bûlgarska pchela* [Bulgarian Bee], no. 46, April 10, 1864.

89. Nikov, *Vûzrazhdane na bûlgarskiya narod*, 210.

90. Snegarov, "Bûlgarskite tsûrkovno-natsionalni borbi," 92.

91. "Appeal of the Bulgarian Municipality of Shumen to Bishops Ilarion Makareopolski and Avksentii of Veles to Ordain their Citizens as Priests," NBKM-BIA, f. 328 [Nikola Vaptsarov], a.e. 6, 54–55.

92. Todor Burmov, *Bûlgaro-grûtskata tsûrkovna razprya* [The Bulgarian-Greek Church Fight] (Sofia: Sv. Sinod na Bûlgarskata tsûrkva, 1902), 221–22.

93. Nikov, *Vûzrazhdane na bûlgarskiya narod*, 266–70.

94. Ibid., 277.

95. Snegarov, "Bûlgarskite tsûrkovno-natsionalni borbi," 94.

96. According to Orthodox canon law, the minimum number of bishops necessary for the election of a new bishop is three. Orthodox theologians, therefore, consider that for a church to be autocephalous, it needs to have at least four bishops. Archimandrite Kalinik, "Kanonicheskoto uchenie na Pravoslavnata tsûrkva za avtokefaliyata" [The Canonical Teaching of the Orthodox Church on Autocephaly], *Dukhovna kultura* [Spiritual Culture] 2 (February 1965): 13.

97. In the case of Goths, the leaders of the Bulgarian Church Movement pointed to the Bible, written in the language of the Eastern Goths. It is known also as the Wulfila Bible and has recently been the object of special research. See the 2004 Project Wulfila conducted by the University of Antwerp, Belgium, available at http://www.wulfila.be (accessed January 9, 2013).

98. Nikov, *Vûzrazhdane na bûlgarskiya narod*, 292.

99. Ibid., 293.

100. Daniela Kalkandjieva, "Balkan Orthodoxies: Church-made Nations or State-made Churches," research project conducted at the Center for Advanced Studies, Sofia, in 2006.

101. Nikov, *Vûzrazhdane na bûlgarskiya narod*, 293.

102. The territorial dimensions of both Churches were set out by V. Teplov. Teplov, *Greko-Bolgarskii tserkovnyi vopros*, 5–8.

103. Nikov, *Vûzrazhdane na bûlgarskiya narod*, 301–4.

104. Traditionally Bulgarian historiography has considered February 28, 1870, as the birthday of the Bulgarian Exarchate. During the last twenty years, some scholars have proposed a revision of this date and its replacement by February 27, the date that corresponds to when the decree was recorded in the Muslim Calendar. In fact the decree was prepared in advance, but its exact date remains unclear. Meanwhile, since 1870 what has been celebrated by generations of Orthodox Bulgarians is the date of the announcement of the decree for the establishment of the exarchate. Therefore this date is supported by the majority of Bulgarian historians. Plamen Mitev, "Dva diskusionni vûprosa ot rannata istoriya na Ekzarkhiyata" [Two Disputable Questions Concerning the Early History of the Exarchate] in *Bûlgarskata tsûrkva prez vekovete* [The Bulgarian Church throughout Centuries] (Sofia: Universitetsko izdatelstvo "Sv. Kliment Ohridski," 2003), 196–200.

105. This fact was explicitly stressed by Marin Drinov in his study "Bolgare i Konstantinopol'skaya patriarkhiya" [Bulgarians and the Patriarchate of Constantinople] (Moscow: n.p., 1871), 324–25.

106. Golubinskii, *Kratkii ocherk istorii*, 325.

107. Nikov, *Vûzrazhdane na bûlgarskiya narod*, 323.

108. Hristo Temelski, "Tsûrkovno-narodniyat sûbor ot 1871 g." [The Church-People's Council in 1878], in *Tsûrkovno-narodniyat sûbor, 1871 g.* [The Church-People's Council, 1878], ed. Hristo Temelski (Sofia: Glavno upravlenie na

arhivite pri Ministerskiya sûvet, Universitetsko izdatelstvo "Sv. Kliment Ohridski," 2001), 10.

109. Petko Slaveykov was famous for his close connections with the Russian embassy in Constantinople. In 1861 he played a major role in the kidnapping of Josif Sokolski, the Exarch of United (Greek Catholic) Bulgarians.

110. Boneva, *Bûlgarskoto tsûrkovno-natsionalno dvizhenie*, 1034.

111. Ibid., 1029.

112. Markova, *Bûlgarskata Ekzarkhiya*, 29.

113. Nikov, *Vûzrazhdane na bûlgarskiya narod*, 311.

114. These were the dioceses of Pirot, Niš, Samokov, Kyustendil, and Veles. Nikov, *Vûzrazhdane na bûlgarskiya narod*, 308–10.

115. Nikov, *Vûzrazhdane na bûlgarskiya narod*, 368.

116. Metropolitan Dorotheos of Sofia was not included in this provisional synod because by that time he was in conflict with his flock. Markova, *Bûlgarskata Ekzarkhiya*, 142.

117. Nikov, *Vûzrazhdane na bûlgarskiya narod*, 364.

118. Dimov, *Ne si pravi kumir*, 44.

119. *Protokoli na dukhovnata komisiya za preglezhdane na Ekzarkhiiskiya Ustav i vsichki deystvuvashti dnes vav vedomstvoto na Bûlgarskata pravoslavna tsûrkva tsûrkovni razporedbi* [Proceedings of the Ecclesiastical Commission Appointed to Review the Exarchate's Statutes and All Administrative Acts in the Bulgarian Orthodox Church] (Sofia: Sinodalno izdatelstvo, 1920), 7.

120. Although the Churches of Russia, Serbia, Romania, and Jerusalem did not sign the decision of 1872 declaring the schism with Bulgarians, they observed it and avoided communion with the Bulgarian Exarchate until 1945, when the schism was abolished.

121. On September 22, 1908, the Bulgarian government proclaimed its state fully independent from the Sublime Porte and Bulgaria was declared as an independent kingdom.

122. The 1879 Bulgarian Constitution was in force until 1947, when the communist regime imposed a new one. The Statutes of the Bulgarian Exarchate (1871) also defined the synod as the supreme spiritual power in the exarchate (Articles 3 and 4).

123. After the Reunion of Southern Rumelia with the Principality of Bulgaria on September 6, 1885, its metropolitans joined the Sofia Synod. Thus Exarch Josif and his administration in Constantinople remained in charge only for the Orthodox Bulgarians in Macedonia and Edirne Thrace.

124. Svetlozar Eldûrov, "Bûlgarskata Ekzarkhiya v borbata za Makedoniya i Odrinska Trakiya (1879–1911)" [The Bulgarian Exarchate in the Struggles for Macedonia and Edirne Thrace (1879–1911)] in *Dûrzhava & Tsûrkva—Tsûrkva & Dûrzhava v bûlgarskata istoriya* [State and Church—Church and State in Bul-

garian History] (Sofia: Universtitetsko izdatelstvo "Sv. Kliment Ohridski," 2006), 327–29. See also Cyril, Patriarch of Bulgaria, *Bûlgaskata Ekzarkhiya v Makedoniya i Odrinsko sled Osvoboditelnata voyna, 1877–1878* [The Bulgarian Exarchate in Macedonia and Edirne Thrace after the Russo-Turkish War, 1877–1878], vol. 1 (Sofia: Sinodalno izdatelstvo, 1970).

125. Nina Dyulgerova, "Pravoslavieto—element ot vûnshnopoliticheskiya instrumentarium na Ruskata imperiya prez poslednata chevûrt na XIX v." [Orthodoxy as an Element of the Foreign Policy Devices of the Russian Empire in the Last Quarter of the Nineteenth Century] in *Bûlgarskata parvoslavna tsûrkva—traditsii i nastoyashte* [Bulgarian Orthodox Church—Traditions and Present Day Situation] (Sofia: IK Gutenberg, 2009), 148–61.

126. Eldûrov, "Bûlgarskata Ekzarkhiya," 330.

127. Ibid., 342.

128. Ibid., 330.

129. Vanya Stoyanova, "Ekzarkhiyskiya institut v Tsarigrad (1913–1925)" [The Exarchate's Office in Constantinople (1913–1925)] in *Bûlgarskata pravoslavna tsûrkva—tradtsii i nastoyashte*, [The Bulgarian Orthodox Church—Traditions and Present Day Situation] (Sofia: IK Gutenberg, 2009), 132.

130. State Archives of the Russian Federation (GARF), f. [fund] 6991, op. [inventory] 1, d. [file] 16, 33. Agreement on the abolishment of the Bulgarian schism signed by the representatives of the Orthodox Churches who attended the election of Patriarch Aleksii of Moscow and All Russia, February 7, 1945.

131. The list of Bulgarian Church hierarchs has been compiled from *Chronicle of the Bulgarian Orthodox Church* (Sofia: Balgarski bestselar, 2010), 369–515; Dimov; and Boneva, *Bûlgarskoto tsûrkovno-natsionalno dvizhenie*, 1083–96.

132. Since the establishment of the Bulgarian Exarchate in 1870, its diocesan hierarchs have had the rank of metropolitans, while bishops have had no such administrative capacity. The Episcopal dignity was a mandatory condition for a cleric to be included in the list of candidates for a widow-diocese.

133. In 1874 Metropolitan Ilarion was elected by the diocese of Kyustendil and left that of Lovech, which was taken by Metropolitan Josif in 1876.

Contributors

Bojan Aleksov is a lecturer in Southeast European history at University College London's School of Slavonic and East European Studies. His recent articles include "One Hundred Years of Yugoslavia. The Vision of Stojan Novaković Revisited," *Nationalities Papers* 39, no. 6 (2011): 997–1010; "The Serbian Orthodox Church: Haunting Past and Challenging Future" *International Journal for the Study of the Christian Church* 10, no. 2 (2010): 176–91; and "The New Role for the Church in Serbia," *Südosteuropa* 56, no. 3 (2008): 353–75.

Daniela Kalkandjieva is a researcher in the Scientific Research Department at Sofia University. In 2004, she defended her doctoral dissertation on "Ecclesio-Political Aspects of the International Activities of the Moscow Patriarchate, 1917–1948." Her publications include *Bûlgarskata pravoslavna tsûrkva i dûrzhavata, 1944–1953* [The Bulgarian Orthodox Church and the State, 1944–1953] (Sofia: Albatros, 1997); "A Comparative Analysis on Church-State Relations in Eastern Orthodoxy: Concepts, Models and Principles," *Journal of Church and State* 53, no. 4 (2011); "The Bulgarian Orthodox Church and the 'Ethics of Capitalism,'" *Social Compass* 57, no. 1 (2010); "Pre-Modern Orthodoxy: Church Features and Transformations," *Études Balkaniques* 4 (2010); and "The Bulgarian Orthodox Church" in *Eastern Christianity and the Cold War, 1945–91*, ed. Lucian N. Leustean (London: Routledge, 2009).

Paschalis M. Kitromilides is professor of political science at the University of Athens. His latest publications include *An Orthodox Commonwealth. Symbolic Legacies and Cultural Encounters in Southeastern Europe* (Aldershot: Ashgate Variorum, 2007); the chapters on the modern history of the Ecumenical Patriarchate in the *Cambridge History of Christianity*, vol. 5 (Cambridge: Cambridge University Press, 2007); *Adamantios Korais and the European Enlightenment* [as editor] (Oxford: SVEC Voltaire Foundation, 2010); and *Enlightenment and Revolution: The Making of Modern Greece* (Cambridge, Mass.: Harvard University Press, 2013).

Lucian N. Leustean is a senior lecturer in politics and international relations in the School of Languages and Social Sciences at Aston University, Birmingham, United Kingdom. He studied international relations, law, and theology in Bucharest and was awarded a doctorate by the Department of Government at the London School of Economics and Political Science. His recent publications related to this project include *Orthodoxy and the Cold War: Religion and Political Power in Romania, 1947–65* (Basingstoke: Palgrave, 2009)—winner of the George Blazyca Prize in East European Studies by the British Association for Slavonic and East European Studies; *Eastern Christianity and the Cold War, 1945–91* [as editor] (London: Routledge, 2010); and *Eastern Christianity and Politics in the Twenty-First Century* [as editor] (London: Routledge, forthcoming 2014). He is the founding editor of the Routledge Book Series on Religion, Society, and Government in Eastern Europe and the Former Soviet States.

Dimitris Stamatopoulos is associate professor in Balkan and late Ottoman history in the Department of Balkan, Slavic, and Oriental Studies at the University of Macedonia, Thessaloniki, Greece. He was a member of the School of Historical Studies, Institute for Advanced Study, Princeton, for the academic year 2010–11. He has published many articles on the history of the Orthodox populations in the Ottoman Empire. He is the author of *Μεταρρύθμιση και εκκοσμίκευση: προς μια ανασύνθεση της ιστορίας του Οικουμενικού Πατριαρχείου τον 19ο αιώνα* [Reform and Secularization: Toward a Reconstruction of the History of the Ecumenical Patriarchate in the Nineteenth Century] (Athens: Alexandreia, 2003); *Το Βυζάντιο μετά το Έθνος: το πρόβλημα της συνέχειας στις Βαλκανικές Ιστοριογραφίες* [Byzantium after the Nation: The Problem of Continuity in Balkan Historiographies] (Athens: Alexandreia, 2009); and has coedited (with Fotini

Tsibiridou) *Οριενταλισμός στα όρια: από τα Οθωμανικά Βαλκάνια στη σύγχρονη Μέση Ανατολή* [Orientalism on the Edge: From the Ottoman Balkans to the Contemporary Middle East] (Athens: Kritiki, 2008). His current interests focus on the relationship between religion and politics in the Balkans and, more specifically, on the process of secularization and the rise of civil society.

Index

Agatangel, Metropolitan, 99
Agathangelos, Ecumenical Patriarch, 33, 36
Aksakov, Konstantin, 92
Alba Iulia, 122, 143, 149–50, 153
Alexandria, 25, 60–1, 185
Âli Paşa, Grand Vezir, 61, 189
Ambrozie, Father (Popa Tun), 108
Amvrosije, Bishop, 100
Anaplasis, 56
Anastasie Gribanovski, Metropolitan, 148, 163
Andreiu Şaguna, Metropolitan of Transylvania, 70, 135–9, 143, 160, 162
Androutsos, Christos, 63
Anthimos III, Ecumenical Patriarch, 33
Anthimos IV, Ecumenical Patriarch, 33, 43, 45–6
Anthimos V, Ecumenical Patriarch, 33
Anthimos VI, Ecumenical Patriarch, 5, 33, 46
Anthimos VII, Ecumenical Patriarch, 33
Antim, Bishop, 100
Antim, Metropolitan, 99
Antim, Metropolitan of Preslav, 185
Antim, Metropolitan of Vidin / Exarch, 182, 187, 192, 199
Anton of Hohenzollern, Prince, 122
Antonie Sokotov, Metropolitan, 146, 162
Apostolic Canon 34, 11
Aprilov, Vasil, 173
Arad, 137–9
Arcadie Ciupercovici, Metropolitan, 100, 162
Archbishopric of Ohrid, 178–9, 186, 188–90
Archdiocese of Odessa and Kherson, 147
Argos, 37
Aristarchis, Nikolaos, 46
Arsenius, Archbishop of Larisa, 62
Asociaţia transilvană pentru cultura şi literatura română—Astra (The Transylvanian Association for Romanian Culture and Literature—Astra), 138
Association for the Dissemination of Greek Letters, 55
Atanasie, Bishop, 132, 134
Athanasie Mironescu, Primate Metropolitan, 161
Athanasios of Nicomedia, 29
Australia, 204

Index

Austro-Hungarian Empire, 6, 13, 101, 103, 115–16, 131–2, 137, 140, 143, 149, 158, 160, 203
Averkii, Metropolitan of Vratsa, 201
Avksentii, Metropolitan of Veles, 182, 185, 200

Bacău, 113
Balkan journal, 81
Balkan Wars, 9, 26, 77, 82–3, 89, 125, 195–6
Banat, 5, 68, 101, 131, 149–51
Banja Luka, 78
Bărnuțiu, Simion, 135
Bartholomew, Bishop of Kalavryta, 53
Basil II, Ecumenical Patriarch, 157
Belgrade, 4, 13, 76, 83, 85–91, 97, 99, 204
Bem, General Iosif, 136
Béni von Kállay, 79, 81
Bessarabia, 5–6, 8, 13, 101, 131, 144–9, 151, 160, 204
Bezdin Monastery, 134
Biserica Ortodoxă Română (the Romanian Orthodox Church), 155
Blaj, 135–6, 145
Boehm, Christopher, 93
Bogomoljci movement, 75
Bosnia and Herzegovina, 10, 72, 77–83, 88, 96, 204
Bosporus, 29
Bozveli, Neofit, 174
Brașov, 104–6, 133
Brătianu, Ioan, 122
Breuilly, John, ix, 7
Britain, 34, 39–40, 45–6, 53, 115
Bucharest, 12–13, 102, 104–5, 107–8, 116, 118–20, 123, 145, 148, 150, 156, 186, 203
Buchenau, Klaus, 92
Budapest, 77, 84, 138–40, 143, 149
Bukovina, 5–6, 8, 11–13, 77, 101, 131, 137, 140–4, 149, 151–2, 160, 204
Bulgaria, 5–6, 8–10, 19, 22–3, 51, 78, 95, 157, 164–201, 203–4

Bulgarian Church Movement (National Church Movement—*tsûrkovno-natsionalno dvizhenie*), 170, 172–5, 177, 179–83, 186, 189, 197–8
Bulgarian Exarchate, 5–6, 11, 19, 22–3, 35, 51, 54, 88–9, 156, 164–201, 203
Bunyan, John, 90
Byzantine Empire, 6–7, 9–10, 12, 52, 73, 86, 88, 96–7, 132, 154, 165, 167, 178–9

Calinic Miclescu, Primate Metropolitan, 161
Câmpia Turzii, 150
Capodistrias, Ioannis, 25, 36–9, 105
Caragea, Ioan, 104
Caransebeș, 137–8
Carol I, Prince, King (United Principalities of Wallachia and Moldavia), 4
Catargiu, Barbu, 116
Catargiu, Lascăr, 121
Cathedral of Arad, 139
Cathedral of Athens, 54
Cathedral of Belgrade, 86, 97
Cathedral of Chișinău, 146
Cathedral of Iași, 1–2, 109
Catholic Consistory of Lemberg, 141
Cernăuți, 13, 140–2, 144
Cetinje Seminary, 95
Chesarie, Bishop of Buzău, 107
Chișinău, 106, 144–9
Chișinăuskie eparkhialnye vedomosti (The Chișinău Eparchial Gazette), 146
Chomakov, Stoyan, 186
Chrysanthos, Archbishop (Cyprus), 24
Chrysanthos, Ecumenical Patriarch, 33
Chrysogelos, Nikolaos, 37
Chrysostom, Bishop of Drama, 23
Chrysostomos Papadopoulos, Archbishop of Athens, 37, 63
Church Fund of Bukovina (*Fondul Bisericesc din Bucovina*), 141
Church and School Autonomy (*Crkveno-školska autonomija*), 71, 74–5

Index

Church-People's Council (*Tsŭrkovno-naroden sŭbor*), 191–2
Church of Saint Sophia in Constantinople, 9
Cluj, 134–5, 138, 152
Compiègne armistice, 149
Congress of Berlin (1878), 4, 88, 193
Conon Arămescu-Donici, Primate Metropolitan, 131, 151, 161
Constantin Popovici, Archpriest, 147
Constantinople (Istanbul), 11, 17, 31, 124, 126, 132, 156, 167, 174, 176–7, 187, 195–7, 199, 203
Constantinos V, Ecumenical Patriarch, 33
Constantios I, Ecumenical Patriarch, 33, 37–8, 46
Constantios II, Ecumenical Patriarch, 33
Count Ignatiev, 19
Count Nesselrode, 107
Count Nikolay Ignatieff, 184, 186, 189
Count Philip of Flanders, 121
Crete, 4, 186
Crimean War, 19–20, 50, 53, 166, 173, 175, 177
Crişana, 101, 131
Croatia, 67–8, 73, 76, 80, 92
Cuvânt Moldovenesc (The Moldovan Word), 148
Cuza, Prince Alexandru Ioan, 2, 4, 116–22, 127, 130, 159, 172
Cyprus, 19, 24–5, 48
Cyril I, Ecumenical Patriarch, 26
Cyril II, Patriarch of Jerusalem, 23, 45–6
Cyril VI, Ecumenical Patriarch, 26, 32
Cyril VII, Ecumenical Patriarch, 33, 113

Dalj, 72
Dalmatia, 10, 75–7, 143, 204
Damalas, Nikolaos, 57
Damian, Patriarch of Jerusalem, 156
Daniel, Metropolitan of Syros-Tinos, 53
Daniil Vlachovici, Archdeacon/Bishop, 141, 162
Danube River, 66–7, 83, 118, 163, 186, 193
Deligiannis, Theodoros, 61

Deligiorgis, Epaminondas, 22
Demidoff, Anatole de, 102
Dialismas, Konstantinos, 56
Dimetrie Sulima, Bishop of Bender and Akkerman / Metropolitan, 144, 146, 162
Dimitrije Branković, Bishop, 99
Dimitrije Pavlović, Metropolitan / Patriarch (Serbia), 4, 99
Dionisie Lupu, Metropolitan of Wallachia, 105–6, 161
Dionisije I, Bishop, 100
Dionisije II Ilić, Bishop, 100
Dionisije II Popović Nišlija, Metropolitan, 99
Dionysios of Ephesus, 29
Dionysios V, Ecumenical Patriarch, 33
Dniester River, 103, 144, 147
Dobrudja, 101, 131, 163, 196
Dodecanese, 4
Đorđe Nikolajević, Metropolitan, 100
Đorđević, Vladan, 88
Dorotheos, Metropolitan of Sofia / Metropolitan of Skopje, 185, 187, 200–1
Dositei Filitti, Bishop of Buzău / Metropolitan of Wallachia, 103–5, 161
Dositej Jović, Bishop of Boka-Kotorska, 77
Dosoftei Herescu, Bishop, 140–1, 162
Drina River, 78
Drinov, Professor Marin, 173
Đurić, Milan, 89
Durkheim, Émile, 7

Easter Action (*Velikdenska aktsiya*), 181–2, 190
Ecumenical Patriarchate, 3–4, 7, 10, 14–33, 34–5, 52, 66, 68, 79, 82, 85, 96, 101, 109, 113–14, 119, 124, 126, 155–6, 166–7, 171–3, 176–7, 181–3, 186, 190–2, 197–8, 204
Efemerida (newspaper), 106
Egypt, 27
Emperor Basil II, 178
Emperor Charles I, 149
Emperor Franz Joseph I, 71, 80, 82, 136–7

Emperor Joseph II, 68–9
Emperor Leopold I, 67
Empress Maria Theresa, 68–9
Enlightenment, 15, 24, 34, 51, 68
Epirus, 4
Ermis o Logios, 28
eschaton, 11
ethnarch, 3
ethno-phyletism, 5–6, 11, 20, 51, 165, 193, 205
ethnos, 11
Eugenie Hacman, Bishop / Metropolitan of Bukovina and Dalmatia, 12, 99, 137, 142–4, 162
Eusebius Mathopoulos, Archimandrite, 58
Evantias, Ioanichie, 119
Evangeliká (Gospel Riots), 61–2
Evgenije Letica, Metropolitan, 83, 100
Evgenios of Anchialos, 29
Evgenios II, Ecumenical Patriarch, 33

Farmakidis, Theoklitos, 34, 38–40, 43, 47–9, 52–3, 62, 180
Feraios, Rigas, 54
Ferdinand of Coburg-Gotha, Prince, 9
Filantropia hospital, 105
Filaret, Metropolitan of Moscow, 183–4
Filaret Beldiman, Bishop of Apameea, 109–11
Filaret Scriban, Archimandrite, 111–14
Focșani, 103
Fotiadis, Dimitrios, 46
France, 34–5, 39–40, 45, 53, 112, 114–16, 121
Frăsinet, 102
French Revolution, 3, 7, 11, 15, 27, 38, 101, 103, 133
Fuad Paşa, 61

Gabrovo, 173
Galicia, 13, 76, 140, 142
Gavriil Bănulescu-Bodoni, Metropolitan, 104–5, 144–5, 158, 161–2
Gavrilo Zmejanović, Bishop of Vršac, 74
Gedeon, Manuel, 16

Genadii, Metropolitan of Veles, 201
Georg Ludwig von Maurer, 35, 38–9, 41–2
Georgije Branković, Patriarch, 98
Gerasim Zelić, 76
German Anđelić, Patriarch, 72, 98
Germanos, Bishop of Kastoria, 23
Germanos IV, Ecumenical Patriarch, 33, 46
Germanos Kalligas, Archbishop of Cephallenia / Archbishop of Athens, 60–1, 64
gerontismos, 20
Gedeon of Sofia, 182
Georgije Branković, Patriarch, 72, 75
Ghenadie Petrescu, Primate Metropolitan, 161
Gherasim Adamovici, Bishop, 133, 161
Gherasim Raț, Bishop, 139
Gherasim Saffirin, Bishop, 129–30
Giannaras, Christos, 58
Glasul Basarabiei (The Voice of Bessarabia), 148
Golescu, General Nicolae, 121
Gračanica Monastery, 97
Great Idea (*Megali Idea*), 3, 9, 49, 52–7, 62–3, 172
Greece, 3–4, 7, 9–10, 17–18, 34–64, 95, 157, 165, 171, 203
Greek War of Independence, 9, 24, 28–9, 101
Grigore Ghica, Prince, 106–7, 111
Grigorie Dascălul, Metropolitan of Wallachia, 106, 161
Grigorii, Metropolitan of Russe, 201
Gregory of Derkoi, 29
Gregory V, Ecumenical Patriarch, 3, 26–30, 32, 54
Gregory VI, Ecumenical Patriarch, 19, 33, 40, 43, 46, 186
Grenzer, 68
Gurie Grosu, Metropolitan, 147

Hansen, Teophil, 96
Haralambie, Nicolae, Colonel, 121
Hatt-i Humayun, 20, 31–2, 175–6
Hellenic school, Nicosia, 24

INDEX

Hellenism, 10, 15–16, 24
High School of Chios, 28
Hilandar Monastery, 66
Hitchins, Keith, x, 132
Holy Alliance, 36
Holy Association, 61
Holy Myrrh, 46, 126, 186
Holy Trinity Church in Pera, 31
Hopovo Monastery, 69
House of Magnates, Budapest, 138–9
Hrišćanski vesnik (Christian Herald), 90
Hungary, 67, 70, 80, 85, 87, 135–6, 149, 154
Hurmuzachi, Doxache, 142
Huși Seminary, 112

Iacob Stamati, Metropolitan of Moldavia, 161
Iacov Peatnitki, Archbishop, 162
Iancu, Avram, 135–6
Iași, 1, 108–12, 118–19, 131
Ierotheos Mathopoulos, Archbishop of Patra, 58
Ignatie Babalos, Metropolitan, 105, 161
Ignjatije I, Bishop, 100
Ignjatije II, Bishop, 100
Ilarion, Bishop of Argeș, 107
Ilarion, Metropolitan of Kyustendil, 201
Ilarion, Metropolitan of Lovech, 187, 192, 199, 201
Ilarion, Metropolitan of Tûrnovo, 199, 201
Ilarion Makariopolski, Bishop of Kukush, 174, 180–2, 185, 187, 189
Ilarion Roganović, Metropolitan, 99
Inocențiu Micu-Klein, Bishop, 133
Inochentie movement, 147–8
Ionian Islands, 4, 27, 53
Ioan Lemeni, Bishop, 135–6
Ioan Mețianul, Metropolitan of Transylvania, 140, 161
Ioan Moga, Father, 136
Iosif Gheorghian, Bishop / Primate Metropolitan, 129, 161, 163
Iosif Naniescu, Metropolitan of Moldavia, 161

Irinarh Popov, Archbishop, 146, 162
Isaia Baloșescu, Bishop, 162
Isakie Polokenski, Archbishop, 162
Islam, 32, 50, 67, 77, 94, 96, 167
Islaz proclamation, 107
Istoriya Slavyano-Bolgarskaya (Slavonic-Bulgarian History), 10, 168, 178–9
Iuliu Hossu, Bishop, 155
Ivanova, Svetlana, 169–70

Jeremiah IV, Ecumenical Patriarch, 32
Jerotej Mutibarić, Bishop, 99
Jerusalem, 23, 25, 44–6, 110, 156–7, 185, 192
Jewish communities, 73, 117, 127, 132, 154, 167
Joachim II, Ecumenical Patriarch, 19, 23, 33, 182
Joachim III, Ecumenical Patriarch, 23, 26, 32–33, 80
Joachim IV, Ecumenical Patriarch, 33, 124
Josif, Metropolitan of Lovech / Exarch, 192, 194–5, 199, 201
Josif Rajačić, Bishop/Metropolitan/Patriarch, 70, 76, 98–9
Josif Sokolski, Archimandrite, 183
Josip Stadler, Archbishop, 81

Kaïris, Theofilos, 43
Kalinik, Bishop, 100
Kallinikos V, Ecumenical Patriarch, 32
Kalliope, 28
Karađorđe's First Uprising, 4
Karadžić, Vuk, 69, 84
Karatzas, Konstantinos, 46
Karlovci Congress (1861), 11
Karlovci Metropolitanate, 10, 13, 65–77, 79, 81, 83, 85–6, 93, 97–9, 133–4, 136–7, 139–40, 143, 161–2
Kedourie, Elie, 7
Kiev Academy, 68
Kiev Pechersk Lavra, 183
King, Jonas, 48
King Carol I (Romania), 121–31, 153
King George I (Greece), 53

King Ferdinand (Romania), 150–3, 157
King Leopold II (Belgium), 121
King Milan Obrenović (Serbia), 4, 88, 91
King Milutin (Serbia), 97
King Othon (Greece), 3, 35, 39–40, 43, 45, 53
Kingdom of Serbs, Croats and Slovenes, 4, 65
Kiril, Metropolitan of Skopje, 201
Kirilo, Metropolitan, 99
Kisselev, General Pavel, 106
Kitromilides, Paschalis, 8
Kolettis, Ioannis, 44
Kolokotronis, Theodoros, 39
Konidaris, Gerasimos, 37
Konstantinos Typaldos-Iakovatos, Metropolitan of Stavropol, 45
Korais, Adamantios, 10, 15, 36–8, 54, 180
Kosovo, 88, 94, 97
Krastevich, Gavril, 185, 188
Krka Monastery, 76
Kukush, 180
Kyprianos, Archbishop (Cyprus), 24

Lajos, Kossuth, 135
Lavrentios, Metropolitan of Kyrenia, 24
Law of Nationalities, 71, 140
League of Nations, 149
Leontije Lambrović, Metropolitan, 99
Livno, 82
Lobanov-Rostovski, Prince Alexey, 184
Logos, 56
Lucian Triteanul, Bishop, 155
Lukijan Bogdanović, Patriarch, 75, 98
Luminătorul (The Light), 147

Macedonia, 4, 20, 23, 36, 51, 88–9, 97, 179, 180, 187, 191, 193–6, 199, 204
Macedonian Orthodox Church, 204
Mackenzie, Frances, 90
Makrakis, Apostolos, 55–8, 60–1
Maramureș, 101, 131
Mărășești, 153
Mardin, Șerif, 58
Marković, Svetozar, 91

Matija Nenadović, Father, 84
Mavrokordatos, Georgios, 47
Mehmed Asim Pașa, 78
Mehmet the Conqueror, 26
Melchisedec Ștefănescu, Archimandrite/ Bishop, 112–14, 127–8, 147, 163
Meletie Lefter, Bishop of Roman / Metropolitan of Moldavia, 110, 161
Meletii, Metropolitan of Sofia, 201
Melentije Pavlović, Metropolitan, 85, 99
Meletios, Metropolitan of Kition, 24
Meletios III, Ecumenical Patriarch, 33
Meletius Metaxakis, Archbishop of Athens, 62–4
Melissa, 28
Metropolitanate of Bukovina and Dalmatia, 12, 77, 143
Metternich, Klemens von, 36
Michael the Brave, 9, 122–3, 150–1
Michael Petrovich, 93
Mihail Sturza, Prince, 109–10, 112
Mihailo Jovanović, Metropolitan of Belgrade, 4, 76, 87–8, 90–1, 97–9
Mijatović, Čedomilj, 90
Miletić, Svetozar, 71, 73
Miloš Obrenović's Second Uprising, 4, 84–5, 91
Milutinović, Sima, 94
Minchoglu, Nikoli, 178
Miron Cristea, Bishop of Caransebeș / Primate Metropolitan / Patriarch (Romania), 5, 150–2, 156, 161
Miron Romanul, Metropolitan of Transylvania, 139, 161
Misail Apostolidis, Archbishop of Athens, 47, 54, 64
Mișcolț, 135
Mitrofan Ban, Metropolitan, 95, 99
Moise Fulea, Father, 136
Moldavia, x, 1–2, 4, 6, 8–9, 17, 20, 28, 36, 101, 103–4, 106, 108–17, 122, 131, 134–5, 139–40, 144, 147, 150, 157–9, 161–3, 166
Monastery of Palaiokastritsa, 58

Montenegro, 10, 92–6, 98–9, 204
Moruzi, Alexandru, 103
Mostar, 78, 82–3
Mount Athos, 27, 66, 110, 174
Muhammad, 56

Napoleon, x, 27, 66, 76, 83
Napoleon III, 120
Naşterea lui Hristos (The Birth of Christ), 147
Natanail, Metropolitan of Ohrid, 173, 201
National Assembly in Troizen, 36
National Orthodox Society of Romanian Women (*Societatea Ortodoxă Naţională a Femeilor Române*), 152–3
Nazarenes, 74, 90
Nectarie, Bishop of Râmnic / Metropolitan of Wallachia, 105, 161
Neofit, Bishop of Râmnic / Metropolitan, 107, 161
Neofit Nevodcikov, Archbishop, 162
Neofit Scriban, Father, 1, 8, 111–14, 119
Neophytos Metaxas, Bishop of Attica / Bishop of Athens, 47, 53, 64
Neophytos VII, Ecumenical Patriarch, 32
Neophytos VIII, Ecumenical Patriarch, 33
Neroulos, Iakovos Rizos, 37, 45
Nestor Ioanovici, Archimandrite, 134
Nicodim Munteanu, Bishop of Huşi / Metropolitan of Moldavia / Patriarch, 148, 161
Nicolae Hutovici, Archpriest, 134
Nifon Niculescu, Bishop, 163
Nifon Sevastias, Bishop of Râmnic / Metropolitan of Wallachia / Primate Metropolitan, 108, 118, 161
Nikanor Ivanović, Metropolitan, 95, 99
Nikodim Milaš, Bishop of Zadar, 76–7, 99
Nikola Petrović, Prince, 95
Nikolaj Mandić, Metropolitan, 100
Nikolopoulos, Vasileios, 56–7
Nikov, Petŭr, 169
Njegoš, Sarajlija, 94
Novocerkassk, 147
Novorossiisk, 146

Obradović, Dositej, 69, 83
Odessa, 147, 173
Ohrid, 10, 48, 165–6, 173, 178–9, 186, 188–91, 195, 201
Oikonomos, Konstantinos, 43–5, 47–9, 62
Okey, Robin, 80–1
Organic Statute (*Regulamentul Organic*), 106–8, 114, 117
Ortakoy, 185
Ottoman Empire, 3–8, 10, 14–15, 17, 51, 54, 66, 75, 82, 93, 101, 103, 113, 116, 125, 158, 164, 168, 170, 174, 177, 181–2, 185–6, 188, 190, 195, 203

Paisii, Metropolitan of Plovdiv, 182, 186, 200
Paisii of Hiledar, Father, 10, 168, 178–9
Pajsije, Bishop, 100
Palauzov, Nikola, 173
Panachrantos Monastery on Andros, 53
Panaret, Metropolitan of Plovdiv, 182, 185–6, 200
Panaretos, Archbishop (Cyprus), 25
Pantelejmon Živković, Bishop, 99
Paparrigopoulos, Konstantinos, 10
Papoulakos (Monk Christoforos / Christos Panagiotopoulos), 52–3, 55
para-ecclesiastical organizations, 57–60
Paris, 28, 38, 110, 113, 149
Partenie Clinceni, Bishop / Metropolitan of Moldavia, 161, 163
Partenii, Metropolitan of Nish, 200–1
Pašić, Nikola, 91–2
Patriarchal Great School, 31
Patriarchate of Peć (Ipek), 10, 65–7, 88, 93, 166, 191
Patriarchate of Tŭrnovo, 10, 165–6, 178, 188–91
Pavel Lebedev, Archbishop, 146, 162
Pavlović, Inokentije, 99
Peloponese, 36, 52
People's and Church Congress (*Narodno-crkveni sabor*), 70–1
Petar Jovanović, Metropolitan, 86, 99

Petar I Petrović Njegoš, Bishop (Saint Peter of Cetinje), 93–4, 98–9
Petar II Petrović Njegoš, Bishop, 94, 99
Peter the Great, 35, 49, 170
Peter Jovanović, Metropolitan, 85
Petmezas, Athanasios, 56
Petrović, Danilo, 94
Petrović, Karađorđe, 83, 85, 94
Petrović-Njegoš clan, 93
Peychovich, Ivancho, 189
Philological Gymnasium in Limassol, 24
Philological Gymnasium of Smyrna, 24, 28
Pimen Georgescu, Bishop/Metropolitan of Moldavia, 150, 161, 163
Piraeus, 45, 53
Platon Rojdestvenski, Metropolitan, 148, 163
Plovdiv, 177, 182, 184–7, 193–4, 200
Poland, 157
Pope Leo XIII, 81
Prečani, 85–6
Preslav, 10, 165, 185
Procopius, Bishop of Oitylos, 53
Procopius Georgiadis, Archbishop of Athens, 55–7, 60, 64
Procopius II Oikonomidis, Archbishop of Athens, 61–2, 64
Prokopije, Bishop, 100
Prokopije Ivačković (Procopie Ivașcovici), Bishop/Metropolitan/Patriarch, 13, 98, 139, 162
Prokopovič, Theofan, 49
Protestantism, 58–60, 74–5, 90, 93, 117, 175
Prussia, 115, 117
Prut River, 144
Putna Monastery, 141

Queen Olga (Russia), 61–2

Radu Șapcă, Father, 107
Rakovski, Georgi, 179
Ranke, Leopold, 84

Rastko Association, 88
Rastko Nemanjić, Prince, 9
Roman Catholic Church, 68, 75, 79–82, 89, 92–3, 98, 108–9, 117, 124, 127, 132, 141–2, 144, 154–5, 175, 180, 183, 198
Romania, 4, 7–8, 10, 17–18, 35, 68, 70, 73, 89, 101–63, 171, 188, 192, 196, 203–4
Romanian Greek Catholic Church, 132, 134, 145, 154–5, 159
Rome, 24, 132–4, 155
Rum Millet, 3, 7, 49, 54, 67, 166–71, 174–6, 192, 197
Rumelia, 20, 193–5
Russian Biblical Society, 145
Russian Empire, 6, 18–19, 34–5, 37, 39–40, 46, 49, 53–4, 68, 73, 91, 93, 95, 98, 101, 103–4, 107, 109–10, 115–16, 125, 147, 149, 158, 160, 170–1, 173, 178, 180–1, 183–5, 189, 195, 203
Russian Orthodox Church, 26, 35, 38, 40, 69, 92, 101, 109–10, 148, 156, 178, 183, 188, 192, 198, 204
Russian Orthodox Church outside Russia (the Karlovci Synod), 148
Russian Revolution, 147–8, 156

Saint Charalambos, 29
Saint Dimitrios, 26
Saint Eleftherios, 29
Saint Ilie Monastery, 141
Saint Ivan of Rila, 169
Saint Parascheva, 1
Saint Petka of Tûrnovo, 169
Saint Sava (Prince Rastko Nemanjić), 9, 87–8, 96
Saint Sava Church in Belgrade, 97
Saint Sava School in Bucharest, 105
Saint Sava Society, 97
Saint Spyridon Church in Nafplion, 37
Saints Cyril and Methodius, 88, 190
Samuel Teleki, Chancellor, 133
Samuilo Maširević, Patriarch, 98

INDEX

San Stefano Bulgaria (*Sanstefanska Búlgariya*), 193–4, 196–8
Sarajevo, 78, 82–3
Sardinia, 115
Sava, Bishop, 188
Sava Kosanović, Metropolitan, 81, 100
Sava River, 83
Schinas, Konstantinos, 42, 44
Scholarius, Gennadius, 12
School of the Logos, 55–7
Secularisation of monastery estates, 4, 117–18
Serafim, Metropolitan of Sliven, 201
Serafim Ciceagov, Metropolitan, 148, 162
Serbia, 4, 10, 17–18, 35, 65–100, 135, 155, 157, 171, 188, 192, 203
Serafim, Bishop, 201
Serghie Leapidevski, Metropolitan, 147, 162
Šibenik, 76
Sibiu, 70, 133–8, 140
Sifnos, 56
Silvestru Morariu-Andrievici, Metropolitan, 100, 162
Simeon, Metropolitan of Varna, 201
Simoniaká scandal, 56
Skopje, 88, 191, 195, 200
Slatina Monastery, 109
Slava (the Family Patron Saint Day), 87, 94, 96
Slaveykov, Petko, 190
Smith, Anthony D., 9–10
Societatea Istorico-Arheologică Bisericească din Basarabia (The Historical Archaeological Society of Bessarabia), 147
Society of Saint Sava, 88
Socola Seminary, 108, 111
Sofia, 11, 182, 185, 187, 193–7, 199, 200–1
Sofronie Miclescu, Bishop of Huşi/ Metropolitan of Moldavia, 110–11, 113–14, 117, 161
Sophronios III, Ecumenical Patriarch, 33, 60
Soveja Monastery, 111
Spiridon of Gabrovo, Father, 168

Stănislăveşti, 102
Stefan, Exarch, 197
Stefan Knežević, Bishop, 76, 99
Stefan Stanković, Metropolitan, 98
Stefan Stratimirović, Metropolitan, 69–70, 76, 83, 98
Stephen, Exarch, 20
Stephen the Great, 2, 9, 122–3
Stojadinović, Milica, 90
Stoyanov, Georgi, 189
St. Petersburg, 104, 110, 144–5, 170, 173–4, 178, 183–4
Sturza, Alecu, 110
Suceava, 152
Sultan Abdul Aziz, 78
Sultan Abdul Mecid I, 30
Sultan Abludhamid II, 31–2
Supplex libellus Valachorum, 133, 135
Şuţu, Alexandru, 105
Syllogos, the Greek Literary Association of Constantinople, 25
Symphonia, 7, 9
Synaxis of Elders, 54

Tanzimat reforms, 60, 78, 171
Taxim square in Istanbul, 31
Telegraful Român (The Romanian Telegraph), 138
Teoctist Blajevici, Metropolitan, 100, 162
Teodorović, Arsenije, 87
Teodosije Mraović, Metropolitan, 99
Teofil Bandella, Metropolitan, 99, 162
Theodorian-Carada, Mariu, 130–1
Theoklitos Minopoulos, Archbishop of Athens, 62–4
Theological Institute in Cernăuţi, 142
Theological Institute in Sibiu, 140
Theological School of Halki, 25, 44–5, 61, 86
Theological School of the Patriarchate of Jerusalem, 44
Theophilus Vlachopapadopoulos, Archbishop of Athens, 55, 61, 64
Thessaloniki, 26, 180

Thessaly, 4, 12
Third Ecumenical Council, Ephesus, 24
Thrace, 20, 23, 51
Three Hierarchs Church in Iași, 112
Tisa River, 150
Titov, Russian ambassador to Athens, 45
Transylvania, 5–6, 8, 11–12, 68, 70, 101, 122, 130–41, 143, 145, 149–51, 153, 158–61, 204
Treaty of Adrianople (1829), 39
Treaty of Berlin (1878), 194
Treaty of Bucharest (1812), 144
Treaty of Edirne (1829), 175
Treaty of Hünkâr İskelesi (1833), 40
Treaty of Karlovci (1699), 75
Treaty of Kuchuk Kainardji (1774), 101, 175
Treaty of Lausanne (1923), 4, 156, 204
Treaty of Neuilly (1919), 149
Treaty of Paris (1857), 113
Treaty of Požarevac (1718), 75
Treaty of Saint-Germain (1919), 149
Treaty of San Stefano (1878), 125, 193
Treaty of Sèvres (1920), 62
Trefort Law (1879), 139–40
Trikoupis, Charilaos, 57, 61
Trikoupis, Spyridon, 38, 44
Tsankov, Dragan, 183
Tsar Alexander I, 104, 145
Tsar Ivan Asen II, 165, 173
Tsar Nicolae II, 148
Turcescu, Lucian, 11
Turda, 134
Tûrnovo Constitution, 194

Unio trium nationum, 132–3
United Principalities of Wallachia and Moldavia, 2, 8–9, 17, 101, 159, 172
United States, 148, 204
University of Athens, 29, 47, 54, 61–3
University of Cernăuți, 144
University Theological Institute in Sibiu, 140

Valasopoulos, Ioannis, 56–7
Vamvas, Neophytos, 48
Vârșeț Seminary, 135
Vasile Mangra, Metropolitan of Transylvania, 140, 161
Vasile Moga, Bishop, 134–5, 161
Vaso Pelagić, Archimandrite, 78
Veles, 88
Velestinlis, Rhigas, 27, 29
Venedikt (Kraljević), Bishop, 99–100
Venetian Republic, 75–6, 81, 93
Veniamin Costachi, Bishop of Huși / Bishop of Roman / Metropolitan of Moldavia, 103, 108–10, 159, 161
Veniamin Roset, Bishop of Roman, 110–11
Venijamin, Bishop, 100
Venijamin Kraljević, Bishop, 76
Venizelos, Eleftherios, 62
Victor, Metropolitan of Nish, 201
Vidin, 166
Vienna, 12, 28, 69, 77, 79, 81, 84, 88, 96, 105–6, 109, 132–6, 138–40, 142–4
Visarion Ljubiša, Metropolitan, 99
Vlachos, Stavros, 47
Vladimir Repta, Metropolitan, 100, 162
Vladimir Sinikovski, Metropolitan, 147, 162
Vladimirescu, Tudor, 106
Vogoridis, Stefanos, 30, 46
Vojvodina, 70

Wallachia, x, 1–2, 4, 6, 8–9, 13, 17, 20, 36, 101–8, 112–18, 122, 131, 134–5, 139, 144–5, 147, 157–9, 161, 166, 170, 172
Weber, Eugen, 95
Wlassics, Gyula, 140

Ypsilantis, Alexander, 28

Zambelios, Spyridon, 52
Zhefarovich, Christophor, 168
Zoe (Life) organization, 58
Zografski, Partenii, 180

ORTHODOX CHRISTIANITY AND CONTEMPORARY THOUGHT

George E. Demacopoulos and Aristotle Papanikolaou, series editors

Ecumenical Patriarch Bartholomew, *In the World, Yet Not of the World: Social and Global Initiatives of Ecumenical Patriarch Bartholomew*. Edited by John Chryssavgis. Foreword by José Manuel Barroso.

Ecumenical Patriarch Bartholomew, *Speaking the Truth in Love: Theological and Spiritual Exhortations of Ecumenical Patriarch Bartholomew*. Edited by John Chryssavgis. Foreword by Dr. Rowan Williams, Archbishop of Canterbury.

Ecumenical Patriarch Bartholomew, *On Earth as in Heaven: Ecological Vision and Initiatives of Ecumenical Patriarch Bartholomew*. Edited by John Chryssavgis. Foreword by His Royal Highness, the Duke of Edinburgh.

George E. Demacopoulos and Aristotle Papaniklaou (eds.), *Orthodox Constructions of the West*.

John Chryssavgis and Bruce V. Foltz (eds.), *Toward an Ecology of Transfiguration: Orthodox Christian Perspectives on Environment, Nature, and Creation*. Foreword by Bill McKibben. Prefatory Letter by Ecumenical Patriarch Bartholomew.

Lucian N. Leustean (ed.), *Orthodox Christianity and Nationalism in Nineteenth-Century Southeastern Europe*.

John Chryssavgis (ed.), *Dialogue of Love: Breaking the Silence of Centuries*. Contributions by Brian E. Daley, S.J., and Georges Florovsky.